Dr Treacy was awarded the "Top Aesthetic Practitioner in the World 2019" at the MyFaceMyBody Global Awards (Las Vegas). He won the 'Doctor of the Year' UK 2019 (Las Vegas) and 'Doctor of the Year' UK and Ireland 2018 at the Safety in Beauty Diamond Award (London). He won the Royal Society of Medicine (London) Research Poster Award 2019. He is among a few doctors in the world to have won the coveted AMEC Trophy three times (Paris 2014 and 2016, Monaco 2019) for varied research relating to the use of stem cells and platelets in treating cancer cachexia and reversing skin necrosis. He won the MyFaceMyBody Trophy in London (2016) for medical research and was Highly Commended (London 2012 and 2013) for studies relating to the use of platelet-rich plasma, growth signalling factors and 633nm red light in both facial rejuvenation and hair transplant. These types of procedures are now popularised and being used by clinicians all around the world. He was given the CCME Medal for "Excellence in contributions to Aesthetic Medicine" (Mexico 2016) and was Highly Commended in "Doctor of the Year" Category (London 2016).

He is recognised as one of the most influential aesthetic practitioners in the world being named for the third time amongst the MyFaceMyBody "Ultimate 100 Global Aesthetic Leaders" (Las Vegas 2019, Los Angeles 2018, London 2017). He received the MyFaceMyBody Specialist Award (London 2018) for research contributions to the field of Aesthetic Medicine. He was awarded a Laureate in Aesthetic Medicine by the Azerbaijani College of Medicine and given the Beauty & Anti-Ageing Trophy (Baku 2017) for contributions to the field of Aesthetic Medicine. He was awarded the 1st AIDA Trophy for his research in Aesthetic Medicine (Abu Dhabi 2017). His research has strongly influenced this specialist area where he has developed global protocols relating to dermal filler complications and wound healing, as well as pioneering techniques for HIV facial lipodystrophy facial endoprostheses and radiosurgery venous thermocoagulation. He won both the "Irish Healthcare Award for Medical Research" (Dublin 2017) and the "British College of Aesthetic Medicine Award for Medical Research" (London 2017).

Dr Treacy was Chairman of the Organising Committee of Royal Society of Medicine (London) Aesthetic Congress 2019, Chairman of the Irish Association of Cosmetic Doctors, and the Irish Representative of the British Association of Cosmetic Medicine. He serves on the editorial boards of five international aesthetic journals. He is author and co-author of many articles in peer-reviewed scientific journals and has contributed to chapters of medical books.

Dr Treacy is a fellow of the Royal Society of Medicine and the Royal Society of Arts (London). He is Chairman of the Ailesbury Humanitarian Foundation and is the driving force behind countless humanitarian efforts that impact the lives of children in communities across Africa, Haiti, and the Third World. To this end, he has opened orphanages in Monrovia, Liberia, and Mirebalais, Haiti. He practices cosmetic medicine in his clinics in Dublin and Cork. He is an advanced aesthetic trainer and has trained over 3,500 doctors and nurses from around the world. He has featured on *CNN, Dr Drew, RTÉ, TV3, Sky News, BBC,* and *Newsweek.*

To Marie Loftus, who helped me initially to edit this text and to both my parents – my mother who instilled in me a passion for education and my father who had a gift for making me believe in myself. Also dedicated to my good friends and medical colleagues Dr Ercin Ozunturk and Dr Mo Herzenhorn who both died unexpectantly after succumbing to Covid 19.

To Annie

memories of life

Patrick 2022

Dr Patrick Treacy

THE NEEDLE AND THE DAMAGE DONE

AUSTIN MACAULEY PUBLISHERS™

LONDON * CAMBRIDGE * NEW YORK * SHARJAH

A CIP catalogue record for this title is available from the British Library.

ISBN 9781528977302 (Paperback)
ISBN 9781528977326 (ePub e-book)

www.austinmacauley.com

First Published (2021)
Austin Macauley Publishers Ltd
25 Canada Square
Canary Wharf
London
E14 5LQ

To my friend Frances Kenny, who co-authored part of my story, giving me the inspiration to keep writing on days when my passion ebbed, and, on many nights, taking pen to paper helping me to document the painful memories of the deaths of my mother and father and of my lost love.

Table of Contents

Prologue

I am writing this in isolation during lockdown in my Dublin home because of the SARS-CoV-2 pandemic now sweeping across the world. At the beginning of the year, we looked forward to the start of a new decade, and no one even knew that the corona virus COVID-19 even existed. The virus has spread to almost every country, infecting over one hundred and twenty million people whom we know about, and many more whom we do not. This figure is widely expected to reach possibly two hundred million and will devastate economies and disturb modern society on a scale that most living people will have never witnessed. Isolation is the ideal time for introspection. What things would one have done differently in hindsight? If I had made different career and personal life choices, how would my life have turned out? For a start, I would probably be writing a vastly different memoir.

History shows us that these pandemics often change the world for the better. They shine a light on what is broken in our society and possibly also how to fix it. When the Black Death first came to Europe in the 14th century, and Ebola to Africa in the 21st, the populous often turned against the medical teams trying to deal with the situation. The coronavirus pandemic, likewise, has led to increased prejudice, xenophobia, and racism against Chinese people. During lockdown, I wrote another book on this very topic.

This book in many ways is an updated version of my previous memoir *Behind the Mask*. The first half focuses on my rather adventurous journey into the world of medicine, while the latter half is related to what I have achieved since reaching there. It includes much of my pioneering research and international accolades, both from an early age to that within the new field of Aesthetic Medicine. Together we share the developments behind new procedures for treating HIV lipodystrophy patients, using patient's platelets and stem cells to help their hair growth, establishing protocols to reverse dermal filler vascular occlusions, and restoring epithelial tissue after the profound damage caused when these type of products are accidently injected into facial arteries. In fact, it was while discussing the award winning HELPIR technique that I developed to correct this damage with my staff in a bar in Dublin one evening, which give rise to the working title of this book '*The Needle and the Damage Done*'.

Writing this manuscript has given me a chance to remember so many people and places, and to reflect on my life. I have now lived through three global pandemics, HIV/AIDS from the last century, the later SARS, and this one. Each of them changed my life in their own way, and like many others, I await the outcome of the present one. The first one, HIV/AIDS, certainly changed my life, and left me with some sadness and regrets. However, it also subsequently drove me to visit the affected nations of southern, central, and eastern Africa in some humanitarian role. It also encouraged me to write a book on how pandemics change societies. Before this present pandemic happened, I had just received two important accolades, 'Top Aesthetic Practitioner in the World 2019' and 'Top Aesthetic Practitioner UK and Ireland 2019' (London). I was honoured that the MyFaceMyBody organisation gave me a specialist award for contributions to aesthetic medicine. I was given multiple international awards for work for my research into wound healing from Miami, Monaco, Dublin, Paris, and London. As we reach the final phase of lockdown, I am enlightened to learn that the recently discovered messengerRNA vaccines appear to successfully protect against the associated diseases of SARS Covid2 successfully. The pandemic deprived me of previously arranged lecturing opportunities in Taipei, Monaco, and Toronto. Rather, ironically, I was supposed to present MyFaceMyBody awards to aesthetic doctors in China last summer.

Pandemics bring with them times of radical change in their wake. They give us a possibility to remake a broken society into something better. My practice of medicine will change when we return to work and it is assumed virtual consultations and conferences will become the norm. I have already done Skype and Zoom conferences to Los Angeles, Saudi Arabia, London, St Petersburg, and Tbilisi, and am invited to host a television show in Paris in the fall.

Dr Patrick Treacy
Dublin March 2021

Foreword

I first met Dr Patrick Treacy in February 2010, shortly after the dreadful earthquake that nearly destroyed a great part of Haiti. I was blown away by this total stranger's kindness. Dr Treacy stood amid the debris of what once was our school and our home, holding an envelope. My heart opened to him immediately. I was amazed by the powerful speech he was making about the natural disaster that had struck the country.

My wife and I, at that stage only knew that he was an Irish doctor. We stood there in disbelief when he simply presented us with a cheque. In his eyes, we saw hope. He was ready to offer himself to humanity. Walking with him in the neighbourhood, I was filled with joy to see him comforting, touching, loving all these unfortunate people who were left with nothing. Dr Treacy interacted with them and made them laugh.

Soon after that, he invited us to come to his country to walk in the path of many great men by commemorating the annual Doolough Famine Walk with the people of Ireland. He said, 'Archbishop Desmond Tutu walked with us and three years later South Africa was liberated! Come and walk in his path for Haiti.' I strongly believe that the compassion and the love he has for the poor, the weak and the unfortunate would impress anyone on this planet, because he carries the world's problems on his shoulders.

It is a great honour to have been asked to express myself in the foreword of this book written by this remarkable man. Dr Treacy is a faithful servant with a strong personality, a friend of humanity. In this time of racial protest sweeping America, Patrick Treacy, is without borders and sees everyone in this world with one colour – the colour love. Yes, he is colour blind.

I am proud to present his new book, and trust it will speak to millions of hearts, as it did to mine.

Bishop Pierre-Pressler Dorcilien
Restoration Ministries, Mirebalais Haiti

Introduction

I have a story to tell, and if you follow me to the end of this book, you will understand why I have decided to write it down. It is a story that exposes many personal intimacies, from my financial struggles as a young doctor, to my time as the personal dermatologist to one of the most recognised faces in the universe, Michael Jackson. It is the story of how I got to know the singer as a friend and witnessed the personal agonies he suffered during the treatment of his vitiligo, of watching him cry as he took off his wig and showed me his scarred scalp. It is the story of how I smuggled cars to Turkey to finance my college studies and how I had to have a piece cut out of my leg to debride an HIV needle-stick from a Dublin heroin addict, in the days before there was any treatment for AIDS. However, it is also a story of overcoming adversity, to pioneering a whole new field of medicine, of winning many international awards and being voted 'Top Aesthetic Physician in the World' by my peers in the Bellagio, Las Vegas.

I never speak publicly about my patients, but in Michael's case, I have decided to make an exception. After watching the recent documentary, 'Leaving Neverland' myself, many questions remain. Some critics say that it is more a testimonial than journalistic endeavour, as people defending the singer were not involved or interviewed. I can only attest to the fact that anytime I saw Michael around children, including his own, he acted with total respect and love towards them.

This story begins with my childhood in Garrison, a small village in rural County Fermanagh. In the early pages, I nearly lose my life in Northern Ireland's ethno-political conflict, and I witness the death of our bread delivery man, Jack McClenaghan, one spring day in May 1979. Retired from the Ulster Defence Regiment (UDR), he was out making deliveries when the IRA motorcyclists fired their bullets. His next stop would have been our house. From my earliest childhood, I dreamt of travel and adventure, of living amongst the Marsh Arabs that Wilfred Thesiger wrote about, of experiencing the thrill of flying with the

Royal Flying Doctor Service, like on the TV series from Broken Hill in New South Wales, Australia. If life is about living out your childhood dreams, then I have long since achieved that ambition, lived those adventures. I will tell you how I was captured by Saddam Hussein's army near the town of Halabja, while working as a doctor in Iraq.

As my story unfolds, you will see how my parents were influential in determining my decisions. My mother instilled in me a passion for education. She was determined that her children would all go to university and encouraged me to study medicine at the Royal College of Surgeons in Dublin. My father, meanwhile, had a gift for making me believe in myself. He had a variety of passions, including local history, and together we would spend our Sundays exploring the megalithic tombs in the West Fermanagh area. In those historic places, if we listened closely to the wind, we could almost hear the spirits of our ancestors and the heartbeats of the generations of people who came before us. He showed me places where teachers had once run Catholic hedge schools, trying to hide from the ever-watching British Armies. You will understand my gratitude to him when I tell you about the night, he cut down the expensive billboard outside our garage and used it to build some soundproof boxes that I needed for my research but couldn't afford to buy. They helped me win both the British Amateur Young Scientist of the Year title and the Irish Aer Lingus Biochemist of the Year title. I treasured these memories and later recounted them to Michael Jackson after he told me of his hugely different childhood.

Determined to become a doctor, I recall having to raise money for medical school after Margaret Thatcher stopped my grant. After qualifying, while working in a hospital in Dublin in 1987, disaster struck: a needle, which I had used to draw blood from a patient with HIV, accidently jabbed me in the leg. Overwhelmed by the emotions this incident stirred up, I emigrated to New Zealand, and then started a peripatetic existence, working as a doctor in Baghdad, California, South Africa, Australia and elsewhere. Thankfully, I never caught the disease. On returning to Dublin, I set up the Ailesbury Clinic, championing treatments such as the novel use of lasers, dermal fillers and botulinum toxin. This new field of medicine gave me the opportunity for research for which I won many awards over the years.

Central to the early part of this memoir is my personal journey: my efforts to escape the Troubles, cope with the fear that I might have contracted HIV, try to get over my lost love and later to detail some of the pioneering research for which

I have won many international awards over the past few years. As you read it, we will stand together at the Berlin Wall on the night it falls, and in Moscow on the night the Soviet Union ends. You will visit Iraq where I was arrested as a spy while documenting the gassing of the Kurds. We will see how I helped pioneer a whole new field of medicine from a small room in an apartment in Dublin and how the rich and famous eventually came to get treatment in those small rooms. You will read how cosmetic medicine developed into its own specialty and how, within ten years, I was invited to lecture to doctors worldwide, mainly about techniques that were started in Dublin. These included treating HIV lipodystrophy patients with facial implants, treating migraine with botulinum toxin, using a patient's own platelets and growth factors to try and make them look younger. Later, you will hear how I scaled up our clinic worldwide, only to have to close some of them again as we faced the terrible Irish recession.

As Ben Franklin said, 'Out of adversity comes opportunity,' and I wrote this book largely as a means of filling the time that the recession and the lockdown created for me. It has also been cathartic, cleansing my mind of some memories that had remained with me. This is the story of my personal journey, of surviving life, of how I got to where I am.

1. The Early Years

Garrison, the picturesque little fishing village where I grew up, lies perched on the border of the Republic of Ireland, snuggled into the scenic shores of Lough Melvin and is favoured by tourists from all over the world. The older boatmen told stories of famous people, like Charlie Chaplin, having once visited the locale to fish for salmon and trout. The regular influx of different nationalities to the area meant that, although it had a distinctly rural character, it wasn't insular. I learnt my first Bob Dylan songs on guitar when I was twelve, from some long-haired Americans who stayed at the local youth hostel. The village had a caravan park, two hotels and a smattering of public houses, so when I was young, the place was a hive of activity in summertime.

The conflict in Northern Ireland, which we euphemistically called "the Troubles", pitted Protestant neighbour against Catholic. Since our garage served both sides of the community, our family tried to remain impartial. In fact, we would sometimes have a known IRA volunteer standing with a UDR reservist, waiting for my father. That was the nature of the conflict: the fields had to be tilled, the broken harvesters repaired, but when twilight came, the guns were loaded. The cultural differences could be seen and heard all around us. They were in the colours of our school jackets, which newspapers we bought, and sadly, the games we played. Sometimes difference was more subtly felt – an intangible, steely force honed by years of hatred and mistrust. My father's favourite piece of advice was: 'If you have to say something, say nothing.'

As young children, the conflict skimmed above our heads like the stones we threw across Lough Melvin, and Garrison was a wonderful place to grow up. There were seven in our family: four boys and three girls. When we were young, we had the freedom of the nearby lakes and green fields, our daily adventures limited only by our rural imaginations. We spoke a dialect all our own. '*Bad cest to you, ya havral!*' was a common expression that evoked misfortune on another and was probably only understood within a twenty-mile radius of Garrison. Our country naïveté was offset by a wonderful sense of community spirit; neighbours looked out for one another and helped those who needed it, whether with food or labour. Of course, the price of this was a loss of privacy, but that didn't particularly bother us. Everybody knew – and *wanted* to know – everybody else's business.

Early years as the man in the middle

My parents were devout Catholics, and both had taken the "Pioneer pledge", promising that they would never drink alcohol. They were decent, industrious people who worked long hours to provide for our family. We weren't given to open displays of affection in our house but I knew I was well loved – it was shown in other ways, like in the small handcrafted toys my father spent hours making, or the long, unsociable hours my mother worked in her shop, saving all she could for our education. The shop supplied the villagers with their daily needs, but because it was attached to our home, it was really more like a prison for my mother as people came from seven in the morning and thought nothing of knocking on the door for a packet of cigarettes on their way home from a dance in Bundoran at three in the morning.

On weekends, our father would take us to the local cinema in Ballyshannon and sometimes, on Sundays, to the dodgem cars in Bundoran or the nearby unspoilt beaches in Rossnowlagh. He excelled at telling stories and had an unending repertoire of legends about our forefathers and how they had lived hundreds of years earlier. I loved these stories, as they belonged to the atmosphere of the village and, more importantly, who we were as a people.

My father, Pat, was a mechanic by trade and, as such, was involved in the daily affairs of the local community – fixing the outdated cars and machinery which were the economic lifeblood of our neighbours' lives and harvests. He had been raised in Corramore, a townland about two miles up the road from our house, and had spent his entire life in the village, so everyone knew the "seed and breed" of him, as they say. Similarly, my mother, through her grocery shop, knew the financial circumstances of our neighbours; every year she waited until they sold their livestock at the harvest fair in Ballyshannon before receiving payment for the provisions of the previous year. I remember her working late into the night, adding up lists of debtors, too tired to say the rosary. She often fell asleep during the *Joyful Mysteries*, giving me and my brother, Raymond, an opportunity to sneak upstairs and listen to the latest hits on Radio Luxembourg. In those childhood days before the Troubles began, the sounds of the Beatles and the Rolling Stones led us to believe that England was a wondrous Shangri-La across the Irish Sea.

Everyone in our family was expected to help in the business after school. My sisters – Anne, Bernadette, and Caroline – mainly helped my mother in the shop. The boys – Sean, Raymond, Brian, and I – usually helped in the garage, often working late into the evening if my father's workload was particularly heavy. These roles were not set in stone and we all helped wherever we were needed. When I was young, I loved to spend the long dark winter evenings with my father by an open fire in his old bicycle shop, built before the garage opened. He and his friends gathered around a brown HMV valve radio, listening to what was happening in the outside world. These were the days before television, and I remember how the neighbours told each other stories and laughed away the winter nights. The shop was filled with broken gramophone springs, brass carbide lamps and the warm tones of the old radio. Some of the news from the radio, like the assassination of President John F Kennedy in 1963, was incredibly sad and I still remember how they all fell silent. Almost every Catholic household in the locality had a framed photo of JFK, twinned with one of the Pope, hanging in their living room. Kennedy was considered an honorary Irishman and a decent human being who was going to set the world right. The memory is deeply ingrained because I had never heard of anyone dying like that – assassinated – but, more importantly, because it was the first time, I had seen my father cry, so I cried too.

Sometimes, he and his friends stayed up until the early hours of the morning listening to heavyweight boxing matches like the big Cassius Clay vs Sonny Liston fight in 1964. On nights like this, the bicycle shop was charged with excitement, the men jumping to their feet and punching the air at imaginary opponents. When Sonny Liston withdrew, they became even more excited and the voice of the man who claimed to float like a butterfly and sting like a bee crackled into our shop: 'I *am* the greatest!' Shortly after that fight, he changed his name to Muhammad Ali.

When I was eight, my father decided to expand his business by building a dedicated garage and having petrol pumps installed. This required local contractors to dig a large hole in front of our house to accommodate two fuel tanks. The JCB digger operator was called Danny Keown, and he was helped by a local man who was nicknamed 'Big Bad John' after a Jimmy Dean hit. We, kids, enjoyed chatting to them while they worked, as they were the first adults, we'd spoken to outside of our own family circle.

Such was the excitement on the morning the petrol pumps arrived that I decided to skip school and hide in my bedroom. I wanted to be with my father and my Uncle Johnny, who was helping to install them. My mother was furious when she discovered me and insisted that I go to school immediately. My father, sensing my disappointment, took a different view. 'Sheila, it's a big day for all of us, he just wanted to be here to see it,' he said. 'Tell Master Regan he's sick – he'll remember this day long after that old school is gone.' I couldn't articulate it at the time, but this felt like a rite of passage, as if my father was treating me as a grown up for the first time. It later transpired that he was right: Devenish No. 2 Primary School closed in 1972, but the old petrol pumps are still standing.

I remember every detail of that day, including the proud look on my father's face when the electricity supply to the Regent Super pump was connected and he filled his black Austin A40 Devon with his own petrol for the very first time. He shook the droplets from the nozzle, put the hose back in position, then scooped me up, placed me in the open boot of the car and drove the short mile into Garrison to buy me a celebratory ice cream. Those were the days before health and safety regulations gained a stranglehold, when childhood was full of excitement and wonder.

My father didn't always agree with my antics, however. One day, when I was about ten and my brother Raymond was six, an elderly farmer called Johnny Keenan arrived at the garage driving a light blue A30. Johnny was small and stubby, with patchy white hair. His car had been Austin's answer to the Morris Minor when it was launched in 1951, but fifteen years had passed since then and it had aged and rusted. My father was out on a job, so the old farmer addressed himself to me.

'Would you be able to fix that hole in her, Sonny?' he said.

Johnny pointed to a large rusty perforation that had recently grown in the front wing on the passenger side. To others, I was called PJ, to distinguish me from my father, Pat. But Johnny Keenan always referred to me as 'Sonny'.

'Sure, I can fix it with Isopon filler, Johnny. Do you know what the colour of her is on the logbook so I can get an exact match?'

'It says sky blue on the tax book, Sonny,' he replied, tightening the rope belt around his coat before leaving. 'I'll pick it up in the morning.'

Although we had a new DeVilbiss paint spray-gun, Raymond and I decided the job was too small to warrant using it or even going to the bother of mixing paint from our suppliers in Enniskillen. Cans of spray paint hadn't been invented, or if they had been, they hadn't reached Garrison. After a little deliberation, Raymond remembered that our mother had tins of sky-blue gloss household paint on sale in the shop, and he ran off to fetch some while I began to fill the hole.

We worked late into the evening and, in a magnanimous gesture, when the wing was completed, we decided to balance the slightly different colours by painting the entire car. Raymond climbed onto the roof to apply some finishing touches, and we had a struggle to get him back down without ruining the job or getting him covered in blue paint. When we were finished, we stood back to admire our handiwork. It had been no mean feat for two small boys armed with paint brushes and two cans of gloss paint, but we had pulled it off. Exhausted but happy with our night's work, we went inside and fell into bed.

The next morning my father called us into the garage. He was standing, hands in pockets, staring open-mouthed at the elderly gentleman's car. For a moment, I thought he was awestruck by our work of art. He wasn't.

'What did yous pair do to Johnny Keenan's good car?' he roared as he paced alongside the offending vehicle, shaking his head. 'Yous have destroyed the man's car and he's coming for it this morning!'

My father was a mild-mannered man who dreaded any type of confrontation with his customers and was sometimes known to hide in the house when the more challenging ones arrived. There was George Blair from Garrison Post Office, with his continually revving engine; Fonsie McGovern from the Melvin Hotel, with his broken outboard motors and, to top the lot, Vincent Kennedy from Glen Cross, with his disassembled lawnmowers. Each of them was one of God's children, and part of my father's never-ending technical nightmare. To be honest, I enjoyed their company, especially Fonsie, who always treated me as an adult. They were all characters who used our garage as an extension of their own workshops, but their endless trivia often got in the way of our other, paying customers. My father, thinking he would have to face Johnny Keenan's fury, politely sought refuge in the village for half an hour while his two prepubescent sons were left to deal with the problem.

True to form, Johnny Keenan arrived exactly when he said he would, to collect his car.

'That's a newer model than mine,' he said, looking with rheumy eyes at the sparkling blue vehicle which my father had parked at the back of the garage. 'Where's my own?'

'Daddy went out to Garrison in it,' I replied, unable to make the confession.

'Will he be long, Sonny?'

'I don't really know – he was gone before I got up here,' I mumbled. As is the custom of rural farmers, Johnny started to explore. He proceeded to get into the car and found his prayer book and rosary beads in the front pocket of the dashboard.

'He must have taken all my stuff out of the car before he left. I wonder why he did that?' he said, still not making the connection.

A difficult fifteen minutes of shrugging shoulders and skirting the issue passed before my father returned and parked his car down the road at the petrol pumps, still not daring to come into the garage.

'Your father is in a black car, Sonny – he just pulled up at the pumps,' Johnny said, perplexed.

After a while, my father relented and slowly made his way back up to the garage to join us.

'Well? Did you tell him yet?' Dad asked.

'No, not yet,' I muttered, my eyes fixed on the toe of my shoe. 'That's a newer model than mine, Pat,' Johnny said to my father as he got into the front seat. 'Is it an A35? Naw, it couldn't be – they'd have trafficators!' he mused, referring to the little orange stalks which used to pop up in the centre of the door frame before electric indicators were invented.

I couldn't take it anymore.

'Johnny, that's your car,' I blurted out. 'Me and Ramy painted it for you last night.'

'My car?' He scratched his head slowly as he took another look. '*My* car?'

'Well, if that's my car, I'm a very happy man and yous can have a fiver each for the bother you put into it!'

He took his wallet from his pocket and handed my brother and me £5 each.

Of course, it didn't really cover the filler and labour we'd put into it, or my mother's paint, or the possible repercussions of having such an advertisement driven around the countryside, but Ramy and I didn't care – we were in the money!

I learnt a valuable lesson that morning: own up to your actions, however hard it may be, because nothing is worse than waiting for the hammer to fall. I have often wondered whether Johnny later spoke to my father in private about the incident.

*

The Northern Ireland state, which I grew up in had only been in existence for a few generations. Although children didn't actively participate in the politics of the day, the fact that Catholics and Protestants were segregated in unique school systems meant we were taught two quite different versions of history. This left lingering marks on us, much like the thumbprints the priest left on our foreheads on Ash Wednesday, but not as easily washed away.

The problems between our communities started after the partition of Ireland in 1920, when a small group of Irish Republican Army members in the North dedicated themselves to achieving a united Ireland. The new Northern government passed the Civil Authorities (Special Powers) Act (Northern Ireland) 1922, giving the Protestant police force power to do almost anything they deemed necessary to eradicate this danger. Unfortunately, long after the threat had been dealt with, the Act was still used against ordinary Catholics. Many Catholics were not allowed to hold jobs in the public service, and Protestants were given priority on housing lists. The new brand of democracy was not "one man, one vote", but "one *house*, one vote" and, as Protestants generally owned more property than Catholics, their community held the reins in politics.

Despite this discrimination, two significant events had taken place in the social upheaval of post-war Britain that favoured the Catholics: the introduction of social welfare and free university education. The poor of Britain no longer needed to send their children out to work to help support the family, so they sent them to school instead. In this new socialist world, the Labour Party had unknowingly sown the seeds of a new, well-educated generation of Irish Catholics, who would no longer be willing to accept the status quo. Indeed, my generation was the first to benefit from the new, "fairer" scheme.

*

My primary school teacher, Master Regan, lived next door to us. He was in his late fifties, with a shock of white hair, and he brought us to school in Garrison each morning in his brown and white Hillman Minx car. This didn't entitle us to any special treatment; in fact, sometimes, after my older brother had been mischievous at school, we had to endure the odd silent journey the following morning.

In those days at Devenish No 2 Primary School, I would imagine the world outside of our village. The world map on the wall was like a door to another universe, one where they spoke those strange languages, I'd heard on the wooden shortwave radio in my father's bicycle shop. At break time, I would carefully take down the large school atlas from the top of Master Regan's cupboard and then the very essence of my day would change. My finger would run across the red expanse of the Soviet Union, following the snaking route of the Trans-Siberian Express from Minsk to Tomsk and beyond. The imaginary train's whistle would blow in short, steady blasts, telling me it was arriving at a station in a place far away from Garrison. Images of snowy Siberian landscapes, of red setting suns that cast long shadows along the carriages, filled my boyhood imagination. By the time the train reached Irkutsk, it was usually time to leave the atlas aside for another day.

One day, a missionary priest visited our school and I remember how his eyes hardened, almost glazed over, as he told us how the pagan Russians had no religion and were destined to go to hell. He was taken aback when the teacher allowed me to mention the towns on the route of the Trans-Siberian Express. When my mother seemed to agree with the missionary, I discovered there were lots of people out there who were destined for damnation and felt lucky to be born into the one true faith.

Mr Regan was one of the best teachers I have ever met. He had a great love of life and was passionate about nature and about our cultural heritage. He taught us the old language, Gaelic, and all things Irish. In class, he explained that our family names were important parts of our heritage and taught us local history. 'P J,' he told me once, 'your townland is called Knockaraven, a word that comes from the Gaelic "Cnoc an Aifrean", which means "Hill of the Mass".'

We learnt about our religion, and about how the English had banned our forefathers from practising their Catholic faith and had executed our priests for performing the sacred ritual of the Mass. Master Regan told us about the lookouts who watched from rocky vantage points to warn of approaching English troops and that one of these was located near Glen Cross, close to where my father was born. He taught us to be proud that our ancestors had stuck to their religious convictions amidst such adversity, and that we should be thankful to have a proper school, as Catholic education in that period had been carried out in secret hedge schools, groups of students hiding from view behind large hedges.

Master Regan explained to us that the village's name, 'Garrison', was a reference to a barracks erected by the Protestant King William of Orange when he halted in the village before the Battle of the Boyne in 1690. William's victory in that battle had secured the Protestant ascendancy, and British rule in Ireland. The local Orange Order provoked much antagonism when they marched in his memory through the village of Garrison each year.

In 1967, I passed the entrance exam to St Michael's Grammar School. I was to be plucked from the innocence of childhood and sent to a far-off boarding school in the market town of Enniskillen. This was normal for a rural student from my area, as there was no grammar school close to our village at that time. Although the seminary type school I was headed to have a wonderful academic reputation, the prospect of leaving my parents behind at such a young age unnerved me.

My brother, Sean, who was four years my senior, was already at St Michael's, but mostly I felt that I was now on my own, fending for myself in a strange world where I was subject to loneliness and, often, cruel bullying. I knew that I had to come to terms with my new situation, but, although I never doubted the pedagogical prowess of the priests to whom my education had been entrusted, theirs was a strict style that could never inspire the same sense of wonder and desire to learn that Master Regan's approach had.

I often lay awake in the dormitory and listened to others crying softly late into the night. We lived a regimented existence, rising at eight every morning to attend Mass in the chapel and taking breaks throughout the day for prayer, the Angelus at noon and the rosary every night. Although I came from a religious home – my father went to Mass every morning – this religiosity was overwhelming. During weekly confession, we sat in the large wooden pews waiting our turns, watching as the other unfortunates walked up behind the main altar to tell the priest their sins. Everybody immediately knew if a student had admitted to masturbation as the priest loudly chastised him in front of the rest of us. The humiliated boy would then have to walk all the way back to his seat amidst the hushed chorus of his friends. It was public mortification without a right to defend oneself. I hated it.

Corporal punishment was legal in Ireland at that time and we were regularly strapped for small infractions of the rules. The instrument used was made of compressed leather, which was brought down hard across the palms of our hands. The Dean, whom my older brother had nicknamed 'Stokey', was particularly cruel. He had us choose which colour leather we'd like used on us – black, brown or white – increasing the time we spent in anticipation of our punishment. After school hours, boys debated which colour was the best. Tactics were discussed too, such as dropping our hands slightly when the leather was about to make contact. That required perfect timing and, in my opinion, didn't really work, although some boys swore by it. It took a lot of willpower not to withdraw your hand as you saw the strap coming. If you did so, the punishment would perhaps be doubled and dished out by an even angrier man.

We were also subjected to ear and hair pulling and the occasional knuckle to the shoulder or side of the head. This wasn't really considered a punishment, more a reinforcement of whatever point the teacher was making to a boy he didn't think was paying enough attention. I'm sure one Irish teacher, in particular, was responsible for many later cases of baldness.

Some of the boarders couldn't take the school's strict regime and ran away – a futile exercise, which only made matters worse for them when they returned. It was difficult for some young rural boarders because, in those days, if they went home and told their parents the teacher had hit them, they were often informed that they must have done something to deserve it. Although some of the priests were later accused of abuse, I never witnessed any during my time at this school.

Life at the seminary followed regular patterns and, every month, we could see a film in the recreation hall. I looked forward to this and fondly remember the black and white 1938 biographical drama about Father Edward Flanagan's work with disadvantaged boys in *Boys Town* and the 1953 colour epic *Shane*, starring Alan Ladd. From time to time, we were also allowed downtown to the Ritz Cinema to see recent Hollywood films such as *Butch Cassidy and the Sundance Kid*, *Doctor Zhivago* and *The Sound of Music*, films that reinforced a sense of decency and social mores that I had learnt at home and still carry with me to this day.

*

My father couldn't come to collect me every weekend. It was a fifty-mile round trip from Garrison to Enniskillen. On top of the time the journey itself took, he was likely to be stopped by the British army and asked a series of tedious questions about the nature of his trip while his car was searched. Apart from this ordeal, there were still five children at home, and my mother had her hands full. At times, I remained at school for as long as three months without seeing my family and, eventually, I learnt to get over the separation. On weekends at the school, we amused ourselves by playing soccer, which I wasn't very good at. It was annoying to be picked second to last for the team and, for a while, I took up hurling, eventually becoming a reserve on the Fermanagh team. There was no rugby at our school, but, for Gaelic football, we had a new pitch, which we were all immensely proud of and enjoyed playing on.

Sometimes we went to the handball alley, but what I most enjoyed were the few occasions when we were allowed downtown to Enniskillen, where I had the opportunity to meet with my old Garrison neighbours – mostly farmers who came to the weekly mart on Belmore Street. It was always a real pleasure to meet them and hear all the news from home that hadn't been included in my mother's letters.

With my mother in Garrison

In the summer months, many of the younger students went to the Donegal Gaeltacht to live for a while amongst native Irish speakers and hopefully improve their native tongue. My mother had been born in this county and we were well used to her speaking Irish to our ourselves and our neighbours when we were growing up.

'*Suí síos ansin le do thoil*,' she'd say while offering someone a place to sit.

It was a wonderful opportunity to meet girls from Mount Lourdes Convent in Enniskillen, and many friendships forged amongst the wild hills of Loughanure, Annagry and Ranafast in west Donegal still survive to this day. While there, we'd jump on the backs of bread delivery vans and hitch lifts to the nearby villages. This is how I first met the Irish traditional group, Clannad, who were performing in their father's pub in Crolly, mixing cover versions of the Beatles and the Beach Boys with traditional music. We continued our friendship in later years when we met again in the clubs of Dublin.

After the Gaeltacht, I went home to spend the rest of the summer helping my father in the garage. He was old school, having trained as a mechanic in the days

29

before cars had microprocessors and computer sensors. He always left the more complex technical problems to me and Sean, who was naturally talented and became my mentor in the garage during my teenage years. There was nothing he didn't know about car engines and, much to the consternation of some of our neighbours, he loved to race cars along the local roads. Despite that, the villagers really missed him when he left Garrison and moved up to Lisburn to start a family of his own. As hormones developed, I developed an interest in some of the local girls in Garrison. Things came to a head when I was caught in a sexual embrace by the local priest outside the community centre. I managed to escape but he got my red corduroy jacket, which had a Rolling Stones badge and a drawing of Jesus Christ that identified me immediately. When he came to our house later, I stood up to his abusive tirade and stated that he had absolutely no right to dictate my moral behaviour and that the Catholic Church's dictatorial control of our destinies was akin to totalitarianism requiring subservience they would never get from me. I could see my mother smiling in the corner as she told me stories about these people that had forced a friend of hers to have more children against medical advice, resulting in her fatality. The local priest left in disgust screaming about communism, damnation, and the fires of hell. We all said nothing, knowing a small battle had been won in our kitchen that night. From the late 1980s, allegations of sexual abuse of children associated with Catholic institutions and clerics in several countries started to be the subject of sporadic, isolated reports. In Ireland, beginning in the 1990s, a series of criminal cases and Irish government enquiries established that hundreds of priests had abused thousands of children over decades.

*

At sixteen, I won several awards, including "Northern Ireland's British Amateur Young Scientist of the Year" and the "Republic of Ireland's Aer Lingus Biochemist of the Year". My winning project showed the effects of different sound waves on plant growth. Many of the judges thought it was ahead of its time. My research secured me a personal introduction to British Prime Minister Harold Wilson at the London International Youth Science Fortnight in 1974. My parents were proud of my academic achievements when they were later printed in the *Fermanagh Herald* about a young Catholic boy meeting a British prime minister. Throughout these years, I lived in two totally different worlds – the rural and the academic – and it seemed as though I had a foot in each.

2. The Troubles Begin

The world I was growing up in began to irrevocably change in 1968, when the newly formed Northern Ireland Civil Rights Association (NICRA) began a series of peaceful protest marches against discrimination, calling for "one man, one vote" and the repeal of the Special Powers Act. The members of the organisation used the language and symbolism of Americans who followed Dr Martin Luther King. In October of that year, a march in Derry was met with a violent backlash from the largely Protestant police force, the Royal Ulster Constabulary (RUC). Three days of rioting followed, and many Catholic homes were burnt to the ground.

Undaunted, in January 1969, thousands set out on a peaceful march from Belfast to Derry and were attacked by loyalists and off-duty policemen who carried bricks, bottles and iron bars. The marchers retreated to Catholic areas, where they erected barricades to stop the police from entering. Police were seen to side with loyalists and the rioting got worse over a period of two days, spreading to other towns across Ulster. There were murmurings of rebellion when we watched the news and saw the burnt-out houses and the horror these riots had left in their wake. Fifteen hundred refugees were moved across the border and took up residence in the Republic.

Irish Taoiseach Jack Lynch said he could no longer stand by and see nationalists under attack in Northern Ireland. He deployed the Irish army to the borders of the six counties with medical aid and a plan called Exercise Armageddon. The planned invasion of the six counties was halted when the British army arrived and ring-fenced Catholic areas in Derry and Belfast, protecting them from further attack. Catholics who believed the presence of the British army would bring stability, though, were in for a rude awakening. Soon after the army arrived, it became obvious that most of its men held the same views as their RUC counterparts, and one was as likely to be stopped, questioned

– and often abused – by somebody with a Liverpool or a Leeds accent as by someone with an Enniskillen accent.

This was a new age of television journalism, and little could be hidden from the eyes of the world. Even though I was still a teenager and unable to assess the situation properly, I was incensed at the treatment of the protesters and the brutality of the Northern Ireland security forces. Although I had been exposed to some conflict in my early life, I had never experienced anything on this scale. I saw a creeping coldness replace the warmth that had long characterised the people of Northern Ireland. Neighbours who had been friends for many years now began to take a different attitude towards each another and even schoolchildren were careful about who they spoke to.

It was during this increasing tide of turmoil that a new church was consecrated in Garrison. Along with Patsy Tracey, the son of the local contractor who had installed our petrol pumps, I was let out from St Michael's for the day to attend the ceremony. Although he was younger than me, we were great friends and I was delighted when he joined me as a boarder in far-off Enniskillen. One of the most popular pastimes there was to take the red phosphorous material from three or four match heads, pack it into the hollow barrel of a key, tamp it down with a nail, tie it with string and bounce it quickly against a wall, making it to explode with a "bang". It was a childish game we played to see who could make the loudest noise, but I suppose if we had been picked up by the British army with these "bangers" in our possession, we might have been perceived as the IRA bombmakers of the future.

The old stone church in Garrison, where Patsy and I had served together as altar boys, had outlived its usefulness and residents had been collecting money for a long time to replace it with a new structure, even seeking donations from as far away as America. When the goal was finally achieved, we were all invited to attend the grand unveiling. Residents were bursting with pride, and local women had festooned the altar with bouquets of fresh flowers, ready for Canon Hackett to arrive and preside over the inaugural Mass.

All the villagers were dressed in their Sunday best. Patsy sat behind me as Canon Hackett started his welcoming speech from the lectern. We had been messing around with bangers on the way, and I had slipped mine into my pocket as we went in to attend the ceremony. At some point, Patsy must have become bored because he slid his hand into my pocket and retrieved the banger. He was trying different nails for size when the banger exploded in his hands. Canon

Hackett teetered sideways in shock, and a group of men who thought he was injured ran to form a protective circle around him. Smoke and a sulphurous stench filled the air, children began to cry and someone in the congregation shouted that the Canon had been shot! For a few moments I believed he had been shot too, because I hadn't felt Patsy take the banger. It was only when I turned and saw the horror on his face that I realised what had happened. I remember my mind whirring through a list of excuses that might save him from discovery, but nothing materialised in time. As the last wisps of smoke cleared, it was obvious who the culprit was.

The whole village was in an uproar and, once they got over their shock, the priests vented their anger on Patsy and his extended family. As the weeks and months wore on, I genuinely thought that the incident would be forgiven and forgotten. But that wasn't the case. It was a harsh reaction and totally undeserved – it was indisputably an accident. With the wisdom of passing years, though, I suppose the reaction must be seen in the context of the changing circumstances in the previously tranquil village.

*

My father played the box accordion, and during the summer, we would attend *Céilís*, small social gatherings where people perfected their Irish dancing to the musical accompaniment of jigs and reels. In hindsight, he was exceptionally good, and the sessions were always enjoyable, but my musical tastes were maturing and veering more in the direction of T Rex and David Bowie. This began to separate me from some of my childhood friends in Garrison, who were listening to the country music that the showbands played in the Astoria in Bundoran. Musical tastes in rural Ireland were important as they defined where one went to dances, what one talked about and probably even who one would eventually marry.

At fifteen, I started going to dances. One of the first bands I followed was the hard-rock band Thin Lizzy, which had formed in Dublin a few years earlier. Their lead singer, Phil Lynott, was a tall, thin black man with a huge Afro and a strong Dublin accent. This was unusual, as not many black people lived in Ireland at the time. Thin Lizzy later found fame on *Top of the Pops* in the UK with their hit single *Whiskey in the Jar*, but on the night, I first saw them, they were just another fledgling band.

It was a slightly older friend, Thomas Maguire, who brought me to see Thin Lizzy in the Holyrood Hotel in Bundoran. When Phil took to the stage, he had a great personal presence, performing with a bottle of champagne in one hand and a microphone in the other. Tommy and I decided to grab a bit of Thin Lizzy memorabilia. As the singer raised the bottle to his lips, I ran forward and made a grab for it, but he moved his body sideways and I accidentally ended up with the gold chain from around his neck dangling in my hand. I didn't know what to do with it, so I looked at Tommy and we both ran and hid behind the bar at the back of the hall.

Phil stopped playing and demanded the return of the chain, which he said his mother had given to him. Anyone who was a fan of Phil Lynott knew how precious his mother was to him. The dancing crowd parted before me like the Red Sea but, unlike Moses leading the Israelites, I was completely in the wrong and had to make my way back up to the stage to return the item. Phil took the chain, smiled and handed over the rest of the bottle of champagne for Tommy and me to finish, even though I was too young to drink.

*

That summer, I started a little business from home, fixing radios and televisions. One of my first customers was an aged bachelor called Paddy McGuinness, who was a great lover of *The Gay Byrne Hour* on *RTÉ*. He told me his radio was broken and asked if I could fix it. It was a 1959 Bush transistor model with a dial that moved a red line across the different stations to the right wavelength. Paddy was accustomed to finding his favourite presenter at a point on the dial, which he had marked on the side of the radio with a red pencil line. During the repairs, I had to retie the old, tethered cord over the tuning spindles, and Gay Byrne was inadvertently moved further along the bandwidth. No matter how hard I tried, I couldn't convince him that he was still listening to *RTÉ*. Even though I waited until it was time for Gay Byrne to come on and brought the radio to Paddy's house to let him hear the show, he still wouldn't believe me – he accused me of tuning in some English station where he wouldn't be able to hear the Sunday Gaelic Athletic Association (GAA) football game. I eventually had to send across to Manchester for a new tuning cord before he would take the radio back from me. The characters in the village pubs, Gilroy's, and Casey's, would joyfully recall this story whenever I visited home in later years.

Paddy McGuiness wasn't the only villager who loved the Sunday game. Gaelic football was immensely popular in west Fermanagh, and the GAA tended to maintain the Catholic cultural traditions of the parish. The organisation had been banned by the British government in 1918 for its association with the nationalist cause, and the GAA had immediately reciprocated by expelling civil servants who had taken the oath of allegiance to the Queen of England. This had alienated some Protestants, who already viewed the organisation with suspicion. Still, the GAA was immensely popular, with every county in Ireland participating in intensely fought football and hurling competitions each year. This was part of the Irish psyche and, in the days before television became popular, many people spent their Sundays listening to these matches on the radio.

County Leitrim lay less than a mile from us, across the border, in the Republic. As technology improved and we became glued to colour televisions, a lot of homes in nearby Leitrim still owned old valve radios powered by four-volt glass batteries, which required weekly recharging. Every Saturday evening, these radio owners would leave our bicycle shop, cycling in small flotillas with the glass batteries attached to the spring carriers on the backs of their bikes. My father got good business from them, but as the demand for the service decreased, he relocated the chargers from the bicycle shop up to the garage, where my brothers and I worked, modifying all types of old demolition cars for rallycross competitions. In this sport, villages pitted their best drivers against each other on summer Sundays, churning up fields that had been made available by local farmers. It was a great way of disposing of the old Ford Anglias and Morris Marinas when stricter regulations forced them off the road.

One night, when I was using an arc welder to build a safety cage on a Mini, I accidentally ignited the hydrogen gas being emitted from the batteries, and they exploded, scattering shards of glass all around me. The next evening, the Leitrim football fans started arriving to collect their batteries in preparation for Sunday's match. By the time four or five hostile customers had arrived, we realised that Leitrim were playing in the Connaught provincial final and the spark had ignited more than the batteries. Eventually, Dad hit upon the idea of inviting them all down the following afternoon to watch the match on a colour television placed on a box in the garage. Some of the farmers pitched in and brought along a crate or two of Guinness, and my mother made tea and sandwiches. It was a great afternoon, and everybody was happy – except me. I had to replace their batteries out of my pocket money.

At the end of the '60s, ideological differences in the IRA led to a schism and the formation of the Provisional IRA, known as "the Provos". The prime minister of Northern Ireland, Brian Faulkner, introduced a new law giving the authorities the power to detain Catholics suspected of republican activities indefinitely without trial. I remember everyone in the village being shocked when some of our neighbours were lifted. Many of those who were interned had no affiliation with any paramilitary organisation. The years 1970-72 were to prove the bloodiest period of the Troubles, and the conflict came closer to Garrison. Five bombs exploded in Enniskillen in the space of a fortnight. A permanent gloom slowly descended over the county, our trips downtown were reduced and we were told to report signs of anything out of the ordinary. As fifteen-year-old boys in St Michael's, we were no longer immune to what was happening in the larger world around us.

The state of Northern Ireland was descending into anarchy and the government responded to the worsening situation by opening a second internment camp, at Magilligan, overlooking Lough Foyle. As the conflict deepened, five armed men entered the youth hostel in Garrison and planted a bomb, which destroyed the building. The Melvin Hotel, which my father's friend Fonsie McGovern owned, was blown up some days later, during a Catholic wedding reception. The local IRA issued a statement saying that it was retaliation for allowing members of the security forces to stay on the premises.

The Troubles then spread like a forest fire along the Fermanagh border, with the nearby village of Belleek being the target for several bombs, including one at the Carlton Hotel and one at the Custom House. Things worsened when a twenty-minute gun battle between the British army and the IRA broke out in the main street of Belleek. No day passed without an incident and before long came the inevitable deaths, with fellow Fermanagh men RUC Constable Raymond Carroll, from Enniskillen, and RUC Sergeant Peter Gilgun, from Belcoo, dying in a rake of machinegun fire. After a spate of further shootings, hijackings and explosions, the border roads around Garrison were closed, bringing desolation and economic misery to the little village where I grew up.

The West Fermanagh IRA responded to these closures by taking forestry worker Thomas Fletcher, who was a private in the UDR, from his home and shooting him in the shed where my father and I used to go to fix his tractor. They asked five of Fletcher's farmer friends, who were also members of the UDR, to leave their homes, which they did, fearing they would otherwise meet the same fate; these were my neighbours, people I met every day, customers in my father's garage. The British army then cratered all access roads from the Republic of Ireland into Garrison, allegedly to stop cross-border activities and close off Provisional IRA escape routes. Still not content, they then brought in helicopters and blocked the roads with concrete boulders and massive iron barricades.

All this further polarised our community. Local Catholic farmers were separated from their farms in the nearby Republic, while Protestants would have been quite happy never to see the roads open again. Garrison became the knot in a rope as the security forces and the IRA played tug of war for the community's hearts. The British army had added an extra hour to the journey from Leitrim to Garrison. Sadly, it was almost impossible for some farmers to make the trip, and my father's business suffered more than most as he was dependent on the Leitrim trade. He had once worked as a creamery manager across the border in Rossinver, so he was well known and liked over there.

While all this was happening, I continued at St Michael's, listening to news reports of bombings or shootings, holding myself in a kind of suspended animation until I had heard who the victims were. I worried that my parents, or one of my siblings, might be in the wrong place one day, that a simple decision to walk into a particular shop or bar might end their lives and I would never see them again. Like many others, I developed a conscience regarding the escalating conflict and, one day, joined a civil rights demonstration of about 1,500 people at the Gaol Square in Enniskillen. I listened intently as facts regarding the level of government discrimination in Fermanagh were read out to us by the speakers. Frank McManus, the chairman of the Fermanagh Civil Rights Association, told us that although the county had a Catholic majority, more than three hundred Protestants were employed in government offices, and only thirty Catholics. Many were incensed to learn that there were only three Catholic school-bus drivers in the county and that the minister of education in Stormont had said he saw no reason to believe that the seventy-five Protestant appointments were made other than on the grounds of merit.

The crowd were seething at such blatant discrimination, but they became even further infuriated when they learnt that thirty-five Fermanagh county councillors were Protestant and only seventeen were Catholic. Everybody knew that this was due to the manipulation of electoral boundaries and the spoiling of electoral votes. Many listening wanted to go and storm the civic offices, as it was obvious that something had to be done. It was time to stand up and be counted.

No doubt many there were inspired by the recent Nobel Prize winner, Martin Luther King, who died trying to end racial segregation and discrimination.

As the months passed, civil-rights marches were repeatedly attacked by Protestant loyalists and by the RUC. Some of my friends wanted me to attend a march planned for Derry on 30 January 1972. From the outset, my mother told me she would be unhappy about me attending it. So, I stood and watched as the car loaded with friends stopped on our street – and then left without me. Although annoyed with her decision at the time, maybe it was providence, as that day will forever go down in the annals of history as Bloody Sunday. The British army opened fire on the civil rights protesters who were marching peacefully through the streets of Derry and twenty-six unarmed citizens were shot – five of them in the back, as they ran away. Seven of the fourteen who died were teenagers like me. Father Edward Daly, from Belleek, flashed across television screens around the world, waving a bloody white handkerchief as he tried to rescue the injured while dodging the bullets.

In the aftermath, the British government held an inquiry that exonerated the soldiers, who claimed they had been fired upon first. It was widely considered to be a whitewash, but subsequent inquiries held to the same view. The Provisional IRA gained hundreds of new recruits as a direct result of Bloody Sunday. It would take the British almost forty years to admit that the army had fired without provocation and that the deaths were "unjustified" and "unjustifiable". There were protests in most Fermanagh villages and I joined the Garrison Civil Resistance, which led the way in efforts to reopen the Garrison-to-Rossinver border road. The situation worsened daily, and two Enniskillen detective constables were blown up in an explosion on the Belleek-Garrison road. Both sides suffered dreadfully, and it seemed there would be no end to the impasse. The landscapes and sounds of my village became less and less familiar, as I settled down to study for my A-level examinations.

Despite the impending civil war, I passed all my exams. I decided to study for a degree in biochemistry at Queen's University in Belfast, considered one of the better third-level institutions in the British Isles. My choice of field was influenced by the award I had received in Dublin the year before. I was excited at the prospect of meeting new friends – especially some Protestants, from whom I had previously been educationally segregated. I knew that living in Belfast would require me to adapt to new circumstances, but I was optimistic and hopeful for my academic future. I had no intention of pursuing a career in medicine at this stage. My only exposures to the profession had been an examination for an outbreak of measles by Dr McCollum in his satellite clinic at Gilroy's pub and the lingering smell of carbolic at the Erne Hospital in Enniskillen when I went there to get some stitches after being bitten by a pregnant laboratory rat.

I began at Queen's University in the autumn of 1974 and entered my fresher year with relish. When the various societies and clubs set out their stalls, trying to entice new members, I joined them all. There was the Motor Club, the Music Club, the Wine Club and the Debating Society. In my excitement, I even joined the Queen's Gliding Club but left when I found out it was part of the Royal Air Force Officers' Training Corps. Although I loved the thought of flying planes, that association might have raised a few eyebrows back in Garrison. Queen's certainly held true to its policy of non-sectarianism, and there were no restrictions enforced anywhere on campus. However, policies are made with good intentions and, outside the auditorium, students naturally gravitated towards their own communities.

During my second year, I moved into the halls of residence, the Queen's Elms. Our building, Alanbrooke Hall, was mainly Catholic; others were mixed or mostly Protestant. Many students had political affiliations – and not always benign ones – and seemingly innocuous remarks made on campus could lead to repercussions outside of the university. Belfast itself was a city battle-scarred from the years of the Troubles, with twisted metal from bombed-out bars, clubs and cars littering its sidewalks. On nearby Lisburn Road, which was largely Protestant, the British flag flew from houses and lampposts, a reminder to all that the marching season surrounding Easter had just ended. Although the Catholic Falls Road was decorated in symbolism of a more Republican nature, openly displaying the Irish tricolour would have been a defiance of the Flags & Emblems (Display) Act of (Northern Ireland) 1954 and considered treasonous.

One day, my father decided to oblige a friend by taking him up to Belfast. I was delighted. I looked forward to seeing my father's new yellow-and-white Ford Consul 375, which he had recently bought from the father of Formula One driver, John Watson. When he arrived, I was horrified to discover he had parked the car on the Protestant Sandy Row, with a picture of the Sacred Heart on the left side of the windscreen and a badge displaying his Pioneer pledge on the right. I pleaded with him to move the car or, at the very least, remove the holy picture, but he refused, believing that doing either would be a denial of his religion. Eventually I gave up and decided to let things take their course.

I took them to the Europa Hotel, and I was sipping a pint of beer when a bomb exploded outside. Both men jumped up, instinctively checking out their environment and wondering what on earth was going on. Later, my father would tell everyone that I hardly blinked – it was a regular occurrence in my world, and I would adapt to it. That's not to say I didn't care, because I certainly did. In fact, I found the violence repulsive. Miraculously, the car was still intact when Dad went to drive home, and I remember mentally crossing my fingers as he opened the door, praying that his faith had been justified.

During my time in Alanbrooke, I became involved in organising a music club in a concert hall shared by all the residences. We mostly employed bands from Belfast and the surrounding area. There were several good bands in Dublin, including the Boomtown Rats, but, try as I might, I couldn't encourage them to travel north of the border after a massacre involving a well-known Dublin-based group, the Miami Showband. The band had been travelling home from a gig in County Down, when they were stopped at a British army checkpoint for what they thought would be a routine search. The checkpoint was manned by members of the UVF, who placed an explosive device in the van, which was supposed to detonate later. The bomb exploded prematurely, and the rogue soldiers opened fire on the members of the showband, killing three and wounding two.

*

In the summer of 1977, I applied for a J-1 student visa so I could go and work in New York. On the way, I stayed with my brother, Sean, who was at that time living in London, and we went to see Bob Marley and the Wailers play at the Rainbow in Finsbury Park. The concert was part of the Exodus tour and I had just bought his new LP with *Jamming* and *Three Little Birds* earlier that day. While in London, Bob Marley was diagnosed with malignant melanoma, a kind of skin cancer, after doctors found a lesion on a toe, he'd injured in a soccer game in Hyde Park. At the time, physicians recommended having the toe amputated. However, he opposed the surgery as he adhered strongly to the tenets of his Rastafarian religion, subscribing to a millenarian, Afrocentric interpretation of Scripture that took hold in Jamaica in the 1930s. Bob believed that amputation was sinful because Leviticus (21:5) states, "They shall not make baldness upon their head, neither shall they shave off the corner of their beard, nor make any cuttings in the flesh."

The first part of this verse gave rise to the belief in wearing dreadlocks, and the second is the basis for a belief that amputation is sinful. Marley was born on February 6, 1945, to Norval and Cedella Marley. Cedella was eighteen at the time, a native of Nine Mile, a rural village with no electricity or running water. Because of a growing interest in Jamaican Reggae, I looked forward to a day when I could visit the island and possibly see the area that he grew up in.

While in New York, I stayed with my Garrison childhood pal, Thomas Maguire, in the Irish suburb of Woodside, in Queens. My J-1 visa entitled me to a temporary Social Security number and the ability to work in the United States for a year. Within a few days, I got a job buffing floors in a new apartment complex called the Manhattan Plaza, on 8th Avenue and 43rd Street, just around the corner from Hell's Kitchen. The building provided accommodation for Equity actors who were out of work and breakfast was sometimes shared by people like Woody Allen, who for a time lived in the building. That summer was filled with memorable musical events: I skipped work and watched Elton John and Kiki Dee sing their duet *Don't Go Breaking My Heart* in Central Park and witnessed the agony on America's brow when she learnt of the death of Elvis Presley. Although Memphis medical examiner Dr Jerry Francisco announced that the immediate cause of death was cardiac arrest and declared that "drugs played no role in his death", most people remembered the words of journalist Tony Scherman wrote that "Presley had become a grotesque caricature of his sleek, energetic former self. Hugely overweight, his mind dulled by the pharmacopeia he daily ingested, he was barely able to pull himself through his concerts."

Later that summer, the citizens of New York were stalked by a serial killer nicknamed "Son of Sam", and I was with some friends in the Hamptons when he was captured there.

Often, at the hour of day when New York's humidity would drive its citizens inside, behind air-conditioned walls, I would wander down to the little cafés and bistros off Broadway and chat to the playwrights and actors there. It was a smorgasbord of American life, a celebration of theatre culture, a place where one could observe the city through the differing lenses of history. One lazy afternoon, I was fortunate enough to meet Jackie Onassis, who was speaking at a protest meeting across the road against the closure of the Lion Theatre and have a worthwhile conversation about Ireland with her.

Searching, sometimes wandering alone, wondering what I would do with my life, I befriended an old Jewish man in Broadway who remembered meeting George Gershwin when he was a child. He was a pleasant man, with lively eyes and greying hair, who discussed my career options with me with the wisdom of an elder. One day, while sharing an afternoon coffee, he held a silver *chai* necklace before my face and said, 'You should become a doctor. I feel inside me that you have great healing power.' Although I had considered the possibility before, this old man's conversation filled me with a sense of inner peace. It was as if medicine had always been my destiny and my search for fulfilment was now within my grasp – my days of wandering alone were over.

Graduating in Hons Biochemistry in Queen's University Belfast 1978

Surrounded by all this excitement, it was difficult to imagine leaving New York and returning to the hate-filled streets of Northern Ireland, especially to spend my life standing behind a laboratory desk somewhere in Belfast. While there, I decided to bide my time and do an honours research year in biochemistry while looking at my options for studying medicine. I found student life in the capital tolerable, but that was about to change....

3. The Attack

In October 1977, the Troubles in Northern Ireland worsened, mainly due to the continuing protests against internment. British Prime Minister Edward Heath decided to send an additional 1,500 British army troops to the province. Tensions on campus matched those of the outside world, and Catholic students were incensed by a British Union Jack that had continued flying over the Protestant-dominated Sinnot Hall student residence for months after the summer marching season had ended.

One morning we awoke to find an Irish tricolour flying from the roof of Alanbrooke Hall. It remained there, fluttering defiantly in the wind, for a few days before it was taken down. The action was seen by many residents of the Queens Elms as treasonous because the flag symbolised a united Ireland. This open resistance to established authority soon became the talk of the university. The mood on campus became distrustful, as students tried to figure out who was brazen enough to have done such a thing. The RUC came and interviewed residents, to try to determine who had decided to redress the imbalance.

As a result of this provocation, hostilities developed in the halls of residence and, one morning, a fellow student committee member of Alanbrooke Hall came to me with an envelope he had received in the post. It contained a bullet. For a moment, I looked at him in silence. It was a warning, and we both knew it would be foolish not to take it seriously. As the Catholic president of our hall of residence, I might be first in the line of fire should someone decide to follow through on the threat.

The situation was not improved by the fact that the Fermanagh ex-Westminster MP Frank McManus had been sleeping on my floor in Alanbrooke Hall during his nights in Belfast. He had been chairman of the Fermanagh Civil Rights Association, and he intended to become a solicitor, so he was attending law lectures at the college. His provocative voice in defence of civil rights for Catholics was well known to his adversaries.

During 1978, the violence on the streets of Belfast reached a new level of intensity, with a series of tit-for-tat murders. Innocent young Catholics were chosen at random for torture and murder by a loyalist Protestant gang, known as the Shankill Butchers, in retaliation for the deaths of British army soldiers by the IRA. The Butchers had murdered at least twenty people, and residents of the streets from which they operated were protecting the killers' identities. Many Catholic students, like me, who were involved in university politics, suddenly became targets, and some were killed. I remembered Micky Mallon, a student from Toomebridge who had been horribly tortured in a Protestant paramilitary club before being shot four times in the head. One of my classmates told me that he had heard of a student who had been horribly tortured, his body hung over Shaw's Bridge with a large fishhook embedded in his neck. The Shankill Butchers' power base was in an area close to where I lived. I learnt to be vigilant about my own safety, especially as I had a high profile and the flag incident had still to be addressed.

The attack, when it came, took me completely by surprise. Perhaps I had dropped my guard because the weeks since the bullet incident had passed so quickly. It was just past midnight when two or three men appeared from the darkness outside a disco in the Student's Union and tackled me, pinning my shoulders to the hard concrete. They kicked and punched me, their blows raining down with furious speed. Instinctively, I curled up into a tight ball and tried to protect my face. The blows continued, each more savage than the one before, as my pleas for mercy whipped the attackers into a frenzy. I heard the sickening crunch of the bones in my leg breaking and felt the agony of something hard hitting my ankle. As the pain became unbearable, I said a prayer, silently begging God to save me. Suddenly they stopped – somebody had interrupted them. I lay there on the concrete, unable to move. The pain in my left ankle was excruciating, and I felt warm blood trickle onto my neck and down onto the ground from a wound at the back of my head. I was thankful to be alive. Eventually, some passing students found me and phoned an ambulance to bring me to the accident and emergency department of the nearby City Hospital on the Lisburn Road. A doctor there stitched the open wounds on my head and told me that the attackers had broken bones in my left leg, and I would need an operation. The next morning, the orthopaedic surgeon arrived. 'Your left ankle is badly shattered, and it'll require some reconstruction with the help of titanium plates, I'm afraid,' he told me. Belfast orthopaedic surgeons were amongst the best in the world, because of the vast experience they had gained in managing patients from bomb blasts, punishment beatings and kneecappings. I knew I couldn't be in a better place.

That evening, some friends and family arrived to see me. After eight years of war, the daily terrors of the Troubles had taught them how to put a brave face on things. I was later transferred to Musgrave Park Hospital to receive carbon-fibre implants to replace my ankle ligaments.

A few days after my ankle operation, I went back to Fermanagh to recover from my injuries. While there, I began considering the practicalities of going back to college and restarting a degree in medicine. It would mean sacrificing a lot, starting life again as a mature student with no money, having to fund six extra years at college. No one in our family had ever studied medicine before, and this made it more difficult to discuss my thoughts with my father, as he wanted me to take over the family business. My brother Sean was living in Lisburn, and Raymond was a construction engineer with Taylor Woodrow, building universities and airports for King Khalid in Riyadh, Saudi Arabia.

The opportunity to discuss my career plans with my father arose one evening when we were building a new outhouse beside the garage.

'I hear you're thinking of going back to Belfast to study medicine. What's the point in more book-learning when you could take over everything, we've built up here together?' he asked, casting his eye around the place.

The last thing I wanted to do was insult my father by turning down his offer of inheritance. I knew how hard he had worked all his life and how proud he was of his achievements. But I had outgrown the desire to remain in the village that had nourished me.

'Who put the notion into your head?' he said. 'There's never been a doctor in our family.'

'Nobody did,' I said, thinking for a moment about the old Jewish man. 'I just want to do something worthwhile with my life.'

My father and I had always been remarkably close. From a young age, he had always made me little presents shaped with his own hands. When I was seven, he made me a red spinning top and, later, a fishing rod with a carved wooden spool. Before I left for St Michael's, he assembled a magical chain-driven merry-go-round, which he sculpted from the sprocket wheels of old broken bicycles.

For a moment, we looked deep into each other's eyes and a lifetime passed between us in the silence. I hated seeing the sadness in his eyes. My father and I worked late into the evening, long after the sun had set. We never talked much about the subject of my inheritance after that.

Meanwhile, Northern Ireland was in chaos, caught in a spiralling ethno-political conflict between unionists, who wanted it to remain part of the United Kingdom, and nationalists, who wanted it to unite with the Republic of Ireland. These antagonistic views were based on different cultural extractions and religions. The Protestants had genetic and traditional links to the border hills of Scotland and northern England, while we, Catholics, saw ourselves as the descendants of an ancient race that had inhabited Ireland's green patchwork hills for millennia. Fanning the flames of the ethnic conflict was institutionalised discrimination by the majority Protestants against the minority Catholics.

Everyone I spoke to was convinced that if I remained in Belfast, I would be subjected to more attacks, and that I might even be killed. And the daily reports on the radio of bombs and murders in Belfast made me less and less interested in living in a city where life seemed to have so little value. But I didn't want to spend my time working in a laboratory – I was determined to pursue a career in medicine. So, after my plaster cast came off, I went to Belfast for an interview with the medical department at Queen's. While waiting for their decision, I lived at home and earned some extra money teaching A-level physics to sixth-form convent girls in Mount Lourdes Grammar School in Enniskillen.

One Saturday morning in May 1979, I heard rapid gunfire and went out to Carty's shop near the main street in Garrison, where I found a few people gathered around something on the ground. When I got closer, I realised it was our bread-delivery man, Jack McClenaghan, lying on the footpath beside his van. I can still see his red blood running down the guttering. After others established that he was dead, his body was covered. I turned away from the hideous scene, engulfed in sadness. His only "crime" was that he had been a member of the Ulster Defence Regiment – a reserve force of the British Army, which became operational in 1970. During the '70s, a few Catholics trusted the security forces, as some of their members were complicit in the ongoing sectarian murders, and there was a belief that countless innocent people had been murdered by agents of the state. Unfortunately, whatever the rights or wrongs of the situation, many of my own neighbours probably also saw Jack McClenaghan in this light.

Over the years, my mother, Sheila, had built up a friendly relationship with Jack when he delivered fresh bread to her shop. She often brought him into the house for a cup of tea and listened to news and gossip from the county town of Enniskillen. I went home to tell her the bad news and found her in the shop. She was visibly horrified.

'I've been meaning to talk to you for a while,' she said, 'and this only brings it all to a head.'

Our home was incorporated into the business, and the front room was always occupied. At any given time, there could be three of us wandering in and out to eat, answer the phones, listen to the radio, or watch television. The "good" room next door, where the family photos were displayed, was always tidy and kept for visitors, except at Christmas when we all sat together to enjoy our lunch. So, I was a little surprised when my mother closed the shop early and asked me to join her there. She made herself comfortable and told me to sit down.

'I don't think it's safe for you any more in Belfast,' she said, tears in her eyes. 'If you really want to do medicine, I think you'd be better off finding a college in the Free State.'

My mother had grown up in the south, in the Republic of Ireland, and had made many connections over the years, including with members of the Irish Senate and university professors. Over the years, she had made most of the academic decisions in our household. It was through her persistence that all seven members of our family were educated – five of us went to university.

'I've had a chat with an old friend, Professor McKenna, in the Royal College of Surgeons in Dublin, and he said you can go there for an interview next week,' she said.

I hadn't even considered Dublin as an option. If I was fortunate enough to get another grant, I had presumed it would be for a British university. Consequently, I had only applied in Belfast and Edinburgh.

'I've also talked to some people in the Department of Education in Belfast and they said if you are accepted in Dublin, they'd be willing to give you a further grant for a degree in medicine, for another six years,' she said.

I looked into my mother's worried eyes and noticed how her hands clasped and unclasped in her lap while she talked about my future.

'You'll be safer there, P J,' she said, and that was that – she said no more on the subject.

4. Starting Medicine

The Royal College of Surgeons was unusual in Ireland in that one-third of the student body was Irish, one-third was European and American, and one-third was from the rest of the world. This meant that students attending there forged friendships with people from all over the world, which endured for decades. The college authorities found accommodation for me with a family near St Stephen's Green, but I spent many Saturday mornings dissecting rats and dogfish in the back garden of my classmate's, David Keane, house in Sandymount. His poor mother never knew what we were going to arrive home with next in those black plastic bags.

In the evenings, Owen Brady, Simon Donnelly, and I would often go down to Jervis Street Hospital and hang around in the Accident and Emergency Department, hoping to get a chance to assist in sewing up patients' injuries. Owen's father worked as an orthopaedic surgeon in the hospital, and we gained a lot of valuable experience from the staff there. With their help and supervision, I quickly became proficient at suturing lacerations. Many of the senior staff there came to trust me, but they never let me do anything beyond my capabilities.

During my first year, I spent a lot of my time socialising in the Bailey Inn and Davy Byrne's, which became known as "Lecture Theatre 3" and "Lecture Theatre 4". My friend, Simon, knew Robbie Fox, who ran the Pink Elephant Night Club, and I have fond memories of meeting Def Leppard, Paul Cleary and the Blades, and Clannad and their friends U2 there in those memorable days of Dublin rock.

There was a derelict bit of land beside the college, called the Dandelion Market. The site, originally part of the Taylor-Keith bottling plant in St Stephen's Green, had become a cultural nirvana, bustling with stalls selling punk badges and Sex Pistols posters. The punk culture was in decline, but still had some diehard Dubliner fans who dressed in bin liners and exuded a sense of nihilism towards politics and economics. The Boomtown Rats and the Vipers were in their ascendency, while bands like Stiff Little Fingers and the Undertones could still be heard at the college parties.

One Saturday in the Dandelion Market, I watched U2 perform – it was the first time I had seen them. They played there on weekends, and we became friends. Later, I watched them on Saturday mornings on Dave Fanning's *RTÉ* television show and, even further on, I went drinking with the Edge in Strings Nightclub on Leeson Street. My friendship with the band continued long after the old market closed.

Before long, an academic year had passed, and it was time to plan how I would spend my summer vacation. Some students joined the Overseas Electives Scheme (TOES) and went abroad to treat patients in the Third World. This required some experience in performing surgical procedures, especially caesarean sections, and appendectomies. The rest of us, who were still much too inexperienced for this, thought about ways of earning enough money for the next year at college by working abroad.

*

Royal College of Surgeons students hung out together in Rice's pub near the college. Although it seemed that most of them had bottled gherkins and lived in camping sites near Munich, two students in the year above me convinced me that it was much more lucrative to work in Germany as a house painter. They wanted me to join them that summer and assured me we would easily find jobs through some Dutch employment agency. One of the students, Damien, still had contact details from working there the previous summer. The trick, he said, was to convince everyone that we were skilled workers worth hiring, and not just unskilled students looking for summer work.

During the early '80s, Germany was the destination of choice for British migrant workers, as it promised large hourly rates for those who could hold down jobs as bricklayers, joiners or painters. The migrant labour scheme was largely run by Dutch agents from Nijmegen, who employed seasonal labourers who didn't pay union fees or public taxes. This system irritated ordinary German workers, who often earned lower rates of pay but still paid their dues. My friends wanted us to take advantage of this unconventional scheme and try to bluff our ways into lucrative jobs as painters or decorators.

In June 1980, over a few beers in Rice's pub, Damien and I decided to pool our meagre resources and travel to Germany. We crossed to Hamburg and, after contacting the Dutch agents, took the train south to Mannheim, where we were given comfortable lodgings at the Hotel zum Autohof in Landstrasse. It was quickly noticed that we had arrived without painters' overalls or brushes, and some painters from Liverpool cheekily asked whether we were students. That evening, we went out to a Herties store and spent the last of our savings on proper decorators' uniforms and equipment. The next morning, when the boss saw us in our brand-new uniforms, he realised we were probably students and exploded into a tirade of abuse.

'*Was is das?*' he said, pulling at the straps of my uniform.

My inability to speak German just compounded the problem, but I felt I had to say something before we lost our jobs.

'*Deutschland über alles,*' I replied, innocently meaning "German overalls".

The boss looked me up and down for a moment.

I then realised from the look on Damien's face that I had just uttered the opening stanza to the Nazi national anthem, '*Deutschland, Deutschland über alles, über alles in der Welt.*' When translated, it meant, 'Germany, Germany above all, above everything in the world.' It was a nationalistic statement which had evidently struck the wrong note with the Yugoslavian boss. He turned back to the other workers and laughingly said, '*Ja…*fuck the Queen!'

Damien, who had acquired some German the previous summer, stutteringly explained that we had wanted new clothes to impress and that we were Irish. The old Yugoslavian boss laughed heartily when he realised my innocent mistake. He patted me on the back and gave me some cans of paint to carry into the back of a small VW minibus.

'I like Ireland – IRA,' he said.

A couple of painters from Belfast who were waiting on us in the van overheard this. When the van started moving, one of them introduced himself as Billy.

'You know, none of that auld IRA stuff here, son – we still think you're both students from Dublin!' he said.

'But I'm from Northern Ireland,' I replied.

'Leslie, your man, says he's from Northern Ireland,' he said to his friend. 'Who did you work for then, back home in Northern Ireland?'

For a few moments, I hesitated with my answer. Once again, our careers as budding painters lay in the balance.

'I worked with Robert Dickie for a while in Enniskillen,' I replied, quoting the name of the wholesaler who supplied my mother with house paint in our shop.

It hit the right note, both politically and professionally.

'OK, fair enough, and where did you meet that other boy from Dublin?'

'Oh, he's a painter by trade, and I met him on the last job we were at, in Hamburg.'

The minibus eventually pulled up outside a modern clothes boutique, which was due to open in a few days. The boss left the Belfast painters in charge of delegating the work.

'He wants a tortoiseshell effect on those panels at the front of the shop – you could do that,' Billy said, handing me some small cans of bronze and brown paint. 'A good tip here is to rub the acrylic with a bit of alcohol before lacquering it with polyurethane.'

I knew from the worried expression on Damien's face that we were now in deep and there was little he could do to help me.

'We'll see you in a few hours then, wee son,' he said, before disappearing with Leslie and Damien inside to paint the interior. 'Remember, this place has to be open by Monday.'

I knew that unless some miracle occurred, there was no way that I could bluff this highly specialised technique. I decided to have a coffee and think through my options. Across the street was a statue to Karl Benz, who reputedly produced the world's first automobile in Mannheim in 1885. Behind the statue was an antique shop with a large collection of faux-tortoiseshell antique shelf clocks in the window. It was a long shot, but I thought that maybe the owner knew how to repair the paintwork on them, and he could give me a quick lesson. I had nothing to lose, so I took off my overalls and put them into a plastic bag and went inside to chat with him.

'Can you repair the tortoiseshell paint on these clocks?' I asked in faltering English.

'*Ja*, of course, I am *repareering* one just now,' he replied.

'Is it difficult? I have one at home in Dublin. Can you show me?'

'Well, first you need this *gelbe* paint to get a good reflection,' he answered.

'*Gelbe*?'

He lifted a large spray can of yellow enamel from the counter and waved his hand in front of his mouth to encourage the English word to come out.

'Yellow?' I guessed.

'Yes, yellow is best for this – that's the secret!'

He sprayed some of the yellow paint onto the old clock and allowed it to dry. Then he buffed it with fine sandpaper and a glaze mixture of an almost translucent darker acrylic paint. He proceeded to show me how to apply sienna, burnt umbers, and mild blacks in swirling layers of differing translucencies and opaqueness. It was a simple technique, and the outcome appeared to depend on patience, and some final deft brushstrokes. The older man took pride in showing me his work, and before long, an hour had passed. I asked him if I could buy the paint spray can for twenty Deutschmarks, but he just slowly smiled and gave it to me. We had become friends and, before I left, he also gave me some acrylic colours. I made my way back across the square to where the van had dropped us off.

Thankfully, nobody had come down to check my work while I'd been gone. I took out the spray can and, with free-form strokes, began turning the outside of the boutique into something that looked like a cross between a Jason Pollock action painting and the cover of the Beatles' *Yellow Submarine* album. Gaining confidence, I painted some brown and bronze around in little glazed circles. As people stopped to watch me, I was conscious that the building was beginning to look more and more ridiculous. With little to lose, I began to experiment with some of the other paints, adding "scales" of different shapes and sizes and laughing quietly as I thought about the day my brother, Raymond, and I painted Johnny Keenan's car. There must be something I'm missing in my appreciation of these unplanned artistic creations because when the owner arrived to inspect the work that afternoon, he appeared to be thrilled with the result.

I was even more amazed when he brought Billy and Leslie down to look at this new *modern* specialist effect, which he felt was totally in keeping with the look of his boutique. The other painters looked at me and gently nodded their approval, but I quietly wondered what they'd have thought if the owner hadn't liked it.

'Where did you learn to paint like that?' said Billy.

'Oh, an old farmer called Johnny Keenan from Garrison in County Fermanagh taught me a long time ago,' I said, smiling to myself, happy I'd survived the first day.

After a week, the Belfast painters left to work in Augsburg, and Damien and I started restoring the exterior of a large secondary school in Mannheim. In early August, we got tickets for the German Formula One Grand Prix in nearby Hockenheim, which was only a few miles up the road.

We were saddened to learn that Patrick Depailler had been killed during practice sessions. Jacque Laffite driving a Ligier won the race that year, but my heart was quickened by the Ferrari drivers, Gilles Villeneuve, and Jody Scheckter, when they passed me each time. And that's how my lifelong love for this Formula One team began – I later followed them to other racetracks around the world.

When work at the school in Mannheim finished, the agents transferred us to a new job in Heidelberg. This was a baroque tourist town with an old castle where Mario Lanza had filmed *The Student Prince*. It brought back memories of watching the film while I was a student at St Michael's in Enniskillen. In Heidelberg, we were joined by Bernie, an amicable young painter from Liverpool who had been working with the company for more than a year. Our first job together involved painting the interior of a private house in the old part of the city. The property was owned by a pleasant older woman who trustingly left the three of us working downstairs while she went out to do her shopping. The snug house was airtight, and before long, we were all getting "high" on the vapours of the high gloss paint we were using.

'Better open some windows, lads, before one of us passes out!' I said.

'It's a bit late for that,' said Bernie, pointing to a cage in the kitchen where a small canary lay upside down, dead.

'Damn! We'll lose the job over that,' Damien said.

'No, we won't!' said Bernie, opening the cage and deftly pulling the canary's head out through the bars to make it appear that the bird had accidentally choked itself.

'Now, everybody upstairs – we'll paint up there and just wait till she comes back.'

Eventually, we heard noises at the front door. Standing stock still, paint brushes in hand and open-mouthed, we waited until we heard the old lady turning the key in the lock. After a few minutes, we heard her emit a small shriek. The noise jarred us into action. We all started talking at the same time, each wondering how best to handle the situation. The consensus was that Damien spoke the best German so he should go down and talk to her. He descended the stairs slowly, obviously dreading the task. After ten minutes of comforting the old lady, he returned to join us.

'Well, what's the story?' Bernie and I asked at the same time. 'You'll never believe this!' he replied.

'She got a shock when she saw the canary all right, but only because it was dead when she got up this morning, and she'd gone out to get a box to bury it in! Now she thinks it had a revival for a while.'

Damien's concern for the old lady earned us cups of tea and biscuits and a glowing recommendation to the boss when he arrived later to inspect the work.

After Heidelberg, we travelled south to Munich, the capital of Bavaria. The city lay in the foothills of the German Alps and was home to the greatest beer festival in the world: Oktoberfest. The Dutch agents put us up in the Hotel Winhart, in the south end of the city. I loved it all, the *Weisswurst*, the *Weissbier,* and the oom-pah-pah bands in the Hofbräuhaus. After the violent streets of Belfast and the economic problems of Dublin, it was great to be in a city that exuded a hearty feeling the Germans called *gemütlichkeit.*

At the end of summer, we visited the Oktoberfest with another five million revellers. A long shadow was cast over the event when a bomb exploded, and thirteen people were killed. The horror of it brought back fading memories of Belfast.

*

In the fall, I returned to the Royal College of Surgeons to resume my medical studies for another year. My new courses included biochemistry, physiology and anatomy and, in that 1980-81 academic year, I won the Norman Rae Gold Medal, earning me a place in "gold" script on one of the large wooden plaques that adorned the hallway of the college. It was my fifth medal in the college. My ambition to study medicine was beginning to pay dividends and when the year ended, and the summer came around, I decided to return to Germany with another of my classmates. The Dutch agents found our work near the McGraw Kaserne US military base in Munich, where we shared basement lodgings with eight British painters. Within a short time, we had struck up a friendship with Kenny, a professional painter from Hartlepool, and Nicholas, a music engineer from Brighton. With his connections, Nicky was able to get us into the after-parties in the Sugar Shack nightclub, where he introduced us to a lot of visiting celebrities. That summer, we partied with Bob Dylan, Santana, Kraftwerk, and The Cure.

Also, that summer, US President Ronald Reagan escalated the Cold War by threatening to place Pershing II missiles in West Germany. He wanted to throw the outdated ideology of Marxism-Leninism onto the trash heap of history. Like Margaret Thatcher, he was impressed by the economic theories of Milton Friedman, who advocated reducing expenditure on social services such as education. Shortly after my return to the Royal College of Surgeons, I saw this policy in action when I received a letter informing me that the British government was going to take away my educational grant. I would have to pay my way at one of the most expensive universities in the world. My future in medicine now hung in the balance, as it was being sacrificed on the official altar of Conservative politics.

5. Living in Istanbul

The next summer, 1982, I left for Munich with another classmate, who was also from Northern Ireland and was in an economic situation like mine. Germany was by now going through a severe economic recession, and the tide was turning against the working practices of the Dutch agencies. As a result, all painting and decorating jobs in Munich had dried up for migrant workers.

We eventually found jobs painting a large gantry hoist crane at the Krauss-Maffei Wegmann (KMW) Panzer tank factory. The work had to be completed over a weekend and involved painting an iron structure suspended above an assembly line of Panzer tanks. With some ingenuity and the help of a spray gun, we finished the job in less than two hours. I wished my father could have been there to see the Panzers below us – with his love of engines, it would have been a real treat for him.

When I was in Germany, my mother sent me a letter posted to Ireland from the deputy dean of medical education at the University of Cape Town, offering me an elective in cardiac surgery that summer. It would have been wonderful to work in the same hospital with the team that had performed the first heart transplant in the world under Christiaan Barnard. Although I didn't accept this wonderful invitation, I remained determined to work in South Africa at some stage, preferably when Apartheid had ended.

By mid-June, some Germans began refusing to work with casual British and Irish labourers unless they had proper papers, and many migrants found it difficult to find work anywhere in Germany. Some British labourers ended up living in squats, or even homeless on the streets, as things were also bad in England. As the recession deepened, tradespeople looked for other sources of income, and I was among those who rented out their bodies in clinical drug trials at the Iphar Institute for Clinical Pharmacology, just outside Munich. These trials paid handsomely, and a lot of the lads used the money to survive – and try to get back on their feet.

Around this time, things were looking bleak for me: I had little hope of saving the tens of thousands of pounds required to pay my college fees for the following year. But, just about then, I met a brickie called 'Geordie Ian' in an English pub named The Coach and Horses, where many of the newly unemployed labourers drank. He told me that a few of his workmates were delivering Mercedes sports cars from Munich to Istanbul. He said that the Pakistani businessmen involved were looking for British and Irish drivers with clean licences and they were paying five thousand Deutschmarks per trip. It would take many trips to secure the funds that I needed, but Ian said he intended to go on the next "Turkey run" and told me I could join him if I wished. It sounded like a wonderful adventure for me. My college friend was more apprehensive, warning that the whole thing sounded too good to be true.

'Nothing is that easy in life,' he said. 'Let's see what they're up to before we commit ourselves to anything. I don't fancy spending the next few years in a Turkish prison.'

The opportunity to learn more about the operation came a few days later when we met the Pakistani businessmen who ran the car operation, at a Wendy's hamburger restaurant in Arnulfstrasse. It was an ideal location for a meeting as it was near the main railway station, where all the rail lines in the city converged. My college friend opted out, but I decided to see what it was all about. There were labourers from all over the UK – some from Glasgow and Sunderland, and others from Nottingham – all eager to go on an adventure to the East.

I spent some time talking to some of Ian's friends, who had already made the trip. They said the only prerequisite for the job was a clean international driving licence and a British or Irish passport. They had been well looked after by the Pakistani businessmen, put up in a good hotel and paid well for their two weeks in the sun. They assured us that many German students drove Mercedes on export plates down to Turkey, where they were four or five times more valuable, but the Pakistanis who ran the operation preferred to work with fluent English speakers.

'How long does it take?' I asked one of the drivers.

'About three days, but if you're in a hurry, you can do it in thirty-six hours,' he replied.

An immaculately dressed Pakistani man in a blue sheen suit came over to us. I was told he was Mohammed, the boss.

'Do you want a drive? We are going to Istanbul tomorrow and one of my drivers can't make it. I need someone to take a two-year-old Mercedes 500 SL there. I'll need a clean driving licence and your passport to get the export documents, and your visa – do you have these with you?'

I felt very uneasy about handing my passport over to a stranger, but the other drivers assured me that it was OK. When he returned with the documentation, about twenty minutes later, all doubts fled my mind, and I grew more excited about the trip. It was late August, and I didn't want to desert my classmate. I asked him to come with me, as a passenger, on my first Turkey run, and he agreed.

The following morning, we headed south to Turkey, birthplace of St Paul, the land of tall minarets and sweet baklava. Our journey would take us across Austria's snow-peaked Alps to Yugoslavia and Eastern Bloc Bulgaria.

On the second day, while we were having a meal in Belgrade, "Nottingham Ray" offended some Serbian locals by getting up to dance on the restaurant table with the red, blue, and white Yugoslavian flag draped on his shoulders. His claims that his grandfather had died trying to protect Yugoslavian Serbians during the Second World War went unheeded, and they rewarded his family's efforts by stealing the seventeen-inch light alloy rims off one of our Mercedes. The incident lost us a day's travel time, but my idea of buying some wheels from a local scrapyard put me well in line to be team leader.

We reached Istanbul on the afternoon of the fourth day and parked the cars in the Sultanahmet neighbourhood. There we visited the infamous Pudding Shop, which had featured in Alan Parker's film *Midnight Express*, about an American student called Billy Hayes who was sent to prison in Turkey for trying to smuggle hashish out of the country. We were given lodgings in the dilapidated old part of the city, which had been the capital of two of the world's greatest empires – the Byzantine and the Ottoman.

The hotel was comfortable, and, from my window, I could see the ruins of the former Hippodrome of Constantinople, where Roman chariots once raced in the afternoon sun. Below me, the street vendors cried "Kebab! Kebab!" and mournful seagulls screeched and circled, looking for whatever scraps they could find before swooping down over the hooting ferryboats, labouring their ways upstream. The next day, we handed the Mercedes over to some Pakistani businessmen, who promised us lots of work if we wanted it. I could accumulate funds by smuggling cars, but I would have to take some time off from college to make enough trips to get together the amount I needed.

Meanwhile, we stayed in Istanbul. It was my first encounter with an Islamic city, and I bathed in its wondrous sounds: the muezzins calling the faithful to prayer, and the rich tapestry of musical styles that celebrated the diversity of contemporary Turkish life. It is said that St Augustine once wrote, 'The world is a book and those who do not travel read only one page.' Well, Istanbul was my Bible, my Koran, my Torah, and I wanted to read it right through to the last chapter.

*

It was early September 1982, and the Pakistanis said that the next Turkey run from Munich would not be for another three weeks, so I decided to stay in Istanbul for a while and gather my thoughts. On those balmy sunny afternoons, I'd often sit reading in the elegant gardens of the Blue Mosque and learn some Turkish from the local children. We would begin by counting the six minarets nearby: '*Bir, iki, üç, dört, beş, alti.*'

The building got its nickname from the magnificent blue haze created by the blue and white Iznik floral-motif tiles that decorated its interior. Other times, I'd go to the riverbank and wait until the evening sun set and the towers melted into the rivulets of violet colours in the evening sky. Russian cargo ships would pass on their way upriver.

To save money, I moved to a cheaper hotel near my boss, Mohammed, and every Wednesday night, we'd meet at the Sultan Bar at the Sheraton Hotel. I was interested in getting to know how he operated and toyed with the idea of exporting my cars to gather the funds necessary to complete my degree. He wanted to do another Turkey run in October before the weather in Germany started to deteriorate, so I went back to Munich and met two British drivers, Nicky and Richard, and drove some older BMWs to Istanbul.

When I arrived, I found a cheap hotel on the Asian side of the Bosporus strait, near some older wooden summer houses that lined the waterfront. This meant taking a twenty-minute ferry ride to Sultanahmet each morning to meet the other drivers. It was a nice journey, and the ferry moved along at a leisurely pace, as boys clanged little bells and served glasses of sweet tea to the seated passengers.

On those mornings, I often leaned over the railings and thought about my family back home.

Ahead of me lay the great land mass of Anatolia, the gateway to the East, the approach route to Iraq and Iran. Sometimes on that journey, when I looked eastwards, my mind played tricks with me, and the very essence of the air appeared to change. Slowly, the people on the boat seemed to take on a drearier look. Maybe it was the prominence of their cheekbones or the shapes of their eyes that reminded me that they were descended from nomadic tribesmen of Central Asia. It could have been the styles of their cloth caps or collars, as Turkey had only adopted a Western style of dress some fifty years before. It made me slightly fearful, but I knew that one day I would travel east into Anatolia. I wanted to experience the modern state of Turkey and its amalgam of differing traditions.

*

As the summer days shortened, I left Istanbul and returned to Munich. It was early in the winter of 1982, and I was horrified to see how many British tradesmen were without work, sleeping rough on trains parked in the Hauptbahnhof at night. Some were reduced to sharing free food with the homeless at the Klosterkirche centre in St Anna Platz. Others told stories of being attacked by employees of private-security firm Schwarze Sheriffs, who patrolled the U-Bahn stations at night in menacing black uniforms. What amazed me was that most of the labourers still preferred to live in Germany rather than return home to Britain. Maybe worse lives awaited them there, maybe they were all running or hiding from something, or maybe they were just like me – too embarrassed to go back home until they'd completed what they had come to achieve.

The snow had already started to fall in Munich, and I allowed some friends to sleep on the warm floor of my hotel for a few nights. I phoned home as often as I could, but it was difficult for me, as my family – especially my father – missed me terribly. I always tried to keep his spirits up, but I'm not sure if I ever really succeeded. Hardest of all was the fact that I would have to tell my family that I was staying in Munich for Christmas. I missed my family, but hadn't enough money to travel back to Ireland, and was determined to finish what I had set out to do – to raise enough money for my medical fees. The icy winds came off the Bavarian mountains for most of December and chilled me to the core. The citizens of Munich prepared themselves for the cold days ahead by heating a selection of hot beverages, including mulled wine, which they sold in little markets.

The weather remained cold until February when Mohammed contacted me and asked me to drive a new Mercedes 280 SL to Alanya, a coastal town in the southwest of Turkey.

He gave me ten thousand Deutschmarks for the journey and told me to keep the car for a month and put as much mileage on it as possible so that the Turkish authorities would think it was second-hand. One afternoon, on my travels around the Gulf of Antalya, I met a beautiful blonde German girl called Monika lying on the beach. After a few days of friendship, I noted that her father drove an old blue Mercedes saloon with Hamburg plates and, every day, he parked it in the same place by the Mediterranean shoreline. One night, while drunk and leaving Monika back to her hotel, I accidentally ended up in the wrong bed – with Monika's mother, whose screams were enough to awaken the whole floor. I had to hide outside for over an hour until the furore had died down. I could have died when Monika introduced me to them some days later, and her mother said, 'Haven't I met you somewhere before? Your face seems so familiar.'

Despite this disastrous introduction, we all ended up the best of friends, and I told them about the smuggling scam selling the Mercedes in Turkey. When Mohammed later arrived and offered her father three times the market value of his old car, her father suggested that Monika stays with me for a few more weeks in Turkey – we could make our way back up to Istanbul, and Mohammed would pay for the car whenever we arrived there. It was a wonderful idea, and, for the next few weeks, we travelled together, taking the long route back to Istanbul, exploring the plains of central Anatolia and one of the famed underground cities of Cappadocia.

One morning, we reached a small eastern village with the snowy peaks of Mount Erciyes just visible behind us on the distant western horizon. I knew we were now nearing the gateway to Iran and thought about the wondrous ancient cities of Isfahan and Tehran across the border. On that peaceful morning, I lay back on the grass, looking up at the cobalt blue sky, without a care in the world. Monika lay beside me; a gentle breeze fluttered her light cotton dress. In the stillness of the midday heat, the tinkling of nearby sheep bells created a soothing sound that convinced me that we should travel further east. I knew it would be dangerous, as Iraq had invaded Iran just a few months earlier and, by all accounts, the conflict was a bitter one.

'Why don't we travel over the mountains to Iran? We could still take a few more weeks together, and it'd be a wonderful adventure. You'll probably have to wear a veil over your face,' I said and laughed.

'Oh, I'd love to see Iran,' she replied.

Iran, in that period, was changing its destiny in the world. Ronald Reagan had just been inaugurated as the fortieth president of the United States, and the world had witnessed the release of the hostages who had been held in the US embassy in Tehran for over a year. The recent SAS assault on the Iranian embassy in London had created problems for British citizens, who had to wait more than six months just to get visas, and I considered asking Mohammed to obtain me some from his usual passport contacts at the embassies in Istanbul. When I chatted with him about it, he told me he could get one for my Irish passport and Monika's German one from his friends easily.

Monika and I returned to Alanya and started to plan for the journey. We went into a store and bought some black burqas for her, as we were determined not to create any suspicion in Iran and to respect the Islamic tradition. I spent the next few weeks reading some books and informing myself better about the history behind the Islamic Revolution. I learnt that the problems had begun about five years earlier when the Shah's information minister published an article that slandered Ayatollah Khomeini as a tool of British neo-colonial interests and a "man without faith". The next day, theology students in the city of Qom had exploded in angry protests. The Shah's security forces put down the demonstrations, killing at least seventy students in just two days. Up to that moment, secular and religious protesters against the Shah had been evenly matched, but after the Qom massacre, the religious opposition became the leaders of the anti-Shah movement.

*

The Shah was subsequently overthrown and replaced with an Islamic republic headed by Khomeini. After a few days, Mohammed returned to Alanya with our passports, with our Iranian visas inside. When he left, he hugged me and warned us that the journey would be dangerous, that there were many stories of tourists who went into Iran and never came out again. And then we set off to the east.

As we drove across Turkey, towards the border at Bazargan, I thought about our future and considered how religion appeared to be at the core of nearly all the strife in this region. To the west were the ethnoreligious memories of the Turkish-Greek wars, to the east, the Afghan *mujahedeen* were waging an Islamic *jihad* war against the Soviet Union, and to the south, Israeli Jews were in open conflict with nearly all their Muslim Arab neighbours. Whenever eternal salvation is at stake, compromise is extremely difficult, as any threat to one's religious beliefs is perceived as a threat to one's very being. I remembered my father showing me the Mass rocks around Garrison and wondered whether we were all any different. The journey to the border was forbidding and became more so when I discovered that the English spelling on my Iranian visa was completely wrong. One stamp said "acompiagned by Monika" instead of "accompanied by Monika", and the blotched-out dates were equally worrisome. I didn't want to startle Monika, but my faith in Mohammed to get the job done had been misplaced. I couldn't believe that I hadn't noticed the printing errors earlier. If the Farsi on the passport stamp were as bad as the English, we would soon be in serious trouble. A cursory look at Monika's German passport left me in no doubt that our visas were probably not official embassy documents. We crossed the border at Bazargan, where the guards searched our car boot but took only a cursory look at our passports before waving us through.

So, this was Iran, a nation in the throes of a cultural revolution, one where centres of learning were being purged of Western influences and converted to the dogmas of Shia Islam. It was important that people didn't think we were from Britain or America, and we travelled carefully, mostly on smaller roads, away from the army roadblocks. Even though we were ultra-cautious, we were detained after a few hours, about three kilometres from Tabriz. In some ways, it was my fault, as I had dropped my guard and stopped to take photographs of a line of older people being shepherded onto a waiting bus.

There had been recent reports in the media that older people were being sent to the frontline battlefields to attack the Iraqi soldiers in "human waves", and I took a chance in snapping some interesting pictures for an article I intended to write for my local newspaper, the *Fermanagh Herald*. My curiosity aroused suspicion, and we were eventually taken in for questioning by the local police. The police were not immediately hostile, and our story – that we just wanted to travel together on a romantic journey through an exotic land – seemed to have a ring of truth to it. After all, we both carried passports from neutral countries, and they could see we had already been living in Turkey for a few months. In earlier times, it was not unusual for busloads of Western travellers to pass this way to see the mosques of Abyaneh, the Chehel Sotoun and the Alamoot Castle. They took us to the police station, and we waited while they developed our photographs. Surprisingly, they never mentioned the entry stamps, and I wondered again whether Mohammed had put us in this dangerous situation. They held us overnight, during which time they asked me about the photographs that I had of the bus, which could just have been a day trip for older people down to the coast. But they focused more on Monika's father's car, saying that we had no import papers to bring it into Iran. I shrugged and told them that the customs officials at the border had let us through, so I hadn't realised it was a problem. Although it was an unnerving time, I never really felt threatened by the Iranian police.

Eventually, we were brought before a judge who fined us. We didn't have enough money to pay for our release, and Monika didn't want her parents to know that we had been arrested in Iran, so we decided we should try to sell the car to pay for our fine. We sold the car to secure our freedom and exchanged the remaining Iranian money we got for it for some gold rings that we would try to sell later. We then caught a bus back towards the border.

From Sero, on the Iran side, we took a dolmuş shared taxi to the Turkish town of Yuksekova, where we stayed overnight. The next morning, Monika just wanted to feel Western again, having worn shawls and long dresses for so long, so she was wearing a type of hot pants. A crinkled old matriarch took exception to the way she was dressed and beat her soundly around the legs with a small stick, much to the amusement of onlookers. 'She's an agent from the Ansar-e-Hezbollah!' I joked, about Iran's religious police.

We exchanged the rest of our Iranian money and travelled by bus back to Istanbul, where we finally parted at the airport. I gave Monika some Deutschmarks to give to her father. I cried as we hugged each other closely, thinking about how different it all could have been. For us, the adventure of travelling to Iran was over, and, in many ways, we were lucky to have survived it.

Playing guitar on a Greek ferry going to Ios 1983

In late March 1983, I decided to take a break from Turkey and went to live in Athens. On the way there, I met an Australian backpacker who gave me an address for cheap lodgings at the Athens Connection Hostel in Ioulianou Street. The price per room was 450 Drachma a night, or one could share a spot on the open roof for 150. Better still, one could work at the hostel, meeting the trains and handing out advertising leaflets to passengers, in exchange for free accommodation and drink. The roof was fine, and it was there that I met a Swedish dental student called Pia. We shared an interest in travelling and, after a brief courtship, we decided to join forces and venture into some of the nearby towns of the northern Peloponnese region, where, rumour had it, one could find work picking fruit on the apricot farms.

Pia really wanted to travel to the Greek islands, but it was too early, as the tourist season didn't start for another few months. We found work picking apricots in Kiato, a small coastal town set amongst the olive groves northwest of the Isthmus of Corinth. The farm was owned by a middle-aged widow called Maria, whose husband had recently been killed in a car crash. She needed whatever assistance we could give her. Every morning, Pia and I helped her prune the apricot trees and collect the fallen branches and, for the equivalent of two pounds a day plus free accommodation, we spent some of the happiest days of our lives there. My most abiding memory of that little village was sitting in the saffron sunsets with the older men in the coffee shop, sipping espresso. One morning, Maria banged excitedly on the door of our room, waking us up. There had been an earthquake in the early hours of the morning, and some villagers were injured. I got into Maria's Suzuki pickup and brought some of the injured a few kilometres down the road to the doctor's house. It was surreal passing houses where men were chalk-marking the buildings with large "alpha", "beta" or "delta" symbols, depending on whether they were still habitable or would have to be torn down. News spread that thieves had taken advantage of the catastrophe and stolen antiquities from the local museum.

There were a lot of casualties, and I spent most of the morning helping the doctor to splint limbs, clean wounds, and suture injuries. The stitching experience that I'd obtained in Jervis Street Hospital proved invaluable. That evening, I had to sew a girl whose beautiful face had been torn apart – two great lacerations ran from the corner of her mouth and nose to the bottom of her chin. By the time the sun had melted back into the waters of the Aegean, I had placed more than forty sutures in her face with a threaded needle. When I'd finished, her mother broke into tears and cried a dozen thankful "efharistos". The old doctor heard the commotion and entered the room. There, between the pride in his eyes and the smile on the young girl's face, I reconfirmed my destiny in life – I wanted to return to medical school as soon as possible.

A few weeks later, Pia and I left Kiato to return to Athens. When we parted, she wrote in my travel book, 'Nar du kommen till Goteborg – your private dentist from now on.'

6. The Last Turkey Run

In April, I returned to Munich. Mohammed was again looking for drivers, this time to take some cars to Van, a town in eastern Turkey. We had a long chat, and he told me he was willing to give me six thousand dollars because of what had happened in Iran. He seemed genuinely embarrassed and tried to assure me that the visa was real. I had to admit that, when we'd been detained in Iran and questioned, the validity of the visa was never called into question. I wanted to believe him. With the money from the next few runs, coupled with a donation my mother had promised, I would have enough to complete my education. Perhaps, as he said, English spelling just wasn't a strong suit with officials in the Iranian embassy in Istanbul. My sixth sense was furiously sending up flares, but I chose to ignore them. In the end, we shook hands when he agreed to allow me to sell some cars myself.

The drivers had a small send-off in The Coach and Horses before we left. We were joined by Pat, a lad from Dublin who was trying to make some money to go and meet his wife and young son, who were living in New Zealand. I'd met Pat at a Van Morrison concert in Athens and told him about the Turkey run. Then there was Scottish Alan, a miscreant who tended to sleepwalk at night – often with other people's wallets. After five days, we arrived at the Hotel Emrah near Aksaray Junction in Istanbul, and Alan was given the choice of either staying in another hotel or returning to Munich. Thankfully, he decided to return.

The next morning, Mohammed came to the hotel and collected our passports to bring to customs. Because of my discomfort at what had happened in Iran, I decided not to trust him, and I follow him to see where he was going. He drove his BMW from the hotel to somewhere near Sultanahmet, where he parked. I followed in a taxi and watched as he ducked down a dimly lit laneway. I paid the driver and then followed Mohammed at a discreet distance. There were no obvious hotels in the area, but I presumed he might have friends there and had decided to visit them. He knocked on a door, and an old Turkish man answered, adding to my belief that this was a social call and I had wasted my time. However, I waited for a moment or two and then peered through a small window at the front of the house.

I watched as Mohammed handed the old man a small bundle of our blue and green passports. The old man chose one of them and slowly selected a page, working under the light of a flickering bulb, which threw wandering shadows across the room. The Turkish leader, Mustafa Kemal Atatürk, stared authoritatively down from the far wall. My heart sank. Some voices in the alleyway startled me, and I pressed my body into the doorway to avoid detection. It suddenly occurred to me that I might not be in the best of neighbourhoods. My heart raced. After a while, the voices disappeared, and I went back to the window again and watched while the old man placed a heavily inked entry stamp on a green-covered passport. He blew on the ink and held it for a few minutes under the warm yellow bulb. Within minutes, the forger was finished. Mohammed examined the stamps before handing him some money.

I was unsure of what to do next. There was little point in confronting them, as it might terminate my relationship with Mohammed and jeopardise the six thousand dollars, he owed me. I wandered slowly back to the hotel, deep in thought. This world of nods, smiles and friendly handshakes was new to me, and, entrenched in the arrogance of youth, I had been foolish enough to think I knew what was going on and could handle it. Even in Queen's University, where a gloss had been deftly painted across the political divide, you knew who the "enemy" was. You knew that if you scratched the surface of any given student, you would eventually see the green or orange shine through. This was a lesson I would never forget. Back at the hotel, I told Pat what I had seen. We sat up most of the night talking and decided it was best to wait until we had been paid before confronting Mohammed.

Faced with the evidence, there was little he could do. Mohammed shrugged and stutteringly explained that the German export cars required an entry stamp on arrival in Turkey, which they all acquired at the Edirne border. He told the authorities that they were en route to Damascus and Saudi Arabia. It was illegal to sell them in Turkey, but Mohammed had a "friend" in customs who had given him his exit stamp, and the passports were modified to say they had exited on the Syrian border.

'You see, it's no big deal. The border guard is paid, the drivers are paid, the new owners are delighted, and the Turks are happy that no illegal cars remain on their soil,' he said. He shrugged and laughed. His flippant attitude infuriated Pat, who lunged before I could stop him. He caught Mohammed by the lapels of his very expensive suit and slammed him against the wall, cursing and threatening to kill him for putting our freedom at risk.

When everyone calmed down, a new deal was negotiated. It was decided that I would get another ten thousand dollars to leave my car in Van. Mohammed knew he had little choice, as the Mercedes was in my name and I could leave with it to Syria at any time. Pat said we should split the money fifty-fifty, and he would take the risk by driving the car there. It suited everybody. Mohammed would get his car delivered and knew that it was in my name, so the driver could not abscond with it. All I had to do was sit tight until Pat returned, and I would get paid for doing nothing.

A long week passed until Pat returned. He and I both continued to stay at the Hotel Emrah, where I met Jackie from Alberta, Canada. From an upper-middle-class background, she had refined manners and often used to dress up in expensive jewellery to accompany me for a kebab dinner at a local restaurant. I enjoyed our rambling conversations, basking in the fact that she seemed to take our rather bohemian lifestyle in Turkey as a type of colonial adventure from another period. We spent many afternoons chatting about politics with university students in the little cafés around Topkapi. Many felt that their new constitution was to protect the state from the actions of its citizens, rather than to protect individual liberties.

I loved the way Jackie could intelligently engage in any conversation, the way she delicately held my hand while we were walking, her ability to see the history in the buildings around us, and the little notes and poems she left for me on my pillow before we went to sleep.

'I ebb, I sway, I dance, I kick I drag, am slug-like
But up again, on again, I'm high I'm swept away by it all.'

We were still hanging out in Istanbul when Mohammed arrived in early June with a convoy of ten cars. He had mentioned to me that he wanted to do one last big run before leaving to live in America. The drivers were accommodated in hotels in Sultanahmet, and soon everyone was aware of their presence, due to their rather boisterous behaviour. It was good to hear English voices again, especially the conversations about Munich and David Bowie's Serious

Moonlight Tour concert in the Olympiahalle. The tour was launched in support of David Bowie's album *Let's Dance* and performed in Brussels and Frankfurt before Munich. I reflected on memories from Munich, the after-parties in the Sugar Shack and Mad Max's and how my life had become such a roller coaster. One day, I was kissing Nena from "99 Red Balloons", and the next I was living with some unemployed labourers in a squat.

Over the next few days, the drivers became increasingly concerned. They said that Mohammed had been edgy for days and they had not received their passports back from him. Others heard he was having difficulty selling the cars they had brought into Istanbul. He had even berated one of them, "Lazy John", for being too loose with his tongue and telling the locals he was importing used Mercedes for sale. They were also concerned that they might not be paid and would run out of money and not be able to stay in the city. I didn't have much sympathy for Mohammed, as these English lads thought that what they were doing was legitimate, so why wouldn't they discuss their work with the locals? My advice was to stay away from local pubs, wait until they got their passports back and were paid, and then forget about the Turkish car-export business. I intimated how I thought the business operated and let them decide whether they wanted to be involved with Mohammed anymore. However, the drivers' paths and mine were now entwined, and destiny was soon going to play an even bigger role in all our lives.

*

Recently, there had been a lot of terrorist activity in Turkey. A group called the Armenian Secret Army for the Liberation of Armenia (ASALA) had killed some Turkish diplomats to draw global attention to the Armenian Genocide of 1915. The incident had occurred during the First World War, when the Turks expelled Armenians to Syria but didn't provide food or water for the journey, resulting in the deaths of as many as 1.5 million Armenians. One sunny afternoon, the drivers and I were down in the Grand Bazaar having a meal in a small café. It was one of those balmy days when you would expect little to happen. We were chatting about Mohammed when there was an explosion, and a lone gunman appeared out of nowhere amidst the confusion and fired randomly into the crowd. The bazaar was soon in complete turmoil, with smoke and people screaming and running for the exits. A young German girl ran towards us, covered in blood, and we lay her down in the alleyway. Watching her dying on the ground, I was horrified at how close I had come, again, to being killed. We later discovered that the gunman had killed two people and wounded twenty-one. I decided to leave Turkey as soon as possible.

I agreed to meet Mohammed to find out what was happening to the cars. We met at his hotel, and he told me he was having major problems with the Turkish customs officials, as his Syrian friend had died suddenly from a heart attack some months before. The Turkish customs had been suspicious of him for some time and had waited until British passports stamped with his dead friend's name appeared. They had already seen the stamp on Lazy John's passport, and the word had gone around Istanbul, ensuring that none of the normal buyers would touch the cars.

'You also need to be careful Patrick – that stamp shouldn't have been used since last February or March. You have to make plans to get out of Turkey immediately,' Mohammed told me.

Customs moved quickly to put a stop to the illegal importations. Good fortune dictated that I was dining with Jackie in a nearby restaurant when police cars with blue flashing lights arrived at the drivers' hotel. I had already told her of the danger, and she clasped my hand tightly as the colour drained from her cheeks. We just looked at one another for a moment, knowing that this could mean the end of our relationship or even prison for me. We watched as four of the British drivers, including Lazy John, were taken away by police. Erkan, our waiter, stood by the door, shook his head and said, 'They make too much noise.'

I had to think fast. Customs was probably looking for me too, as, likely, they had seen me associating with Mohammed and the other drivers. My money, clothes, and passport were still at the Emrah Hotel, and I didn't know if the police were going to raid it as well. We would have to make our way back there and warn Pat about what was happening. Jackie gathered up my belongings, and we joined Pat at the hotel.

'Mohammed's on the Asian side of the city, and he doesn't know what's happening to his cars and the drivers. Let's let him know,' I said.

'Let him hang,' Pat replied. 'That bastard wouldn't do it for you.' I remembered how desperate I had been when Mohammed first gave me a job and how he had been good to me when the chips were down. We had become friends, often socialising together, and I felt that he had been more than generous in his financial dealings with me. I knew that Pat and Jackie wouldn't understand, but

I felt a peculiar sense of loyalty towards him. Thankfully for Mohammed, the other drivers didn't know where he lived – but it wouldn't take the authorities long to discover his whereabouts.

I said goodbye to Pat and Jackie and took the ferry across to the Asian side. It was a short trip, twenty minutes or less, but it seemed to take an eternity. As the boat churned its way through the dark waters of the Bosporus, my heart quickened as I thought about what might happen to me. I held on, white-knuckled, to the deck rails, imagining my mother's face as she was told that her son, the potential doctor was in a Turkish jail.

I met Mohammed at his hotel and told him related what had happened. For the first time in our acquaintance, he seemed afraid. He looked crumpled, worn out as if he hadn't slept for days. He thanked me for the update and advised me not to leave by the Edirne border crossing but, instead, to take the bus to Izmir, where I could get a ferry to Greece. Embarrassed, he asked if I could give him something to help him leave the country. I fumbled through my knapsack, extracted five hundred Deutschmarks, and handed them to him. He hugged me for a few moments; then his eyes caught mine in shared recognition of the wonderful adventures we had had together.

'Goodbye, Patrick, you are a special, brave person,' he said. 'Good luck when you get back to medical school – and become a great doctor!'

I left Mohammed and caught the next ferry back to meet Jackie. My heart was beating wildly. I knew how difficult it was going to be to say goodbye to her. I stood on deck by the rail and watched how the evening sun made the needle-like minarets of the Blue Mosque melt into the waters of the Golden Horn. My fellow passengers were mostly urban Turks, and they gathered around in respectful silence to watch the balconied minarets descend into the waters as the skyline of the old city receded into the far horizon. It was almost like nature was providing a requiem for my adventures in Turkey. It had been on the same waters, which Jason was fabled to have negotiated with the Argonauts, that I had first fallen in love with the country.

From the port, I caught a taxi back to the restaurant to find Jackie. Together, we went to the Büyük Otogar Bus Station so that I could start the ten-hour journey to Izmir. There were tears in both our eyes as I boarded. As we said our goodbyes, she handed me a small, scribbled note, which I read as we passed the city of Bursa. *'P J, Just one great adventure after another! I'll meet you in*

Dublin at any time if you want. Remember this. My destiny is not to serve, it is to create. I am a woman. Jackie xxx'

7. The Greek Islands

The next day, I caught the ferry from Izmir to Chios in Greece. Hostilities between Turkey and Greece ran very deep, and I watched the disembarking Greeks shake the dust from their shoes before leaving the end of the gangway; even minute particles of Turkish soil were viewed as contaminants. Since Greece had won its independence from the Ottoman Empire in 1832, it had faced Turkey in four major wars.

I went to Athens and, from there, caught a ferry to the island of Ios, where I lived for the next two months, mostly chilling out with my memories and meeting girls – lots of girls. It was a hedonistic lifestyle, mostly dedicated to the pursuit of sexual pleasure. During that period Dublin seemed very far away. As one friend wrote in my travel diary:

'Hot sun, hot sand and you
For a while we all become one
The sand and sun and then us
I look out on sea and sky
Blue on blue and again you
And wish this would last forever... forever... forever...

– Diamond Debbie Vancouver'

I stayed at Papa Antonia's hostel, at the top of the village on Ios. I shared my room with some Swedish and Danish backpackers, and we formed a band that practiced on a small beach near Scorpion's disco. Before long, I started dating Trine, who came from Skanderborg in Denmark and, when the band split up, we returned to the Athens Connection Hostel to try to find work. However, we were both bitten by the free life of the islands and working the dusty old streets of the capital for a few dollars a day didn't appeal to us. So, one night, we decided we had had enough and took the advice of some American tourists we'd been serving. We said goodbye to the owner, Thasos, and caught the ferry across the darkening waters of the Aegean to the volcanic isle of Santorini. It was early morning when we arrived.

Lonely seagulls swooped and cried around us as we slowly ascended the 587 cobbled steps up the face of the red hill. Somehow, we felt at home again. Maybe it was seeing the sparkling blue waters of the Aegean or smelling myrtle and eucalyptus in the air – whatever the reason, we were both alive again. Trine and I went further up the hill, passing along rows of whitewashed houses where old men gathered to gossip away the morning. We eventually found a small hostel on a back road that snaked its way towards the village of Firostefani.

In the afternoon, we hired scooters and found a quiet black-pebble beach on the east side of the island, shaded by a bank of tamarisk trees. We lay back on the beach. I watched as Trine pulled her blonde hair up into a ponytail and started reading John Irving's *The World According to Garp*, which I had carried with me from Turkey. I realised that I was falling in love with her – we were similar spirits, and I wanted to travel further with her.

That evening we sat together on the steps in Oia, on Santorini, as the last church bell pealed, and the orange and red sun tried to set the surface of the sea alight. If ever there was a place on earth to be in love, it was there. As the sun descended further into the sea, it seemed like the volcanic caldera was still alive, turning the sky into a mixture of violet, mauve and pink. I reached out, pulled Trine into my arms, and hugged her tightly. There were many things about our developing relationship that I wanted to say to her. She knew. As I looked deep into her eyes, she said, 'Patrick, what are you thinking?' I wanted to say that I was falling in love with her, that I wanted to take her to another place, a gentler one, far from the violence of Northern Ireland, the bombs of Munich and the gunmen of Istanbul. There are times in life when things are said that can change a person's destiny forever. I had gone through a lot to fulfil my dream of becoming a doctor, and I couldn't let that go. I looked out across the magnificent palette of colours reflected on the Aegean waters, unsure if our relationship could survive everyday life in Dublin. Resting my head in the hollow of her shoulder, I said, 'Oh, I don't know – just thinking about food tonight. Why don't we find a little courtyard restaurant that only Greeks go to?'

She looked at me sadly. Something was lost in the moment, and we both recognised it. Her eyes softened as she sensed that I was on another journey through life – one that didn't include her. We hugged each other tightly for a long time before getting up and making our way back to the scooters.

'OK, let find a little restaurant, and we'll get drunk,' she said.

'Let's spend all of those traveller's cheques I have from Munich,' I said.

We laughed, but I also knew my inability to deal with my emotions had weakened the bond that had developed between us.

We travelled south on Santorini until we reached a remote village called Akrotiri. There, we found a little courtyard restaurant with green creepers on flaking white walls, and farm animals wandering near the entrance. The locals stopped dining when we arrived, and they watched us intently as we waited by the doorway. An older woman came by but left us standing where we were, seemingly unwilling to give us a table. The smell of *magiritsa* soup cooking wafted on the night air. After some time, we nodded across at the old woman, even smiled politely, but she muttered under her breath and stayed away.

Eventually, we took our seats at a long wooden table under a pomegranate tree. A squeaking metal fan with three and a half blades provided the only sound. Despite our best efforts to get some attention, we couldn't get served, and I became increasingly annoyed as the other diners began to giggle amongst themselves.

Eventually, an old man approached us from one of the other tables and said, '*Ti na kanoume?*' What can we do?

'*Retsina!*' I declared, demanding wine, striking the wooden table in defiance.

An instant hush descended on the gathering, and many mouths opened in anticipation of what was going to happen next.

'And *magiritsa!*' I continued.

I glanced across at Trine, all the time wondering why the older woman was so unwilling to serve us. Another customer got up from his chair and talked to the old woman. He spoke gently, all the time retaining eye contact with her as if he was eager to see her response. The old woman slowly smiled, cackled something aloud and then went back inside to the kitchen. She returned a few moments later with a bottle of *Retsina* and a large platter of food. A young girl appeared with a jug of water and glasses and placed them on the table. There was something likeable about the old gentleman, and I thanked him for his help. I smiled at the other customers, hoping they would forgive my previous rudeness to the woman. The old man was eager to know if we came from Australia and the other guests wished us '*Kali orexi*', Greek for 'Enjoy your meal'.

The girl brought us more food, and we feasted until every plate on the table was empty. She then went upstairs and returned with a small candle, which she lit and placed on our table. I watched its flickering flame and noticed how its golden glow fell upon the edges of Trine's face; its light raised our spirits, giving us a thirst for more *Retsina*. I'm sure the fact that we were in love played a role in our desire to remain there as long as possible. I told her that I would be going back to medical school in a few months, and it was probably better for both of us to start facing that fact. 'I know that, Patrick,' she replied.

We stared into each other's eyes for a long time before asking the old gentleman if he would get the owner to fetch us another bottle. The old woman reappeared, small beads of sweat gathered on her forehead and placed another bottle of *Retsina* on the table. Soon it was past midnight and time for us to make our way silently back to our hostel near the village of Thera. A thousand stars glinted in the night sky as I reached for some traveller's cheques to pay for our meal. The old woman took one and studied the writing under the glimmer of an Aegean moon. She examined it for a long while before handing it to one of the guests at the table. He passed it around from person to person in the dusky light, each one reading aloud my name and the value in dollars. Then, a younger man started laughing, and the others joined him. He turned to me and said, 'Mister Patrick Treacy, this place is not a restaurant – you have been eating and drinking with my family in our private house!'

Trine and I eventually parted in August 1983. I continued my travels without her. In Cyprus, I met John, a Buddhist from Dunfermline, who wrote these memories in my diary:

'Here we all are in Limassol, Cyprus en route to Israel, as Eddie Grant would say, living on the front line. However, Bob Dylan would probably have explained it better. The Exodus from Genesis has begun. I'm glad I met someone at last who both understands the system and reads the Guardian.'

After Cyprus, I travelled to Israel and stayed with a tantric Buddhist sect in Haifa for a few days. It was a convivial atmosphere, not at all what I had expected in Israel. I parted company with John and went to visit some *kibbutzim* in the Judean Hills, before making my way to Jerusalem. I took accommodation at the Hotel Zefania, where I met Wolfgang, a student from Dortmund who wanted to travel south to Egypt. Everywhere we went, the Israelis were zealous in their attempts to educate us on the moral war that was raging over the Palestine question.

Politics aside, the ideology of the *kibbutz* impressed me, and Jerusalem was a wondrous city with many sights from ancient Christianity. These included the Church of the Holy Sepulchre, where Jesus was buried, and the Chapel of the Ascension, where he later ascended into Heaven. As I walked along Via Dolorosa, the route that Jesus walked to his crucifixion, I thought of how my parents would have loved to visit these places, and I was determined to bring them when my education was complete.

As the days passed, I started making plans to go back to college, but first, I wanted to visit Bethlehem, where Jesus was born. Wolfgang and I took a bus there and got off in the dusty square outside the Church of the Nativity. An elderly Arab man approached us; his mottled teeth stained in the different hues of the olive-wood rosaries he carried.

'*Salam!*' he said, as his teabag eyes beseeched us to buy his wares. He followed us along the square, gaining the attention of the Israeli police, who rather forcibly moved him along, instructing him to stop annoying the tourists. I had seen enough of this type of behaviour in my childhood and, in mild defiance of their actions, I called him back and deliberately bought some rosaries from him. I felt that whatever we thought about our fellow man, there, outside the birthplace of Jesus, there should have been some sense of human compassion – or his time on earth was wasted.

A guide brought us through a small entrance into the church, which tradition held to be the birthplace of Jesus of Nazareth. We made our way through a small basilica lined with Corinthian columns, which had been donated by King Edward IV of England to hold up the roof. The guide told us that the original roof had been stolen by the Ottoman Turks and melted down to make ammunition for a war against Venice. We reached an underground cave where a fourteen-pointed silver star set into the marble floor enshrined the site where Jesus was born. This was the cradle of Christianity and the birthplace of the person who shaped my beliefs and conscience. There are few moments in life when one feels humbled, and this was one of them. I stayed there a while trying to absorb the spiritual presence of the place and whispered a small prayer asking Jesus to help me in my studies when I returned to college. It was an overwhelming experience, and I carried it with me for many days as I travelled overland across the sands of the Sinai desert to Egypt.

The winds of change were turning in favour of Egypt, as Israel was pulling out of these lands and dismantling Israeli settlements. We arrived first in Alexandria and then went on to the cockroach-ridden Oxford Pension in Talaat Harb Street in Cairo. It was there that I parted company with Wolfgang, as he was heading further south through Africa. He wrote a few words of wisdom in my travelogue.

'P J, I have concluded after many years of travelling that life is basically about finding something to eat. Be sure to make it back to college, man, and do Africa at another time.'

It was with these rather profound words that I returned to the Royal College of Surgeons in Dublin in the fall of 1983 to try to continue my studies in medicine. It took some time to sort out my absence with the college, but they were tolerant when they understood the circumstances surrounding my decision.

Graduation from Royal College of Surgeons 1986

I qualified in June 1986 and, as I stood there taking the medical degree scroll from the registrar of the college, I reflected on the many life experiences that had brought me to that point in my life. I thought about the recent death of my father, and how he would have loved to see me standing there that day.

8. Now a Doctor

My medical career began at James Connolly Memorial Hospital in Blanchardstown in the autumn of 1987. The hospital was initially built to treat tuberculosis, which plagued Ireland in the period after the Second World War. During the 1950s, the village of Blanchardstown was considered far enough outside the city limits to construct "open-air" wards in which to treat this communicable disease. After the discovery of Isoniazid in the late 1950s, the rate of tuberculosis started to fall, and the hospital lost its specialised role. By the early 1980s, the burgeoning population of Dublin meant that the hospital was upgraded and integrated into the accident and emergency service for north Dublin.

That autumn, the new Fianna Fáil government introduced severe budgetary cuts across all departments, including health. This meant all accident-and-emergency cases in one side of the city were taken to just one designated on-call hospital. This arrangement, known as "supercall", put enormous strains on the system as staff had no previous knowledge of a patient's medical condition and no access to their records. These were the circumstances when I worked as a casualty senior house officer at the hospital.

The medical staff struggled to keep up with the workload. Sometimes we admitted more than sixty medical patients and the same number of surgical patients in one night. We often worked through the weekend without any sleep – that was just the way it was, and we accepted it. Junior doctors worked long hours, often in the absence of senior consultants and provided a service to the best of their abilities.

Late one night, amidst this mayhem, I was called to see a new, wheezing patient, who had been brought in by ambulance. He was a young man of seventeen, about five and a half feet tall, emaciated, with unkempt brown hair and sunken eyes that stared vacantly, when they focused at all. I suspected he was a heroin addict even before I saw the tracks on his limbs, where the veins he used to inject himself had hardened. This was the ugly face, the *other* face of Dublin in the '80s – the high unemployment, grey rainy streets and mass emigration; it was the Dublin portrayed in U2's song *Bad*.

'He's an asthmatic on Ventolin, inhalers, and he's recently been given steroids from his GP. He wasn't bad earlier – called us himself,' said one of the ambulance men, who had stayed until the medical staff arrived. That was the extent of the medical history I would receive, but the patient's blue facial hue told me he was going downhill rapidly. I put on a pair of gloves; he needed an intravenous line inserted straight away so that I could draw blood for analysis. The fibrotic nature of his main vessels caused some concern, but I gained access in a vein near his right ankle. I drew off about ten millilitres of dark bluish-red blood into a large syringe to distribute it into the relevant haematology and biochemistry containers and put the tubes on the bed beside the patient.

Blood would also have to be drawn from one of his arteries: an immediate oxygen analysis was needed to get a base level before hooking him up to our piped supply. The test is very painful but necessary; it would determine the oxygen levels in the blood coming from his lungs and their ability to function. In preparation, I began to examine the radial artery in his wrist.

One of the student nurses tried to get a temperature reading from the patient, who was becoming distressed. I searched his wrist again, hoping to find a bounding pulse, which would alert me to where his artery was. Unfortunately, my patient thought I was looking for a vein and, to be helpful, rolled over to show me his other leg.

'I have one here,' he said, pointing to the last open vessel through which he could inject heroin.

As he rolled, the bedding caught on the syringes, tossing them onto the floor. I felt a sharp stabbing pain as the syringe full of blood embedded itself in the side of my right leg. I grunted from the pain, and the patient looked down and saw what had happened. He turned even paler than he had been already.

'Doc,' he said. 'I'm HIV-positive.'

There have been few occasions in my life when I have known that four words could change my very existence. This was a disease which had only been discovered a few years before. Everyone who contracted it died – there was no known cure.

I saw the look of shock on the face of the nurse standing beside me. I knew her. She was in the same year as my girlfriend, Trish.

My body stiffened. I hesitated for a moment before pulling out the syringe. Although I knew I should act quickly, there were no procedures in place to tell me what I should do. I grabbed some Betadine– an iodine-based antiseptic liquid – and applied it to the wound.

I went upstairs to the operating theatre, where an old classmate was preparing to assist with surgery on an elderly patient with a neck-of-femur fracture. I took him to one side.

'I need you to do something particularly important for me,' I said. 'I want you to excise part of the skin and muscle of my right leg just below the knee.'

My friend looked at me in some confusion but trusted me enough to agree to my request without question.

'I just got a needle-stick injury from an HIV-positive patient. I want you to cut out the area around it like you are removing a malignant melanoma, OK?'

'Oh God!' he said, his face full of compassion. 'It had to happen to one of us sooner or later.'

'I'll put on another pair of gloves,' he said, and immediately set about excising a large lump of skin and underlying muscle from my leg. As he worked, a slow, circling wave of fear began in my stomach, making me feel nauseous.

'What's going on out here?' shouted the theatre sister, who had come out to see what was holding up her surgeon.

'Patrick got an HIV needle-stick injury.'

'What? And why did you bring that in here?' she bellowed.

'Cancel the hip operation and open up Theatre Two!' she called to the other scrub nurses, giving a major eyeroll in my direction.

I was left in no doubt that the theatre sister thought I had brought damnation on her theatre. For the first time, I realised that I was now the patient.

When my friend had finished with the operation, he sat me down for a chat. 'What are you going to do now?' he asked. 'And who'll take out the stitches?'

'I don't know yet, maybe I'll do it myself, but it's fairly obvious I'll not get much sympathy around here,' I said, nodding in the direction of the angry theatre nurse.

I knew it could be arranged through the emergency department, but that would mean opening a medical chart, and my HIV blood tests would then be available to my colleagues. I slowly made my way back downstairs. All heads turned towards me, and I realised that by the next day, every other person in the hospital would know what had happened.

I wandered over to see how my patient was doing. In a way, I felt cheated, as he had completely recovered from his attack and was sitting there using a nebuliser and chatting to the student nurse beside his bed. He apologised again as soon as he saw me, and I assured him that it wasn't his fault. Medicine was the choice I had made in life. I was a doctor, trained to treat illness and, unfortunately, these things happened.

I stayed in the department, treating patients until my shift was over. There was no risk to anyone I treated, though, as the virus, even if it had entered my blood, still hadn't had time to replicate. That could take another three to six months. During the night, I saw chest pains, kidney stones, gallbladder pains and whatever else the medical river of life washed up.

When my shift was over, I walked outside to the car park and stared at the Dublin skyline for a long time. It was November, and the morning air was damp and cold. Slowly the implications of what had happened dawned on me – for the next few years, I was going to have to play a waiting game to see whether I'd seroconvert and develop the illness. This was a time before the creation of the internet, when information about diseases had to be gained by reading papers published in medical journals. Rumours and myths about HIV abounded – many physicians openly stated that the infection could spread through saliva, tears, sweat, mosquitoes, and casual contact. Others said that if you kissed someone with the disease, you could die from it. James Connolly Memorial Hospital had just discarded a new gastroscope, worth tens of thousands of pounds when it was discovered that one of the patients who had used it had been HIV-positive. In that respect, as physicians, we were just as ignorant of the facts concerning this virus as the public.

I drove across the city to the cosy apartment I was renting on Serpentine Avenue in Ballsbridge. Exhausted, I climbed into bed but, even though it was nearly 9.30 am and I had worked all night, I couldn't sleep. I just lay there wondering how I would break the news to Trish.

Even though we hadn't moved in together, she spent most of her spare time with me at my apartment. I had met her soon after I started work at James Connolly Memorial. She hadn't been particularly impressed by my advances, but eventually, my persistence had won out. We'd been dating for nearly eighteen months; we had already met each other's parents. Trish's father, like mine, was a mechanic and had died. Her mother was a matron at the hospice, so we had medicine in common. When I took Trish to visit my mother for the first time, she brought a wreath for my father's grave, which won her instant approval.

Sometimes Trish and I would sit for hours, listening to Pavarotti, planning our future – the places we would see together and even how many kids we would have. There were plenty of nursing jobs available in Australia, and we had given some consideration to emigrating thereafter she qualified. Many of our friends had already taken up the opportunity, and that added to the appeal. The prospect of losing her terrified me. It wasn't that I didn't trust Trish to stand by me – I knew she would – but should I ask that of her?

With Trish on holiday in Portugal 1987

I stayed at home most of the day, trying to catch some sleep. I would close my eyes, and the enormity of the event would wash over me. I prowled my apartment, waiting for some sense of peace, but it never came. The needle stick didn't necessarily mean I would seroconvert and, logically, I knew that, but my mind continued to flick through the pages of a future riddled with AIDS.

I thought about the actor Rock Hudson, who had recently announced to the world that he was dying of AIDS. His gaunt appearance and nearly incoherent speech were so shocking that his announcement was broadcast all over the world for weeks. He had originally told everybody that he had inoperable liver cancer, as HIV was considered modern-day leprosy. People with the disease were stigmatised, not only in the employment arena but socially. The spectre of his illness loomed large in my mind's eye and made me realise that if I ever seroconverted, there would be no place to hide: the ravages of the disease would eventually show on my face, and its incumbent prejudices would be mine to deal with.

As evening fell, I considered the possibility of just keeping what had happened to me private. I didn't have the disease, so why should I broadcast the fact that I might? Why should I worry those who loved me? These were just fleeting thoughts as the darkness enveloped the night sky – I knew I would have to tell my girlfriend and my family, especially my mother. I tried to plan how best to break the news without causing too much upset, but it was futile.

Trish was a nurse and was every bit as aware of the danger as I was. She also had probably already heard about what had happened to me from friends at the hospital.

It was late in the afternoon when Trish arrived at the apartment. Smiling, she handed me a small container of potpourri to place on the kitchen table. She said she had bought it in the supermarket on her way. I just looked at her, noticing how her blonde hair fell loosely over her pretty face, partially hiding the blue eyes that always held such love when they looked into mine. We had taken many journeys together, but this one would be different. I was unsure of what exactly to say, and my silence caused her to speak.

'It's not like you to be so quiet. What's the matter? Has something happened?'

'Yes, I had a needle-stick injury at the hospital, and the patient has HIV,' I said, the words tumbling over themselves in their rush to leave my mouth.

'No,' she said quietly. 'No!'

She lifted her hands and held them against her cheeks, eyes widening in disbelief.

'What does it mean?' she asked, the tears already welling up in her eyes because she knew exactly what it might mean.

She moved towards me and wrapped her arms around my neck. We stood like that for a long time, as if our lack of movement could shield us from any calamity. Tears ran down my face as I told her how it had happened and about the staff's reaction. I told her how nervous I felt about the wait for the results.

My emotional reaction took me by surprise. There had been no tears at the hospital, and I hadn't had time since then to think the situation through. Perhaps it was her closeness, the fact that she loved me, and would love me no matter what, that was the impetus for my suppressed emotions to surge to the surface.

We sat on the sofa holding hands. She reassured me that I might never catch the disease. Suddenly I was tired, emotionally drained. Trish held me tightly, stroking my hair and telling me all the things I wanted to hear. Through her tears she said she would never leave me – if anything, she wanted to cement our relationship more firmly and talked of getting engaged, perhaps starting a family immediately, just in case I became ill later.

'You know, I got a surgeon to cut a big lump out of my leg,' I said, pulling off the dressing and showing her the stitches winding down the inside of my right leg. 'I did that immediately after it happened. I cleaned it with Betadine and went straight up to the theatre.'

Perhaps I wanted her to tell me I had done exactly the right thing, had saved the day – and myself in the process.

Trish tried to comfort me by telling me that they were making progress on the treatment for HIV every day and, even if I seroconverted, it could be many years before I became seriously ill. Who knew what might be available by then? Someone might even find a cure. Realistically, we both knew there wasn't too much hope of that, but we managed to convince ourselves.

I was very appreciative of all Trish's assurances and grateful that I had someone who loved me unconditionally the way she did. It certainly helped me through that time, when I was trying to come to terms with what my future might hold.

*

The hospital authorities, conscious of their responsibility to me as an employee, made an appointment for me to see a doctor at the Royal College of Surgeons, a specialist in virology. I was happy to go along with this and felt it more appropriate to start investigations away from the hospital, somewhere my colleagues would not have access to the results.

On the way to my appointment, I noticed an article in one of the morning papers that said a global HIV crisis was developing. It said there were already 150,000 cases of HIV diagnosed worldwide, and worse – each one of these people was expected to die. The article was critical of President Reagan's inability to focus attention on the need for AIDS research, education, and treatment. It filled me with dread. When I got to the appointment, I sat down across from the doctor.

'When did this happen to you?' she asked, writing some notes. 'It happened just three days ago.'

'Well, let's do the tests and see how things are with you,' she said, pulling on her surgical gloves. 'At least you have the benefit of knowing that the medical people who have contracted AIDS or died of the illness are very few – only four, in fact, to date – and each one had a distinct history of the blood being directly injected. It seems IM-IM transmission of the illness is not as serious as we are led to believe.'

She was alluding to the fact that most needle-stick accidents are caused by a medical professional receiving a prick injury to the finger muscle from an HIV patient who had just received an intramuscular injection. However, this was certainly not the situation with me. I had been injected directly with a 10-millilitre syringe full of HIV venous blood, putting me into the IV-IM classification.

'And what about IV-IM transmission?' I asked, almost not wanting to hear the answer.

'Oh, that's a different situation, and everyone to date with IV-IM transmission has died. The last one happened in London I think – a nurse accidentally got some blood injected into the back of her hand from a syringe full of blood lying on a worktop,' she said, unaware of the nature of my needle-stick case.

I turned towards her, my anger rising.

'I got HIV blood injected from a full syringe directly into my leg,' I said. 'The blood was from a vein and still in the syringe when it fell from a height and stabbed me.'

I watched as a deep red blush of embarrassment made its way slowly up her face. The doctor may have been many things – academic, kindly, brilliant in her way – but she had no experience as an HIV counsellor.

'Oh, I'm sorry – no one told me that,' she said, refusing to hold my gaze.

I was sitting with a scared academic, a research doctor who was probably unused to taking a proper medical history, and who had said the wrong thing completely.

'I could've told you, if you'd asked,' I said, unable to keep the sarcasm from my voice.

I left the consultation feeling disgusted that a doctor could heighten my fear and increase my sense of isolation. There had been many times up to that point in my life when I had had to tell patients' relatives that their loved ones wouldn't make it through the night. It took special discretion to impart this terrible news.

In my view, the professor entirely lacked this skill. I felt that medicine had completely let me down. The environment in which I practiced my profession caused the accident, yet my own colleagues would probably stigmatise me. Now, one of its experts had coldly told me that I was going to die.

I felt that I had to get out of Ireland until I could come to grips with what was happening. At first, it was a passing thought, but, as I made my way home, the idea took root.

My thoughts over the next few days were distracted from my predicament by the news that the IRA had detonated a bomb at Enniskillen's war memorial during a Remembrance Sunday ceremony – killing eleven people and injuring sixty-three more. The "Poppy Day Massacre" cast a dark shadow over the whole of Northern Ireland, and particularly rural Fermanagh. It was hard not to feel repugnance at what had occurred.

When my blood test came back later in the week, I got the good news that I didn't have the virus. I was elated, but I knew that the virus often didn't show up for years and that this was only the first test – I would have to be screened every three months for the next three or four years.

Trish joined me, to provide moral support when I went home to tell my mother and the rest of my family about what had happened. The drive seemed endless, and yet Garrison was only a couple of hours from Dublin. On the journey, Trish talked about having a child just in case I caught the disease. It was an incredibly selfless gesture, borne out of love, but bringing a child into the world with the possibility that it might grow up fatherless didn't sit well with me. I was unsure if I would have been able to do the same thing for her if our circumstances had been reversed – watch someone I loved ebb away, getting closer to death each day.

I needed to get away and face this thing on my own.

My family's house lay nestled beside a small copse of trees. The petrol pumps stood out front, and the large garage and several outhouses lay to the rear. This was where I had been hugged, praised, and chastised in equal measure throughout my childhood, and its familiarity wrapped itself around me like a blanket. When I got my mother alone, I sat down with her at the kitchen table.

'I've something to tell you…' I began.

'Don't tell me you and Trish are getting married!' she said, smiling. I wished I had been visiting with such joyous news, something for her to look forward to, rather than to dread. There was nothing I could do about that, so I told her, hesitantly at first, what had happened, and the implications.

'Oh, no! What does Trish think about it?'

'She's been brilliant, but I've applied for a job in New Zealand.'

'In New Zealand? God, you couldn't have chosen a place any further away!'

My mother was a stoical woman who usually gave good advice, and I wanted to hear what she had to say on the whole subject. Her advice was not to rush into anything. She adopted a "what will be, will be" policy and thought I should take my time. In taking this approach, she was thinking of Trish. I explained to my mother that, rightly or wrongly, I needed to spend some time alone.

My contract in James Connolly Memorial finished in December, and I got many jobs offers, all of which I rejected, aiming for New Zealand instead. I knew Trish wouldn't be happy, because she still had six months to go on her nursing contract in Dublin, but I thought I could take the time I needed, and she could join me later.

*

I took a trip back to Queen's University in Belfast to do more research about the virus. I hoped to chat with Professor Max Lewis at the Medical Research Centre (MRC) on the Lisburn Road, whose opinion I felt I could trust. But, before I went to see him, I wanted to go to the university's library and do some reading. I still had access to the computers, and I checked PubMed, an extensive database of articles on biomedical topics.

From what I read, it seemed that Luc Montagnier in France and Robert Gallo in the United States had both discovered the same virus in patients with AIDS, and the most promising hope for treatment came from a team with expertise in viral diseases working at Burrough-Wellcome & Company. Preliminary trials showed some therapeutic effects in humans, and a new drug called Zidovudine or azidothymidine (AZT) was receiving accelerated approval status.

The window in the library looked down upon the city streets of Belfast, where I had almost lost my life years before. It was late evening and, as I sat there alone, I took a letter from Professor G D Barbezet at the Department of Medicine at the University of Otago out of my pocket and read it again:

'Dear Dr Treacy,

It was a pleasure to speak to you on the phone last evening. I am sorry to have awoken you but at least it is good news. We are setting things in motion to have your letter of appointment sent to you through official channels and to have these processed through New Zealand House in London. We look forward to meeting you and welcoming you to New Zealand.'

*

I met Max Lewis the next day and he consoled me and said there was little he could add to what I already knew. After that, I returned to Dublin and told Trish I was moving to New Zealand – indefinitely.

Trish wasn't happy and didn't understand why I wanted to go so far away, but she acquiesced to my decision, asking if I would buy her a friendship ring to wear until we met again. She just wanted to solidify our relationship in some way before I left, but I felt she was hinting at our engagement, and didn't agree to it, convincing her that we didn't need a ring. I honestly believed it at the time.

9. The Asthma Epidemic in New Zealand

From the window, I could see the snow-capped mountains of New Zealand's Southern Alps, stretching like the backbone of a fossilised animal below the plane as it carried me closer to Dunedin. We passed near Mount Cook, a snow-capped monolith of rock, known to the Maori as Aorangi, "the cloud piercer". They called the surrounding land Aotearoa – the "place of the long white cloud", and I could see why.

One hundred miles to the south lay Dunedin – the capital city of the Otago region, and almost the last stop before Antarctica. I lay back in my seat, closed my eyes, and thought about my new job as a respiratory registrar in Dunedin Hospital. It would be challenging; New Zealand had the world's highest incidence of asthma deaths among young people. The situation was causing international concern, and special protocols had been put in place in Dunedin to ensure patient survival. Some doctors said the cause of the spike in asthma mortalities was related to the New Zealand flora, but most were sceptical about that theory, as the incidence had soared overnight, and the plants had been there for a long time.

The woman in the next seat noticed the copy of the *Irish Medical Times* that I was reading and started a conversation.

'Do you come from Ireland?' she asked. 'Are you going to work in Dunedin?'

I nodded that I was.

'Ah, I was at Ireland's Rugby World Cup game against Canada, and afterward, we went to a new, wee Irish pub beside the hospital,' she said. 'You'll like it there – it's called The Dubliner, and they even have Guinness on tap! It's run by Bob and Judy Walsh, and they're both from Dublin. I'm sure they'd love to see you. They probably don't get too many Irish in these parts.'

Dunedin had just hosted some of the matches for the first Rugby World Cup, which New Zealand had won. Indeed, the sport had evolved into a national pastime in this country, where – in contrast to South Africa – a Maori player could proudly stand side by side with the grandson of a former British soldier and they could chant the famous Haka together. I was looking forward to visiting the grounds and even possibly catching a match or two there.

When the plane landed, I loaded my cases into a taxi, which carried me through the rainy streets of Dunedin, towards the hospital quarters. The city was amongst the best-preserved Victorian and Edwardian cities in the Southern Hemisphere, and it was charming. Most of the streets were named after familiar avenues in the Scottish capital, and many people referred to it as "the Edinburgh of the south". My mind drifted. In Dublin, I had been happy, surrounded by friends, in the company of someone who loved me and who I loved. And yet I had left it all behind to live in a new country, surrounded by strangers. When I reached the hospital, I was given some keys to my room, where I stayed alone for many hours, quietly unpacking, and thinking about Trish's parting words, promising to stand by me no matter what happened.

As evening fell, I decided to take a stroll around the city I had adopted as my new home. Near the main gate of the hospital was a hotel called Captain Cook, which had a lively bar. Three hours and four Steinlagers later, my memories of home had slightly faded. Sitting beside me was a sheep drover, whose eyes simmered in an alcohol-induced red haze.

'You know, Irish,' he said, 'when you take everything into account, New Zealanders are a bloody great race of people! We have the best rugby team in the world, we had the first welfare state, and we discovered the atom. What the fuck has the Irish ever done?'

I didn't think it appropriate, considering his state of inebriation, to tell him that although some credit New Zealand-born Ernest Rutherford with splitting the atom in 1917, the man who got the official credit was Ernest Walton, who was born in County Waterford and studied physics at Trinity College Dublin.

In a way, my new Kiwi "friend" had lifted my spirits by giving me something to think about other than Trish and my family. After that conversation, I found myself chatting to quite a few of the locals and thinking that life in New Zealand wouldn't be so bad after all.

My first morning at the hospital passed pleasantly if a little frenetically at times. There were two consultants in charge of the respiratory unit. Professor

Malcolm Sears, an expert in the epidemiology of respiratory medicine, was known internationally as one of the first to use inhaled steroids in the management of asthma. He was a friendly, open man, and I felt lucky to be working with him. Dr Robin Taylor had recently migrated from Belfast and seemed a little more reticent.

My intern was a New Zealander called Graham, who proved to be competent and efficient. It was gratifying to be working as a registrar and to have an intern who could keep me informed about which patients required admission and which were waiting to be seen in Casualty. Up to that point I'd been the one doing all the running around.

On that first morning, I had just started exchanging pleasantries about life in Ireland with Professor Sears when Graham entered the room and told me I was needed in Casualty.

'It's a pneumothorax! And Mike Ozimek, the registrar from Cardiothoracic, wants to watch you put in the chest drain if that's OK.'

'How's the patient?' I inquired.

'She's a tall, thin girl, so it's probably a primary spontaneous pneumothorax, and she's breathing OK now.'

This meant that the gas leak that had collapsed her lung had occurred of its own accord and wasn't secondary to another lung condition. When the leak is small, it usually resolves itself and needs no further treatment, but when it is large, it quickly leads to chest pain and shortness of breath and requires the insertion of a chest drain into the lung to allow the air to escape. I followed Graham to Casualty and placed the chest drain.

That afternoon, I attended Dr Taylor's. Outpatient clinic, where I saw mostly tuberculosis patients who were Vietnamese boat people who had been accepted for residency by the New Zealand government. Graham and I entered the room where Dr Taylor was discussing an X-ray with a patient and her interpreter. Dr Taylor smiled as I walked in.

'Ah, Patrick – Am I on the call today? I can't remember!' he said. 'Yes, it's fairly quiet. I admitted a pneumothorax up on the ward.'

'Good man – drain in, that's what I like to hear!'

He turned and resumed his conversation with the interpreter for the boat people.

'Do you recognise this?' he asked, handing me a copy of the X-ray.

I could see a cavity in the upper lung and knew that it was active TB. 'Yes, that's tuberculosis.'

'Correct, but a wee bit quieter next time – I haven't told her yet,' he replied. 'Well done. Where were you working before you came here?'

'James Connolly Memorial in Dublin.'

'Ah, that was an old TB hospital in the past,' he said and smiled.

When the clinic finished, I chatted to the interpreter for a while, trying to find out more about my new patients. I learnt that the Vietnamese boat people had begun taking to the open seas after the US-Vietnam war and that over the twenty-five years that followed, more than 1 million of them had fled the communist regime and became refugees.

I felt privileged to be able to treat these desperate people who had faced such hardship on the open seas. Although most couldn't speak English, I could imagine the horror they'd seen and was impressed by how they seemed to accept their fate with dignity.

Over the next few weeks, I had several interesting patients under my care, including a Southlander called Ann Crawford, from the mining town of Invercargill. At fourteen, she had been struck down with a respiratory illness, which resulted in her spending much of the following eight years in hospitals. In March 1984, she had travelled to Harefield Hospital in England for treatment and had become New Zealand's first heart/lung transplant recipient. When I saw her, she was suffering from continual infections in the bases of her lungs, most likely a result of a packing deformity that left the new lungs effectively too large for her thoracic cage. She had recently written a book about her experiences, called *Pumps & Bellows*. We remained good friends throughout those difficult times, and I was always there when she returned to us for treatment. She bore her illness well and without complaint. She died a year later, but her bravery and good humour remained until the very end.

One day, I was approached on the ward by a naval officer, who asked if I would be willing to screen some young recruits for asthma. He came from the Toroa base of the Royal New Zealand Naval Volunteer Reserve, which was in nearby Andrew Street. There had been naval reserves in New Zealand since 1860 when local citizens volunteered to train as part-time sailors to help the regulars defend the country and her interests if required. The ward sister said that the two previous respiratory registrars had done the check-ups on the young cadets, and it was up to me. I thought it would be an interesting diversion, one that would get me out of the apartment for a while each week, so I said I would do it.

The officer invited me down to the naval base to meet some of his colleagues and to see their maritime museum. After a few weeks, I agreed to attend the main naval base in Davenport, Auckland, to undergo formal training and get my stripes as a surgical lieutenant commander. Initial difficulties with my Irish passport were overcome by granting me a New Zealand permanent residency with the proviso that I return at least once every four years to renew it. My life was settling into a routine, and the Naval Reserve was a nice pastime outside the hospital. There was a social aspect to it and a sense of pride and belonging.

While in Dunedin, I looked up one of my father's best friends, Bartley O'Reilly, who had travelled from Garrison and settled in Dunedin many years before. I vaguely remembered him as one of the men who had gathered around the fire in the bicycle shop, but he had left while I was still young. Bartley's emigration to New Zealand had come as a shock to my father, and I knew he had missed him terribly. I would spend time with Bartley and his wife, Vicky, whenever I could, visiting their home and listening to stories about the scrapes he and my father had got into as kids.

Once, Bartley told me a story about my father when he was only ten or eleven years old. It was back before the Second World War, when Irish villagers used to come together to *Céilí* and play music in a neighbour's house. One night they had gathered at Paddy the Yank's to listen to jazz music being played on a portable wind-up gramophone. Paddy had become very Americanised after living in New York for a few years, and he was so proud of his jazz collection that he had even devoted a bedroom in the house to it, hanging his Louis Armstrong records on little nails around the bed. That evening, my father and Bartley cheekily changed all the records for Irish traditional music. It was very embarrassing for the poor man, as he had advertised the jazz night, and the two boys got in trouble with their parents. My grandfather had laughed all night at what had happened to Paddy, which only added to the night's enjoyment.

I remember Bartley sitting back in his chair, smiling at the memory. I smiled too. It was special for me to hear stories about my father from another time and place – I still felt his loss and missed him dreadfully at times.

Vicky worked for the New Zealand Postal Service, which was going through a major restructuring at the time.

'Oh, you should have been here in the '50s,' she would say. 'You know, we had the highest standard of living in the world back then.' It was true that there was a period during the 1950s when New Zealand was at its peak as an agricultural economy and had the highest living standard in the world. In the 1970s, though, life began to change. The social order became frayed, and violent crime was reported on an almost daily basis.

'I lay all New Zealand's problems squarely on the fact that Great Britain went into the European Community and closed down the market for our commodities,' Vicky said.

She wasn't alone in expressing this sentiment. New Zealanders felt very bitter about Britain abandoning them, and they hated the French for taking advantage of the British market.

After a few weeks, I realised that there were other unresolved social problems causing resentment in New Zealand, when a police station in Dunedin was bombed by a motorcycle gang called the Mongrel Mob. Their name originated from comments made by a district court judge, who had called them "nothing but a pack of mongrels". They had a network of more than fifty chapters throughout New Zealand, each likely to bomb police stations or shoot at those in uniform. Most of these gangs inhabited the North Island, but there was an increasing rise in incidents – such as drive-by shootings – on the South Island.

One evening in early summer I was rambling through an area of town that was unfamiliar to me. I spotted a small bar at the top of Princes Street and decided to go in for a drink. The place was dark and nearly empty except for a few Maoris seated by the counter. A jukebox was playing in the corner as I asked the bartender for a bottle of Steinlager. One of the Maoris greeted me with an instinctive nod as the heavy, opening bass beat of Midnight Oil's latest hit, *Beds Are Burning* started to play.

A bearded Maori man who was sitting to one side of the jukebox with his arms folded began staring at me as I paid for my beer. We listened as the poignant words of the song about aboriginal injustices in the Australian outback grew louder and louder. I knew I had stumbled into the wrong place: there was an undercurrent of unfriendliness, and one wrong move on my part might bring it bubbling to the surface.

Without a word, the bearded Maori man rose and walked towards me. His jacket carried the faded insignia of a red bulldog, which I recognised as the emblem of the Mongrel Mob. He leaned across me, stubbed his cigarette out in an ashtray in front of me on the bar and exhaled a cloud of smoke into my face. Up close, his *tā moko* tattoos made him look ferocious.

'Why don't you drink in your bar, *pākehā*?' he said.

'I don't have a particular bar. I've only just arrived in Dunedin,' I said.

The other Maoris watched the encounter, their russet eyes mirroring a cry as if to the right some historical wrong.

'*Pākehā*, this hotel is for the family – for *whānau.*'

Dublin or Dunedin, it was all the same to him – I was a *pākehā*, a member of the race that had dispossessed his people. Without an argument, I got up, nodded to the barman, and slowly walked to the door. No one followed me, although I was half expecting them to, and I imagined they were watching me as I walked away.

In February, I learnt that the Pogues were going to be playing at a music festival in Dunedin called Febberfest 88. They had recently released a single called *Fairytale of New York*, which had gone to number two in the UK charts. The band had been founded in 1982, and had begun as Pogue Mahone, the Anglicisation of the Irish *póg mo thóin*, meaning "kiss my arse". Singer Shane MacGowan fronted the band, and they had used the irreverent name to snub the authorities.

On the night of the concert, I went to the Captain Cook on Albany Street to meet some friends. They knew truly little about The Pogues and gathered around to listen as I told them. My medical colleagues were impressed to learn that I had gone to medical college with two of Shane's first cousins and that his uncle was Professor William McGowan, who had performed the first renal transplant in Ireland in 1963.

'He has another uncle, Uncle Leo, who has an Irish pub in Frankfurt. And the taxis have stickers there with "VIP" – Visit the Irish Pub,' I told them.

I lifted my drink and noticed the drunken sheep drover I had met on my first night in Dunedin. He was looking over at me, obviously annoyed at the attention I was receiving. He approached our table.

'Well, Irish, do you know any New Zealand bands? Loose Change and Sang Froid are playing the Febberfest this year. I bet they're much better than these Pogue guys!'

He then pointed at the label on his bottle of Speights. 'Do you know what "SPEIGHTS" means?' he asked.

Some of the hospital staff advised me not to bother answering him.

'Superior Piss Enjoyed in Great Hotels in The Southland,' he said, sneering.

I smiled politely at him and went on chatting about Shane MacGowan.

Soon we left for the small ballroom where the band was playing. The rafters were decked in Irish green bunting, giving the feeling that St Patrick's Day had arrived a month early.

After what seemed like a long wait, Shane, dressed in a white T-shirt and a red necktie wandered onstage. He balanced a tin whistle with a Guinness bottle in one hand as the band started playing *The Broad Majestic Shannon*. By the time they sang *Fairytale of New York*, the crowd was swaying to the rhythm, and I was proud to be Irish. When the concert ended, I felt tall in the crowd, trying to catch the many eyes that had shared the musical culture of my nation. On the way out, I noticed the drunken driver.

'Do you know what the Irish meaning of "SPEIGHTS" is then?' I asked him.

'Shane's Pissheads Enjoy Irish Guinness Here in The South!'

I left him without waiting for his response and went backstage, where I met Shane and partied with the band until late the following morning. Although he had a concert in Auckland the next day, to his manager's dismay, he was only too happy to stay with me in Dunedin, chatting and sharing stories about the "old sod".

I missed Trish and looked forward to the day when she would join me. At first, I wrote to her and phoned whenever I could, reading her letters repeatedly, delighting in each loving word and soaking up every little bit of information about home. There were times when I almost knew them by heart, and they would come to mind throughout the day. Unfortunately, the longer I stayed in New Zealand, the further I fell behind in my correspondence with her.

Trish complained in one of our telephone conversations that she felt lonely and neglected and wondered why, if I loved her so much, I didn't put pen to paper. Of course, I reassured her that I still cared for her as much as I had on the day I had left and that all my plans revolved around her. I may have related how crammed my days were: I had work and, on my days off, I visited Bartley or attended naval training and never seemed to have a spare minute. She seemed to accept my explanation, if I promised to do better in the future – which, of course, I did. After I hung up, I thought no more about it. But on the other side of the world, Trish was only beginning to think.

As the months progressed, the high mortality rate from asthma continued to climb, causing growing concern in the hospital. It seemed that the problem did not exist in every hospital, and suspicion began to fall on a drug we were using called fenoterol, which was made by the German pharmaceutical company Boehringer Ingelheim. The Wellington Asthma Research Group was convinced there was an association, but the drug representatives said the group's studies were flawed, and the New Zealand Department of Health asked that they be repeated. Meanwhile, patients were dying. My own feeling on the subject was that, if there was doubt about a drug, its use should have been suspended pending further investigation.

One day on the wards, I was discussing the problem with my intern, Graham.

'How do you manage asthma differently in Ireland?' he asked. 'We give IV aminophylline on admission.'

'To everyone?' asked Professor Sears, who was listening to our conversation.

'Yes, to everyone,' I replied.

'And what if somebody comes in already on this medicine?' he asked.

'We give it to them as well.'

'That doesn't make a lot of medical sense,' he said. 'If the patient is already at therapeutic levels of theophylline, you're only exposing them to the side-effects of the drug. You would be better off using some beta-agonist there instead.'

I couldn't disagree with the professor – he was right. The medication we were using in Britain and Ireland had been around for more than a hundred years. It had first been extracted from tea leaves in 1888 and used as a diuretic. Hirsch, in Frankfurt, used it as a treatment for asthma just after the Great War and it survived in the role despite having many side effects. The newer beta-agonist drugs like Ventolin and Bricanyl had been in use for many years. What we didn't know at that time was that the newer German medicine we were using in Dunedin, fenoterol, was much more toxic than the aminophylline or theophylline that I had used in Dublin.

I'd already left New Zealand by the time the suspicions about the drug became irrefutable. When taken repeatedly, it had detrimental effects on the heart. In 1989, the New Zealand Department of Health acted to restrict the use of fenoterol. The epidemic of asthmatic deaths in New Zealand was over.

*

As the time approached for my second HIV test, I became very anxious. The test was done anonymously through the usual channels in the hospital. It would change my life if it came back positive, but I would just have to deal with it. Meanwhile, I didn't want my colleagues to know there might be a problem or to look at me differently. Trish was the first person I rang when I received the news that I was still negative. I could sense her relief and excitement at the other end of the phone. She was missing me terribly in Dublin but didn't seem committed to travelling down to join me in New Zealand.

One morning in September, I got another letter from Trish. Reading it was one of the hardest experiences of my life – she wanted to end our relationship. I went through her previous letters looking for clues of when she might have made the decision. Each perusal only added to my misery but didn't gain me any insight into why a love that had been so strong could suddenly have died. I spoke to her on the phone, but she made it clear that there was no going back. She said that she didn't want to see me and that she wanted to spend some time in self-reflection. She suggested I do the same. I wanted to respect her decision, so I decided to give her the time she needed. But I had no intention of losing her – I couldn't. I would return to Ireland.

My journey home from New Zealand took me by way of Thailand and India, countries that have given the world some of its oldest beliefs and philosophies. I would have loved to spend months travelling through these ancient kingdoms. Of course, that was my head speaking. My heart had already decided that I shouldn't spend too long, just in case Trish solidified her relationship with her new boyfriend, and I was pushed out of the picture.

10. Back to Ireland

I looked out of my hotel window in Bangkok just as the sun lifted itself out of a bed of soft clouds on the horizon, sending shafts of sunlight in all directions to awaken the surrounding countryside. This was Thailand, the former Siam, a land that had inspired one of my father's favourite films, *The King and I*. However, time, moves on, and the old kingdom of Siam had disappeared with time, just like my father. The hotel concierge recommended visiting a Buddhist temple on the west bank of the Chao Phraya River, called Wat Arun. With a heavy heart, I caught the Tha Tien express ferry and made my way across to the temple. We arrived at the sun rose high enough to begin streaming over its imposing Khmer-style spire. The glistening light display could be seen from every corner of the city. The magical effect was caused by little pieces of Chinese porcelain and coloured glass which caught the light. I could see why it was called the Temple of Dawn.

Some monks in saffron robes were already up and attending to their duties. I watched them march in single file along the tree-lined riverbank. Some were carrying aluminium begging bowls, while others carried small birdcages. They clapped their hands to the rhythmical beat of a melodic mantra. These daily alms rituals, *tam bun*, are part of the Buddhist philosophy of giving and creating merit to gain good karma, and it takes place all over Thailand.

A small wind rose as I stepped off, the boat, and the mantra grew louder as the monks gathered around, happy to accept money from the tourists who were travelling with me. Their leader, Praydoor, greeted me in perfect English, his young face exuding an air of self-assured dignity. I felt at ease in his company and asked him questions about Buddhist philosophy. I felt that he sensed my pain. He told me that all personal suffering was caused by craving, and when that stopped, the pain of loss would end. He bowed and then lifted a small cage.

'Why don't you let the bird carry away your suffering as it flies to freedom?'
'How much does it cost?'

'Just a few baht.'

I was annoyed by the simplicity of the symbolism and told him that I didn't agree with caging wild birds to set them free. He told me that he had raised the bird from birth, and now it was old enough to survive on its own. He said that if something is trapped with, in a cage, it is good karma to release it and give it freedom. I gave him some money. I felt that he was trying to tell me to let Trish go.

I stayed for another few days in Bangkok, but soon it was time to move on.

On the morning that I arrived in Delhi, I hired a 1950s-style black and yellow Morris Oxford taxi to take me on the three-hour journey to visit the Taj Mahal in Agra. The romantic mausoleum was built by Mughal emperor Shah Jahan in memory of his third wife, and it was one of the places Trish and I had prioritised on our list of things to see. I was apprehensive about visiting it alone, knowing it was a symbol of eternal love.

My route took me along the Grand Trunk Road, one of southern Asia's oldest and longest major highways. From the front seat, I watched the vortex of bicycles, rickshaws, bullock carts and pedestrians that formed the lifeblood of the Indian highway crisscrossing and passing us in every direction. A Krishna figurine dangled from the vehicle's front mirror, moving hypnotically to the rhythm of the potholed road beneath us. After two miles of clanking, the car gave one last metallic groan and ground to a halt. A stony silence filled the cab as my driver got out and opened the bonnet to survey the damage. A tattered strip of electrical cable hanging under the engine indicated that our dynamo was missing.

The frantic driver started pacing around the vehicle, cursing his luck and looking impatiently for the missing component.

'It cannot be far. I see one of the bolts,' he said, before tumbling into the crowd and bending down to pick something up out of the dust. I was preoccupied with some desperate cycle-rickshaw drivers who had stopped, looking for customers, so I hardly noticed the man in the white *dhoti* coming towards the car. I suppose he could have been a Hindu holy man, but he looked too dishevelled. He walked, with a slight limp, up to where I was standing outside the car.

'Master Sahib is this what you're looking for?' he inquired, thrusting the generator in my direction. 'My name is Chandrapal and, please, Sahib, I am travelling to Calcutta – could you aid me in my journey?'

I looked at the man, tall in the crowd, his body covered in the only possessions he owned in the world. His craggy, lined face was worn, like the sculpted staff he carried. He moved closer, grinning. His eyes were piercing and yet at peace, indifferent to the chaos that surrounded us. There was a certain aura about him, and I sensed that he would be interesting company for the journey. He lowered his head and looked over at the driver, who had taken the dynamo from him and was busily repairing the taxi.

'This taxi is fully booked out!' the driver said, without even bothering to lift his head from underneath the half-open bonnet. 'Please leave! You can see that we have no more places in this vehicle.'

I indicated that I would pay for the man's passage, but the driver's eyes widened, and he gesticulated with his finger, excitedly signifying there was to be no more talk about carrying this holy man in the taxi. The driver said that he had never agreed to take me to Calcutta, which was a few days away, and that he was returning to Delhi that evening.

I turned back to the poor man and said, 'Sorry, Chandrapal, but he's the boss.'

He agreed, standing away from the car in poised silence, passing no remark on the taxi driver's intolerance, which we both knew was probably caste-driven, the unspoken way of life in India.

'Here are some rupees,' I said.

'I do not want to carry money – it would buy me only trouble. If I had your money, then the robbers would follow me, and I would not sleep at night.'

'But if you had my money, you could pay for a taxi to go to Calcutta!' I replied.

'I never buy what kindness can give from the heart.'

'Here, take this money and get an autorickshaw to take you a little further on your way to Calcutta.'

I placed some money in his aluminium bowl. He began murmuring some Hindu mantra as I got back into the taxi. He drifted away, walking behind a passing bullock cart and timing his steps to the rhythm of the creaking wheels. From the back window of the taxi, I could see him pausing and looking into the begging bowl to count his takings. Then he lifted something high into the air and gave it a fling – my money!

*

When we finally reached it, I found that touring the Taj Mahal was difficult for me. The symbol of eternal love only reinforced my sense of loss. I knew that if I had acted differently, Trish would have waited for me. But I had felt that I just couldn't commit to our future until I knew my own.

After visiting the Taj Mahal, I took a so-called "super air-conditioned coach" to Calcutta. There were windows missing, and although passengers had queued to receive numbered tickets, people sat wherever they liked. While there, I went to see Mother Teresa's Missionaries of Charity and found her oasis of humanity to be a special place, where the spiritual worlds of the living and the dying met. This was a place where people crossed over to the other side in dignity and love. They cried with outstretched hands from their beds when they heard I was a doctor, each wanting to live, and I felt a great sense of empathy. It reinforced my desire to use my profession, wherever possible, for the betterment of humanity.

*

When I returned to Ireland, I began working in Our Lady's Children's Hospital in Crumlin as an accident-and-emergency senior house officer (SHO). Some of the scenes I witnessed there were truly heart-breaking, like when I watched a mother carry a dead three-year-old burns victim to his sister so that she could kiss him goodbye. Both children had been in an upstairs bedroom when a fire had broken out. Medicine can tear your heart out, but one quickly learns that the best doctors are those who remain dissociated and stoical – the next tragedy is only waiting around the corner.

When I met Trish, at first it seemed as though she wanted us to get back together, but then she changed her mind. Eventually, she left Ireland to work for the summer in the United States. This gave me a little more insight into how she must have felt while I'd been away. This was the place where I almost expected her to be at my side and, if it was possible, I missed her even more now that I was back. Slowly I began to realise that it was harder for the person left behind they met the same friends and visited the same places, only now they did it alone. The person who left was, at the very least, meeting new people, sharing new adventures and not burdened by the constant reminders of what they were missing. It was too late – she wouldn't see me.

After the accident and emergency rotation, I began work as an orthopaedic SHO. My consultants were Mr Frank Dowling and Mr Ossie Fogarty, both excellent orthopaedic surgeons who specialised in placing Hartmann's rods for paediatric scoliosis and introducing limb-lengthening techniques to height-challenged patients. The techniques were becoming popular since the discovery that the pooled pituitary human growth hormone being used on pituitary dwarfs was infected with the HIV virus and causing deaths. It seemed impossible to escape this virus, which left a trail of destruction wherever it appeared. In that year, we discovered that babies on the hospital wards with HIV-positive blood tests were suddenly becoming negative when they reached six months old. The tests were showing false positives due to the mother's blood still circulating in the child's system. The age of antiretroviral drugs had arrived; they were being used on the new born – and they were beginning to work.

*

In 1989, while I was working at Our Lady's in Crumlin, several parents asked me to accompany a group of one hundred very sick children to Lourdes, a small town in the foothills of the Pyrenees that is famous for its miraculous cures. I agreed to go because I felt it would be interesting to see the sick children, I treated every day in a completely different environment. Many were dying, and some had brain tumours, with large swollen heads secondary to unresolved hydrocephalus. I spent a lot of my time in Lourdes administering intravenous diazepam to fitting epileptics, sometimes treating as many as five patients at one time. It was sad to see the children suffering, but they faced their illness with resigned dignity, and their parents handled them wonderfully as well. We all knew that many of the children would not see out the rest of the year, but the parents were tireless in their devotion and never gave up their hope for a cure.

The Lourdes authorities asked me to sit on a committee that oversaw the criteria for miraculous cures. There had been about two and a half thousand recognised medical "cures" there since 1858 and, of these, sixty-four were accepted by the Catholic Church as miraculous. I accepted their invitation, and for many years, we communicated, and they sent me medical notes of potential miracles for perusal. The authorities were extremely conservative in their acceptance of any unexplained patient survival not readily explicable by medical or scientific means, and I was fascinated by the interaction of religion and medicine. It still intrigues me to this day.

After my six-month rotation in paediatrics ended, I decided to remain in Ireland. It was the fall of 1989, and I had established a line of communication with Trish, who had by now returned to Ireland. I wanted to give it until Christmas to see if we could put the relationship back together again.

Part of me felt that it would be advantageous for me to do the preliminary parts of General Practice in case I decided to go overseas again; at least I would have some specialist qualifications. Eventually, I opted to do Obstetrics and Gynaecology in Our Lady of Lourdes Hospital in Drogheda, County Louth. The Medical Missionaries of Mary ran the hospital as an international training hospital. The obstetric unit was built away from the main hospital, so it had certain independence. I worked with three obstetric consultants: Mr Liam O'Brien, Mr Finian Lynch and Mr Michael Neary. The actions of the latter would later cause national outrage: it would be discovered that he had carried out an inordinate number of caesarean hysterectomies. Some patients had expressed concern over their procedures to me, which I had noted in their charts. This would be used in the High Court later. The Irish Medical Council suspended Michael Neary after an inquiry found that he had carried out nearly two hundred peripartum hysterectomies in the previous twenty-five years, often on women with one or no children. The average consultant obstetrician carries out five or six of these operations in their entire career.

I found it extremely difficult to live without Trish, and every phone call just made the situation worse. It's a strange thing: sometimes the more you try to show someone that you love them, the further away you drive them. At that point, all the flowers and fast cars in the world can't bridge the gap, it's all or nothing, and women can sometimes be cruel without meaning to be. Men express their emotions differently and often carry a heavier burden consequently.

Heartbroken, I decided that I needed to leave Ireland again and continue my HIV tests in another environment. I decided to apply for a position at the PARC Irish hospital group in Baghdad, Iraq. This was a country that I had always wanted to visit, a country that was once considered to be the cradle of civilisation, home to Babylon and Nineveh.

In late 1989, while I was contemplating this move, the world around me started to change forever. During October, many Eastern-bloc citizens started to defy their Marxist regimes and strike for freedom. The movement for political change had started with Solidarity (*Solidarność*) in the shipyards of Poland and had spread from there. After weeks of mounting civil unrest in East Germany, the government there announced that it would allow its citizens to visit West Berlin, starting on 9 November. Many thousands of people gathered near the Brandenburg Gate.

As the crowds in Berlin grew larger, I knew this was a historic time, and I wanted to share the moment when the people gained their freedom from the outdated communist regimes that had once ruled them with iron fists. So, I arranged to go to Berlin. Just before I left, I received a letter which carried a blue-and-red official postmark from the PARC hospital complex in Baghdad. It offered me a medical locum position there for an initial period of six weeks.

I arrived in West Berlin and found a small room in a hotel on Schöneberger Strasse. The owner was a pleasant man with old-fashioned Germanic manners, slightly bent and rather aloof. I went across to the half-opened window of my room and peered outside. It was freezing on the streets outside, and the palm trees in the Iraqi hospital brochure with my job offer made Baghdad seem like a tropical paradise. The moon had risen, and a cold wind was starting to blow, biting like frozen needles into the edges of my face. It made a whistling sound and, before long, its presence had filled every corner of the small room. In the distance, I heard the haunting melody of Beethoven's *Ninth Symphony* and thought how appropriate it was that this work should commemorate the ending of the Cold War and, with it, the old order that had shaped the world my generation had grown up in.

Crowds were building up on the streets below and, amidst the blare of a hundred alpine horns, a few people attempted to sing the enduring Lutheran hymn *Nun Danket Alle Gott.* They beckoned for me to join them in their march to the Wall and, on that cold November night, I walked along the crammed pavements of Potsdamer Strasse to the green copper chariots that graced the pillars of the Brandenburg Gate. There, I climbed up on a scaffold of clasped hands and secured a foothold on the side of the concrete edifice. Somebody threw me up a small hammer and, under the glow of an array of klieg lights, I symbolically broke a piece of rubble from the wall. The people below me cheered, and a knot of emotion rose in my throat as I looked out at the thousands of people below me in a sea of flashbulbs and flickering sparklers.

For a moment, the crowd became silent. In the blur of emotion, I became fearful of the new political system that I was helping to create. The Soviet Empire had collapsed, but nobody was willing to look far enough above their bottles of Sekt to care about exactly what would take its place? Below me, some people joined in the chorus of a song coming from a tape player. Their words broke into my thoughts and, like a stone dropping into the pond of life, ripples spread out as others sang loudly in the frosty night air. It was a tune of Bob Dylan's, and it seemed to capture the moment – *The Times They Are a-Changin.*

The night the Berlin Wall fell

11. Moving to Baghdad

Back in Ireland, I began reading as much as I could about the political situation in Iraq. Reports in the media told of a world ruled by a brutal dictator called Saddam Hussein, who had created a totalitarian society based on the ideologies of Nazism and Stalinism. His tyranny was likened to the darkest days of the Jewish ghettos, Iraq portrayed as a modern-day Nazi Germany, awash in a sea of propaganda. Amnesty International said there was evidence of civilians being tortured in vats of acid, and of parents being forced to watch as torturers gouged out the eyes of their little children. I bought a book called *Republic of Fear*, which told of the secret police – the Mukhabarat – who maintained strict control of the population through disappearances and targeted assassinations. Some British papers intimated that the ruling Ba'ath Party were using chemical weapons against their people.

The medical staff who lived in Baghdad during the worst years of the Iran-Iraq War tended to paint a different picture. They told of a country with modern highways and great nightclubs and hotels with seven-star ratings, a land where women had the freedom to work in high-powered legal, medical and government jobs, a place where there was a higher level of literacy than in Ireland. 'Even the poor Arabs who live in the marshes have schools and electricity,' one told me, 'and that's more than some of our neighbours in the west of Ireland.' They assured me that alcohol was freely available in Iraq, unlike in some of the other Gulf states. Most considered Iraq a modern nation, which didn't take a fundamentalist line, and this level of religious tolerance led hundreds of western Christian medical staff to practice there in the early 1990s.

I found it difficult to marry these conflicting views on Iraq, but I would see things for myself.

The journey to Baghdad found me sandwiched between Sarah, a young Irish nurse, and a jowly Scottish engineer called Donald. The pretty blonde nurse's distinct Dublin 4 accent told me she had probably trained in St Vincent's

University Hospital. My other conversationalist, by comparison, carried the more rhotic accent of Scotland's capital, Edinburgh.

Donald was a tall man with a welcoming smile, whose greying sandy hair was swept back from his face. He told me that he was a professional naval diver and spent his time searching for unexploded mines in the waterways around the southern Iraqi city of Basra. These devices had been left behind after the Iran-Iraq War and had to be cleared from the Persian Gulf to ensure safe passage for ships travelling upstream. It would take them years to finish the project, as many of the mines were adrift in the open sea. 'Do you want some Johnny Walker?' Donald asked, smiling as he poured some duty-free whiskey into a glass and handed it across to me. 'Take a decent wee drop. With the restrictions on foreign currency, it might be the last you'll get of any *good* Scotch whiskey until you come back.'

I could see he was a seasoned traveller who had been to Iraq many times, and I took the opportunity to find out some of what he knew about the country.

'Do you ever see any of the mass public hangings?' I inquired. 'You'll never see any of that – it's all drinking and parties.'

'Surely, not all the media reports are wrong?' I asked.

Softening, he poured me another whiskey.

'Ah, don't believe all you read in the papers. You're going to love it out there and wait till you see the nurses' parties – you'll probably still be going back there in two years,' he said and laughed.

Donald eased my anxiety, and I almost wanted to believe him, but I also remembered my classmate Mohammed al Sadr in the Royal College of Surgeons. He was an Iraqi political refugee who carried – deeply embedded in his back – the scars of torture inflicted by Saddam's Ba'ath regime. More than once, he had broken down in tears as he recounted how his mother had been murdered while she slept. Like many other Iraqi students studying medicine in Ireland, he would never return to his native land. For the next six weeks, I was going to live under the regime his family had fled from, so it was natural to be apprehensive – but deep inside, the prospect excited me too.

Sarah settled herself more comfortably into her seat and smiled across at me.

'Are you looking forward to working in Iraq?' she asked.

'Well, it's easy money. What about yourself?' I asked.

'The hospital staff before us worked when Iranian missiles were falling on the city. If they can do that, then we should be OK. I've spoken to some of the nurses working there now, and they say it's all right,' she said.

'I suppose we'll just have to find out for ourselves.'

*

When the plane came to a halt on the runway in Baghdad, I looked through the cabin window at the twinkling night sky. After what seemed like an awfully long wait, we were allowed to disembark. The air outside was still. There was hardly a trace of wind to soothe the burning landscape.

We collected our luggage from the baggage carousel and joined the phalanx of people waiting for immigration officials to check their passports. Some soldiers in green fatigues eyed us warily, readjusting their guns. I stared straight ahead, trying to avoid their gazes, as my backpack contained banned newspapers and magazines which highlighted the world's growing uneasiness about Saddam Hussein. Although our colleagues in Baghdad were looking forward to news from home, it was advisable not to carry it through the airport. A heavyset man standing in front of me in the queue shifted nervously from one foot to the other, his breathing long and laboured. He frequently turned around, keeping an eye on the soldiers always. I put a little distance between myself and this anxious stranger. A combination of exhaustion, whiskey and fear made me feel nauseous. The bright lights of the airport swirled around me. If the soldiers searched and found the newspapers, my time in Baghdad could be over before it began – or I might face an even worse fate. Sarah, who I had left behind in baggage claim, came over to me. 'Welcome to Baghdad, the cradle of civilisation and home for the next six weeks,' she said, pointing up to a colourful mural of Saddam Hussein seated on a chestnut stallion. The artist had portrayed the Iraqi leader as a gallant Arabian knight leading his troops into battle. I later learnt that this portrait remembered the Battle of Qadisiya, during which the Iraqi cavalry brought the great Persian army to its knees and changed the course of Islamic history. I stood in awe of the symbolism of the picture, amazed that I had arrived in the ancient land of Mesopotamia, home of the Hanging Gardens of Babylon and the Garden of Eden.

The line moved again and soon it was my turn in front of the immigration official.

'*Salaam alaikum*,' I said, trying to speak a little Arabic.

'*Alaikum as-salaam*. Papers,' he demanded, not bothering to lift his eyes from his desk.

He was younger than I had expected, probably still in his early twenties, and I was surprised that he was wearing casual Western-style clothes. I handed over my passport. He fingered the pages of the book methodically, painstakingly checking the colourful visas I had collected from my many travels around the world.

'Have you been to Israel?' he robotically asked.

'No,' I replied as my visa had just been stapled to the page, and I had since removed it.

It was apparent from his cold manner that there would be no pleasantries exchanged. He looked up at me, checked the photograph on the passport, and then stamped it with the words, 'This visa is considered invalid for entry into Iraq if the bearer obtains an Israeli visa on his passport.'

'What are you going to be doing in Iraq?' he asked.

'I am going to work in a hospital,' I said.

'If you going to work in the hospital, you must take one of these,' he said, giving me a slip of paper. I opened it slowly and read its contents.

'Dear Passenger,

Please note that according to the Revolutionary Command Council Resolution No 229 dated 16/4/1987 you should call within five days of your arrival to Iraq at either Alkindi, Alkarama or Alkadhmiya Hospital in Baghdad or the preventive health centres in the governates for AIDS Laboratory Blood Tests. Otherwise, you will be submitted to a fine of five hundred Iraqi dinars or six months' imprisonment, in case of not paying the fine.'

I finished with the immigration officer and went to join Sarah, who by now had got ahead of me. 'Everybody has to be tested for AIDS before they can work,' I said to her.

The test the Iraqi government was requiring me to take would establish, for the fourth time, whether I was HIV-negative. I intended to take it as soon as possible.

'Well, look on the bright side, Patrick,' she laughed, 'at least you know that every nurse in Baghdad is HIV-negative.'

We walked together towards the door of the arrivals lounge, where there was another large portrait of Saddam Hussein, dressed in a red-and-white chequered *kaffiyeh*, an Arab headdress. Icons of leaders signify power in the Middle East and, if his portraits were anything to judge by, the "Father of the Nation" was a very powerful man indeed. This was my first exposure to the personality cult of Saddam Hussein. A nearby sign read: 'Don't for one moment think that the Revolution is unaware of what you are all doing. Remember that the Revolution is everywhere, and it has its eyes wide open.'

The automatic doors opened, and a stifling blast of hot air hit us in the face. We said our goodbyes to Donald, who promised to meet up with us when he came to Baghdad.

A welcoming committee was waiting to meet Sarah and me. We were approached by a smiling, dark-haired guy in his mid-twenties, who shook hands with me and said, 'Hi, I'm David, one of the cardiology registrars. And this is Paul, one of the medical SHOs. I think you know each other – your fame goes before you!'

I immediately recognised an old friend I had played guitar with at college. We chatted as we walked from the airport terminal, across the parking lot.

The night air was heavy, and it clung to my skin like an invisible cloth. Above us, a brilliant crescent moon hung sideways in a deep rose sky, bathing us in its light. The sweet smell of roasting chestnuts wafted from a nearby vendor's stall. A hawker exhibited piles of men's shirts on the pavement in neat rows, next to a display of cheap watches. Paul lifted one of the watches and gazed at the image of Saddam smiling from between the moving hands.

'Big ERIC gets his face on everything out here. Be careful – he misses nothing,' Paul said.

'Who's Eric?' I asked.

'ERIC – Eternal Ruler in Command,' he whispered. 'That's what we call Saddam.'

He told me that it was best to talk in code about anything that related to the Ba'ath regime or its policies, as the country was overrun with Mukhabarat, secret police, who continually listened to conversations and phone calls.

'You can't tell them apart from the ordinary man in the street, so it's best to be careful at all times,' Paul said. 'You won't find anyone willing to talk about life in Iraq.'

Suddenly Donald's conversation made more sense to me. Like a lot of foreigners living in Iraq, he had learnt never to mention the dark side of the Ba'ath regime, even in drunken conversation.

Paul continued, 'I hear they're going to put you into Staff Health. You'll be given your own jeep.'

'What's it like?' I asked.

'Brilliant, it's a bit of a doss, you'll probably have every waster in the hospital coming to you looking for a day off. But at least you'll get the use of your own Nissan Patrol. It's shared between you and Patricia, the Staff Health nurse.'

We approached a green-and-white jeep bearing the Ibn al-Bitar Hospital insignia. It was surrounded by a group of irate taxi drivers, as David had been parked right in the middle of one of their ranks. An unshaven man with an obvious limp approached us and begged for some dollars. I presumed he had been injured in the Iran-Iraq War; he wouldn't be the last of these people we would meet in Baghdad that year.

'Be careful they don't confiscate your jeep. Look at this new circular on parking that was sent round today,' Paul said, reaching into his pocket and taking out a slip of paper.

'To all staff, Ibn al-Bitar Hospital,
A drive to tighten up the traffic regulations is taking place, in particular in Basra and also in some parts of Baghdad. A directive has been given to apply the maximum penalty for illegal parking, breaking of speed limits, driving through the red light and reckless driving. The penalties for expatriates could amount to confiscation of the vehicle and a ban on re-entry to Iraq. Such offences for Iraqi staff could result in imprisonment for a year. Personnel using vehicles, particularly for social purposes, are reminded of their responsibility in the event of the vehicle being confiscated, stolen, or damaged.

–Hospital Administrator'

'A year in jail for parking in the wrong spot – that's a bit over the top, isn't it?' I said.

'Well, just be glad we're not driving your Nissan Patrol to the airport tonight, or we'd definitely all be locked up for a year,' Paul said.

'Why do you say that?' I asked.

'Oh, it's a big scandal in the hospital now. Did you hear about Farzad Bazoft – the *Observer* journalist? He was caught at the airport with soil samples he'd taken from a missile plant. He was with your staff nurse in the Staff Health Nissan Patrol. They say she'll get a life sentence.'

I learnt that Bazoft was a reporter who had arrived in Baghdad a few months earlier. He'd met Daphne Parish at the Mansour Melia Hotel, where he was staying. The two became friendly, and he used her as a cover to investigate an explosion that had occurred at the Al-Iskandaria military complex, about 30 miles south of Baghdad. Rumours had circulated that many hundreds of Egyptian technicians working in the plant had been killed.

Bazoft attracted attention to himself when he started asking the hotel staff questions about whether the facility made rockets, failing to realise that the secret police were everywhere. The nurse supplied him with sterile containers from the hospital to gather soil samples from the affected area. When Bazoft tried to leave the country, he was arrested at the airport, carrying sensitive photographs and the soil samples, which bore the Ibn al-Bitar logo and therefore were easily traced back to the nurse.

'The Iraqis now say that Bazoft is an Israeli spy,' David said. 'They came and took Dee from the hospital. I saw her leaving with Dr Raad and two dudes in black suits. Some of the other nurses have tried to get in to see her. She's in a crap place, full of cockroaches, and nobody speaks English there. She made a Christmas tree out of old copies of the *Baghdad Times*.'

'At least it's putting it to some use,' Paul said, laughing. 'The Nissan Patrol you've been allocated has the most famous licence number in Iraq!'

We made our way to the centre of Baghdad on a modern highway, which we shared with tooting Toyota pickup trucks and orange-and-white taxis, all frantically jostling and competing for more favourable positions. As we reached the suburbs, the landscape changed. Older men wearing long white *dishdashas* wandered along the streets and chatted to hawkers selling cans of Pepsi and packets of Marlboro cigarettes from little stalls illuminated by chains of flickering bulbs. At last, we crossed the Tigris, passing over the Al Sinak Bridge, and entered the sector that was to be our new home.

The expatriates had nicknamed this area of the city "Saddamsville", which comprised rows of twelve-storey apartment blocks with neatly landscaped gardens and date palms. Soldiers on sentry duty outside a nearby military complex watched our vehicle as we drove along the broad boulevards of 14th of July Street and made our way along the edge of Zawra Park towards the

117

impressive concrete structure of the Al Rashid Hotel, where I was to stay during my locum.

'Wait till you see this place,' Paul said. 'If most big hotels in the West are five stars, then this is seven stars!'

The Al Rashid was set amidst twenty acres of lavishly manicured gardens. My friends told me the building was designed by Swedish engineers to withstand a bomb attack, and its eighteen storeys pivoted on an oil suspension system, so finely balanced that the manager could tell when uninvited guests were staying over in some of the top floors.

A gentle breeze blew as we entered the courtyard. It was hot that night in February, and a wedding party sat under the shade of some acacia trees. The women's outfits were especially elaborate, with large hoop skirts and long veils. The people were friendly and soon we were dancing with them under the bright Iraqi moonlight to the rhythmical sounds of musicians with small reed flutes and hand drums. The music reminded me of my time in Istanbul, but the tone was Arabic and mysterious.

'Patrick, you'll have to meet The Hajj – he's a legend,' David said, pointing to a tall European man in the distance.

He explained that the friend we were meeting had earned his nickname while working in Saudi Arabia, where he had gone on the pilgrimage to Mecca disguised as a Muslim, wearing white garments called *ihram* that pilgrims donned as part of the tradition of shedding signs of their wealth while undertaking the journey. Only Muslims are supposed to enter Mecca, and it was said by hospital staff in Baghdad that an English traveller, Richard Burton, was the only other non-Muslim European known to have performed the feat nearly one hundred years earlier.

'It's amazing what you can do with a split tablecloth and a jeep fan belt if given a chance,' The Haj said in the bar later, laughing.

*

The next morning, I got up and made my way across to the nearby hospital, a whitewashed, low-slung building set in a small garden lined with pomegranate trees. There was a tiny open courtyard with a tiled pavement that led to the Staff Health Clinic. The morning started easily. Pauline, the staff nurse, had already dealt with the trivial problems concerning staff.

Once we had introduced ourselves and she had shown me around the clinic, she took a deep breath, smiled and opened the door to show me where a group of Indian porters sat shivering, their faces peering out at me from the depths of the woollen blankets they had wrapped themselves in. This was a common occurrence, even when the outside temperature climbed over forty degrees Celsius. There were about ten of them, waiting for some antibiotics and hopefully a day or two off work. During my time in Baghdad, I grew used to their contrived performances and even found a certain charm in the way that different cultures portrayed their illnesses.

That day, one of them had a fever. His name was Anwar, he was an assistant chef, and he had severe Giardia gastroenteritis, which required his immediate release from work and a hefty course of Metronidazole. This taught me to examine everybody and not to stereotype the different nationalities too easily.

Part of my duties was working in a walk-in casualty service, seeing Iraqi patients who had previously been admitted to hospital. Late in the afternoon, the first of these patients arrived: a couple from Najaf, a town south of Baghdad. The husband, a slight man with refined features, introduced his wife and told us she had previously been one of our renal dialysis patients. His English wasn't good, so we needed the assistance of Nadia, our interpreter. His wife, clearly uncomfortable, deferred lying down, preferring to remain in a distorted position in front of my desk. I noted how she tried to smile but looked too exhausted even to let go of the black handbag she grasped with the fingers of an older rheumatoid patient.

'She can't open her mouth,' her husband said in broken English, gesturing to her face, his loving eyes filled with sadness.

'How long has she been like this?' I inquired.

'For a few days – they just drove up from Najaf,' Nadia replied.

I was told that her face had gone numb the night before and that at one point, she had been unable to breathe or see properly.

'Can she open her right hand?' I asked, realising that she couldn't let go of her handbag.

'No,' he answered.

'I think she's got tetanus,' said Pauline, mentioning a previous case.

I had to admit that it certainly looked like tetanus, but the patient hadn't had any fever, malaise, or even headache before the symptoms appearing. It was a baffling case.

'Has she any numbness around her lips now?' I asked.

The patient nodded, and I realised that she also spoke some English.

I asked Pauline to draw some blood and to ask the lab, which was only next door, to get the results back to me as soon as possible. I thought I knew what was happening, but didn't want to say, as I was only starting my medical rotation and my diagnoses would be under scrutiny.

When the blood came back, my suspicions were confirmed. The patient was suffering from reduced levels of calcium in her blood, causing the nerve endings to fire continually, producing a constant spasm of the muscles around her jaw. I wondered whether the condition would have been easier to diagnose in Dublin, where I could have got a better history of the problem from the relatives. I informed the renal registrar, who agreed that we should give her some calcium gluconate. The effect was immediate, and the patient regained her normal countenance within a few minutes.

Pauline looked over at me, and her thumbs-up suggested that we would work well together over the next few months.

I returned to the Al Rashid Hotel that evening, excited after my first day at work. David had agreed to collect me and bring me along to "The Villa", a sort of Irish social club in the Mansour area of Baghdad, where hospital staff went to relax in the evenings. He said that we could catch a coach there from outside the Commissary, a small shop on the complex that sold Irish provisions. After we got there, a blue-and-white Mercedes coach pulled up. In the distance, a forlorn mullah struggled to communicate to the city through a faulty microphone. The coach's driver, an older adult, descended and started talking to my friends. I guessed, from his black-and-white turban-like head wrap, that he was not Arab – possibly Kurdish.

'This is Hassan,' said Paul, introducing me. The driver smiled.

'*Choni?*' I said, greeting him in the forbidden Kurdish tongue, which I had learnt from friends in Istanbul.

'*Bash'm supas ey to?*' he replied, astonished and smiling, returning my greeting.

He gripped my hand firmly. I instinctively knew that we would be friends.

'Where are you staying, Patrick?' asked Hassan.

'I hear they might be moving you to Room 908 in one of the residential apartment blocks,' David said.

'Oh no – not 908!' Hassan said, holding his hands to his head and laughing loudly about the apartment's infamy. It was a shared apartment, and my new roommates were party legends in Baghdad.

On the way to The Villa, David told me that Hassan had lost his sons in the Iran-Iraq War. They had been forced to fight for Saddam and, as a consequence, he hated the Iraqi Arabs. I knew from a *Sunday Times* article that I had smuggled into Baghdad from Ireland that the Iraqi air force had dropped mustard gas on the little town of Halabja and killed thousands of people, while the watching world said nothing. Part of the reason was that the US initially tried to blame Iran until ITN television footage showed this not to be the case. I wanted to travel to the Kurds' homeland in the northern mountains and learn more about their culture, but Paul said that was considered dangerous and was actively discouraged by the hospital authorities.

That evening, after spending some time in the Villa, we all went to a party in Block 2 of the residential apartment complex. It seemed that everyone from the hospital was there, and they had gathered huge platters of pizzas, samosas and chicken legs, cooked up in the hospital canteen earlier in the day. The haunting melody of Sinead O'Connor's *Nothing Compares 2 U* was playing loudly from a CD player. Some innovative people had chopped up large blocks of ice in the bath to make a modified fridge.

'So, you're joining the Ba'ath Party!' said one of the male nurses, laughing.

The party was soon in full swing. Most of the people present were Irish and British female nurses, and David was correct when he said they outnumbered the males by about ten to one. During the evening, I again met Pauline, the Staff Health nurse with whom I would be working for the next few weeks.

'Don't sleep in tomorrow morning,' she said. 'I wouldn't like you to miss those Indian porters with their "total body pains". They'll be lining up for a day off work at eight o'clock.'

Pauline told me that most of the hospital porters were Christians who came from Goa in India. An enterprising lot, they ran the black market in currency at the hospital.

'We have to stay on the right side of them to get a good deal, but you can't be too soft, or they'll skive off work at any opportunity,' she said, winking, before introducing me to Venugopal Naidu who acted as our go-between in these matters on behalf of Staff Health.

'I hear you might be staying in Room 908. Those guys are the hardest drinkers in the block. When they throw a party, it usually lasts all week.'

'Did you hear what they did the other day? They say Pat McGlynn found a donkey wandering in some fields beside Block 34 and brought it up to his apartment in the lift. When Chris Duckling aka "the Duck" – found it, he fed him enough gin and tonic to get the poor donkey drunk and then rode it through the hospital courtyard.'

'Actually, Pat's here at the party – come on over,' Pauline said. Pauline introduced me to Pat, a likable male nurse from County Donegal, in the northwest of Ireland.

'What's this I hear about you keeping animals in the apartment?' I said to him.

'Which animals do you mean?' he replied.

'I heard about the donkey getting drunk up there,' I said. 'Is it true?'

'Oh God, yes – for a minute there I thought you meant the chickens.'

'Chickens!'

'Yeah, we had two chickens, called "Curry" and "Supreme", living outside on the corridor for a while. They were leftover extras from last year's Christmas party. The hospital management made us get rid of them, so we gave them to Hassan, the bus driver.'

I left Pat and wandered around the room. My eyes fell on a printed notice displayed in a prominent position on one of the walls.

'All Residents Blocks 34 and Block 2

All staff holding parties have a responsibility to ensure that attendance is by invitation only

No amplification is to be used outside the apartment

Apartment occupants have a responsibility to keep the noise level at parties at an acceptable level

Any damage to apartments is the responsibility of the occupants

The hospital administration must clear all social notices before they are placed on the notice board.

Signed: John Duffy, Hospital Administrator, Mrs. Anne Morgan, Director of Nursing, Mr. Joe McMullan, Medical Director of the Ibn al-Bitar Hospital.'

It was the first time I had seen a directive on the official way to the party, signed by such senior hospital staff. While I was reading the notice, Sarah sneaked up behind me and whispered in my ear, 'Fancy meeting you here.'

Sarah told me that news was breaking on the *BBC World Service* that Nelson Mandela had just been released from Victor Verster Prison in South Africa. In the '80s, like many other students, I had joined the anti-apartheid demonstrations outside South Africa House in London and protested for his freedom. I took Sarah's hand and we danced for a while before moving outside to the balcony, where we sat chatting and listening to the loud music. I pushed all thoughts of Trish to one side and, a little while later, we left the party and went back to the Rashid to have a few drinks in the residents' lounge before going to bed.

Morning came early, and I read Sarah's note on my pillow, explaining that she had gone back to her apartment to change for work. I got up and made my way along the busy streets to the Ibn al-Bitar Hospital. A small group of barefoot children played together on the side of the road, while a little boy carried a glass of sweet tea, in a pear-shaped Turkish glass, to an old man seated on a shabby armchair by the side of the road. The old man nodded to me serenely, and I responded with the traditional greeting, '*Marhaban. Kayf haluk?*'

That evening, David and Paul arrived at the Rashid to bring my luggage over to Room 908, and then took me downtown to have a closer look at the city before sunset. We passed through narrow streets, which were full of toothless old men sitting and chatting together, through shabby areas with flaking plaster shopfronts and alleyways full of young children playing and vendors selling mangoes from little stalls. David and Paul pointed out Saddam's Presidential Palace; a group of Northern Ireland lads had constructed the fine fretwork on the building. From the outside, it looked like an ornate mosque, with neat rows of sandy bricks laced with intricately carved arabesque portals and windows. On the roof, there was a blue-and-white tiled dome that exuded the grandiose ethos of the Ottoman Sultans.

Underground, the building was completely different. It was, in effect, a vast underground command structure, designed by Swiss engineers to house a communications centre, a generating station and a barracks for hundreds of men. It stretched eighty feet into the ground and was supported on a hard rubber foundation with springs, designed to withstand the shock waves of enemy bombs. This nation was preparing for an invasion.

As we approached Al Kindi Street, a jeep load of armed soldiers swerved in front of us, forcing us to pull over. David cursed under his breath. They jumped out and surrounded our vehicle, looking at us through narrowed, suspicious eyes.

The soldier in charge lowered his Kalashnikov and approached the passenger-side window.

'Papers!' he demanded.

David passed his residence permit to me, and I obligingly passed it on to the soldier at my window. His dark, unwavering eyes looked at me for what seemed like a long time. I had seen that look before a mixture of edginess and suspicion – at British roadblocks in Northern Ireland. He glanced at the permit, slowly looked at each of us in turn, as if memorising our faces, and then silently passed the papers back. I thought he tried to smile before waving us on, but I may have imagined it.

'Just say nothing – *ciúnas*!' Paul said to me, meaning "quiet", invoking the way Irish people over the centuries spoke together whenever they didn't want other nationalities to understand them.

David took his residence permit from me and stuck it into the pocket of his shirt. He turned on the engine and moved back onto the carriageway.

'I hear they're restricting the import of Heineken into Iraq again,' he said as if nothing had happened. 'If we don't book some this evening at the Commissary, we'll have to get some crates of that Shahrivar piss instead.'

We followed the highway for a while before approaching a grotesque monument straddling the highway. It consisted of two gigantic crossed sabres made of cement, held in an upright position by clenched fists pointing in opposite directions. From the apex of the structure, an Iraqi flag fluttered in the gentle wind.

'This is the Iraqi Arc de Triomphe,' said David. 'It was built to commemorate the so-called victory over Iran. The hands are modelled on those of Saddam himself.'

12. Room 908

The door to Apartment 908 was the open, and the music was playing loudly inside. It was early evening, and there was no one at home. I assumed my roommates were downstairs with friends. The apartment looked like it hadn't been cleaned for years. There were unwashed cups and plates everywhere. Surprisingly, the same level of squalor didn't extend to the toilets or shower area, where the smell of cologne made it seem like a real bachelor pad. This was it – Room 908, with its abandoned frying pans and empty beer bottles, another enchanting abode in the ebbing hourglass of my life. I left my luggage beside an empty bed and waited for my flatmates to return.

Chris arrived sometime later and opened some beers.

'What's with all the black PVC tape on the windows of my room?' I asked, pointing to the crisscrossed duct-tape strips, which looked like leftovers from a previous party.

'That's to stop the glass shattering down on top of you if you're hit by a stray missile in the middle of the night,' he replied. 'It was needed during the War of the Cities, at the end of the Iran-Iraq War, but everyone feels it's better to leave it up, as you never know what could happen here.'

A mosquito whined above my head and the black-and-white television in the living room, showing Ba'ath propaganda, flickered on and off to the rhythm of the air conditioner.

'Have you brought over any Irish papers?' he asked, looking at my luggage.

I opened the backpack and dumped the contents on the bed. 'Good lad, well done! How the hell did you get all that lot through?'

He brought the papers into the kitchen, where he cleared a space on the table. My eyes fell on the story about Saddam gassing the Kurds in northern Iraq.

'Have any of you lads heard what happened up in Halabja?' I asked.

'Never heard of it, what's that about?' he answered.

'It's a small town up in Kurdistan, near the Iranian border, and Saddam has killed a lot of people there.'

'Never heard of it, but he's always fighting with the Kurds,' Chris shrugged. 'Ask Hassan, the bus driver – he's Kurdish.'

He then started to read the article about Halabja aloud.

'By all accounts, a combination of mustard gas and other, more instantly fatal, chemical agents caused the massive carnage at Halabja. The injured survivors that reporters saw being treated in hospitals in Tehran and elsewhere last week showed the classic symptoms of mustard-gas poisoning – ugly skin lesions and breathing difficulties. As well as progressively affecting the lungs and skin, mustard gas also impairs the bone-marrow function,' he read.

'I heard about this,' he said, tapping the paper with his finger. 'They say we're treating some of the survivors down in the ICU of the hospital.'

*

Sunrise came earl; its radiant light splintered into shafts by the tape on my bedroom window. From the courtyard below, some schoolchildren began singing a patriotic verse, probably extolling the virtues of their "Great Leader". As I listened, their young voices gained vigour and strength, and the revolutionary verses continued for nearly thirty minutes. Over the coming days, their patriotic singing became my second alarm clock in Baghdad.

I got up and made my way to the hospital. It was already hot outside and the streets were busy, despite the early hour. White taxis with orange panels stalked me, looking for business, while old men on the sidewalks lazily trailed their long *dishdashas* through the dust.

I passed the International Communications Centre, a military complex strategically situated across from the hospital. The building was guarded by a group of young soldiers who stood aloof and neatly dressed, their black boots glinting in the bright sunlight, their red epaulets defining their status as members of the Republican Guard, an elite unit tasked with protecting the president and the important military buildings in the capital.

The day at the hospital began with the usual plethora of staff health problems. One had to be extremely careful regarding confidentiality because if the wide-ranging blood screens in Baghdad showed any communicable diseases, especially hepatitis, it would compromise a career back in Dublin.

That afternoon, I ran an outpatient emergency-room clinic for Iraqi patients who already had been patients of the hospital and who might require readmission. One of my first patients was an Olympic gold-medal winner. He was an older man who was once a weightlifter. Grateful to discover that his abdominal pain did not require admission, he presented me with a large Arabic ring before leaving. Maybe it was a morning for Iraq's unusual personages to grace my clinic, but the next case proved equally interesting.

Before me sat a well-built woman with delicate bone structure and skin that had the smoothness that comes from years of care. She wore a padded red dress and imitation jewellery; her well-combed hair fell seductively around one shoulder.

'I've come for my injection,' she said.

The nurse had left the room, and I searched through the patient's chart for some reference to her malady. The nurse returned with the patient's medicine and proceeded to inject her. As she left, the patient embraced me a little too warmly. I looked at Pauline, hoping for an explanation.

'Well, now you've met Mary,' she said, smiling. 'Do you know who she is?'

'Haven't a clue, but she appears a little strange.'

'Mary is Iraq's only transsexual – she comes here every few months for her hormone injections. She had the job done in London but, God love her, she must have an uphill battle existing in Baghdad.'

After the clinic ended, I walked through the hospital, looking for one of my roommates. Sarah came up to me and guided me towards a new item that was pinned on the noticeboard, saying, 'It's pretty heavy stuff.'

On Friday, February 16, 1990, the Iraqi Ministry of Foreign Affairs informed the British Ambassador in Iraq that Mrs Daphne Parish is to be charged with espionage against Iraq. She is to be tried on February 26 before a Revolutionary Court. The Iraqi Ministry of Foreign Affairs has said that the same charge is to be taken against Mr Farzad Bazaoft. He will also appear in front of the Revolutionary Council on February 26. The British Ambassador was assured that full legal access would be granted to Nurse Parish's lawyer and that a representative of the British Embassy would be allowed to attend the trial.

Sarah and I decided to get a taxi and travel to the Saray Souk in the old city. She was shaken by the development and genuinely concerned about what might happen to her colleague.

'Some say she'll get twenty years or more,' she said. 'And Bazoft could be hanged.'

The driver was friendly and spoke in broken English. I was very much aware that he might report our conversation to the Mukhabarat.

'*Ná bí ag caint*,' I said, indicating in Irish that she should stop talking.

She remained silent for the rest of the journey.

The sun sank into a swirling canvas of saffron and Jaffa-orange hues, adding a wonderful sense of romance to the evening. The souk was packed with people, who lingered by open hemp sacks of cinnamon, tobacco, and turmeric. We walked for about an hour through the labyrinth of mysterious sunlit alleyways and narrow stone streets. Now and then a bearded barterer would call out to the crowd, to be heard above the noise of the clinking tinsmiths. It was exciting to ramble through this mystic terrain teeming with open stalls selling pictures of painted sultans and delicate little filigree silver dishes garnished with etched steel knives and daggers.

However, amidst the bustle and chatter, the buying and selling, there was also suspicion and uneasiness. Occasionally, I saw fear in the eyes of the friendly stallholders who implored us a little too desperately to buy quartz watches emblazoned with the latest propagandist portrait of their Great Leader.

*

Over the next few weeks, I went travelling as much as I could through the little villages that surrounded Baghdad. I had long been fascinated by the memoirs of the Ethiopian-born British explorer, Wilfred Thesiger, who had travelled through this area in the 1950s, on the way from his homeland in Ethiopia to Afghanistan. Aristocratic by birth, educated at Eton and Oxford, Thesiger was a confessed romantic and traditionalist. His adventures fed a deep-seated desire within me, especially his stories of the Marsh Arabs and the rise and fall of Babylon. The ancient city, which has haunted European imaginations for centuries, was only about eighty miles south of Baghdad.

In Devenish Primary School, Mr Regan had taught me how its hanging gardens were once considered one of the wonders of the ancient world, but I had never imagined that I would visit it one day. The Bible stated that Babylon would be destroyed and never rebuilt, a Christian prophecy that Saddam Hussein had been unable to resist proving wrong. When he rose to power in Iraq, he said that

Babylon would once more rise again from the dust. He conceived a grandiose scheme to reconstruct the ancient city, even building on top of the foundation stones of King Nebuchadnezzar's Palace. Archaeologists worldwide were horrified and said that to rebuild on top of these ancient artefacts didn't preserve history – it disfigured it.

On my second weekend in Iraq, I visited the ancient city and sat for a while alone, reading the inscription that Saddam had embossed into the brickwork: 'In the era of Saddam Hussein, protector of Iraq, who rebuilt civilisation and rebuilt Babylon.' Babylon had long been associated with the anti-Christ and was said to have been the seat of power for the tyrant of the world. Maybe, I thought, this was history repeating itself.

*

Sarah and I spent most of our free afternoons in February soaking up the sun and lazing beside the swimming pool in the Mansour Melia Hotel. After a hard day's work, it was a welcome change of environment – the landscaped garden filled with flowering bougainvillea was like an oasis. The hospital staff relaxed by the poolside, tanned their torsos, and fanned themselves with the latest edition of the *Baghdad Times*. For a nominal fee, hotel waiters in light-brown uniforms carried drinks to the guests. These facilities were available exclusively to privileged Westerners, some of whom exuded an air of pretentiousness. Donald joined us there on a few occasions and laughed about how apprehensive I had been on the flight over.

Since Farzad Bazoft's arrest, hospital staff had become more aware of their security and were careful about what they said in front of others. As the date of his trial approached, the atmosphere in Baghdad changed and everybody was on tenterhooks, waiting to see what would happen to the prisoners.

There seemed to be growing antipathy towards the hospital staff, and I perceived animosity in the eyes of the patients in the hospital wards. Even the sickest amongst them clicked their tongues in feigned intolerance at the very suggestion that anything was wrong with their country. From morning to night, the indoctrination of the masses continued, through the two television channels which every home in the city received. International appeals largely fell on deaf ears in Iraq. At one stage, Saddam Hussein personally tried to calm fears by assuring British Prime Minister Margaret Thatcher that the journalist would get a fair hearing.

The morning of March 15 started like any other Thursday. The usual patchwork of cotton cumulus clouds hung along the horizon. By mid-morning, the sun was climbing in the sky and promising temperatures well above forty degrees Celsius.

Everybody at the hospital was looking forward to the "Spring in the Air" party at the British Club in a few days. Some of the hospital staff had formed a rock group called the Baghdad Blues Band, which would play at the party. The local expatriate Hash House Harriers were getting record attendances at their weekly fun runs and had to increase their alcohol supplies for their post-run festivities.

In the late afternoon, I wandered through the bazaars, hoping to get a watch repaired. I left it with an old Egyptian jeweller and headed off to a little restaurant for something to eat. Normally we went to the "liver souk", an area of the bazaar where tasty delicacies were sold from modified wheelbarrows. On this occasion, I decided to try out a newly discovered eatery, nicknamed by hospital staff "the Hole in the Wall Restaurant", because it had a gaping hole – from a missile attack – near its front entrance.

The restaurant was crowded and quite loud. After a while, some Iraqis, who spoke good English, joined me at my table.

'What do you think of the news?' one of them asked.

'Why, what's happened?' I said.

'They hanged Bazoft, and the nurse was sentenced to fifteen years' imprisonment.'

I was incredulous – so much for Saddam allaying fears. I knew that life in Baghdad would never be the same again. Despite the opportunity for Iraq to show leniency, Bazoft had been sentenced to death and had already been executed in Abu Ghraib prison. His body was placed in a wooden coffin and left outside the British Council, which was right beside the hospital.

I listened to their feeble justifications, namely that Bazoft had made a confession of his own free will on Iraqi television and found it difficult to believe that they were thinking clearly. They had been subjected to a substantial propaganda campaign, but perhaps they thought the same of me. We were different people seeing opposite sides of the same coin. I was outnumbered and felt it was useless to argue. The fact that Bazoft had an Iranian background made the execution easier for the Iraqi people to accept. They also seemed proud to have a strong leader who would not waver in his decisions, even with world opinion against him. I thought Saddam was poorly advised in deciding to hang Bazoft. By doing so, he had played into the hands of the Israelis, who wanted to portray him as a dangerous monster who could not be trusted, especially as he had used poison gas on his people.

My head started to spin. I could only surmise that propaganda and malice were being spread from the nearby minaret. Had I judged the population of Iraq so badly? Was it possible that Bazoft could be an Israeli spy?

Suffering from an acute loss of appetite, I made my apologies and wandered back over to the old jeweller's shop. He had repaired the watch while I was away but tried to convince me that he had replaced two of the main bevel wheels. The fact that one of the wheels he said he had taken out of the watch was nearly as big as the back of the watch only infuriated me. Many Iraqi people considered the Egyptian craftsmen to be deceitful, and I had little difficulty in expressing my predicament to some local militia. It was gratifying to see the soulless old watchmaker grovel at the soldiers' request to hand over the timepiece without charging me. Suffice it to say, he got his revenge when the crown wheel fell out of the watch about ten days later.

Back at my apartment, Chris was distressed by the news about Farzad Bazoft and Daphne Parish. He told me that some of the staff had seen Bazoft's body being unceremoniously deposited in a coffin from the back of a pickup truck outside the British Council. There was a derisory note in Arabic attached to the remains. It said something to the effect of, 'Thatcher wanted him back – she can have him back in a box.'

Chris also told me that Donald, the Scottish engineer who had been on the plane with me, had been arrested in Basra and charged with being a British spy. The Iraqi authorities had decided that, in addition to removing dangerous mines, he was placing new detonation devices in the shipping channel on behalf of the British government. Chris, who was English, surprised me when he said, 'He was ex-British army, so who knows who is telling the truth. The best thing is to keep your thoughts to yourself out here.'

The government-run *Baghdad Observer* reported that the verdict passed on the captives was just and that the court had given Bazoft and Parish proper, legal trials. Minister for Information and Culture Latif Nsayyif Jassim stated that the international outcry over the sentences was blatant interference in Iraq's internal affairs. We were warned not to attend the party scheduled to take place in the British club that night. Two nights later, hand grenades were tossed over the wall of the club, and a Polish boy was seriously injured. Only seven years old, he was admitted to Ward E with extensive leg wounds. This ward was reserved for the treatment of Westerners and visiting Iraqi dignitaries.

My roommate, Pat, was working on the ward, and I took the opportunity to visit him. The child appeared to be in good spirits and had been inundated with well-wishers. I wished our young victim well and told him I would come back to visit him again.

'Do you know who just vacated the bed he's in?' asked Pat.

'No – anybody important?' I replied.

'An Egyptian pilot accidentally shot down over the Tigris during the air show last year. He was piloting an Alpha jet, which they'd never seen before, and they thought it was the Israelis coming to attack Baghdad,' Pat said.

'Oh, I heard about him. Didn't one of the nurses shake his hand and tell him how lucky he was to be able to "ejaculate" out of his aircraft?' I replied.

There were definite signs of a shift in Western media opinion about Iraq after the hanging of Bazoft. For many in the Middle East, the image had changed from "Saddam the protector" to "Saddam the tyrannical monster". The following week, the *BBC World Service*, informed us that Dr Gerald Bull, a Canadian ballistics expert working for the Ba'ath regime, had been assassinated in Belgium. The assassination had the hallmarks of an Israeli Mossad killing. Then news broke that Bull had been developing a new Iraqi "supergun" capable of launching nuclear warheads thousands of miles, deep into the heart of Israeli territory.

Some days later, British Customs confiscated forty nuclear trigger devices from a wooden crate at Heathrow Airport being loaded onto Iraqi Airways Flight 238, bound for Baghdad. It was apparent that the Western powers were intent on commencing a battle against the Iraqi regime. But Saddam remained belligerent. On Iraqi television news, he spoke of an Israeli conspiracy. He threatened that he would use his weaponry to drive them into the sea. What the Ba'ath regime needed was a Western public-relations department. Night after night, we watched in awe as the heavy artillery on the roofs of Baghdad's highest buildings lit up the night sky with bursts of practice tracer fire.

The hospital authorities told us that the Iraqi government had evidence that Israel was going to attempt a surprise air strike. It would be modelled on their

1981 attack on the Osiraq nuclear reactor, but this time Iraq would be prepared. There were rumours that an Israeli jet had been shot down over the Tigris, but it may have been the poor Egyptian pilot in his Alpha.

Travelling in Kurdistan

Before long, political demonstrations were being organised in downtown Baghdad, and the Iraqi media whipped up the populace by claiming that the Israeli secret service was plotting with the West to attack them. I watched many of these agitated meetings from a safe distance, feeling it was better not to show my face, as the pent-up anger in the crowds rose to the surface and overflowed.

I found it rather difficult to believe the Western media, which was suggesting that Iraq was positioned at the centre of some great secret doomsday project. There was suggestive evidence that there was another hand at work: intelligence reports leaked from Tel Aviv were probably influencing the Baghdad government's decisions.

Whatever criticism could be levelled at Saddam, his activities were now creating a flurry on the world stage. As the tension grew in Iraq, I heard about a British worker from Northern Ireland who had been found dead in a hotel room.

133

It was alleged that he had worked for Matrix Churchill, a British company based in Coventry, which was rumoured to be involved in the "supergun" project. The company had been bought by the Iraqis as a front for making components, which would allow them to bypass the paperwork required for procuring sanctioned technological materials. Interpol now targeted them, and some of their products had been confiscated from Hungarian lorries at the Haydarpaşa customs, on the Asian side of the Bosphorus, in Istanbul.

The British worker had been discovered in suspicious circumstances after sustaining a fatal head injury. The preliminary medical report stated that his death resulted from a skull fracture sustained during a fall from his bed while having a heart attack. His co-workers thought differently. There were accusations that a taxi, which collected him from a local bar, had been driven by members of Mossad, and that people had seen him being bundled into the back of it. Rumours also circulated that he had presented to an Iraqi hospital the previous night after receiving a head injury. X-rays taken at that time showed no evidence of a skull fracture.

The dead man was transferred to the Ibn al-Bitar Hospital for a post-mortem. The pathologist normally in charge of performing this duty happened to be a patient of mine and had suddenly become ill. I had to decide whether he was fit enough to perform his duties. If I deemed him unfit, a replacement pathologist would have to be flown in from the United Kingdom. For purely medical reasons, I decided that it was preferable that he did not perform the autopsy. Because of the intense suspicion surrounding the death, it was a difficult call to make. His fellow workers were convinced that their friend would not get an objective autopsy and that there had been a dark hand involved in the proceedings. My decision could only add to the controversy. It was the first time that my medical opinion had played a role in politics, and I felt uncomfortable with the responsibility.

Although my involvement, in this case, was small, my administrative position gave me access to some conversations with official parties about another reason why Bazoft had been so readily executed. My diplomatic sources claimed that within a few days of Bazoft's arrest, Mossad had contacted the Iraqi embassy in Holland, stating that Jerusalem was willing to make a deal for *their* man. This alleged conversation convinced the Iraqis that they were dealing with a real spy and sealed his execution. All Mossad had to do was sit back and watch as Saddam proved to the world what a monster he was.

*

I was reaching the end of my locum job in Baghdad, and I decided to return to Dublin, where I would take the opportunity to do a repeat HIV test. If things did not deteriorate in Iraq, I might take another locum position there, which would allow me to work until the beginning of August, when I would take up a GP registrar position in Scotland. I had selected Broxburn, a small agricultural town in West Lothian, about five miles from the Edinburgh Airport.

One Tuesday night before I left Baghdad, a group of hospital staff decided to go to the disco in the Palestine Hotel. We were enjoying ourselves until one of the men from a party beside us began hassling one of the nurses in a very unpleasant way. His unruly behaviour continued until, eventually, I went over to confront the man, warning him to leave the young woman alone. Everybody at the table went silent, and it was only then that I noticed some of them were wearing pistols. The person in question let go of the nurse and looked at me coldly for a moment. Then he got up, brushed himself down and – unexpectedly – shook my hand, apologised and promised to behave himself in our company. I returned to my own table, but my friends had seen what had happened and had become very subdued. The other party left shortly afterward and, as soon as they were gone, my friends began to babble excitedly. The person I had just confronted was none other than Uday Hussein, the feared son of Saddam.

13. The Apparition

I returned from Ireland after spending a few weeks in Dublin as a locum medical registrar. It had taken all my powers not to phone Trish, but I had thought about her every day while I was there. My new duties were more varied than before, covering all hospital departments, including intensive care at weekends. I made it a habit to go to ICU for a personal briefing and learn about the patients who were critically ill. This tended to leave me better prepared for unexpected middle-of-the-night phone calls.

One night, I was called to the wards, where one of the SHOs was having difficulty controlling an asthmatic patient. She was afraid of the cannula needle, probably because she had seen the half-terror in the eyes of the inexperienced doctor holding it. Although he was older than some of the other SHOs, the doctor had recently been an intern at a hospital in Belgium and was finding the rigours of a busy tertiary referral centre in the Middle East rather daunting. 'She's extremely excited and won't allow me to put a drip in her arm,' he said dejectedly.

The patient was surrounded by female family members, all dressed in black *chadors*, who were squabbling with the nurses. Some Iraqi hospitals didn't have a developed nursing system, so the females in the family often acted as nurses. Consequently, they treated our female staff with some condescension.

'Get the family out of the room please,' I said, trying to take control of the situation. Hospital security arrived and took the family into one of the side rooms. With the help of the nurses, I managed to get the hysterical young woman into a supine position and prepared an infusion bag of aminophylline and steroids. It is often preferable to go ahead and insert an IV cannula into the patient to gain access in case of emergency and worry about the legal consequences later.

I had learnt that nearly all the patients in Baghdad screamed while having cannulas inserted, but that they quickly settled on receiving their drugs. Their protests were not about infringement of their personal liberties, but rather a genuine cultural needle phobia. I inserted the cannula with minimum objection and got the patient settled quickly.

I called into ICU, where there were five patients, including two renal transplants and two small children recovering from cardiac surgery. A recent spate of postoperative paediatric mortalities had affected staff morale, and the nurses were sombre and withdrawn. Dealing with hysterical parents who blamed them for their children's deaths was taking its toll. Furthermore, one of the nurses had received a needle-stick injury from a child who had Hepatitis B.

'What about the patient in the corner?' I asked.

'We don't know much about him. He's a twenty-four-year-old transfer from the Rasheed Military Hospital. He's suffering from right and left heart failure. Dave is going to phone us later with all the details about him, but he's chatting away to us at the moment and in great form. His folks are wandering around here somewhere, so you had better get out of here before they nab you as well,' one of the nurses replied.

Later that evening, I was called back to ICU. The nurses were concerned about the young soldier who had been transferred from the military hospital earlier that day. He was standing on his bed, naked and drenched in sweat. He had removed the fluid line from his arm and bright red blood was pouring onto the white sheets beneath him and down onto the floor below. The spectacle verged on a surrealistic scene from a Ken Russell movie. There was a look of sheer terror on his young face; his pupils, in full dilation, were focused right on me. He pointed and shouted a confused tirade in my direction.

I couldn't understand how I had evoked such fervour in a patient whom I had seen for the first time earlier that day. At the same time, his family surrounded me, and his mother threw herself on her knees, beating her head with a closed fist in a wildly excited state. I fumbled my way through the melee to reach the nursing station. The wailing of the haggard older women around the bed had a foreboding rhythm, and the whole scene began to take on the cast of a tribal ritual rather than a high-technology intensive care unit.

'What the hell is going on?' I asked one of the nurses nearest to me, who seemed to be getting more afraid for the safety of the other patients by the minute.

'Apparently, he's seen an apparition. St John the Baptist says he is going to die if he doesn't leave the hospital.'

'And can we not sedate him?' I said.

'He'd already been given twenty milligrams of Valium by IV before he pulled out his drip,' she sighed, frustrated. 'They want to bring him to Karbala, a town about sixty miles from here!'

'Where the hell is security when we need them?' shouted one of the nursing sisters, who had come to see what all the noise was about.

'They've already been here and have gone to the blocks for reinforcements,' one of the staff answered.

'Do we have an interpreter with us?' I asked.

'Yes, Maria is here.'

Maria, an Iraqi Christian, seemed to be at a loss as to what was going on. She looked at me in astonishment, her eyes searching mine for some solution to the problem.

'These are crazy people – they think their son is going to die at eight o'clock tomorrow if he is not brought to Karbala,' she said.

From the nursing desk, I could see the patient, who continued to bleed from the Venflon still stuck in his vein. I noticed that he remained fixated on the spot in the room; presumably, he was looking at the apparition.

'What is the significance of Karbala?' I inquired, knowing that I had heard the name before.

Maria explained that Karbala was one of the Shi'ites most venerated holy places. She explained how a famous battle had taken place there in 680AD, between the supporters and relatives of Muhammad's grandson, Hussein, and the forces of Yazid, the Umayyad Caliph. Hussein and all his supporters were killed. Shi'ites still commemorated the Battle of Karbala each year in the Islamic month of Muharram. It was a ghastly sight: they mourned by flagellating themselves with whips until they bled. Saddam Hussein eventually banned the practice.

These people were fanatical, and everyone believed the patient saw a vision of St John the Baptist, who predicted he would die at eight o'clock in the morning if he didn't go to pray at Hussein's Shrine before then. I asked Maria to tell them this wasn't possible – the patient was sick and couldn't be transferred.

'Patrick, don't you think I've already done that?' she sighed.

'You'll have to phone Medical Director Joe McMullan immediately and tell him about this because there's a crowd of them gathering outside and security can't hold them,' one of the nurses said.

I had just managed to contact him when one of the security guards arrived to tell us that about ten people had broken into the hospital grounds and were heading for the intensive care unit. We could hear scuffles and loud voices in the corridors outside.

'You'll have to contact Dr Raad, the Iraqi director of the Ibn al-Bitar Hospital, as this sounds like it could become quite serious,' Mr McMullan advised.

I had a mental image of what might happen to the defenceless sick children lying in intensive care if these religious zealots broke through the doors. Their assault on the hospital was a dangerous development. A nurse told me that Dr Raad knew about the situation and had decided to call in the army to protect us.

Objects were being thrown onto the roof, and the noise outside grew steadily louder. Dr Raad phoned to say he had come to the hospital and attempt to negotiate with the fanatical mob gathering on the streets outside.

The noise outside began to reach fever pitch. We could hear women chanting in shrill tones as stones rained down on the roof of the hospital. There was a genuine fear that a riot was going to ensue and, before long, other wards started phoning the unit for information. Word started to spread around the hospital that something big was happening outside the gates. The staff coming on duty relayed developments to those still working inside. Meanwhile, the anxious patient remained standing on the bed, continually repeating that he was going to die at eight o'clock. The relatives left to speak with the other members of the Shia sect outside, giving us some respite.

The crowd grew louder and more vehement, and each new wave of protest seemed to agitate the patient more. For a long time, we stood listening to the conflict, then a volley of shots rang out, and there was silence. A while later, we heard footsteps approaching the unit, and we were asked to open the locked door. Dr Raad entered with an army officer and stood looking at us silently for a moment before speaking.

'This is Colonel Adnan, and he has ordered the army to fire shots over the crowd outside to disperse them,' Dr Raad began.

'A judge in a court of law will have to decide tomorrow morning whether the patient can leave the hospital, but until that time he will stay here. You are not in any danger from these people tonight.'

They both turned to the soldier and spoke a few words to him. He appeared to be a little less agitated, but there was a fear in his eyes that even they couldn't remove. One of the nurses managed to get the Venflon out of his arm and apply a small compression bandage. Two armed guards were placed outside the unit.

Taking advantage of the temporary lull, I retreated along the outside courtyard to my bedroom in the doctor's residence. Patients' relatives were sitting under the palm trees, chatting, and smoking below the bright stars of the Baghdad night. A few soldiers with Russian AK-47 assault rifles slung loosely from their shoulders stood by the perimeter walls. There was no sign of any of the soldier's family members within the compound.

I found it difficult to get to sleep knowing that I could be called at any moment, and for a long while, I lay and listened to the crickets singing in the long grass outside. From time to time, a muezzin on a minaret wailed into a microphone and probably woke the sleeping city. I had just managed to get a few hours of sleep before the phone rang again. It was twenty to eight in the morning, and there was a cardiac arrest in intensive care.

As I struggled to put my clothes on, I heard the cardiac beeper of my colleague sounding in the room next door. I wondered which of the patients had crashed and decided it was probably one of the little girls again. I ran out the door, pulling on my white coat, and narrowly missing a pair of veiled Muslim women who were walking along the path.

A group of nurses were returning from an all-night party in one of the blocks and watched me running across the courtyard. Their early morning revelry was changed to concern as they watched my sprint. I took a shortcut, jumping over some shrubs to reach the door of the unit, and arrived on the ward out of breath.

One of the nurses was bent over the body of the young soldier, compressing his chest in a valiant effort to maintain his vital functions. I looked at the cardiac monitor and saw the trace was wildly erratic – the patient was in ventricular fibrillation.

'Ah, no, draw us up 100 milligrams of lignocaine and some adrenaline,' I called to the nearest nurse.

'It's already drawn up and ready to push,' she answered.

'How long has he been like this?' I asked.

'Only about three or four minutes. I called you immediately,' she replied.

'We just *can't* lose him,' I said as if my voice could defy the heavens above.

'Right, charge the defib at two hundred, we'll have to shock him.'

I pushed both drugs into his cannula, which one of the ICU nurses had re-sited during the night.

'OK, stand back everyone,' I said, placing one of the paddles over his breastbone and the other to the left side of his chest wall.

I pressed the button and the electricity discharged into his contracting body. For a moment, we stood frozen and waited for the response to register on the oscilloscope. The jagged lines slowed down to a more decipherable pattern but then continued to change into an almost lethargic pulse. 'No, stand back and let's see what we have. He's had three lots of adrenaline and atropine and remains in asystole. He's been like that now for nearly twenty minutes. If there's no response soon, we'll have to consider calling it a day. I'll try some intra-cardiac adrenaline,' I said, asking a nurse to hand me a long needle.

I pushed the needle into the patient's thorax, but couldn't find any heart muscle, which would have been indicated by the immediate rush of blood into my syringe. The patient looked at me. There was no fear or pain in his eyes. We both knew he was being taken away by a power bigger than my little needle. I tried again, aware that his heart chamber must be distended and at least twice the normal size. I realised at that moment that I should respect the inevitability of death and was withdrawing my needle when the anaesthetist arrived. We reviewed the situation and agreed that the patient had been given every chance but was not going to recover. The arrest was called off. It was just after eight o'clock – the very time that he had predicted he would die unless he was transferred to Karbala. The court would not sit in judgement for another hour.

What power of belief had influenced this patient to predict his own demise? How could we face his family and tell them we thought we knew better, but we were wrong? The great Western concept of pharmaceutical healing was beginning to look a little tattered.

As I was leaving the unit, the young soldier's relatives began to enter. His parents fell on their knees by his bedside, bowed their head and touched his body. There were no emotional scenes from any member of the family. No one pointed the finger of blame. Their response to his death was dignified as if it was an order from the heavens. They unfolded a large carpet and rolled the soldier up inside it. Without uttering a word, they carried the body outside to a waiting taxi. They attached the corpse to the roof of the vehicle and disappeared into the dawn.

14. Journey to Kurdistan

Many of the patients on the oncology ward at Ibn al-Bitar Hospital were suffering from aplastic anaemia, a rare form of bone-marrow cancer, which left them unable to make mature blood cells. It did not go unnoticed that the majority of patients suffering from this condition came from the north-eastern area of Kurdistan, where Ali Hassan al-Majid – acting under direct orders from Saddam Hussein – decided to use Tabun nerve agent and mustard gas against the Kurdish population during the Halabja attack about two years earlier. A video team from the Iranian army had captured the grotesque horror of this bombing attack. Five thousand people, mostly women, and children, had been killed in the first two days, and nearly ten thousand others suffered from injuries that took their lives later. These wretched patients presented in Kurdish hospitals around Sulaymaniyah and future problems associated with cyanide poisoning caused by Tabun went mostly undocumented.

Mustard gas was first used effectively in 1917, by the German army against British and Canadian soldiers near Ypres. Since that time, it has been used in several wars. Doctors discovered as early as 1919 that it caused decreased counts of white blood cells, and it was trialled as a therapy for Hodgkin's lymphoma and other types of lymphoma and leukaemia. The mutagenic and carcinogenic effects of mustard agent mean that victims who recover from mustard-gas burns have an increased risk of developing cancer in later life. It was impossible not to feel the deepest of sorrow for these poor people.

In hindsight, it was probably during an arduous night, taking blood cultures on the oncology ward that I made up my mind to visit the area where the nitrogen mustard gassing had occurred. I had always had a sense of adventure and a desire to experience historical events at first hand. But I was also aware that travel to that part of Iraq was forbidden.

When I floated the idea with my colleagues, who had been in Iraq longest, every one of them considered it too dangerous to attempt such an expedition in the aftermath of the trial of nurse Daphne Parish. Many Iraqis were already pointing fingers at British hospital staff, accusing them of being spies. Perhaps it was the experience of growing up in Northern Ireland that spurred me on, as I had been raised in a place where propaganda reigned supreme, and sometimes it was difficult to tell fact from fiction unless you witnessed it with your own eyes.

Travelling in Kurdistan 1990

In late June, I started to put my plans in place. With a camera and four rolls of film in my orange backpack, I went to the taxi rank outside the Alawi al-Hilla bus station, looking for an English-speaking driver to take me to Mosul, in the heart of Kurdistan. I wandered amongst the drivers at the station, chatting and trying to glean as much information as possible; the secret police came in many guises, so I had to be careful about my choice. I was hoping to meet a Kurdish-speaking driver who wouldn't be afraid to take me from Mosul across the backbone of the mountains to the cities of Erbil and Sulaymaniyah when it was required. In this way, I hoped to avoid drawing the attention of the secret police to my destination – Halabja.

Eventually, I found a friendly young driver, Mohammed, who appeared to possess the right credentials. 'You want to go to Kurdistan?' he asked, in disbelief, when I told him my plan. I chatted to him for a while, trying to gauge his interest in making the journey north. Then we haggled over the price of the trip. I was carrying more than a thousand American dollars, but the cultural norm was to bargain, and I felt it was important to follow tradition. We agreed to travel to Mosul, Erbil and Sulaymaniyah for four hundred dinars. I decided not to mention the visit to Halabja until later.

Mohammed took me back to his house, where he said goodbye to his family and collected a change of clothes. I felt apprehensive about travelling to northern Iraq without telling my friends at the hospital where I was going. It was a conscious decision, though, I didn't want anybody in Baghdad to know about my journey. The larger the number of people who knew, the greater the chance of being caught by the secret police.

I had a strange sense of elation as I left Baghdad behind. The apparatus of the state was everywhere, and the Mukhabarat ruled a nation where violence was legitimised by a network of informers who accepted the situation as some sort of "necessary evil" on the road to progress. As hired workers in this realm, we, doctors, and nurses, at Ibn al-Bitar stood idly by and helped the regime perpetuate this system. Like many other Westerners, we justified it to ourselves, even as the smell of the bodies of so-called "enemies of the state" grew stronger by the day. Although we distanced ourselves from it, we were prostituting ourselves in the cradle of civilisation, selling our souls for blood money supplied by the black gold that lay under Iraq. In my way, I was finally rebelling against the regime, standing idly by no longer.

I peered out the window at the countryside as the taxi followed the signs towards the town of Tikrit, the village of Saddam Hussein's birth. Most senior members of the Iraqi government came from Saddam's own Tikriti tribe, the Al-Bu Nasir, and bore the same surname, "al-Tikriti". The village of Tikrit was special to the Kurds because it was the birthplace of the famous twelfth-century Islamic leader, Saladin, who was Kurdish. Saddam Hussein frequently compared himself to this great leader, but at the same time openly commanded genocide against the sultan's descendants.

As we progressed north, I played my cassette tapes, a mixture of U2, Bob Marley and John Lennon. They brought a sense of comfort as our journey brought us through the fertile plains of Samarra, where we passed fields of golden wheat and farmers harvesting their crops. As evening fell, we reached the mudwalled buildings of the village of Ash-Sharqat, where Mohammed pulled the car over to a little roadside garage. The town had an Arabic feel, with palm trees overlooking single-storey homes, each of which had a little courtyard. The main street was quiet, and there didn't appear to be any soldiers in sight. To the east lay Kirkuk and the oilfields. To the north, one could see the low banks of white clouds that hung around the eastern foothills of Kurdistan.

The garage owner, a jovial man with red-capillaried cheeks and a flowing handlebar moustache, appeared. He approached us with welcoming arms, emitting a string of salutations in both Arabic and Kurdish. He told his son to drive Mohammed's car up to an elevated concrete ramp and proceeded with the oil change. When that was finished, he gave the young boy a few dinars to go off to a tea shop for three glasses of sweet, blood-red tea.

'*Ingelterre?*' he asked as he passed me a glass.

'*Irlanda!*' I said.

'*Ah, Irlanda,*' he said and struck his right fist against his heart. 'Bobby Sands!'

He shook my hand firmly, as though he admired my nationality, or saw us as sharing a common history of oppression and suffering. In many ways, the feeling was reciprocal and was possibly the reason that I was going to visit Halabja. I thought about Bobby Sands and the injustices of Northern Ireland, aware that the British had a long history in this area. Only seventy years earlier, the Royal Air Force had shot and bombed the Kurds as they worked in their fields, to gain control of the new oilfields in nearby Kirkuk. We continued to Mosul, a major trading city and home to more than a million people. It was late in the evening when we reached the outskirts, where we found a hotel near Babatub Square. The city lay on the ancient caravan route that ran between Europe and India, and Marco Polo passed through on his way to China. However, its importance declined with the opening of the Suez Canal, which made it easier to transport goods east from Europe by sea. The discovery of oil in Kirkuk had somewhat restored Mosul's fortunes, and a new pipeline had been constructed to carry the crude product to the Mediterranean ports by way of Turkey and Syria.

Although it was late in the evening, there were a lot of old men still sitting around the square chatting. The narrow streets were bustling with people dressed in Kurdish-style baggy trousers, gathered at the waist, and tapered at the ankle. The women were mostly dressed in Anatolian costume, although many of the older ones wore black *chadors*, highlighting the large number of Sunni Muslims who inhabited the area. The restaurants were already full, mostly offering helpings of a rice dish. When I saw it was *pilav*, I realised that we were only about fifty miles from the Turkish border. Everything was peaceful in Mosul. It somehow seemed devoid of the petty pressures and suspicions of downtown Baghdad. With a few beers on board, I decided it might be a good time to approach Mohammed about the delicate subject of Halabja.

He told me he had been brought up in Sulaymaniyah, about fifty miles from the town.

'Have you ever been to Halabja?' I asked.

'Yes,' Mohammed said, beginning to look uneasy.

'Can I go and see it?'

'No, it is not allowed,' he said, waving his finger in the air in front of me. 'It is forbidden to go there!'

I felt it was better not to pursue the subject. We chatted for a while longer, and then I made my excuses and said goodnight. I had completed the first part of my journey and spent the rest of the evening, carefully updating my diary.

Mosul sprang to life in the early morning. People gathered in little groups outside open-fronted bakeries to buy fresh flatbread, and the smell from the long flat ovens reminded me of eastern Turkey. This was a city that had existed two thousand years before the birth of Christ, and I was humbled to be in the presence of such antiquity, as my guidebook indicated that one of the gates of Nineveh was close by. Mohammed and I went to a bus garage, where we saw some mudbrick towers and reconstructed stone walls, probably the Shamash entrance to the ancient city.

After Nineveh, we left for Sulaymaniyah and the endless expanse of inhospitable, colourless hills where it was nestled. We passed young shepherd boys tending to their flocks as we travelled further east into the low foothills of the mountains. Now and then, as sunlight reflected from the blue-green tiles on the dome of some local village mosque, Mohammed would laugh and say, 'Kurdistani telephones!' and point to where the last flash had occurred. He was referring to the fact that the Kurdish *peshmerga* often used mirrors to signal messages from one village to another in the days before mobile phones. The barren landscape grew more desolate as the daylight colours started to fade, and the hillside anemones faded into the treeless slopes.

We drove through the low mountains, past a succession of little villages, towards the outer boundaries of Erbil, the fourth-largest city in Iraq, stopping for a while near the Kaisary market to take some photographs. The journey to

Sulaymaniyah took us about two hours along a two-lane highway, skirting the city of Kirkuk. We passed some checkpoints near the oilfields in the Baba Gurgur region, where we could see long yellow flames emerging from along the pipelines. Historically, the Kurdish people saw the area around Kirkuk as theirs, as they had lived there for over a thousand years. However, the recent government-planned Arabisation of the area had successfully diluted the Kurdish population.

We reached the town of Sulaymaniyah as twilight approached and rented rooms in a modest hotel on a small square in the heart of the bazaar area. The hotelier was a Kurd called Zamo. Pictures in the hotel of the Imam Mosque in Isfahan suggested that he had close affiliations with Iran; we were getting close to the border. We talked for a little about Halabja, although I was careful not to disclose my interest in the town.

The next morning, over breakfast, Zamo and I got into conversation about Saddam, and how he was not the first person to use poison gas against the Kurds. It came as a surprise to me when he told me that the British had once ruled the area and that Winston Churchill was the first to use gas against the Kurds.

'Have you been up to see Halabja?' I asked.

'No. No one is allowed in, but I've heard there's nothing much to see. The Iraqis have removed all the evidence,' he said.

Over breakfast, I decided to come clean with Mohammed and told him that I was a doctor. I explained that I had treated many patients from the area who had presented with blood diseases and cancers. It was important, I said, that the outside world hears about what had happened in Halabja. He was frightened but I could see he was giving it some thought.

'Only *peshmerga* can take you over the hills to Halabja,' he whispered. 'It's, not safe, and they will need money.'

He left to make some phone calls, and I considered my position with some trepidation. If I were caught travelling with *peshmerga*, Kurdish rebels, into a restricted area, I would probably receive a long jail sentence.

When Mohammed returned, he said, 'It's settled. I'll take you to meet them, and they will take you to Halabja.'

He said he would wait at the hotel in Sulaymaniyah for two days and, if I had not returned by then, he would leave without me. We set off, heading due south for Arbat, hoping to make the mountainous village of Darbandikhana before evening. We stopped for lunch at a restaurant where many Hino and Mercedes trucks were parked, painted brightly in the Baluchistani fashion. The entrance was lit by rows of little red-light bulbs strung around the tree trunks. I stood in the park admiring the vehicles, each with its own regional decoration, with images that probably signified memorable events in the drivers' lives.

Visiting Erbil en route to Halabja

It was a tranquil afternoon, and the sound of Kurdish music lingered in the still air. Several men, who I assumed were truck drivers, were seated around a table drinking tea and playing cards. The one nearest me carried a small, bent knife tucked into his *peshtwen*, that broad plaited sash that Kurdish men use as a belt. They began laughing loudly at one of their group, who I presumed was losing, as he banged the wooden table repeatedly in frustration. The waiter showed us to a table by the window and offered us some sweetened tea in two miniature tulip glasses.

'I can take you no further,' Mohammed said. 'You must wait here, and I'll go get some friends.'

One of the card players stared at me for a few minutes, as if suspicious of my presence. I realised that he had probably never seen a European traveller this deep into Kurdish territory before – but he didn't seem particularly unfriendly. He smiled at me through a mouthful of decaying teeth.

Travelling deep in Kurdistan

Mohammed drove off in the direction from which we had come. I waited alone at the restaurant for several hours.

15. Visiting Forbidden Halabja

Evening came, and still, there was no sign of Mohammed. Strangely, I felt no fear, but rather a sense of living amid history and experiencing for myself what had happened there. Dusk was already falling when he returned with two men; both dressed in loose Kurdish clothes. They shook hands with the waiter, as if they already knew him, before joining me at the table.

'These are my friends – they'll take you to Halabja,' Mohammed said casually.

'Hello, my name is Jamal,' one of the men said, stretching out his hand to greet me.

'And I am Soubhi,' the other said. 'Would you like to eat? Those deep-fried *kibbehs* look good,' he continued, pointing to some food on display.

The waiter brought us bottled water and a plate of Kurdish flatbread.

For a while, we chatted about David O'Leary and Ireland's chances of winning the World Cup in Italy before Jamal got to the point.

'You want to go to Halabja?' he asked.

He leaned back in his chair and gazed at me as though making a private assessment.

'The army has roadblocks around the lake, and it is forbidden to go there except with special permission,' he said. 'You cannot take photographs, or you will be arrested.' He looked at me closely, obviously unsure whether to be amazed at my tenacity or my naiveté.

I leaned forward to meet his eyes and said, 'Do you think it's possible? How much would it cost?'

'It's possible. Two hundred American dollars.' I agreed to the price but felt embarrassed as I had told Mohammed I only had Iraqi money.

Jamal then opened a small bag, revealing some grey-and-white striped traditional Kurdish clothes. I would have to travel in disguise.

Mohammed changed his mind and said he would drive us to the lakeshore and leave us to walk the rest of the way.

'It's only about fifteen kilometres – two hours across the mountains. It is better we don't sleep tonight and go into the village in the morning,' Jamal said.

*

We drove about ten kilometres up the road to a hydroelectric project called the Darbandikhan Dam. The dying sun gently ended the day, casting weary shadows on the surrounding hills. We waited at the hydroelectric dam until about two o'clock in the morning, and then Soubhi advised Mohammed to take a desolate southerly route that ran across the river, to try and miss the army patrols. I wondered whether his friends were *peshmerga*. It surprised me how focused they were, not allowing themselves to indulge in small talk for long, and continually watching the hills around us.

On a deserted part of the road, Mohammed stopped the car and opened the boot to get my knapsack. Jamal retrieved a large assault rifle from the boot and slung it over his shoulder. It was only then that I realised the great risk we were taking. If an Iraqi patrol had opened the boot, we'd have been arrested, and they'd have thrown away the key.

Mohammed's friends had seriously escalated the danger for me, but I said nothing, knowing the rifle gave us a level of respectability in the mountains. He didn't speak as he handed me the orange knapsack and camera.

'I'll see you back at the restaurant,' I said, and he nodded. Jamal sensed my apprehension.

'Have courage,' he said.

The lake beside us supplied a large part of Iraq's fresh water and electricity. It was a strategic location, and the thought struck me that Iranian forces might have crossed the border into Halabja to take over the power station. Maybe Saddam had used poisonous gas to try to force the Iranian army to retreat.

Trekking in single file, we travelled deeper into the mountains. Jamal stopped to have a cigarette, and I noticed the way he covered it with his hands, not wanting to send out a signal. Even in the moonlight, one could see a long way. We walked slowly, passing some herds of black goats, but no words were spoken.

151

Eventually, we reached a collection of shacks on the outskirts of Halabja, where we sat on a stone wall and waited for the dawn. Some dogs barked, and I felt they would surely give away our presence. The sun rose in a blaze of orange and saffron and lit up the surrounding countryside. In daylight, one could see that many buildings had been razed, while others had half-built block walls with sheets of galvanised iron to give them stability.

When the sun was fully up, one of the men went ahead to see if it was safe to enter the town. He returned after about twenty minutes, and we went to meet the wakening townsfolk. On the way into the town, Jamal pointed to an old rusted iron casing. It was about three or four feet long, with a long barrel and a conical top.

'Gas shells!' he said and spat in disgust.

I took a photograph of the casing, amazed that something so crude could wreak so much destruction. The photograph would provide evidence of Saddam's inhumanity to his fellow man.

'There are many cases here, some unexploded,' Jamal said.

It seemed that some families used these unexploded shells as roof supports when building their houses. I thought of how hard it must be to raise a child in this environment, as every day one was reminded of the scourge of war. Jamal hung his rifle on his back as we approached a small hospital near the centre of town.

'Can we go into the hospital?' I asked Jamal.

'No!' he said, wagging his finger in the air. 'Saddam's men there!' We had breakfast at a little restaurant, where people were reticent about interacting with us. I felt quite foolish making an appearance dressed in Kurdish gear. After about thirty minutes, we met someone who was willing to talk about the gassing but said he didn't want to be photographed. The old man was hesitant at first but later talked freely.

'They started shelling early in the morning,' he said. 'Everyone was frightened, and all the children were crying with the sound from the aircraft overhead. Then a smell of garlic filled the shelter, and everyone knew it was a chemical.'

He took a deep breath and allowed it to escape slowly as if remembering took an act of tremendous will.

'My eyes were burning, and they bombed us for hours. When it was over, I discovered my family was dead. The next day, we found my brother with his skin blue.'

I looked into the old man's eyes and realised that I had heard enough. Whatever urgency had brought me here to share this experience was now gone. I was frightened by the horror of it and wanted to get back to the safety of the Ibn al-Bitar Hospital as quickly as possible. This man had looked death straight in the face, and I didn't want to join him.

The sight of demolished buildings in the hills around me bore testimony to what had happened during Saddam's Anfal Campaign, also known as the Kurdish Genocide, of which the Halabja chemical attack was only one small part. I took some photographs as mementos, and we left the town to make our way back along the mountains, moving at a more hurried pace. My guides pointed to small empty hamlets in the far-off hills. The villagers, they said, had been brought by lorry to "resettlement camps" near the towns. We walked back along the lake to the village of Darbandikhan, where a car was waiting to bring me back to the restaurant.

At about one o'clock, Mohammed returned to the restaurant as promised. I was never so relieved to see anyone in my life and greeted him like a long-lost friend. We started our journey home, following the road back to Sulaymaniyah, mostly in silence. The track was narrow, lined with hillside hamlets where children played with their dogs in the dust. Sometimes the road curved, and I glimpsed herds of goats and sheep in the valley below.

Mohammed seemed very apprehensive; his eyes fixed on the rear-view mirror. I glanced over my shoulder and, through the dust in our wake, saw what was causing his concern. There was a green army lorry coming at speed behind us.

'Do you think they're following us?' I asked.

'I don't know – I think so,' he stuttered, shaking his head as though trying to clear it.

We drove onto a narrow dirt track which led to a village. The lorry was still there. There was now little doubt that it was following us.

We cut back onto the main road at the next intersection. Mohammed accelerated in a frenzied attempt to outrun them. Another lorry appeared on the far-off horizon, blocking our path. My skin crawled as we neared it, and the soldiers got out on the road with an array of machine guns slung carelessly around their necks.

I felt goose pimples break out all over my body. We were the only vehicle on the road, and I knew there would be no witnesses if anything should happen to us. Frantically, I pulled off my Kurdish clothes, realising that a European in this attire would only arouse more suspicion. A black-and-grey petrol tanker was parked up ahead, and I shouted at Mohammed to stop the taxi. I jumped out and hid the rolls of film on a small siderail, which carried the fuel hosepipes.

A jeep shrieked to a halt in front of our car, blocking our exit should we decide to make a run for it again. Three young soldiers jumped down and approached us. One of them opened Mohammed's door, screaming as he pulled him from the vehicle. A second soldier pointed his rifle at me through the open door, while a third opened the passenger door and hauled me outside.

My bundle of Kurdish clothes was taken and thrown on the road. They found my camera, and some rolls of undeveloped film, lying on the back seat. These were snaps I had taken of the flames in the oilfields and a large, brightly lit bridge outside Sulaymaniyah. The oilfields were in a strategic location, and I knew they could be interpreted as evidence of military espionage. This would be indefensible in an Iraqi military court. Similar cases had been punished with penalties of up to ten years' imprisonment.

The soldiers proceeded to dismantle the taxi, taking out the back seats and tossing them by the roadside. Their painstaking inspection continued for about thirty minutes before they bundled us into one of the jeeps. Thankfully, during the inspection, the driver of the petrol tanker returned and unwittingly drove off with the pictures I had taken in Halabja. Mohammed tried to plead with the soldiers, but they were not sympathetic. At one stage, the exchange became heated and he was punched viciously in the face. I found myself willing him to be quiet so they wouldn't kill him for talking back.

16. Prisoner of Saddam Hussein

After about thirty minutes, we reached an army complex with a heavily fortified front entrance. The soldiers brought us out into a central courtyard, where we were separated and led to different buildings. We were to be interrogated independently. In all our careful planning, we had not discussed what we should say if we were caught. I was brought down a short corridor to a little cell, about six feet square, which contained a small bed with a filthy mattress. The steel door was locked, and I was left alone. I sat on the bed and tried to gather my thoughts.

The soldiers had taken my passport, camera, and film, but left my watch. I was concerned that it had only been a short time since Daphne Parish had been sentenced, and soon they would realise that I was working at the same hospital. They also had my rucksack and would certainly have my pictures developed. No matter how I tried to organise the thoughts in my head, I kept coming to the same conclusion – I was in trouble.

I could hear noises as if people were walking outside in the corridor, but no one entered my cell. The time passed slowly, and I knew it must be getting dark outside, but still, nobody came to interrogate me. I must have fallen asleep because the next thing I remembered was an older man, dressed in a long white *dishdasha*, standing over my bed. He carried a tray with some jam and flatbread and encouraged me to eat.

'Do you speak English?' I inquired.

He put his hands to his lips and shook his head, indicating that he could not. When he left, the door was locked under the scrutiny of the soldiers on duty outside. I sat down on the mattress and started to eat. Once I had finished, I lay on the bed for a long time, trying to get back to sleep. Night fell and, with it, a darkness entered my spirit. I had read of horrific acts performed in Iraqi prisons, and I prowled the room in silence, wondering what to do next, realising there was absolutely nothing I *could* do. I knew I had to be strong and face the consequences of my actions. Knowing what time, it had brought me some small comfort, and I was thankful they had let me keep my watch.

During the night, there was a lot of shouting in Arabic, and the agonising screams of a prisoner being beaten. My heart hammered in my chest and I hoped it wasn't Mohammed. At one stage, I thought I heard my name being called and feared for the worst. What devastation had I brought on this man by my decision to travel to Halabja? Over the next three hours, the steel doors along the corridor banged open and closed, as other prisoners were arrested and interrogated.

Morning came, and the sun shone through a slit in the passageway under my door. At about ten o'clock, the door of my cell opened, and two men entered. They escorted me down the corridor to a room where a group of soldiers sat smoking around a small table. My passport lay open beside them, and my camera was propped up with the lens facing the ceiling. One soldier spoke to me in perfect English.

'What are you doing in this area? What kind of pictures have you taken?' he asked.

'Mostly farmers in the fields, and a group of Kurds I met in Sulaymaniyah.'

'How do you know the driver of the car you were travelling in?'

'I met him today in a restaurant in a little village near here.'

'Who were the other people who were travelling in the taxi last night?'

I shrugged my shoulders and did my best to look confused.

They had found my Kurdish clothes in the back seat, but they had no way of knowing I had been to Halabja unless Mohammed had talked. On balance, I decided he would never admit to organising my trip, or to any wrongdoing, as he was only too aware of the consequences of such an admission. They continued their interrogation, but I wouldn't admit to being in the taxi the night before.

'Why are you taking photographs in Iraq?' he asked.

'I like the country and the people,' I replied, trying to look as innocent as possible.

'Where are you working here?'

'At Ibn al-Bitar Hospital. You can ring them to check if you wish.' The exchange continued and, as it progressed, I felt less intimidated by the interviewer, although I worried about being lulled into a false sense of security. I told him again that he could verify my story if he phoned the hospital and hoped in doing so that he would let people know where I was.

'What part of England do you come from?'

'I'm an Irish citizen,' I said. 'You have my passport.'

'Where did you go to college?'

'In Dublin.'

'Do you know Trinity College?' he continued.

'Yes, very well, but I didn't go to college there. How do you know Trinity College?'

He stood up abruptly and folded some papers in front of him. He looked at me and said, 'We already know that is where you are working, but we will have to check some other things later in the day.'

The preliminary interview ended abruptly, and an escort took me back to my cell. I was gratified things had gone so easily and sensed that the interviewer had been trained in the West, possibly even in Dublin. There had been no mention of the photograph that I had taken of the bridge, and I could only suppose they were waiting for the film to be developed. Maybe that was what he meant when he said they would be checking out some things later.

The day dragged on slowly and nobody bothered about me for many hours. I realised how hard it would be to serve a jail sentence and thought of all the poor prisoners languishing in jails up and down the country. During the day, I heard a man sobbing and felt it was only a matter of time before the soldiers inflicted this level of interrogation on me. My thoughts turned to Mohammed and what was happening to him. Only my jailer broke the monotony that day, bringing me food on three occasions and allowing me a visit to the outside toilet on another. The soldiers in the corridor never smiled, looking at me as something of interest rather than of concern. I read some of the graffiti on the walls, each word a protest in another language. This was not the script of drunken prisoners, but of those threatened with extinction by the state apparatus of Saddam Hussein.

When night fell, the lights went out and again I was alone in the darkness. It is easy to become hopelessly lost in the silence and isolation. It was important not to allow guilt to take over – that would ensure the absence of objective thought. I wondered if they were playing a game with me and if the level of interrogation would increase with each passing day. They could easily find my driving licence, associate me with the Nissan Patrol that Daphne Parish had driven, link me to the journey to Halabja, and I could end up with a lengthy sentence as a spy – or worse. I wondered what had happened to Jamal and his friend and remembered his words before we started the journey: 'Have courage!'

My mind raced. After a while, I fell into a sort of trance, somewhere between waking and sleeping. I began dreaming about a priest who had taught my religion classes at St Michael's in Enniskillen when I was a teenager. In my dream, he spoke to me in a soft Monaghan accent. 'What is courage? Is it the absence of fear? No, it is the ability to stand up against things that are unjust, knowing that the consequences of your action might be physical injury.' My mind swirled, following the different experiences in my life and taking me right back to where I had started.

I awoke in a sweat and looked at my watch. It wasn't yet six o'clock in the morning, and already there was the noise of people washing in the bathroom area outside. A cockroach scurried across the floor. Normally, I would have killed it, but somehow, I felt guilty taking the life of the only other living thing in my cell. After a few hours, I could wash and was given a light breakfast before the soldiers brought me back to the interrogation room. This time there appeared to be a judge at the table, and I was given the impression that a court was in session.

'How did you get to Sulaymaniyah?'

'I took a taxi.'

'Where did you get the taxi?'

'From the Alawi al-Hilla bus station.'

'Where did you go to?'

'To Mosul,' I said.

'And then where?'

'I got another taxi to Erbil.'

'And from there?'

'I got a taxi to Sulaymaniyah.'

'All different taxis?'

'Yes, all different taxis.'

'And where did you meet this driver?'

'I met him in that small village.'

'Then how do you explain this?' the judge said, sliding a picture across the table that I had taken of Mohammed with the garage owner outside Tikrit.

My heart sank. I had forgotten this photograph. Trying to stay focused, I wondered how many photographs they had developed and what Mohammed might have told them. I decided to say the photographs were not mine, but I didn't know if some of the other pictures on the roll could incriminate me. Was

I in any of them? I remembered changing a roll of film at Nineveh and another at Halabja.

'That picture must belong to the taxi driver,' I said, hoping it sounded convincing.

'And these?' showing me the pictures of Nineveh.

'They are mine,' I replied, hoping there were no photographs of myself and Mohammed together. I didn't think there were, as my camera was complex, and I didn't trust anyone else with it.

'The taxi driver says he brought you there,' the judge said, fixing me with a stare.

'Why would he say that? I only met him this morning,' I said.

'What did you talk about in the taxi?'

'We talked about Kurdistan.'

'What did you say?'

'I told him it is not a real country and it is not recognised in the world.'

My answer resonated with a colonel beside me, who seemed to stand a little taller as he puffed out his chest, giving me an indication of the way, they expected their questions should be answered.

'Have you been to Israel?' he asked, raising an eyebrow.

'No,' I answered.

The judge then produced the *Sunday Times* article about Halabja that I had carried with me on the journey from Baghdad, as it contained the names of people who I wanted to interview.

'Where did the driver get this?'

'I don't know – what is it?'

'It is an English newspaper not allowed in Iraq. You must have given it to him.'

They passed the paper over for my perusal.

I tapped the left-hand corner a few times with my finger and noted that the date on it was Sunday, March 27, 1988.

'It has nothing to do with me,' I said. 'Check my passport – I was in New Zealand then!'

'What were you doing in New Zealand?' the judge asked, clearly unimpressed.

'I was working as a doctor.'

'And why did you come to Iraq?'

'I was always fascinated by the Iraqi people, especially the Marsh Arabs.'

'Have you been to the marshes?'

'Yes, I have been to the marshes.'

'What do you think of Saddam Hussein?' the judge asked, changing tactics.

'I think he has brought a lot of literacy to Iraq, even to the people in the marshes.'

'Is this your photograph?' he said, showing me the picture of the bridge.

'Yes.'

'You will receive one year's jail sentence for this photograph.'

'Why?' I asked in astonishment.

'We think you are a spy, and this is a military bridge.'

'I am not a spy! The bridge had nice lights, so I just took a photograph.'

'Do you think we are stupid?'

'Well, if I were a spy, surely I would have better photographs than these?' I said, becoming agitated.

The soldiers beside me moved in a little closer, in case I tried to do anything rash, I surmised.

'What type of photographs?' the judge asked.

'I don't know – ones of the army and things I suppose.'

The interrogation continued for another hour, covering the same topics. Why had I come to Iraq? Why was I taking photographs of sensitive military structures? Did I know the driver? Was this my newspaper?

I was returned to my cell, confident that I had stood up to the constant barrage of the interrogation, but shocked by the sentence of one year for taking a photograph of a bridge. If I were jailed in Iraq, how would I get my HIV tests, and what if they were positive? Where would I get treatment?

My thoughts turned to Mohammed. Because of me, they had arrested him and found the *Sunday Times* in his possession. Some of the photographs of the oilfields in Kirkuk were on the same rolls as the "garage man", and his taxi had also been identified as being near the hydroelectric dam the night before. I knew he was in bigger trouble than me.

Evening came and, with it, the reality that I could be in prison in Iraq for the next year. I would have to forgo my GP registrar year in Scotland and would have to dig deep in the coming weeks to find the mental strength to face the sentence. Surely, the administration at the hospital would come looking for me and get the Irish embassy to secure my freedom. The next morning the questioning continued.

'The driver says he brought you to Halabja.'

'I was never there.'

'We have witnesses who saw you there.'

'Then bring them here.'

Jamal and his companion were perfectly at ease in Halabja. They only objected to visiting the hospital, which, when I thought about it, was understandable. At least some staff there had to be involved in the cover-up operation following the gas attack. I was pretty confident that no witnesses would come forward, unless they were forced by the army to do so. However, the Mukhabarat had deep tentacles, and anything was possible.

I thought of the advice my father had given me in Northern Ireland: 'If you're going to say anything – say nothing!' Remembering made me think of home, of how my mother would worry about me.

Tears filled my eyes, and the interrogator, misreading the signals, increased his questioning, confident of a successful outcome.

'Where did you meet the driver?' the judge asked again. I said nothing.

'Answer!' a soldier shouted, hitting the back of my head with the butt of his rifle.

I put my hand behind my head and felt the trickle of blood.

'There is no need for such things,' said the judge. 'I am sure the doctor will tell us everything he knows.'

'I've told you everything already,' I said, holding my head in the knowledge that this was only the beginning.

If Mohammed talked, I would probably be sentenced to many years in jail – or worse, be hanged like Bazoft. It was imperative that they didn't discover that the Nissan Patrol on my driving licence was the one used for the journey to the Al-Iskandaria military complex. It would be one coincidence too many.

The questioning continued and they asked the same questions repeatedly. They were trying to cloud my judgement. The judge seemed quite civilised, but I knew that if I diverted, even a little, from a previous answer it would be enough to hang me.

My mind was foggy as I tried to remember the information and my head hurt where I had been hit. They were trying to wear me down, slowly, bit by bit, day by day, and I knew it was going to get worse.

The soldiers returned me to my cell, and I was left alone for a few days, except for the delivery of food and trips to the toilet. At first, I was relieved, but relief was quickly replaced by thoughts of what might happen to me. When I was brought back and forth to be interrogated, I at least felt I had some say in my future. I could put up a good fight. Alone, I could only imagine what my fate might be. Sometimes I would think of Mohammed, and I would be overcome with guilt. Had I followed my lust for adventure to his detriment? These and many other thoughts were still racing through my head on the morning of the fifth day when the door of my cell opened. A colonel, carrying a small handgun, came into my cell and sat on my bed. He left the gun between us, which immediately aroused my suspicion.

My God, this is it – I'm going to be shot by the Revolutionary Council, I thought.

'What do you think of Iraq?' he asked.

I said nothing, just kept my eyes on the gun, wondering if this was a test. 'You think we're all barbarians?' he said.

'No, I don't,' I promptly replied, feeling that denial was in my best interest at this stage.

'Yes, you do – but I know James Joyce and I know Trinity College.' He replaced the gun in its holster, roughly pinned my arm behind my back and frog-marched me out of my cell. *He's leading me away to be tortured*, I thought.

We passed the soldiers guarding the cells and made our way down the corridor. I could almost feel his anger as he bent my arm into a more painful position. What had happened? Had they finally come across my driving licence in the little red pouch I'd carried?

The colonel marched me to the end of the building, opened a door with his key and forced me outside. There was a stone path through the centre of a courtyard in front of me, although it seemed like a long way to walk with my back turned to an armed guard. I stood and looked back at the window in the door where the colonel was standing. He stared back at me but didn't speak. Then, through the bars of the window, he handed me the red pouch. There was some film in it, which they had exposed – and my driving licence. They hadn't put two and two together. He stared at me with cold, indifferent eyes, as if the life had died within them many years before.

'What about Mohammed, my taxi driver?' I asked.

He just stared at me without responding. I turned to walk down the long path, holding my breath, suppressing the desire to run. Would I be shot in the back as an escapee, or had I genuinely been released? The courtyard was empty except for a few soldier's guarding the entrance with Kalashnikovs slung over their shoulders. At the far end of the gate was a portrait of Saddam Hussein in traditional Iraqi dress, greeting Kurdish peasant women. In the distance, I could hear shots being fired, but the casual glance of the soldiers in that direction persuaded me it was probably of no consequence. In a few minutes, I was through the outer perimeter and making my way back down the road. As I reached the end of the path I thought, *I'm free – I'm out of here.*

Eventually, I reached a taxi rank, where I found a driver who was willing to travel the four hundred kilometres back to Baghdad. Nobody at the hospital knew where I had been, and my immediate reaction was not to go back there. What if the secret police were watching me to see where I went or who I met up with? I decided to take the first flight out of the country.

When I reached Baghdad, I phoned Chris and told him to collect my belongings and meet me at the Hole in the Wall. He knew he would have to move clandestinely in order not to arouse the suspicions of the Mukhabarat. After I had recovered my possessions from him, we had a farewell drink, and I asked him to say goodbye to my friends.

'It's been good fun, mate, stay safe. I just can't believe we nearly had another Dee Parish on our hands!' he smiled, shaking his head. Then I went to the airport and caught the first flight to Europe.

*

In August, I met Hajj and some of the Ibn al-Bitar nurses at the Galway Races. We were in the bar, catching up and watching some horse racing on television when the programme was interrupted by a breaking *BBC News* bulletin.

'Quiet, everybody, and listen to this!' said Hajj.

The newscaster said, 'More than a hundred thousand Iraqi soldiers backed up by seven hundred tanks invaded the Gulf state of Kuwait in the early hours of this morning. Iraqi forces have established a provisional government and their leader Saddam Hussein has threatened to turn Kuwait City into a "graveyard" if any other country dares to challenge the "takeover by force".'

The Iraqi army had just invaded Kuwait, stating that it had always been a part of the Ottoman Empire's province of Basra, something that made it rightfully Iraqi territory; the British had made it a separate emirate after the First World War.

Tensions had been simmering for some time. Iraq had accused Kuwait of stealing Iraqi petroleum near the border through slant drilling. Kuwait said it was doing this to compensate for more than $80 billion it had loaned to Iraq to finance the Iran-Iraq War and which Saddam was refusing to pay back.

*

I later discovered that my roommate Chris and his girlfriend, Dr Mary O'Loughlin, had returned to Baghdad from a holiday in Turkey just as hostilities had commenced and had been held there as prisoners, unable to join the overland exodus through Syria. They were among many Western hostages held by the Iraqi regime during this time. All 450 of the hospital staff – British, Irish, Danish and American – were held, and Saddam threatened to place them in areas of military importance if the West attacked Iraq.

In the coming months, celebrity political leaders made their way to Baghdad to try to secure the release of these hostages. Photographs of Saddam with Jesse Jackson were splashed across the newspapers of the world. The singer Yusuf Islam, formerly known as "Cat Stevens", secured the release of a trickle of hostages, but it was the former German Prime Minister, Willy Brandt, who scored the biggest success when he landed in Frankfurt Airport with 174 freed hostages on board.

Around the time of the Gulf War, there was a series of popular rebellions in the northern and southern Iraqi provinces, which were referred to as the Sha'aban Intifada among Arabs and as the National Uprising among Kurds. After the war ended, Saddam Hussein's forces, spearheaded by the Iraqi Republican Guard, sought terrible revenge on the Kurdish people for this uprising, and the streets I had walked in Mosul, Erbil, and Sulaymaniyah ran red with their blood. The vanquished people gathered in the tens of thousands and formed a haunting column of men, women and babies, all blindly stumbling through the snows of the Zakho Mountains, at the mercy of the wolves and the pursuing Iraqi army. Their anguish made the world listen, and my article about my journey to Halabja made the front page of the *Fermanagh Herald*.

17. Scots, Whiskey on the Rock and White Russians

A letter from Chris arrived for me in Scotland:

'Truth is we have no problems (except for leaving!) and are free to move all over the country. Unfortunately, it's not the same for some other companies, who have either taken up residence on the embassy lawn or are languishing in the local power station, etc., but by all accounts, being well treated – food, four beers, two boxes of cigs a day, and all for free! Mary Mac got trapped here when we came back from Turkey. She was at the end of contract and came back for luggage on July 31. All is much as usual. Fr Pat is on the dry (except for gin and tonic) but your replacement is very inferior. Mary Mac is doing a clinic on the embassy lawns once a week, and it's one of the best parties going. Have fun in E'burgh – the street behind Princes St is wall-to-wall pubs, but I suppose you've found that out already.

Keep in touch. Pat says "On-On", in memory of the call sign of the Baghdad Hash House Harriers that we used when out jogging together.

–Chris (Happy Hostage)'

What a role reversal! Just a few weeks earlier, we had said goodbye to each other in a pub in Baghdad, and now he and Pat McGlynn were prisoners in Room 908. I was surprised the Iraqi government had allowed him to get a letter out. I was settling into the life of a Scottish general practitioner, under the tutelage of Dr Nigel Woods and Dr Fergus McRae. Both men worked hard to provide the community with a good level of service. The practice had an on-call room in nearby Bangour General Hospital, which I shared with Lokesh, a plastic surgeon senior house officer from India and another female doctor from Nigeria. General

165

practice was a new way of life for me, and there were some funny incidents. On my very first evening on call, a distressed mother rang and spoke to me in a thick Scottish accent.

'Cud ya cum outa the house? Me bairn's grating,' she said. 'Your bearing is grating?'

'Yes, me bairn's grating terribly all day!'

'Sorry – this is the doctor's – are you sure you don't need a mechanic?' I innocently replied, remembering all the grating bearings I'd replaced in my father's garage in Garrison.

Lindsey, a nurse who also stayed at Bangour, informed me that a "grating bairn" was the Scottish way of saying a "crying child". We laughed about the peculiarities of the Scottish language.

I soon got a letter from the chef at Ibn al-Bitar, Robbie Sweeney, who updated me on what was left of the Baghdad Blues Band.

'The Baghdad Blues Band now consists of Sean, Carl, Declan, Serge (Italian guy!) and Neil from the lab on lead guitar and he is good. Carl got a visa, thank God, for we're getting fed up listening to Declan trying to sing. Luke had joined the band, but, as you probably know by now, he ran out across the border, thank God. We are hoping to be home on December 15 as PARC have proposed this. I'm hoping to buy a pub in Drogheda. Any word from Trish or could you be bothered?

–Robbie'

Robbie sent me photos of him and the former world heavyweight champion, Muhammad Ali, sparring together in Baghdad. This hero of my father's bicycle shop had gone to Iraq and secured the release of another fifteen hostages. One by one, my colleagues from the Ibn al-Bitar hospital started to arrive home, beginning with the transport manager's family and some of the nurses. As Christmas approached, there were 270 Irish Ibn al-Bitar hospital staff still being held in Iraq or Kuwait.

The winter of 1990 was one of the worst on record. The snows began in early December and caused havoc, bringing down power lines and disrupting electricity. There was an enormous rise in callouts for patients with respiratory illnesses. The very young and very old were most susceptible to the flu viruses of that year. By the time the snow ended in February, the severe weather had led to the deaths of about ten people.

In early 1991, it was decided that Bangour General Hospital should finally close and its services should be moved to a new facility in Livingstone. The new hospital had many teething problems. Some were quite simple, like the beds being longer than the curtains. Others, like the nurses' strike for more handover time, created problems for the doctors.

One evening, I visited a sick child in a house near Broxburn, whom I believed had meningitis. As the child was deteriorating, I gave her an injection of penicillin and, deciding not to wait for an ambulance, I drove her to the new hospital in my car. The child lay in accident and emergency for quite a long time. The paediatric registrar helped me perform a lumbar puncture, which confirmed my diagnosis, and Andy Woods, the emergency-room SHO, decided to transfer the sick child to the paediatric hospital in Edinburgh. It was the correct decision, as the child deteriorated in the ambulance on the way. The next day, her sister presented with similar symptoms during a lunch-hour call, and I drove her to the hospital too. My quick action on their behalf was kindly rewarded with free beer by an ever-grateful father during my tenure in Broxburn, which I happily imbibed at the Volunteer Arms public house in East Main Street. Although happy to be accepted within the wider community, I often felt slightly on edge in the bar, as this part of Scotland retained traditions like Northern Ireland's, and proudly sent loyalist flute bands across the water to march on July 12.

In March of that year, I received a letter offering me an accident and emergency registrar's position in St Bernard's Hospital in Gibraltar, a British overseas territory located on the southern end of the Iberian Peninsula. It suited me as I was due to finish up my GP registrar position in Scotland at the end of the year. I ruminated on the possibilities of working in Gibraltar for a while, from there I could travel through Africa and eventually work in Cape Town, where I had already registered as a doctor now that Mandela was free. In the months before my departure, I started dating a design student named Hazel. I asked if she would like to join me in Gibraltar and she agreed.

Dr McRae laughed when he heard where I was thinking of working. 'You'll spend your time there treating tourists for monkey bites!' he joked.

Towards the end of July, some of my patients organised a "Rock rave" in one of the local pubs as a farewell party for Hazel and me. One of my patients, Doris Wilson, made up an elaborate yellow-and-white cake in the shape of a suitcase, with baggage tags saying "Scotland", "Gibraltar" and "Ireland". Then we packed our belongings into my car and set out for the three-day journey to the bottom of Spain.

On our way through France, we stopped over in Montauban to see my brother Raymond, who had recently bought a small farm near the banks of the river Tarn, just off the motorway between Toulouse and Bordeaux. The cold winter of 1990 had killed off his apple crops, and he was finding it difficult to make ends meet. It was great spending time with him, and although I wished I could stay longer, we had a long journey ahead of us. Two days later, we reached the small Spanish border town of La Línea de la Concepción, on the eastern flank of the Bay of Gibraltar.

Gibraltar wasn't like anywhere I'd ever been before. The name of the promontory was derived from the Arabic name "Jabal Tāriq" or "Mountain of Tariq", and it reflected an earlier period when the Moors had ruled this part of Europe. The Rock had been of vital strategic importance to Britain during the Napoleonic wars, a role it maintained during the two world wars when it was a location for British operations against the Germans. As we crossed the border, we were told to wait as two policemen placed barriers on the road. I was amazed when a Boeing 737 landed a few minutes later; the airport runway intersected with the road we were driving on. I had never seen anything like it. Our route took us by the Shell filling station where members of the SAS had shot the three IRA volunteers a few years before.

St Bernard's Hospital was built on the top of a hill, with a medical history dating back to 1567, when it was used to treat syphilis.

The elevated location meant that it was well away from the town, but it also meant that after we visited the bars and restaurants in the town, we had to walk up hundreds of steps to reach our accommodation in the doctors' quarters. However, we were richly rewarded for the climb, with balconies that provided the best view across the strait to the northern coastline of Africa.

Hazel and I shared the quarters with three doctors: Lisa Penrice from Manchester and Ian Franklin from Avon, as well as Marcel and his wife from the Transvaal in South Africa. My Casualty registrar position in St Bernard's was tourists with monkey bites proved quite accurate.

In the evenings, my colleagues and I chilled out in the pubs around Irishtown and discussed the events of the day. We often sat out on the balcony of the doctors' accommodation and watched the setting sun spill orange and purple rivulets of colour into the far-off deserts of Morocco. I told Marcel that I was registered in South Africa and discussed the possibility of working at the Groote Schuur Hospital, in Cape Town, where Professor Christiaan Barnard had performed the first human heart transplant in December 1967. This was where Marcel had his next rotation, and Hazel wanted to travel down to South Africa.

At the beginning of September, Hazel and I went on holiday to Tangier in Morocco, staying at the Europa Hotel. For her, it was an incessant hassle – "official guides" walking after her, vying for her attention. For me, it was great to be back in the Arabic world, with its dagger and tin markets, watching the old men spinning cotton with the help of bicycle wheels. I had to laugh when one of the more persistent local hagglers began speaking to Hazel in Irish. Towards the end of the month, the nurses in the hospital decided to stage a walkout over conditions and felt that the junior doctors should support them. It is always difficult when medicine becomes political because one must continue working with one's colleagues when things settle.

Amid the negotiations, an elderly Moroccan man was admitted through the accident and emergency department. He had been found lying in the street, semi-comatose, unkempt and smelling of alcohol.

At first, everyone assumed that the patient, who was well known to them, was just drunk. Although his initial neurological observations were entirely normal, I had a bad feeling about the case and decided to admit him to one of the surgical wards, where I put him on an hourly examination and requested a skull X-ray.

During the early hours of the morning, the patient developed "racoon" signs around his eyes, and his skull X-ray showed evidence of a fracture. I transferred him to the intensive care unit and informed the locum consultant that we had a possible intracranial bleed and base-of-skull fracture. Over the next hour, the patient's right pupil stopped reacting to light and became fixed and dilated. The consultant agreed that the most likely cause of the patient's dilated pupil was a massive bleed in the subdural part of the brain, which was compressing the oculomotor nerve. In the absence of a brain scan to confirm, we had no choice but to bring him to theatre and drill an emergency burr hole to relieve the pressure. When we opened the surgical instruments, I remember my surprise at seeing how similar they looked to a carpenter's swivel drill and bits. The consultant separated the temporalis muscle before cutting into the periosteum.

'Get the drill bit and start screwing it about two centimetres above and behind the orbital process of the frontal bone,' he said, as I injected more adrenaline into the skin to prevent fresh bleeding. 'Just about there – but be careful, this patient has a much larger skull fracture than we saw on the X-ray.'

I started boring into the patient's exposed skull with a large conical bit. As the bit drove deeper, I became ever more cautious not to burst through and damage the brain underneath. The technical practicalities of being accurate while drilling into somebody's skull were, in all honesty, not very different from what I had learnt in my father's garage, and I switched over to the cylindrical bit while my colleague teased the "freed-up" skull fragment from the delicate dura matter underneath. We removed a large clot, covered the brain with antibiotics and got him back to the intensive care unit. The next day, he developed a fixed pupil on the other side and had to go back to theatre.

Meanwhile, word arrived at the hospital that the Moroccan patient had been assaulted by a local Gibraltarian, who had gone into hiding somewhere on the Rock. Moroccans were Gibraltar's underclass, and many of them lived in squalid, cockroach-infested slum hotels in an area of town called Casemates. They were forced to pay tax but were not allowed to enjoy any of the benefits of citizenship, and if they lost their jobs, they were deported back to their homeland. It was later discovered that the poor man had been battered over the head with a shoe until he became unconscious. His attacker came from a good family, and subsequent rumours indicated that this man had already left Gibraltar and was being treated in a psychiatric hospital in England. The patient lived through most of the following week, but eventually succumbed to his injuries.

In every moral sense, this situation regarding these immigrants was grossly unfair. These people had saved the Rock with their labour in 1969, when the Spanish dictator, General Franco, decided to close the frontier, preventing Spaniards from working there. Almost five thousand came during that period but, as the years passed, the Rock of Gibraltar became their prison cell. The authorities even confiscated the passports of their wives and children whenever they stopped over on the evening ferry that ran from Tangiers to the Spanish port of Algeciras.

Another disturbing aspect of life in Gibraltar, at least in 1991, was the government's apparent willingness to turn a blind eye to tobacco smugglers, who were known locally as the "Winston boys". The smugglers operated openly, using speedboats to cross the strait between Morocco and Spain, with Gibraltar as their base. On any given evening, one could wander amongst the black Phantom speedboats in Gibraltar's extensive harbour and see young men loading cartons of Winston cigarettes, preparing for the run across to Playa de la Atunara. The Spanish Guardia Civil abhorred this smuggling, and often chased the Winston boys with helicopters and speedboats.

*

One of the most interesting people I met on the Rock was Dr Cecil Isola, a sixty-three-year-old politician, whose wife was Irish. He had been born into a political Gibraltarian family, and his ancestors had been on the Rock longer than the British. Cecil was a larger-than-life character, a product of his upbringing at Stonyhurst College in Lancashire, the alumni of which included three saints, seven Victoria Cross winners, two prime ministers and one signatory of the

On ships in Gibraltar

American Declaration of Independence. He had studied medicine at Trinity College Dublin, but after many years of service as port medical officer was getting too old for climbing the sides of ships in the middle of the night to see sick patients on board, and he had handed over this duty to the junior doctors in

171

St Bernard's Hospital. One evening, I was standing on the balcony, enjoying the fiery sunset and thinking about Africa. Marcel joined me, and we talked for some time about my plans to travel overland from Kenya to the southern tip of Africa. Then, my beeper sounded for an emergency. It was a call from the harbour master, asking me to attend a possible heart attack aboard a Yugoslavian tanker.

'Are you on call?' Marcel asked me. 'I hit my nose on the side of a big Indian cargo ship last Tuesday when I was climbing up the rope ladder. A massive wave threw me against her side, and Dr Isola's black bag fell into the water!'

We all knew the dangers of climbing on board these ships late at night with only a small torch to light the way. Often, the crew spoke no English and commands were mistaken. A Russian crew once brought me down into the lower decks to fix an engine while their first mate lay upstairs suffering from an angina attack. However, it was also quite a lucrative business, which we all participated in, so we protected each other on that rare occasion when we were required to attend both the hospital and a naval emergency at the same time. We had a small car at our disposal, which I drove down to the Waterport Gate, where a pilot boat was waiting to take me out to sea.

'What is it?' I inquired in Spanish.

'Chest pain,' the captain replied, indicating that we had better hurry.

The craft thrust its way into the darkness, and before long we were alongside the tanker. It was a calm, starry night, perfect for alighting, and after the crew had thrown down ropes to haul up my equipment, I climbed aboard. The vessel's captain was first to meet me. He walked awkwardly, as if his leg had been injured, and ushered me into a little room.

'This young man is very sick, and I don't want him aboard my vessel,' he began. 'I want you to find bed for him in the hospital – please, you find bed for him?'

I was worried that the patient was seriously ill and indicated that we should go to see him immediately. Lifting my bag from the table, I made my way towards the iron door. It became apparent that the captain had other ideas. With a gesture, he signalled for me to sit down again. From the cupboard, he produced a bottle of Johnnie Walker whiskey and filled up two glasses.

'*Zivjeli*,' he said, handing one to me. 'Please you find my man a bed, we will sail tonight.'

After we emptied our glasses, we descended into the cramped lower part of the ship, passing through different stairwells until we reached the patient. He was

Yugoslavian, probably in his late thirties and dressed in white overalls. Another crew member lay on the opposite bed, anxiously watching. Some others emerged from the shadows, eager to see what was happening. I thought it unusual that the captain allowed them to congregate in this fashion and searched my bag for a stethoscope – my gavel, my truncheon of authority. The patient began writhing and spoke to me in a faint, apprehensive voice.

'*Ulcera*,' he said, pointing to his stomach area.

I noted how his flickering eyes were fearful as he grasped my shirt, as if his life depended on my getting him out of there. He spoke to me in a tired, pleading voice as I felt his abdomen. On examination, nothing seemed to add up. His basic observations were normal, and his pulse rate ticked along at normal speed. As each moment passed, he seemed to be getting worse, the pain increasing.

'*Ulcera*,' he sobbed again.

I began to wonder whether there was a cultural aspect to his pain but remained suspicious – the degree of pain and fear in his voice, the symptoms which were allegedly bothering him just didn't match my findings. Although I didn't want to miss a perforated ulcer, my sixth sense made me consider whether I was being subjected to an elaborate hoax. The captain seemed to share the patient's anguish, and he signalled for me to take the patient ashore. I thought about it for a while and then said to a stretcher party he had assembled, 'OK, we'll have to take him to the hospital.'

The crew members lifted him onto the stretcher, and I followed them to the gangway. On the way, the captain ordered someone to collect the patient's personal belongings so that they could be brought ashore with him. He turned to me and said, 'When you are finished, you fly my man to Dubrovnik.'

'Yes, captain,' I replied cautiously. 'But what's his real problem?' The captain took me back to his cabin and, in the dim light, opened his coat and offered me another glass of whiskey.

'He is a Croatian on this Serbian ship. Yesterday his family were killed, and he wants to go back to fight in the war,' he said, shaking my hand and thrusting the remainder of the bottle of whiskey into my red life jacket. 'You see, I am also Croatian.'

Croatia had just declared independence, dissolving its association with Yugoslavia. He explained that two months before, the border city of Vukovar had been besieged by Serbian troops, and the population suffered extreme hardship. I learnt a lot that night. Although the captain had abused my position as a doctor, sometimes a greater human need may transcend our professional ethics. This is a judgement call that each doctor must make from time to time and live with. The patient had his gastroscopy a few days later, which proved normal, as expected. He hugged me goodbye before leaving for the airport.

*

In early November, I noticed a spectacular yacht, the *Lady Ghislaine*, moored in Marina Bay. For some reason, I was impressed enough to take a photograph of it and show it to my colleagues in the apartment.

It belonged to British media mogul Robert Maxwell. His naked body was found a few days later, floating in the Atlantic Ocean.

Rumours abounded that he had fallen overboard near the Canary Islands, and some speculated that the Israeli intelligence service, Mossad, was involved in his death. He was eventually buried on the Mount of Olives in Jerusalem, across from the Temple Mount, widely discounting that theory. During his eulogy, Prime Minister Yitzhak Shamir broadcast to the world, 'He has done more for Israel than can be said today.'

During December, the commissioner of Gibraltar police asked me to train some of his officers in basic life support. However, the position gave me no special status when the British aircraft carrier *Ark Royal* visited Gibraltar en route to the Gulf War. It had been deployed to the Mediterranean area to monitor Libya, which had proclaimed support for Iraq's actions. I was unsure whether to be proud or embarrassed when word came back that I was the only doctor in the hospital not to be given security clearance to visit the ship. The long arm of Britannia was in action again, and somebody somewhere was working overtime.

I had more luck when the *QE2* arrived en route from Southampton with a sick passenger for disembarkation. The journey only took a few days, and I was always surprised by the number of people who developed the need for specialist help during that short period. The principal medical officer on board the *QE2* was from Staffordshire, a graduate of King's College Hospital, and he had an Irish mother. We bonded instantly, and he gave me a signed copy of his book, *Doctor of the Queen Elizabeth 2*.

'This would be a perfect career for you,' he told me. 'You've accident and emergency, cardiology, and orthopaedic experience. However, it's not for the faint-hearted. You'll be on your own at sea, but you'll have the happiest memories of your life!'

I took the idea a little further and, during the Christmas holidays, went to the London office of Carnival Cruise Lines, to meet Randy Coldham, to seek opportunities as a ship's physician, working from the United States. He thought my CV was perfect and immediately offered me a ship from Miami. However, I still wanted to visit Cape Town, so I decided to wait on another liner leaving from Los Angeles, sailing along the Mexican Riviera the following June.

In the meantime, Hazel went back to college in Edinburgh, and I applied for a six-week tour from Nairobi overland to Johannesburg with a group called Truck Africa. That Christmas, the famous hammer-and-sickle emblem of the Soviet Union was lowered for the last time. I had witnessed the fall of the Berlin Wall in 1989 and the slow disintegration of the USSR. History was being created before my eyes, and now that I had some time on my hands, I thought it would be a shame not to witness the beginning of a new Russia, finally free of communism.

The nation had always fascinated me, right from the earliest days of my childhood, when I would take down the school atlas from the top of the teacher's press and trace the winding path of the Trans-Siberian Express from Moscow to Vladivostok. When I grew older, my mother told me that the vast landscapes that my dream-train traversed were dotted with prison camps and the people were detained against their will behind a great Iron Curtain. Later, at St Michael's College, I discovered the music of Tchaikovsky and Rimsky-Korsakov. Now I wanted to go and experience Russia for myself, especially at this time of political transformation.

*

The Aeroflot jet landed at Sheremetyevo Airport as the evening snow fell outside my window. After an hour's wait, I cleared customs and found the official state taxi that was to take me to the city. The service was provided by Intourist, a travel agency founded by Stalin, and I felt his long shadow hanging over me: an unusual sense of secretiveness prevailed in my conversation with the driver.

We travelled for about twenty minutes before dark grey silhouettes of buildings began to appear through the smoggy haze of the city's chimneys. The streets we passed were surreal, traders and cheap wooden stalls contrasted with the architectural splendours behind them. Their products appeared to be mostly traditional – Russian cigarettes and vodka – but there also seemed to be quite a lot of Western merchandise.

My hotel was a large, nineteenth-century, cast-iron and brick building situated near the street where Boris Yeltsin had climbed up onto a tank to protest the attempted coup by hard-line Communists, just a few months before. I made friends with some guests from Minsk, and we dined together that evening. The waiter was unacceptably rude, but this was something I grew accustomed to experiencing in the dying days of the Soviet Union. The next morning, there were noisy Communist demonstrations outside.

I left the hotel and took photographs of the ragged lines of Russian soldiers who huddled together in the chilly air outside empty supermarkets. They looked uncertain and dejected, and it was difficult to imagine that these men were the remnants of the mighty Red Army, which had stood against Nazi fascism and whose May Day parades had sent shivers down Western spines. Throughout this great nation's history, authoritarianism had always been the rule, but after seven decades, the whole system was collapsing from within. Yet, the citizens of Moscow whom I met still seemed to be the cheeriest of souls and displayed little of the xenophobia that I had imagined they would have. The opposite was true: everybody smiled when they met me.

I wandered the streets to the banks of the Moskva River, where featureless proletarian apartment blocks rose high into the far-off skyline – the dying symbols of a social experiment soon to be lost and gone forever. Enveloped in thought, I followed the sloping cobblestone streets to a great bridge across the river to west of the walls of the Kremlin. A soft snow fell as I entered Red Square, and, for a moment, I thought about how Batu Khan, the grandson of Genghis Khan, had burnt Moscow to the ground

I made my way to St Basil's, a cathedral built in classic Russian style. When Ivan the Terrible completed it in 1561, legend states that he blinded the architects so they could never recreate it. Napoleon allowed his troops to stable their horses there, but his attempt to blow up the building was, tradition has it, prevented by the town's people, who extinguished the burning fuses during his retreat. I did not fail to notice the irony of being surrounded by gilded cupolas, elaborate frescoes and all the iconography of these allegedly pagan people.

It was still snowing when I left the building. A group of soldiers approached me, their jackboots grinding the snow beneath their feet, their greatcoats swishing with each purposeful stride. They questioned me for a moment before posing to have their picture taken. Although we could only communicate in words of two syllables, they seemed open and friendly, curious about Ireland and what the weather was like there.

I caught a taxi with my friends to Belorussky railway station. The dreariness of the building and its dilapidated surroundings reminded me of Kreuzburg, a graffiti-scarred sector of Berlin. Nearby, I noticed many people queuing outside an empty supermarket. There were easily a hundred ragged people, standing in an untidy line outside a shop that was protected by metal grilles. Now and then, an unseen hand lifted the grille from inside and, as the shoppers exited, more were allowed through. I stopped by the queue to take a photograph. Most ignored my camera, turning their backs and concentrating on their places in the queue. I spoke to a female straggler at the end of the line. Her name was Olga Stawislavna, and, unlike me, she was dressed for the Russian weather, with her hat pulled well down over her ears, and her heavy coat stretching almost to her toes. A woollen scarf obscured the lower part of her face and, as a result, accentuated her warm, friendly eyes. Olga's English was good and, even if her heavy Russian accent was a little difficult to get used to, I liked its cadence and tone. I found out that she was a doctor who specialised in HIV/AIDS in children, and that she worked in a nearby hospital. I considered having one last test before going to Africa, although my chances of conversion at this stage were considered minimal. I was surprised when Olga told me that HIV was reaching epidemic levels in Russian cities. It seemed that nowhere escaped the tentacles of the virus.

Having found a shared interest, we talked for some time as the line of people slowly moved forward. I told her that I wanted to experience what life was like for ordinary people in Moscow. To my amazement, Olga invited me to stay in her apartment. She explained that she shared it with two engineers, one male, one female, and dismissed my worries that they might object. When it was her turn to go inside, she seemed to take it for granted that I would accompany her and, of course, I was curious to see the whole process.

We entered what can only be described as a type of supermarket, crammed with empty shelves and small display freezers with nothing inside. It was a bizarre sight. The citizens of Moscow were queuing for basic commodities like bread and sausages. They moved forward in a giant, silent conga line, compliantly awaiting their turn. There was no jostling or shouting, just the occasional soft murmur of complaint at the meagre amount of food available. People come together in times of need, I supposed, recognising the ineffectuality of creating a fuss – surviving as best they can.

Olga collected some bread and salami, sighing, no doubt embarrassed that these scanty supplies would have to feed an extra guest that night. We found a map and she showed me where her apartment was, on a street called Shirokaya Ulitsa near the Metro terminus Medvedkovo. It might seem unusual that somebody would invite a stranger to share their home, but those were different times, and travellers were often met with great kindness.

Olga's Spartan apartment was large and airy. The cold wind whistled through cracks in the wooden sash windows. The building harked back to a more lavish time, with little reminders scattered here and there, like opulent cornices on the ceiling, now crumbling in places due to neglect. Olga and her friends welcomed me into their home, apparently one of the better places to live in Moscow, and I smiled and hid my astonishment that three professional people should live in such a place. There was nothing wrong with it, they had all they needed, but I couldn't help contrasting it to the homes of those with similar educational backgrounds and work experience in the West.

Olga had appeared full-figured in her outdoor clothing but was actually quite petite. She tied her brown hair back from her pale face into a utilitarian bun at the nape of her neck. She didn't use any makeup, except for a little lipstick, and her well-worn clothes would have been thought old-fashioned, even by women of my mother's generation. This obviously wasn't a deliberate choice on her part, as her roommate dressed in much the same way, and both women immediately apologised for their lack of sartorial elegance. It surprised me how much they knew about Western fashion and exactly how far behind they were, so I just said, 'Neechevo, neechevo – pazhaloosta,' ('It's nothing, it's nothing – please'), which I believed was expected of me. This was my first introduction to "real" Russian women, and I discovered that I had unwittingly harboured preconceived notions that the communist ethos meant that they wouldn't care about such things.

In the West, we knew little or nothing about "them" except what we had heard on the news. In the days that followed, I discovered that they had no hostility towards us. Olga and her flatmate both wanted to leave Russia at the first opportunity and work in the United States. It was the first time I had given much consideration to how citizens from other parts of the world aspire just to embrace the life we tend to take for granted.

The next day, while Olga was at work, I paid a visit to Lenin's black Labradorite Mausoleum. Under the direction of the Soviet leadership, this political theorist had been transformed into an "immortal", his cadaver displayed in Red Square like some holy artefact. As the years passed, he became a largely fictional, god-like figure who served to legitimise both the state and those who claimed to be carrying on his original mission. By the time of my visit, the Russian people were confused – documents had been released that implicated Lenin in countless acts of revolutionary terror and barbarity, including his bloody campaign against the clergy and the kulaks. His mausoleum had become a symbol of the hopes and ambitions of a proud race who mistakenly thought they might provide a better life for their people. For more than seventy years, Russian people had stood in lines that often stretched along the length of the square, hoping to view his body. Now, as the wheels of history locked the cult of Lenin and the Soviet state together in a binding embrace, they both spiralled downward, leaving the revered mausoleum an unwanted reminder of a bygone era.

Evenings at Olga's were mainly spent in conversation after meals of salami and bread, their staple diet. My new friends felt that the West looked down on them, viewing them as inferior, not only in dress but in education and science. I told them that their scientists were respected, and the Kirov and Bolshoi ballet schools were also world-renowned. My small revelations pleased Olga and her friends. These people loved their country and they were aware of the pitfalls of communism.

After spending a month in their company, it was time for me to travel to Africa. I had secured a job as a registrar in a hospital in Cape Town and was going to travel there from Kenya overland with Truck Africa. I was due to leave from Mombasa in late February. Thesiger had been fond of Kenya, having spent many years there as a game warden, trying to control poaching. He had been fascinated by its varied wildlife and distinctive nomadic tribes and had made a series of long journeys on foot with camels to Lake Turkana and Marsabit. His description of tribal warriors dancing by moonlight, and the Maasai initiation ceremonies, recounted in his memoir *My Kenya Days*, was one of the things that made me want to travel through the country.

18. The Magic of Africa

As I stood by the waters of the mighty Zambezi and watched it flow over the edge of the Victoria Falls, it was easy to see why it was known as one of the most spectacular natural wonders of the world. Amidst the cavorting rainbows, the capering cascades, and the deafening roar of the largest curtain of water on earth, I felt at home with the real spirit of Africa. We stayed there for a week. In the evenings, we dined in the Victoria Falls Hotel, an opulent building in the grandest colonial style. I felt at home there, amidst the camphorous scent of flowering leleshwa, with the tawny vervet monkeys playing along the rooftop. Nobody wanted to leave that hallowed place, but eventually we did, travelling onwards to Zimbabwe.

The 1992 drought in Zimbabwe was horrific, the worst in living memory. The newspapers carried articles daily about children fainting from dehydration in the primary schools, and the nation once famed as the breadbasket of Southern Africa was experiencing food riots in the streets. I was sorry to see the fledgling nation in such a terrible state. It had always been special to me, even before independence, when it was still known as Rhodesia. My interest started when I shared a house in Dublin with my Rhodesian medical-student roommate, Greg. It was also influenced by Bob Marley's protest song *Zimbabwe*, which he released on the 1979 album *Survival* and played during the independence celebrations one year later. Because of these experiences, the tales of the old Rhodesia and the spirit of the new Zimbabwe had equal shares of my heart.

Whilst there, I wanted to immerse myself in the culture as much as I could. This meant I wanted to visit the grave of Cecil Rhodes, the person for whom the nation was originally named. Few of my friends shared my sense of nostalgia and, in the end, I decided to go to the Matopos Hills and see Rhodes's grave alone, cushioned by the promise that Richard and Victoria would meet me at the Selborne Hotel in Bulawayo a few days later.

The Selborne was the epitome of the former colonial era. With its carved arches and wide balconies, it was affectionately known to expatriates as "the Grand Old Lady of the South". It was there that I met an old couple who owned a tobacco farm some miles from town. Timothy drove a vintage green Austin 40 Farina that had caught my eye on the pavement outside the hotel. It reminded me of one driven by Johnny Keenan, back home in Garrison when I was young.

'Has she the 948cc engine?' I asked him.

'No, she's got the larger 1098cc,' he replied, with a warm smile.

The old farmer, whose grey hair fell over a cragged face, flickered to life as he spoke about his car. Our friendship grew over a few beers in the Selborne bar, and a fuller flush seemed to settle on his tanned face when he told me that he had been born on a farm about fifteen miles from Bulawayo. While the Johnnie Walker flowed, he reminisced about his childhood, fondly remembering journeys into town with his father.

'Africa was vastly different then,' he said. 'The streets of Bulawayo were beautifully decorated with hydrangeas and jacaranda, and everything and everybody had its place! Now the country is destroyed with bloody commie crooks in charge. The Zim dollar is worthless and half the kaffirs have AIDS!'

Timothy reminisced about a time when Rhodesia was called the "breadbasket of the world", and his father would pay the staff by the light of an old hurricane lamp on the veranda. He introduced me to his wife, who was from further south, near the gold fields of Mafikeng in South Africa. She told me she still remembered the day she arrived with her father on a steam train from Mafikeng, to find work at Timothy's farm. I loved their stories. For me, it was a privilege to be able to share an insight into their disappearing world.

They took me to see Rhodes's grave, and on the way, we visited the burial place of their only son. He had died on bush patrol, fighting "terrs" down on the Mozambique border some years before. Looking at their broken-hearted faces as they stood by his graveside, I knew that part of their spirit had died with him. I watched as Timothy sprinkled wildflowers on the ochre rocks around the grave, a symbolic action recognising those daring men who had fought in this inhospitable landscape to forge a new home. Now, President Robert Mugabe had threatened to send them all back to England.

That afternoon, the Zimbabwean newspapers carried headlines of a South African referendum, which promised to finally end Apartheid and lift the ban on the African National Congress (ANC). South African President F W de Klerk said a fundamental turning point had been reached: whites would help create a multiracial government. It was a historic time, and I thought about how the world was changing before my eyes: The Gulf War had ended, the Soviet Union had collapsed, and South Africa was bringing Apartheid to an end. Most amazing of all, I had had a ringside ticket to each event as it happened.

The Okavango Delta

From the wetlands of Botswana, we made our way back again to Zimbabwe, to a campsite on the outskirts of Harare, from where we would finish the journey to South Africa. Life there was strained, as the Zimbabwean police kept a watchful eye on travellers, eager to catch them exchanging money on the black market. April was approaching and my window for working as a doctor in South Africa was diminishing, so I took a minibus south to Johannesburg. From a distance, it looked like a mini-Manhattan rising from the African skyline. The bustling metropolis had developed because of gold being found in the flat hills of the Witwatersrand; it had no natural water supply. This gave it the distinction of being the largest city in the world not situated on a river, lake or coastline.

Johannesburg appeared to represent the free spirit of South Africa, but one had only to enter the city to encounter a different world, where streets patrolled by armed security men were clogged with poverty-stricken urban Africans, begging and hustling. The glass skyscrapers were surrounded by dilapidated Victorian buildings, which housed Indian bazaars and shops for traditional African herbal medicine. For the first time in Africa, we felt uncomfortable as we looked for accommodation in this chaotic mixture of different cultures, all competing to survive in the crowded, modern metropolis.

Rafting on the Zambezi

I awoke early the next day and took a taxi to visit Soweto, as I was keen to do a travel article for the *Fermanagh Herald*. The hostels there reminded me of the squalid conditions of the Moroccan workforce in Gibraltar, where a few hundred men shared one toilet. These were ordinary people, trying to eke out a living, often working long hours in the mines for somebody from another country. My visit to Soweto was a harrowing experience and one that I have never forgotten.

My next stop was Cape Town. I wanted to check out the possibility of finding some locum work at the Groote Schuur Hospital, where Marcel, my friend from Gibraltar, was working. It was a thousand-mile, overnight journey across the barren scrubland of the Great Karoo. The train arrived the next afternoon, and I found accommodation at the Cape Town English Guest House in Long Street. It was quite basic, really, but seemed like heaven to a hardened traveller who had been sleeping on the carpet of the African earth for most of the previous four months. In the room next to me was a tall, blonde-bearded Welsh university student called Simon. We shared some pints in the pubs around Long Street, discovered we had similar tastes in music and, within a short time, had become good friends.

At the Groote Schuur Hospital, I was surprised to find an Irish colleague from Our Lady of Lourdes Hospital in Drogheda.

'You can get a job as a locum working here, but everything has really changed,' Marcel said. 'It's now more gunshots than gallbladders. They've lost most of the better staff, and it's just like any other big African hospital now.'

He told me that there was a nice SHO locum job in cardiothoracic surgery going in a private hospital in Long Street. It seemed the better option. It was near the hotel, and I only had a short time to spend in South Africa before leaving to work as a doctor for Carnival Cruise lines in the United States.

Cape Town was beautiful, a scintillating jewel set in an amphitheatre of mountains at the southern tip of the African continent. I loved everything about the city. I somehow felt I'd lived there before, and on occasion, I felt I could one day make it my home. At evening time, when a thin layer of grey clouds draped Table Mountain, Simon and I would take the cable car up to where the trails of mist blurred the edges of the peaks and watch the sun setting over the shimmering city below. There, on that gigantic rock, poised between the heavens and the earth, we would sit and wait as the evening light descended over the southern tip of Africa.

Then, as the reds of sunset deepened into purples, and a sliver of white moon rose above the horizon, we would watch as the lights of the suburbs below twinkled to life in an orderly fashion. First to light up were the outdoor cafés along the Victoria and Albert Wharf. Five minutes later, the houses lit up on Robben Island, where Nelson Mandela had been imprisoned for so many years. Lastly, the yellow glimmers of the Primus stoves and the dancing bulbs lit by a thousand generators in the Cape Flat townships would brighten the wastelands to the east.

At weekends, we took turns in driving to the greenish-blue hillsides of Stellenbosch and Paarl, visiting the nearby Cape wineries. There are fewer things on earth more pleasurable than to spend a Saturday morning sipping some Pinotage wine amid those transplanted oak and pine trees. The landscapes of the wineries were breath-taking. Small turreted castles were set into undulating green hills smothered with vines nurtured from cuttings taken from France almost three centuries before. My favourite place was Constantia, known as "the Beverly Hills of Cape Town", because of its lush green vineyards and sprawling mansions decorated with magnificent artworks and old Cape Dutch furniture.

Despite the idyllic setting, the older problems of Africa were always close at hand. One night, while we were watching a Pink Floyd tribute band in one of the bars off Long Street, a commotion started at the door. We learnt that a couple of black clients wanted to enter, and the owner of the bar had set his dogs on them. One of the black men was bleeding from a dog bite on his arm, and the dogs were jumping excitedly as a crowd of onlookers gathered. Such was the power of Apartheid that, at first, none of the customers wanted to stand up against this blatant discrimination – this was their bar, and no black had ever had a beer at the counter. We watched in horror as the owner unleashed the dogs on the other man. The band were playing *Us and Them* when Simon left my side to face down the owner and the rest of his thugs. Africa was changing, and they would have to accept the winds of change. A fight started and, of course, I rowed in and ended up getting in one or two punches before we were asked to leave.

Although racism, at least superficially, appeared to be less prevalent in the Cape than the Transvaal, problems with the rising crime rate were everywhere. One morning, when I went out to my car, I found a young African man trying to break into it. The object of his desire appeared to be the cassette player. He told me that he had two small children and no way to feed them. I didn't know whether to hand him over to the authorities. I decided not to.

Instead, impressed with his honesty and tempted by curiosity, I offered to drive him back to the shanty townships of the Cape Flats, where I could elaborate on an article, that I had written for the *Fermanagh Herald* about the townships in Soweto. His eldest daughter, Danile, was a slender girl with coffee-coloured eyes, and a mischievous smile. I played with her for a while and thought about her destiny in this land of Africa.

19. Becoming a Ship's Surgeon

In late May 1992, I flew from Cape Town to Miami to meet Dr Moses Herzenhorn, medical director of Carnival Cruise Lines. He was Bolivian and had worked for many years as a doctor at sea before assuming medical command of the whole Carnival operation. He had ten ships under his control and was responsible for all medical operations aboard them. We shared a pleasant lunch in Bayside, a waterfront shopping area near Biscayne Boulevard. It was a beautiful spring afternoon, and as the sun glinted from the clear water on the bay, it made me feel a little better about leaving Cape Town and coming to America. 'I don't normally put new British doctors on the bigger ships, but I like the fact you have Advanced Trauma Cardiac and Life Support,' he said. 'I'm going to put you on the *Jubilee* over in California. It has a six-bed hospital and a coronary care unit.'

Moses told me that being a doctor at sea is different from being a doctor in any other environment. By way of explanation, he told me that the previous evening, one of his doctors had seen a twenty-seven-year-old galley steward with a painful, swollen testis. It could have been a torsion (a twisted spermatic cord), requiring emergency surgery, or simple viral epididymitis, requiring only painkillers. The doctor had no ultrasound on board to confirm a diagnosis and decided to evacuate the patient by helicopter. Everybody on board saw the dramatic evacuation. Imagine his embarrassment when the smiling patient was waiting on the quayside in Mexico the next morning when the ship docked.

'What would you have done?' Moses asked me.

'I'd have evacuated him and taken no chances,' I told him. Moses drove me back to my hotel by way of the palm-lined MacArthur Causeway, where rows of cruise ships with Carnival's coloured funnels emerged on the skyline like a pack of giant whales' tails. There were also ships there bearing the markings of Royal Caribbean and Norwegian Cruise Lines.

'Welcome to the cruise-ship capital of the world,' Moses said. 'You see that big ship up ahead in the distance – that's the *Ecstasy* – Carnival's newest ship. When you've spent some time in California, I'll bring you back here and put you on that ship. It's the biggest in the fleet and, being in port in Miami, you'll be closer to Ireland.'

I flew to Los Angeles and boarded the *Jubilee*. Once aboard, I changed into my new uniform and made my way to the bridge to introduce myself to the master of the vessel, Captain Giampaolo Casula. Judy, one of the nurses, dropped by to say hello and to give me a beeper. The bridge was mostly staffed by Italian officers. They were chatting together, preoccupied with getting the large ship out of port. I wandered amongst them. The captain, whom I recognised by the four gold bars on his epaulets, lifted his head from one of the maps and glanced at me.

'Ah, Patrick, the new doctor! I've seen your CV, it's particularly good,' he said. 'However, I don't want a good doctor on board my ship – I want a lucky one.'

The captain explained that he didn't want to have to turn the ship back to port with a medical emergency and be late to the next port. He'd have to listen to Miami saying they would have to pay a lot of money to the tour busses and the stores for business losses.

'Try also not to get any "notifiable" diseases,' he continued.

I could see why the captain wanted a lucky doctor. For the first time in my medical career, I would be serving two masters – the Hippocratic Oath and Carnival Cruise Lines. This conflict would later become problematic, when I had to decide whether to treat seriously ill foreign staff in the United States or send them back home with a monetary payoff.

The captain took me to his office and gave me a small blue book with the gold-embossed words "Seaman's Identification and Record Book Republic of Liberia". He opened a page and stamped it with the company seal, recording my first day at sea: May 24, 1992.

On the way back to my cabin, I listened to the clipped English accent of the cruise director on the tannoy, 'Welcome aboard and bon voyage! We're on board the superliner *Jubilee* sailing to Mexico on a seven-day cruise to Puerto Vallarta, Mazatlán and Cabo San Lucas. We hope you have a good cruise – happy sailing.'

*

The evening clinic started at six o'clock. Nurse Judy told me that the infirmary was always busy, and we had a separate crew and passenger clinics daily, each serving about ten to fifteen patients.

Working as a Ships Surgeon on the M/S Jubilee

'The first patient has lost his T-tube – from his gall bladder!' she said.

She introduced me to a pleasant septuagenarian called Stanley, from Las Vegas, who had recently been in hospital for the removal of his gallstones. It appeared that his surgeon removed the stones but left a T-shaped rubber drainage tube behind to allow the bile juices to drain into a small bag. The tube was to be left in place for three weeks and then removed when everything had healed. Unfortunately, the tube was now missing, and the patient didn't know what had happened to it. It had disappeared while he was crossing the Mojave Desert, and the hole in his abdomen was now leaking bile fluid onto his clothes.

'What are we going to do?' said Judy. 'We'll be at sea for the next three days – we could get him seen by one of the surgeons in Mazatlán, but he'll pour off his bile juices onto his clothes, and he's bound to get an infection through that opening.'

I pondered the problem and decided that the tube couldn't have gone back inside. In the end, I decided to manufacture a new tube from a urinary catheter bag. Thankfully, the device started to work almost immediately. I fastened it to the patient with superglue. The tubing was still working the next morning, and the superglue held until we returned to Los Angeles at the end of the cruise. I took great pleasure in reading his letter to me later:

'The following day we drove 290 miles back to Las Vegas, Nevada, and home. I went to the hospital and had a new tube inserted to drain my biliary tract. The "crazy glue" let loose easily, and the hospital personnel had little trouble getting the bag off my side. The surgeon told me you did a great job, and you are a great credit to the medical profession.'

At the end of the clinic, the nurse told me there was a woman in one of the cabins who kept telling staff she saw bees in her room. 'But they've checked, and there's nothing there,' the nurse said.

'She even points to them. They think she's mad!'

She told me that it was difficult to deal with a psychiatric emergency at sea. This type of patient often required constant monitoring in the infirmary in case they jumped overboard.

We went to her suite together. It had a large balcony overlooking the sea. The lady was an elderly German who spoke little English and was travelling alone. She was dressed in a bathrobe, hugging the bathroom door and trying to breathe through the clouds of insect spray provided by her diligent galley steward.

'Look at them everywhere!' she said, pointing to her sparkling jewellery on the table.

I lifted the jewellery and carried it over to her. Her panicked reaction assured me that she thought I would be stung. When I threw some of the glittering earrings into the air, her reaction confirmed my suspicions – she was having a visual hallucination! Her medical history revealed that her doctor in Hamburg had recently put her on Tryptizol for trigeminal neuralgia. It was better known to me as amitriptyline, a well-known cause of visual hallucinations.

The remainder of the first few days provided the usual plethora of passengers with ear barotrauma after flying, crew members with gastroenteritis, falls and injuries. These took a lot of time to document properly, to guard against the risk of an insurance claim.

After three days of sailing, we reached the coastal town of Puerto Vallarta, nestled in the foothills of the Sierra Madre Mountains and beside the tranquil waters of Banderas Bay. I wandered along the cobblestone streets of the esplanade, eyeing the far-off white *casitas* snuggled into the hillsides as if they were suspended in space. The town retained an old-world charm, and donkey carts rattled along amongst the buses and taxis. Things moved slowly; the pace of life seemingly dictated more by the turning of the tides than the raising of tequila glasses. The town was famous, as Richard Burton and Elizabeth Taylor had arrived in 1963 to film *The Night of the Iguana*, and they had settled in the locality after filming ended.

I listened as the noon bell struck loudly from the Church of Our Lady of Guadalupe and watched as older women blessed themselves and said prayers by the little sidewalk stalls. There was something familiar about Mexico. Maybe it was the Angelus bell, the Madonna icons or the rosaries that reminded me of an older Irish generation, my home in Garrison, and my parents preparing us for evening devotions.

A rising breeze carried the mournful chimes of the bell towards the Cuale River, where washerwomen gathered their clothes from the bougainvillea plants and made their way back home to prepare for lunch. Then came the sound of a wandering mariachi band, playing *La Cucaracha* for some American tourists from the cruise ship. The driver of an old flatbed truck hooted loudly as he tried to clear a path around a broken donkey cart blocking his way. A group of workmen stood huddled together on the back of his gaily painted vehicle, uninterested in the altercation.

That evening, I caught the last tender back to the cruise ship, which made a magnificent sight as it lay anchored in the harbour.

A few days later, a galley steward named José came to see me.

'My mother has a problem that her doctor cannot fix – she's very sick – *empacho*!' he said.

I knew from my experiences in Gibraltar that the word "*empacho*" can be a general term for stomach illness. I wondered why he thought I could do something other doctors couldn't, but my mind was made up when he told me that the family lived in one of the little white *casitas* on the hillsides surrounding the town; I would visit his mother and see if I could help.

The next time the ship docked in Puerto Vallarta, we took a taxi up the narrow, winding roads to the little houses in the tropical vegetation on the

190

hillside. The driver stopped outside a tin-roofed house, where an old grey donkey stood tethered to an outside wall. We entered the homestead, and José introduced me to his sister, Maria, who, with typical Latin hospitality, gave me the best seat in the house and a small meal of *tortas fritas de maíz y salsa*. Then he took me to a dimly lit room where his mother was lying on a bed. She raised herself on one elbow to look at me.

'*Tengo empacho*,' she said weakly reaching out to hold my hand. '*Tengo empacho.*'

I bent down and put my stethoscope on her abdomen, thankful to discover that her bowel sounds were present. In the poor light, it was difficult to know exactly what was happening, but her pulse was quite rapid, and I thought she felt feverish. Just as I was going to request a urine sample, José put something furry into my left hand.

It was a small ball of hair.

I looked at him, unsure of what to do. He whispered to me that he wanted me to make it appear that it came from her tummy. I bent over the old woman again, cupping my hands, first concealing the hairball and then producing it for inspection. The old lady gripped my hand and started shouting praises to the Lady of Guadeloupe.

'Thank you, Doctor Patrick,' José said. 'She believes in the old Mexican ways and thinks an evil spirit, or a witch put the hairball in her.'

Although I had been taken advantage of by José, in those few minutes, I learnt more about healing than six years of college had taught me. To make some sense of disease, societies had established their ritualistic behaviours, hoping to gain control. This is how bloodletting, and exorcism had gained popularity. It was still quite normal also to see scars on the bodies of South American crew members from "cupping", that ancient form of alternative medicine in which a local suction is created on the skin. Practitioners believe that this mobilises blood flow to promote healing.

*

Some weeks later, we got a new Italian captain, Leonardo Francolla, who was in charge on a September night when we shared an emergency at sea. It was almost five in the morning when the beeper went off. We were on the second day of our journey, heading along the Baja peninsula with the coast of Mexico on our port side. This meant that we were outside US territorial waters, without the US Coast Guard to help evacuate patients in case of emergencies.

I wandered sleepily down the corridor, wondering what interesting ailment lay ahead of me. Linda, one of the nurses, met me at the door of the infirmary. She looked distressed.

'I have a young woman from New York with severe abdominal pain, probably a bout of gastroenteritis,' she said. 'She has no fever or diarrhoea and her husband is here with her.'

I knew by the look on the nurse's face that all was not well. Walking into the isolation ward, I saw a young girl in her early twenties wearing a light green negligee. She appeared to be in agony, screaming in a New York accent. Her husband stood beside her, holding her hand. I asked him to leave while I examined his wife.

The cause of her pain quickly became apparent. She was in the final stages of labour.

'When did you have your last period?' I asked.

'Four weeks ago,' she said. 'I'm regular as clockwork,' she continued, gyrating in pain to the rhythm of another contraction.

On completion of a pelvic examination, I was shocked to feel that the baby's head was already crowning. Our patient was going to deliver much sooner than we expected. Linda was a good nurse, with obstetric experience, but neither of us was prepared for a birth at sea. Despite my best efforts to gain control of the situation, the baby's head started to appear. I tried to rotate it as I pulled down to get a shoulder out, but there was a spiral of cord loosely wound around the baby's neck, preventing it from moving another inch.

We were at least two hundred miles from the nearest American port. The cord wouldn't unwind, and the infant's colour was a light shade of blue. If I cut it, I might deprive the baby of oxygen – if I didn't, the baby could die. Linda gave the mother some Entonox gas and found me an obstetric kit.

'Vicki, do I cut the cord or not?' I whispered above the wails of a patient who was going through the full pain of labour.

After some tense minutes and a small tear, the baby slowly emerged from the birth canal and started to cry. I cut the cord and the mother took over. The cries of the slippery mass in the nurse's arms brought the father running back into the improvised delivery suite.

'We have a *baby*?' he said, almost crying with delight.

'Yes, a beautiful little girl,' the mother said, smiling adoringly at the baby.

'Oh, she's beautiful!' the father replied. 'Now what will we call her?'

Just then, I realised that I still hadn't informed Captain Francolla, as everything had happened so quickly. I went up to the bridge, and together we put a statement of birth at sea into the log. Then I returned to the hospital, where I learnt that the couple had decided to name their daughter Julianne, after the ship, *Jubilee*. And with that, little Julianne became the newest passenger on board.

The new parents, Scott and Elizabeth, sent me a lovely letter a few weeks after they disembarked. It said Julianne was twenty-four inches long and weighed eleven pounds. She can travel free for the rest of her life on the *Jubilee*. We remain good Facebook friends to this day, as I follow her progress through journalism school in New York.

*

The *Jubilee* went into dry dock for that Christmas period of 1992, and I returned to Ireland. I left that February to take up a position on the *Ecstasy*, sailing from Miami. I was glad to learn that Franklin, the chief steward, and Tom, the head of food and beverage, from the *Jubilee,* would also be sailing. It was nice to have familiar faces on board, and it made life much easier when trying to get favours done, like getting spills cleaned up or meals sent down to patients and staff. One night, Tom phoned to say that a Haitian cook was deeply disturbed and believed he was under a voodoo spell. He thought he would die unless he got off the ship immediately. The situation instantly reminded me of the soldier who had felt he could see the apparition of St John the Baptist and had died in my arms at the Ibn al-Bitar Hospital in Baghdad. Cultural religious beliefs, often promoted by guilt, fear and shame, can have deep mental effects on a patient, so I didn't take the situation lightly.

We transferred the hallucinating patient to the ship's infirmary. Before long, some of his work colleagues gathered outside the door, holding lighted candles and chanting monotonously. They didn't try to gain entry, but the patient became more and more agitated. The nurses were scared that unless we sedated him, he could easily jump overboard. The head of security, David Kelleher arrived and told me that the group outside were chanting to a voodoo spirit, and they wanted to get a Haitian priest on board to exorcise the patient. The drugs we were using could only sedate the patient for short periods, and he showed no evidence of any pathology, infection, or other cause of his almost delusional state. Franklin visited the infirmary and told me about some of the voodoo beliefs that he had encountered as a child in Jamaica. What little I knew about voodoo I had learnt from Hollywood films, but I did not fear it. Eventually, as a last resort, I tried some hypnosis, which I had been medically trained to use in Scotland. The patient appeared to respond, and the nurses asked me to continue. Within about fifteen minutes, he had almost become manageable, but I asked the nurses and security to monitor him overnight until he could safely disembark the next morning and be taken to a hospital in San Juan, Puerto Rico.

Working on the *Ecstasy* was a wonderful experience. I had grown comfortable with the various aspects of my new nautical career and felt confident that I could handle any emergency at sea. It is well known that if the crew trust their doctor, staff morale increases. The new ports we visited with the *Ecstasy* included a route known as "The Western and Eastern Caribbean". The Western Caribbean cruise visited Cozumel, Mexico, the Cayman Islands, and Jamaica; it was followed the next week by the eastern Caribbean cruise to the eastern Bahamas, San Juan, Puerto Rico and the Virgin Islands. Most of the crew looked forward to the western route, especially the white sandy beaches of Ocho Rios and the party atmosphere of a pub called Carlos and Charlie's in Cozumel.

The western route also brought us to the lush green foothills of St Anne Parish, Jamaica, where Bob Marley was buried. Bob's mausoleum was in the hilltop hamlet of Nine Mile, about ninety minutes from where the cruise ship docked. These were the same hills where the spirits of runaway African slaves lingered and people believed in Rastafarianism, a religion based on Ethiopian culture. The belief developed in Jamaica during the 1930s, when labour unrest on the island led to the deaths of striking sugarcane workers.

They believed that their salvation lay not in a white man's heaven, but back in their homeland of Africa.

One of the Carnival pursers, Richard Lloyd, jokingly read some Rastafarian literature he had found in Ocho Rios to me as we made our way up the hillsides to the grave. The brochure quoted from Leviticus 21:5: 'They shall not make baldness upon their head, neither shall they shave off the corner of their beard, nor make any cuttings in their flesh.'

'Ah, so therefore Rastafarians like dreadlocks,' Richard said.

At Bob Marley's Grave

The Rastafari also used other biblical quotations to support their practices, such as Psalms 104:14, which they used to sanctify their use of cannabis: 'He causeth the grass to grow for the cattle, and herb for the service of man, that he may bring forth food out of the earth.' It reminded me of some of the Christian religious zealots in Northern Ireland, who also quoted Leviticus 18:22: 'Thou shalt not lie with mankind, as with womankind: it is *toevah*.' Using the old text as moral guidance has its limitations, as the word *toevah* does not even mean "abomination".

The use of cannabis was not only legal but encouraged at the mausoleum. Some children even sold "spliffs" near the entrance. Respectfully, we took off our shoes and joined some believers sitting on rocks near a small hut. Overhead hung a picture of the former Ethiopian ruler, Emperor Haile Selassie, who visited the island in 1966. One of the men offered me a smoke from a long pipe.

'Ya know mon,' he said, 'Bob himself wrote da song *Three Little Birds* restin' on dat very rock you are sittin' on.'

For a while, he looked at me, calculating, measuring me up as he slowly inhaled again. Silence descended as his eyes glazed over, his speech slowed, and the perfumes of the nearby flowering plants mixed with the sweet aroma of ganja.

'It's all about respect mon,' he said.

Richard and I took the taxi back along the road, up to the tiny hamlet, where we stopped for a while. I looked down over the tin shacks and wondered how a man born into such abject poverty could have been so influential in my life. Religions are often known to reflect the environments from which they emerge, and many of the Caribbean islands – especially Haiti – had developed new religions or maintained their old ones in hybrid forms.

Later in 1993, I joined the *Fantasy* leaving Port Canaveral, close to the famous rocket-launch site from which *Apollo 11* had blasted off on its mission to the moon in 1969. I still remember the pictures of the moon landing on our black-and-white television at home. One morning, I was privileged to watch the spectacular dawn lift-off of the space shuttle *Columbia* on its five-million-mile, fourteen-day journey into space. It was a humid morning and we stood together by the rail of the ship.

It started quietly, a startled bird on the wing, a change in the wind, a faint yellow light at the edge of the far horizon. The light continued to grow as a pillar of fire detached itself from its umbilical tower and started its journey heavenward. I watched in silence, feeling privileged to witness man's challenge to the gods. Enthralled, we watched *Columbia* climb as the bright golden glow softened into saffron and swirled into a canvas of reds and greys that melted back into the light of the coming dawn. The air around us became thin and heady and as everybody started clapping, I thought about the men inside, those special people who regarded the challenge of space travel as part of their daily existence.

*

I continued as a doctor on Carnival's cruise ships until 1994. Because of a deepening love of Mexico, I decided to return to Puerto Vallarta and stay there for a few months before traveling across the country. I intended visiting old friends in Guadalajara, capital of Jalisco, and Guanajuato, home to the mummified remains of locals who died during an outbreak of cholera in the mid-19th century. It was during this period living in Mexico. I discovered that Mexicans have a very different relationship with death and the departed than other nations. The dead are not feared, possibly even revered, and they even have a public holiday to remember their ancestors called the *Día de los Muertos*. It reminded me somewhat of our own Halloween traditions, which had originated from ancient Celtic harvest festivals, especially the Gaelic festival of Samhain. Both probably had pagan roots; Samhain was recognised as Halloween by the early Irish Church and the Spanish moved the Mexican feast day to coincide with the Triduum of All Hallowtide – All Saints' Eve, All Saints' Day, and All Souls' Day.

Later that year, I returned to Dublin and worked in the ER of St Vincent's University Hospital and the Meath Hospital. During that time, I became friendly with Dr Oliver Keenan, who helped me to cope with the fact that Trish was marrying someone else that year. On that day, I sent her a large bouquet and wished her luck. My mother hugged me and said, 'That's the hardest thing you've ever had to do – now let's put it to bed and get on with the rest of your life.'

One day, I saw an advertisement in the *Irish Medical Times* offering work for after-hours deputising doctors in Australia. The thought of sunny days living in Melbourne appealed to me. My application was successful, and the medical group wanted me to start straightaway.

20. The Flying Doctor

I arrived in Melbourne, Australia's second-largest city, in February 1996. It was a nice city, with old green-and-yellow trams that clinked their way through tree-lined avenues, giving the city a feeling of tranquillity and ease of pace. In some ways, it reminded me of Cape Town, as wineries – with exotic-sounding names like the Macedon Ranges, the Yarra Valley, and the Mornington Peninsula – enclosed the city on all sides. I rented a house in Toorak, an expensive suburb filled with art galleries, elegant shops, and picturesque red-tiled period buildings. Nearby was bohemian St Kilda, where houses with white fretwork handrails and ornate wooden windows, once favoured by the gentry, had long been abandoned to students. It was also the centre of the city's red-light district.

One day, over breakfast, I read an article about Men at Work, a Scottish-Australian rock band who were reuniting in an old hotel in St Kilda after a ten-year absence from playing together. They had achieved international success in the 1980s with their hit single *Down Under*. Their farewell concert was within walking distance of my lodgings, and I decided to go and see them. After the concert, as I was making my way back home along Grey Street, I noticed two streetwalkers on one the corners up ahead of me. One was bent over the other, who appeared to be in difficulty on the ground, and she started shouting for someone to help them. I ran over and saw that the young woman on the ground was almost unconscious and considered the possibility she was suffering from a drug overdose.

'Has she taken anything?' I asked, calling for an ambulance with my mobile phone and identifying myself to the switchboard as a Victoria state-registered practitioner.

Within a short time, the ambulance arrived, lights flashing.

'So, Doc, what do you think is happening here?' asked the emergency medical technician (EMT). 'Is she a heroin overdose?'

There was something about her deteriorating condition that made me doubt that. Maybe it was the dilated pupils, the stridor in her breathing, or my sixth sense, but I was unwilling to go along with the obvious diagnosis.

'Has she taken heroin?' the EMT asked her friend. 'Yes, she had some earlier in the evening.'

'I thought so,' the EMT said, rifling through the ambulance emergency bag for some Naloxone, a powerful drug that specifically acts on the brain to counter the effects of a heroin or morphine overdose.

'Do you want me to give the Naloxone, Doc? Will I draw up 0.4 milligrams?'

'No,' I said, still trying to establish the cause of her difficulty.

Her case was baffling. Normally, a heroin overdose would have tiny fixed pupils, but this patient had the exact opposite. The patient was deteriorating before our eyes and had turned blue, but I remained calm and tried to establish the correct diagnosis. Medicine must be exact, as the consequence of a mistake can be the loss of someone's life.

'Doc, you have to decide. We're gonna lose her, and the IV Naloxone won't do her much harm,' the EMT said.

That was not true, as the drug had a lot of side effects, including heart-rhythm changes, seizures, and sudden chest pain, and I knew that it should not be used if the diagnosis was in doubt.

'No, give her adrenaline,' I said. 'Half a mig of one in a thousand IM.'

'Adrenaline? Are you sure?' he said, reluctantly handing me the prefilled syringe. I thrust it into her leg and, almost immediately, the patient started to recover.

Her first words to her friend were, 'Fruit and nut chocolate? I told you I was fucking allergic to nuts!'

As the ambulance team shepherded the two women away, their leader turned to shake my hand.

'You certainly made the right decision there. Who'd have believed it – a bloody allergy to hazelnuts? Fair dinkum to you, Doc.'

*

The work at the deputising agency proved to be rewarding. On any given night, I would see a diverse range of conditions, from a woman going into labour, preparing to bring a new life into the world, to the other end of the spectrum –

an older patient who had reached the end and was dying at home. The Australian medical authorities recognised the problems doctors had working late at night and limited the number of opiates that we could dispense to patients in a month. One had to be resistant to the charms of the chronically migrainous and the pancreatic patient looking for shots of pethidine. It was difficult for me to turn them away, but if I didn't, I would just be a soft touch, and they would make a habit of phoning up when I was on duty. I'd seen it happen to one or two less-experienced colleagues.

As the weeks passed, I gradually got to know the other doctors working for the deputising company. Most came from English-speaking countries, especially the United Kingdom, South Africa, and Canada. Initially, we met only when we passed on the stairs or while handing in our reports.

One day, a doctor asked if I was from Ireland, and I nodded. 'I'm from Mayo,' he said. 'The name's Ray Brennan.'

Ray was a good-humoured sort who had been working with the deputising service for the previous six months. He had a large house in Box Hill, a more Asian part of the city, and was looking for someone to share the rent. As I was living alone in Toorak, I decided to take him up on the offer. We sometimes met up while on duty in the middle of the night and visited patients together. One of these patients, a crocodile hunter, lived fifty miles away in the Mornington Peninsula. He suffered from phantom limb pain in a missing arm, which he had lost to one of the reptiles. It was difficult to drive so far just to give a patient pethidine for pain in an absent limb, but this was a recognised neurological illness and had to be treated accordingly.

Melbourne was a great city for sport, and Ray and I both went to see the Australian rules football, which had many similarities to Gaelic football in Ireland. I adopted the Carlton "Blues" as my favourite, while Ray favoured the Collingwood "Magpies". Both used the Melbourne Cricket Ground as their headquarters, and we looked forward to dressing up in gear and going to the matches. Melbourne was also home to the opening round of the 1996 Formula One Grand Prix. I was lucky to be allowed to work as a medical doctor associated with the track.

In late spring, Ray's mother died, and he went back to Ireland for the funeral. I was at a loose end when he left and decided to try for a position with the Royal Flying Doctor Service in Broken Hill. This was an ideal opportunity to combine work with pleasure and experience some of the Australian outback at the same time. I passed the interview process, no doubt helped by the fact that three of the interviewers had direct or familial connections to Ireland. The fact that I was a qualified GP, an advanced trauma life-support instructor and had many years of emergency-room medicine probably helped as well.

With the Royal Flying Doctors in Broken Hill

Broken Hill is a remote mining city in the far west outback of New South Wales. The station had been the location for the '80s television show *The Flying Doctors*. The town had received its name from an entry in the diary of explorer Charles Sturt, who mined silver ore there in 1883. The break in the hills that the explorer noted no longer existed, having long since been mined away. The Royal Flying Doctor Service (RFDS) was started by Rev John Flynn, superintendent of the Australian Inland Mission about forty-five years later. In the early days, it was called the Aerial Medical Service, and it provided emergency and primary healthcare for people living in remote areas of Australia.

I was excited about my new position, and my colleagues in Melbourne started to tell me stories they had heard about the RFDS. One of them referred to the medical chests that everybody in outback properties had, for treating different conditions. The chests contained prescription-only medication, and the drugs inside could only be used by licence on the telephone advice of an RFDS medical practitioner. To help prevent abuse, the drugs in the chests were coded using a simple numbering system known only to RFDS medical officers. The story concerned an old stockman who called the Flying Doctors one day about his sick wife who had a pain going down her left arm.

'Has she any history of angina or heart trouble?' the Flying Doctor asked.

'Yes, Doc, what am I going to do?'

'Open the chest and take two tablets from tray number six, this is Angised – a heart medicine. Put them under her tongue, and we'll get a plane out to you immediately.'

The plane landed on the old man's property sometime later, and the old man came running up, shouting, 'I think we saved her, Doc!'

However, he proceeded to tell the doctor that when he had gone to tray six, it had been empty.

'So, what did you do?'

'I gave her a number four and a number two, and she came up fine!'

*

There were three doctors in our team: John from New Zealand, Tim from Cornwall, and me. We shared the RFDS house in the town and got on extremely well. On occasion, we had to drive to the hospital in Wilcannia, a small town two hundred kilometres east of Broken Hill. The town had once been one of the biggest inland ports in Australia, on the Darling River, which snaked through, carrying bales of merino wool under the coolabah trees and out to the harbours on the south coast. With the advent of the railroad, the town lost its significance, and many people drifted away.

The hospital was staffed by older nurses, experienced in doing X-rays and stitching whatever lacerations came their way. One of our duties was to do a weekly ward round in the hospital, which was mainly filled with local Barkindji people, eager to be discharged.

'This is George, a forty-three-year-old Aboriginal male with haematemesis for two days,' a nurse told me on one of my visits.

Haematemesis was the medical term for vomiting blood, and it could be profoundly serious in some circumstances, especially if the patient had ripped the lining of the stomach. It was usually associated with excessive alcohol intake, although one had to be careful that there was not a gastric tumour on board. He had been "scoped" a few times at the Broken Hill base hospital, and the nurses usually discharged him with medication after he had settled.

'Well, George, what happened to you?' I asked.

'I fell out with the lady from the lake,' he replied.

I was amused by his reply but thought little more about it and went to see the patient in the next bed. My next patient was something of a surprise: a one-hundred-and-fifty-kilogram male victim of domestic violence. I was intrigued when he also told me that he "fell out with the lady from the lake".

'We've done a skull X-ray, Dr Treacy, and he had a small parietal fracture, but his neuro obs have been OK for the past two days, so we're just letting him home,' the nurse told me.

Next, we reviewed a fifty-four-year-old white female suffering from gallstones, awaiting transfer to the base hospital for removal of her gall bladder. This condition can be extremely painful, and patients are often admitted for analgesia before they are operated on. These procedures had been done in Wilcannia hospital in the past, but the facility had been downgraded as the population had diminished.

After that was a below-the-knee amputee with Type 1 diabetes, who had sustained some facial lacerations when he had fallen from his wheelchair and had been kept in for observation. His home circumstances weren't good, but he seemed to be a favourite with the nurses.

'So, what happened to you?' I said.

When the patient told me, he had "fallen out with the lady from the lake", I had to take the nurse aside and ask her what the saying meant.

'Well, the native Aboriginal population here likes to drink those cheap three-litre boxes of red wine,' the nurse explained. 'They can't pronounce "Cabernet Sauvignon", so they call it by the Renoir picture on the outside. It's of a gentleman rowing a lady in a boat on a lake. It's responsible for a lot of business around here.'

There was little doubt that the Aboriginal population, like many displaced populations everywhere, had a problem with alcohol. It was sad to see these indigenous people, who had lived on this land for nearly 45,000 years, fighting in the parks and letting their children run around unwashed because of this addiction.

On the way back home, I visited an outback pub. The bar was a blurry canvas of khaki Akubra hats, Coopers Brewery beer mats and blue NSW Waratahs rugby shirts. As at most outback pubs, the only women present were those serving behind the bar.

'Where are you from, mate?' said an overindulged Aboriginal jackaroo standing at the corner of the bar. He was a squat man with broad shoulders and a muscular body, and it was evident that many hard years of drinking grog had made him look older than his years.

'Ireland,' he said.

'Ireland? My second name is O'Brien!' he said, taking out his driving licence and throwing it on the bar counter.

During the evening, he became boisterous and got a warning from the barman. Before long, he started shouting at another customer and, when he began fighting, staff intervened and showed him to the door. I watched him as he left; a mischievous grin lit up his craggy face as he came back up to me.

'You know, mate,' he said, 'that's the bloody problem with us Irish everywhere we go, we just can't hold our drink!'

*

About twenty-five kilometres northwest of Broken Hill lay the iconic outback town of Silverton. The town had a brief but spectacular career during the silver-mining era of the 1880s, but fell into decline as the more significant, wealthier mines in nearby Broken Hill became more successful. Silverton was not quite a ghost town, but there were only around fifty people living there. It had appeared in over one hundred films and commercials, including Bryan Brown's *Dirty Deeds*, *Mad Max 2* and *The Adventures of Priscilla, Queen of the Desert*. On weekends, I loved to visit Peter Browne's gallery there, with his collection of VW Beetles painted as emus. It never ceased to amaze me how people there could eke out a living in such a hostile environment.

My favourite hour in the outback was just before dawn, when everything was covered in a blanket of darkness and no wind blew. There was a feeling of solitude in the air, a strange mixture of loneliness and expectation, and I often thought about life in Ireland. There was magic in the awakening morning, as the colours of the sandy environment began to change, and daylight spilled across the plains, washing away the night. On one such morning, I watched an old Aboriginal woman approaching along the dirt track that snaked through the back of the town. She walked with slow shuffling steps, dragging oversized shoes through the red dust, which rose in plumes about her. The dust settled on her ragged clothing, coating her unkempt hair and rounded face, filling in each jagged line.

The old lady was Barkindji, a people supposedly charged with the custodianship of the land and all living things upon it. Her people lived in a collection of dirty tin shacks that nestled around the bank of the Darling River, a sleepy place where children ran naked through the paprika sand and lethargic dogs stretched and scratched in the midday sun. She carried a small stick, possibly to poke for roots or catch one of the lizards that darted across the desert floor. Eventually, she stopped just beneath my patio and began looking at some old stones, which littered the edge of the roadside. For a while, we stared at each other as her unwavering eyes looked deep inside me and told me tales about her people's lost dignity. I watched her for a moment, before turning away, embarrassed by the intimacy. The irreverent cackle of a blue-winged kookaburra called out loudly from a nearby tree, as if he recognised my shame. Suddenly, the old woman got up and left, wandering further out into the bush, turning now and then in the desert landscape as if she was equipped with some hidden scrubland Sat-Nav. In the distance, I watched her continue this ritual, pausing to sit on the ground at regular intervals and wished to get closer to her, to understand all things in the Aboriginal culture that were denied to me.

Another morning, I was on the veranda with Tim, listening to the sounds of a distant thunderstorm brewing and the tinkling of some raindrops on our roof. The atmosphere was full of mystery and one could almost smell scorched rain in the morning sky. The phone rang and, as I was on call, I answered it. It was Maureen, a nurse at Tibooburra, calling to say they had a female patient with acute abdominal pain to be airlifted to the base hospital. Tibooburra was a gold-rush town in red-sand country up at the very corner of New South Wales.

'What's the landing strip like?' I asked.

'Oh, there's no landing strip. You'll have to land on the road.'

The King Air took off and, as we rose high into the sky, daylight began streaming through the aircraft. From my small, circular window, I watched the streetlights of Broken Hill grow smaller and smaller. Soon the plane was alone in the morning sky, with only the drone of its engines to keep it company. The pilot contacted the base station in Tibooburra and requested landing flares to be put in position on the roadway. The desert below us was starting to come to life, and in the faint light, I watched as a group of kangaroos bounced across the saltbush, no doubt startled by the sound of the aircraft.

'I hope they steer well clear of the plane when we're landing,' said Magnus, the pilot. 'I don't want to damage another nose cone!'

The pilot lined up the plane to make his approach, preparing to land due south. There was a roar of engines. The plane flitted on the crosswinds as it approached the bitumen roadway and then landed with a bump.

'Glad to see you, fellas,' said Maureen. 'If you confirm a diagnosis of her gallbladder problem, I'll give her some pethidine for the flight.'

I examined the patient and concurred with the nurse's diagnosis. It seemed cruel that a patient could be left in pain awaiting a diagnosis, but it was vitally important to prevent a situation in which a patient with acute appendicitis, or even an ectopic pregnancy, could deteriorate on board the plane, their symptoms masked by pethidine. As we ascended, I looked across at my patient. She was sleeping, and I considered that without the Flying Doctor Service much of Australia would be completely uninhabitable.

*

While I was working in Broken Hill, a position for a GP with specialist knowledge of dermatology came up in Toowoomba, about eighty miles west of Queensland's capital, Brisbane, and I took it. It would mean leaving the Flying Doctors, but I had done six months and knew a position like this did not appear every day for a doctor trained overseas. What intrigued me about the job was the fact that Queensland was considered the skin cancer capital of the world and the situation would give me an unequalled opportunity to deal with melanomas on an almost daily basis. Dr Carey told me that some of the patients were also part of the melanoma vaccine study at Brisbane's Princess Alexandra Hospital.

Toowoomba was a university town of about 150,000 people, situated in the Darling Downs. The job was mostly general practice and skin-cancer management, initially with Dr Cormac Carey and Dr Peter Beeston at the Wilsonton Shopping Centre; I later worked with Dr Neville Lutton and Dr Jim McConaghie at the James Neil Medical Plaza. It was greatly facilitated by easy access to radiology facilities on the premises.

One morning, Dr McConaghie asked me to see a patient who had had a persistent cough for some time. He had started with a flulike illness but soon progressed to fever and chills. Jim knew that I had worked as a respiratory registrar with Malcolm Sear in New Zealand and wanted an opinion, as his X-ray showed a small basal pneumonia. The patient was a singer by profession, who performed in the local hotels and had been off work for nearly three weeks. He gave a history of severe headaches, lethargy, and joint pain, and I noticed he had a small rash. He had already had numerous courses of antibiotics, which had done little to alleviate the symptoms. Of more concern was the fact that, on abdominal examination, he also had a large spleen.

Dr McConaghie was a seasoned middle-aged physician who had worked out towards the bush, in the isolated towns of Dalby and Goondiwindi. I respected colleagues who based in these environments, as they worked in the absence of radiology and laboratory backup, diagnosing ruptured ovarian cysts and appendixes, possibly delivering babies late at night and allowing God to take away the aged by dawn.

'His Q-fever test is negative,' he said, holding the results in his hand. Q fever is a disease that was first described by an Australian pathologist called Edward Holbrook Derrick after an outbreak of the illness in abattoir workers in Brisbane. It is caused by an unusual bacterium called *Coxiella burnetii*, which is found in ticks, cattle, sheep, goats and other domestic animals. It causes severe headache, respiratory distress and joint pain.

'I think I know what it is,' I said. 'Do you keep budgies?'

'I do,' he said. 'Why?'

'Because you need to give them the antibiotics as well as yourself. I think they're infected with chlamydia.'

Dr McConaghie looked at me with profound interest. He knew *Chlamydia trachomatis* was the cause of the well-known sexually transmitted variant, but I was referring instead to its biological relative, *Chlamydia psittacosis*.

'How did you work that out?' he inquired.

I agreed that the patient had the signs of Q fever, but he had an enlarged spleen on the left rather than an enlarged liver on the right. Although it was a rare condition, I had seen some *psittacosis* cases in respiratory medicine in New Zealand and, once seen, they are never forgotten. This patient presented with a raised pink facial rash called Horder's spots, seen almost exclusively in this condition. The sputum results returned *Chlamydophila psittaci* and the patient returned to full health with a double dose of doxycycline. When I went to see him perform at the Spotted Cow, a historic hotel on the corner of Ruthven and

Campbell streets, he invited me up to the stage and we shared a microphone for Van Morrison's *Brown Eyed Girl*. It was a duet that we went on to perform together on many other occasions during my time in Toowoomba.

Within a few days, Dr McConaghie returned the favour of the difficult diagnosis. The patient was a thirty-three-year-old farmer, suffering from similar flulike symptoms. Some of his joints were quite stiff and swollen, especially in the mornings. It was evident that the illness was more debilitating than life-threatening, but I didn't recognise it.

'He's even got a little rash, but I don't think it's Horder's,' Jim said sarcastically.

The patient was unwell but wanted to return to his duties on the farm. I felt it had to be something transmitted from an animal; my sixth sense told me it had to be a local or tropical illness.

'I get the feeling it is a transmitted infection,' I replied.

'Good guess,' he said. 'We'll hold on to you – it's Ross River virus!'

Dr McConaghie explained that this was a debilitating disease transmitted by saltwater *Aedes vigilax* mosquitoes, endemic to Queensland. The virus was not contagious, but it used kangaroos as reservoir hosts. There was no cure, and the patient often remained debilitated for many months.

'The Ross River is awfully close to here,' he explained. 'It's up in northern Queensland.'

*

Australia was a wonderful place to learn about dermatology, as Queensland has the highest rate of melanoma skin cancer in the world. I had had an interest in this aggressive cancer since I was a student in the Mayo Clinic in Rochester, Minnesota, in 1985, when I wrote my first paper on it. Some of my Toowoomba patients were part of a melanoma vaccine study at the Princess Alexandra Hospital in Brisbane, and I was disappointed when the result did not show as much benefit as we had hoped. I was chastened one day when one of my patients from my Flying Doctor days drove 700 kilometres with his family to see me. He was not part of the Brisbane study, but his condition had spread, and even with the administration of the vaccine, there was little that could be done for the poor man. Such was the nature of malignant melanoma: once the tumour cells start to move into the deeper dermal layers of the skin, their behaviour changes dramatically and the patient has an extremely poor prognosis.

On another occasion, I was examining a truck driver, when I noticed what at first appeared like a recent blood blister under one of his thumbnails. Despite his protestation that it was a jacking injury, I took off part of his nail to have a closer look. There was no blood, just dark pigment. As I had suspected, it was a subungual malignant melanoma; my perseverance in obtaining a diagnosis probably saved his life. He left the hospital later that week dressed in bandages. They had taken no chances and removed the last part of his thumb above the joint.

At the end of six months, I found it more tax-effective to leave Australia and go to live in South Africa or California for a while. During this period, I would also work for a few months as an Emergency Room senior registrar in St Vincent's University Hospital in Dublin.

*

When I returned to Toowoomba from Ireland in the summer of 1997, I rented a new apartment on the southern slopes of the Great Dividing Range, overlooking the hills of the Darling Downs. It was a short distance from the new Grand Central Shopping Centre, where another colleague, Dr Michael Kornfield, had his medical practice. Michael was different from the other physicians in Toowoomba: he had a melanoma scanner and a computerised cosmetic dermatology practice. He also had an old red post-war Cessna airplane and often promised to take me flying in the outback.

One day, Michael asked me to come over to the Darling Downs Aero Club at Wilsonton, where he kept his airplane. I noticed it had the licence number "VH-HRH" on the tail wing and joked with him about flying the "royal" plane.

'At least it's better than the one I had in the Flying Doctors – it was "VH-MSU"!' I said, referring to the medical acronym for "midstream urine".

We plotted a journey that would take us out over the cattle stations and the properties of the Darling Downs, to an air show in Bundaberg. With a wobble or two, we were airborne and looking down on the fertile, green fields of Toowoomba. It was exhilarating to fly by the seat of our pants, without the aid of GPS navigation.

We were flying somewhere over the town of Nanango when Michael turned to me and said, 'Patrick, you really should try and bring Botox into your practice.'

'Botox?'

'Yes, whether you're staying here or considering going back to Ireland,' he said, 'it's the future and will be used to treat pain, spasms in children, as well as wrinkles.'

'OK, why don't I come over to your practice and you can teach me how to do it?' I suggested.

When we returned to Toowoomba, I decided to do some formal Botox® training in Brisbane. During the training session, I learnt that public interest in Botox® had started a few years earlier, when a Canadian ophthalmologist, Dr Jean Carruthers, wrote an article in the *Journal of Dermatological Surgery*, suggesting that a biological bacterial toxin could be injected into somebody's face in order to take away wrinkles. The story goes that she had been using Botox® to treat some patients for blepharospasm when one of her older patients asked her for an injection in her forehead for some wrinkles there. The treatment was successful, and the genie was out of the bottle. Within a short time, news had spread like wildfire of this new wonder treatment that could melt away wrinkles.

Over the next few weeks, I began practicing on some of my friends, and as my experience improved, I started treating a few willing patients. After a few months, sometimes working at home, I began experimenting with other medical conditions, including sweating, flushing, tinnitus and even teeth grinding. These studies were performed on small numbers, and my early trials showed that it was very effective in sweating and teeth grinding, but less so in tinnitus and facial flushing.

One evening in the clinic, an amazing opportunity to continue my research, arrived without warning on my doorstep. Some Queensland police arrived to caution a patient who had scurried quietly into the waiting room. It appeared that she had broken a red light to try and make it to the laundry in time before closing to clean her wedding dress. It appeared this laundry journey was a recurrent phenomenon and that she was being treated by one of my colleagues, Dr Neville Lutton, with high dose Prozac for an impulse control disorder characterised by a long-term urge to clean the dress. He had told me about her condition and said it was related to her having excess sweating and that she felt she ruined her wedding photographs because of her condition. The condition was very disabling, and the laundry seemed to provide some form of release for her.

As she was suffering from a condition called primary axillary hyperhidrosis, I asked if I could treat her with Botox®. I had read about some doctors in Wales using the treatment only a few years before. The treatment was effective, worked within a day and was still working when I returned home to Dublin from Australia. She also gave up taking her medicine as she didn't need the pills anymore. From that impressive start, I began treating patients for sweating, developing my techniques, especially for dilution of the product. Before long, I was also treating hands and feet and enjoyed the response that I got from patients. Maybe, Michael was right after all and there was something to this new wonder product called Botox®.

As I started to become more experienced in its use, I realised that this pharmaceutical could have far-reaching applications, especially when used in conjunction with the hyaluronic-acid dermal filler, Restylane®, as both could change a patient's appearance for relatively little money, and with minimal downtime.

21. Death of My Mother

During the Irish summer, I took some time off from my job in Australia and went to work for a while with Dr Rita Doyle in Bray, a seaside resort about twelve miles south of Dublin. The town straddled the Dublin-Wicklow border and was home to Ireland's fledgling film industry. It was there that parts of Oscar-winning films such as *My Left Foot* and *Braveheart* had been shot.

Rita and I had a similar approach to medicine and got on well together. One evening, while sipping wine in her kitchen, she asked me to mull over the idea of becoming partners, as she was considering setting up a new medical enterprise, which she wanted to call the Bray Family Practice. It would use my experience to provide dermatology, skin cancer screening, and minor surgical procedures within primary care. In many ways, I liked the idea but didn't commit to an immediate answer as Rita had been in bad health for some time, and I wasn't sure if she would be up to the task. In the end, we decided it would be preferable to consider asking one of the other staff, Dr Emma Nelson, if she would also like to become a partner.

I had been working as a doctor outside Ireland for over ten years and the thought of returning home was undoubtedly exciting, but I had already established a sizeable patient list in Australia. In the end, I promised to keep in close contact with both Rita and Emma and to make a final decision about the partnership when I went back to Toowoomba. Over the next few months, I toyed with the idea of returning to Ireland many times, but I was settled in Queensland and had a lot of good friends there, many of whom pleaded with me to stay in Australia. Near the beginning of November, Emma contacted me and asked if we could meet in South Africa if I was going back through there on my way home to Ireland that Christmas.

Emma and I met in Cape Town and spent some wonderful days together, visiting the Cape wineries and discussing the merits of sharing a possible future as business partners. We had quite different personalities, and I knew this would be reflected in the way we treated our patients. I tended to be less of a talker, much more interactive and hands-on. That didn't cause me any concern because patients tend to gravitate towards the doctor, they feel most comfortable with, and we could always swop our dermatology and psychiatric patients.

One afternoon, we visited the bar in Long Street, where I'd had difficulties so many years before. It was under new management, and Emma laughed when I related the story of my Apartheid experience there – her heart was with the African people too. We wanted to visit Robben Island, where Nelson Mandela's cell block had just been turned into a museum. There were rumours that it would be declared a UNESCO World Heritage Site.

Despite the new freedoms, it was quickly apparent to me that South Africa had a lot of problems: street children huddled together and slept openly on Long Street at night, beggars flooded the streets of Stellenbosch, and there was evidence of a rising tide of crime everywhere. It seemed like there was no control over the generation who had been freed from the shackles of Apartheid. Worse still, before we arrived, a pipe bomb had exploded at the Planet Hollywood restaurant on the Victoria & Alfred Wharf, seriously injuring twenty-six people, two of whom later died in hospital.

After some restful days in the Cape, I returned to Dublin, looking forward to spending Christmas at home with my mother. When there, I discovered that she'd had her own mishap only a week before. A slurry tanker, leaking its foul-smelling cargo, had sprayed the walls, path, and roadway as it whizzed past our shop. The thick viscous liquid covered everything, and as she was cleaning up the mess, she had slipped, hurting her arm, and banging the side of her head. She had attended the local doctor, who had diagnosed a Colles fracture and sent her to the hospital – her arm would be in plaster for six weeks. She also said that her face was badly bruised and that she was sore all over. We chatted for a while and she seemed much happier for me to drive up the next morning, Christmas morning, rather than risking it that night.

My mother was a robust outgoing kind of woman when we were growing up. She was a plain speaker: she said what she thought and meant what she said. There were no "sides" to her. When she was happy, she shared it with us, and when she was annoyed, we knew all about it, in no uncertain terms. As a result, I always knew where I stood with her. That Christmas morning, she seemed much frailer than I remembered, but that was understandable – a fall of that nature can be hard on the young, so a woman of her age couldn't be expected to cope with it that easily. Her bruises had changed from a dark purple to that mottled yellow, which means the body is recovering. I took another look at her and noticed that she had bruising to both sides of her face.

'You fell on the left side,' I said. 'Why are you bruised in your right eye?'

'The doctor said the bruises spread there.'

To me, this was anatomically impossible. How could a person bang one side of the face and end up bruised on the other eye? My mother was jaundiced!

I told her I'd be happier if she had a few more tests, just to be on the safe side. She agreed, but I suppose she wasn't expecting to have them during the Christmas period. My biggest fear was that she had pancreatic cancer. From observing her and from what she had told me, all the signs pointed to it, but I wanted to be sure. I phoned her doctor and told him my suspicions. He remembered the events surrounding my father's death and was much more courteous this time and willing to listen. In fairness to him, he organised an MRI scan at the hospital on St Stephen's Day, bringing in a radiologist over the holiday period and doing everything in his power to help.

My worst fears were confirmed the following day. I knew my mother would not have much longer to live. My brother, Brian, and I were standing outside the hospital when I broke the news, and he smashed his fist into the wall, damaging his hand in the process. I was trying to cope with my own emotions, and seeing his distress added to the rising tension and sorrow within me. My mother would have to be told, and I couldn't leave it to a stranger to do so.

She was terribly upset when I told her that my suspicions regarding a pancreatic cause to her illness was now confirmed by the MRI. I told her that I would take her to see Professor John Hegarty, an excellent hepatologist in St Vincent's University Hospital in Dublin, where I had previously worked. We made the journey to Dublin together, and when she asked him straight out if she had cancer, he told her that she did.

'How long have I got to live?' she asked.

'Well, Mrs Treacy, nobody knows for sure, but we're looking at years rather than decades,' he said.

When my mother left the room to get dressed, he turned to me gravely.

'I'd give her nine or ten months,' he said. 'But we can put in a stent, Patrick, and buy her some time...'

*

My mother's illness came as a shock, and it left me determined to move home from Australia to Ireland and be with her while she still had some quality of life and share her last days on earth. We had been remarkably close, and she had helped me through troubled days as only a mother can. I decided to formalise the GP partnership in Bray. At the end of January, I went back to Toowoomba to let my colleagues and patients know that I was leaving. My patients accepted my decision, and we arranged a farewell party in town. It was challenging to leave Australia, where I had built up a good practice.

The days passed quickly when I returned to Ireland, and I spent most of the evenings with my mother in the hospital. Once the stent had been placed in her pancreatic duct, her quality of life improved noticeably. She started to regain her energy, getting out and about and enjoying herself as she had done years before. As she regained her strength and her colour returned to normal, she started to talk about doing things she had always wanted to do, like obtaining a driving licence and possibly visiting her sister in California.

Unfortunately, she seemed to think that she could beat the odds, and it was complicated for me to try to explain that she wasn't going to come out the other end of this illness. I was her son, a doctor, and I think, for a time, she placed her faith in me to make it go away. She was in denial. If there had been any hope of a cure, anywhere on this planet, I would have found it, but there wasn't. In a strange sense, I think she resented the fact that I couldn't make her better. I found it hard to cope with myself, and sometimes black despair descended on me when I thought about it.

While I was in Australia, Rita had converted the garage at her house, and I moved my office in there and began performing minor surgical procedures. It is always daunting to start a new business, and, in the beginning, we were looking at various methods of marketing our differing specialities.

In 1992, I had first used a graphical browser called Mosaic, to pass away the cabin hours while working as a ship's surgeons on the MS *Ecstasy* and being at sea for days when sailing from Los Angeles, California along the coast of the Mexican Riviera. I maintained this interest in computers when Microsoft introduced Windows NT as a graphical user interface for MS-DOS, the following year. Before long, I had become quite proficient with the fledgling operating system and had added SCSI CD-ROMs and external hard drives to my computer when I moved with Carnival Cruise Lines to Miami, Florida. The world wide web still hadn't come into use when I left the ship and by 1997, the total number of websites was still minute compared to present figures. In 1998, I decided to build the first medical general practice website in Ireland. It was called www.bfp.com after the Bray Family Practice and although quite primitive in design, it showed patients many of the services that we were providing. I added on the other doctors in the "About Us" section and printed up some purple-tinged business cards to give out to the patients. Bray Family Practice started to grow in leaps and bounds and, within a short time, patients began attending from all over Ireland for the removal of sebaceous cysts, ingrown toenails and screening for malignant melanomas and other skin cancers.

The Loreto nuns in Bray in this period kept me entertained with their stories about Africa, and they also kept me up to date with all the gossip from Gibraltar and Queensland, where they had sister convents. The Loretos were active in every continent, operating some 150 schools worldwide, educating over 70,000 pupils. They strived for greater justice and peace in the world, and their community was engaged in a variety of ministries be it either literacy programmes, spiritual direction or managing shelters for homeless women. Their Celtic complexions were no doubt coveted by some, but it was prone to skin cancers, including melanomas because of the equatorial locations they tended to work in. This meant they had to be examined every few years from the backs of their necks to the soles of their feet.

One day, I was somewhat surprised when one of the older sisters, from whom I had treated some early facial pre-cancers with liquid nitrogen refused any further examination. This was particularly surprising as I never found any of the nuns prudish and they were always willing to undress for examination without complaint. After some persuasion and highlighting warnings about the dangers of melanoma, she hesitantly agreed to allow me a limited inspection or her legs, arms and feet. It was then that I noticed she was wearing two or three packages under her black tunic, tightly strapped to her abdomen with coils of silver duct tape. The older nun slowly started to blush with embarrassment, taking on the expression of a suicide bomber who had been discovered by security. It was then that one of her colleagues, Sr Cyril re-entered the room and seeing my surprise, intervened and started laughing quietly,

'Don't worry, Patrick – Sr Magdalene is not carrying drugs down to South Africa!' she smiled and continued, 'She's just been out to see Bono at his house in Dalkey, and he kindly gave us a donation of a few thousand euro!'

'If she carried that through the customs in Johannesburg, they'd only follow her out the road and steal it from her later. I'm afraid, you'll just have to finish the examination next year when she returns back again.'

I knew of Bono's benevolence to the nuns in the past and was aware of the dangers of carjacking and robberies in South Africa. We had a laugh together when I mentioned it to him the next time we met. Over the next few months, the practice continued to grow but my partner's health continued to deteriorate, and my worst fears materialised with an ever-increasing workload. After spending many months of working every other weekend and missing the chance to spend more time with my dying mother, I knew I had to start looking for a practice of my own eventually. I would be sorry to leave Bray but knew that most of my patients understood what was happening and many of them would follow me back to Dublin.

When the nuns arrived again some months later, Sister Cyril approached me and asked politely, 'Are you still using your business cards for Bray Family Practice!'

'Yes,' I replied but to be honest, I had rather forgotten about them and paying for the website as my interest in the practice was beginning to wane. 'Why do you ask?' I inquired.

'Because the nuns in Gibraltar say that the website has nothing about the practice on it.'

'Oh, let me see!' I said.

I went to the computer and typed in bfp.com in the address bar, aware that I hadn't paid the hosting company for some months. There in all its glory was a new pornographic website in place of my own called "Bonding for Pleasure".

'Oh, I'm so sorry, Sr Cyril, I was totally unaware that somebody else has taken over that website address!'

I am still unsure if she ever believed me and I wondered about the hundreds of other business cards that I had distributed amongst my own medical colleagues as well as my patients. It is difficult to know whether it was contributory, but I never met any of the Loreto nuns after that until I had an opportunity to meet another great missionary, Sr Cyril Mooney, at their Bray convent many years later.

Sr Cyril was home from Kolkata, where she had been working as a teacher for more than 50 years. She was a wonderful humanitarian and had received India's highest civil award, the Padma Shri, for her mission to educate the street children of the poverty-stricken city. Under her guidance she had opened the doors of the Loreto Sealdah school, to the poor, helping some 450,000 people to significantly improve their circumstances and help battle the inhuman conditions in the Indian shanty towns. I had met her originally when viewing a film about her work in India at the Irish Film Theatre and she had invited me back for some tea at the convent.

Everything went well and we shared some stories about Mother Theresa who had worked with her in educating street children in Kolkata. Sr Cyril shared a story with me about once scolding Mother Theresa for inviting children into the Loreto Sealdah school without her permission. When Mother Theresa found out that Sr Cyril was on the warpath, she mounted her scooter and went back to the convent to hide for a while. It appears that the Irish nun must have been a formidable foe because the poor lady went missing for a while and was found three hours later hiding in a cupboard. We were all laughing soundly when one of the older nuns approached me with a top-up of tea and said quietly,

'Are you still building the websites, Patrick?!'

I didn't recognise her, but no doubt my expertise in information technology had gone way before me.

My mother remained relatively well for about ten months or so, and then her body began to give out slowly. As the cancer spread, it caused some gastric bleeding, and she had to be hospitalised for prolonged periods. Between hospital visits, she stayed with me in Dublin and often asked me to marry before she died, wanting to see me settled with a family of my own. It was heart-breaking to see such a strong woman, who had never taken a holiday and had given her whole life to her family, waste away before my eyes. Towards the end, we decided to take her home to Garrison to die in her own bed. My sisters always attended her until she died. The months following my mother's death were difficult for me, emotionally. I had spent so much time looking out for her health that the loss of her as a parent didn't really hit me until she was gone.

22. Setting up the Ailesbury Clinic

Although I had a great relationship with the patients in Bray, things were becoming more difficult for me there by the day. In the end, I decided to move my medical equipment back up to my house in Enniskillen, with the help of my good friend, Peter Hanley. We rented a van and left Dublin. But sometimes life has a way of throwing a curveball right into one's path: we were about halfway there when a classmate phoned to tell me about a medical practice for sale on Ailesbury Road in Ballsbridge.

I went to see the practice the next morning. The clinic was located on the ground floor of an apartment complex on Ailesbury Road, long considered the best address in Ireland. It was in the embassy belt, between the Spanish ambassador's residence and St Michael's College, one of the best private secondary schools in Ireland. There were other, well-established, second-generation dental, psychiatric, and physiotherapy businesses operating in the complex. Initially, it had been owned by an orthopaedic surgeon, Jimmy Sheehan, who had left to co-partner the opening of Ireland's first high-class private medical facility, the Blackrock Clinic, in Dublin in 1984. Since that time, it had been owned and operated by a plastic surgeon, Dr Gerry Edwards, until he had tragically died before his time.

The Ailesbury Road clinic was within walking distance of my apartment and seemed the perfect place to establish a new practice.

'Well, what do you think?' asked Peter.

'It's perfect!' I replied.

*

As we approached the end of the twentieth century, many technical innovations emerged almost at the one time to address the effects of facial ageing. These included Botox®, hyaluronic-acid dermal fillers and the invention of the IPL laser for hair removal. The new century ushered in a new era of thinking in medicine, in which stem cells and cloning might revolutionise the treatment of chronic disease. Many felt that if we could harness the power of stem cells or fibroblasts, we could repair damaged skin, burns, acne scarring and even, potentially, eradicate wrinkles. Looking around the adjoining rooms, I knew this was an opportunity to design an aesthetic clinic to my exacting artistic standards and included into the design, interior glass doors, fake ionic columns and painted the stucco with gold-leaf paint. It required a three-phase electrical system to carry the increased load of my lasers, and the telephone system was upgraded to handle an internet connection. I made the office totally paperless and used scanners to update the patients' records.

However, not everyone agreed with my ideas, and the early days were financially tough, mainly because the banks could not understand the new field of medicine that I was trying to create and were unwilling to invest in the project. First, I was turned down by Anglo Irish and Sean Quinn, both of whom had filed for bankruptcy before the end of the decade. The main cause of Sean Quinn's substantial stake in the Anglo-Irish Bank, which was built-up during the boom years. His interest in the bank related to its success during Ireland's Celtic Tiger years which led to it being heralded as the Best Bank in the World in 2007. Rather than buying shares, he chose a financial instrument called contracts for difference (CFDs) which allowed him to bet on the share price of the bank. The CFDs fell and Anglo-Irish Bank crashed during the financial crisis. In September 2008, the Irish government took the ill-fated decision to guarantee the banks including Anglo as the property market collapsed tipping the nation into ten years of recession.

My own bank, the Ulster Bank, had similar reservations and eventually, Allied Irish Bank lent me the money. I completed the purchase before the end of the week, and then went down to the Companies Registration Office and registered "Ailesbury Clinic" as a business name. It was from these humble origins in that two-room apartment that the whole concept of aesthetic medicine and the now famous Ailesbury Clinic brand was born. Within ten years, the idea of aesthetic medicine would become a global phenomenon, and Ailesbury Clinic would employ over twenty-five staff and have offices in London, Cork, Belgrade, Istanbul, and Dubai.

While the clinic was being fitted out, a childhood friend from Garrison, Patsy Keenan called from Atlanta and invited me to the United States Grand Prix being staged for the first time at the iconic Indianapolis Motor Speedway. We hired a large Winnebago and a few of us took it on the ten-hour journey from Atlanta, through the historic towns of Chattanooga and Nashville to the Midwest state of Indiana. It was just the break I needed. On route, we pulled over at a pole dancing club somewhere near Louisville, and Patsy paid a few extra dollars to one of the dancers to try and convince him that she once sat in front of him at a Primary School in Rockfield, Ballyshannon, before her mother took her away to America. He was absolutely convinced that she was telling the truth and the fact she was Afro-American did not seem to diminish his belief. Interestingly, it was the same primary school that my mother had attended as a child as well.

*

During 2001, I continued to work in the accident and emergency department of St Vincent's University Hospital while my Ailesbury Clinic client patient base grew. Patients seemed to like the Australian concept of a walk-in clinic for minor surgery and in that period, I focused on developing the new field of aesthetic medicine, still mostly in its infancy and yet to evolve in any specific direction. Over the next few months, I was caught in that dilemma of whether to see some general practice patients to maintain payments towards my rather hefty mortgage but knew that it would also be difficult to discontinue a medical relationship with these patients if my idea of practicing aesthetic medicine evolved. I found myself at the cutting edge of this new field of medicine and knew that there was a terrible antipathy amongst my colleagues towards the use of Botox®, especially when used for cosmetic reasons. It was as if nobody, except me could see the future emerging field of aesthetic medicine.

Around that time, I was writing some articles about my experiences with HIV patients in South Africa for the *Irish Medical Times,* and I discussed the problem with the editor, Aindreas McEntee.

'What hope have I attracting patients for Botox® when my own colleagues are writing in the Sunday papers against it?' I questioned.

The recent *Sunday Tribune* had just published a controversial frontpage article entitled "Botox Will Leave a Trail of Disaster for Many Years to Come". It was penned by one of my plastic surgical colleagues with whom I had ever worked with in James Connolly Memorial Hospital. The sensational piece was misleading as it was accompanied by an image of a girl with extremely pouty lips. It was obvious the paper or the doctor was confusing Botox® with dermal fillers and it made me consider whether I should reply, to this misconception.

Aindreas replied, 'Patrick, you're going to have to first educate your colleagues about the medical uses of Botox®,' and he invited to write a series of articles relating to its common use in dermatology and other aspects of medicine.

'That's a great idea!'

'Let's do it!'

We titled the first of the four-part series "*Mapping the Long Journey from Sausage Poison to Wonder Drug*". The first article recorded the history of botulinum from its discovery by Émile Pierre-Marie van Ermengen, a Belgian bacteriologist working at the University of Ghent who, in 1895, isolated Clostridium botulinum, the bacterium that causes botulism, from a piece of ham that had poisoned thirty-four people. The last part of the series predicted that "Botulinum Toxin Will Revolutionise the Practice of Conventional Medicine".

In the first of similar situations, I took pen to paper to defend Botox®, and the newspaper published my letter of complaint in the first few pages of the next Sunday edition, along with an apology.

Soon afterwards, the manufacturers of the product, Allergan, asked me to be their official spokesperson in Ireland. At the time, it was considered brave by my hospital colleagues to take a medical stand on the issue, but it wasn't long until many other media people, who didn't subscribe to the scaremongering, came knocking on my door. The rebranding of the wrongly maligned pharmaceutical had begun. That summer I attended the 2001 FACE Conference in London and got involved in a discussion on the treatment of axillary hyperhidrosis with Botox®. It began after a lecture by an eminent dermatology professor regarding the benefit of using starch to delineate the area where the patient was sweating from under their armpit. I stated that in my opinion the use of the starch test during treatment of axillary hyperhidrosis was unnecessary as the sweat glands tend to correspond with the region of the hair follicles in the underarm region. To negate the test would save physicians and patients quite a lot of time during the procedure and make it much simpler. As I had already treated about twenty cases in this fashion without having to repeat one of them, I stood my ground under his challenge. I remain unsure if the lecturer ever forgave me for teaching the audience a less complicated method, but it certainly saved many a patient up and down the United Kingdom from sitting in waiting rooms all wrapped up in Snapwrap®.

While at the FACE conference, I was approached by an English medical colleague who had a patient who developed a droopy left upper eyelid after treatment of Botox®. The Botox was probably put too close to the eyelid and weakened one of the two muscles that lift the lid. His patient was distressed, and I stayed in London on Monday morning to meet the patient. Her left eye as partially closed, and she wondered whether it would remain like that until the effect of the botulinum wore off. I used some 0.5% iopidine to treat her. These eye drops are usually used in glaucoma to lower eye pressure and work by stimulating another muscle to work a little harder, and so it helped temporarily to open the eye. It was the first time that I had used Iopidine (apraclonidine) although I had read about it in textbooks. I told the patient that the Botox® effect on the primary eyelid "lifter" still had to wear off, and this could take about three weeks. In the meantime, she would still have to use the drops. The word got around that I was a good person to whom to refer aesthetic complications, and I remain firm friends with this doctor to this very day.

Meanwhile, Michael Ryan at *RTÉ*'s *Nationwide* produced a colourful, edgy fifteen-minute television programme on the growing phenomenon of Botox® in Ireland, which included video clips of patients treated at Ailesbury Clinic. After that, *RTÉ*'s *The Afternoon Show* went one step further and showed a patient receiving Botox® injections live in the *RTÉ* studio for the first time in Ireland. Over the next six to eight months, I was invited back on a few more occasions to both *RTÉ* and TV3 to inject different dermal fillers on live television. My friend, Michael Brady, who was now CEO of 98FM, asked me to do an interview on the radio about rising trends in cosmetic medicine, both focusing on botulinum but also Isolagen®, the new fibroblast treatment for wrinkles. This was indeed a seminal period for aesthetic medicine in Ireland and many of the programmes were later shown on *RTÉ*'s *Reeling in the Years*, a programme showcasing the news stories that changed the culture of Ireland over the last few decades. Meanwhile, patients were voting with their feet; despite the apprehension of some of my colleagues, the new field of aesthetic medicine was here to stay.

*

That summer, I went back to Cape Town, eager to interview Health Minister Manto Tshabalala-Msimang about the treatment of HIV patients and the overhaul of the pharmaceutical industry in South Africa, for the *Irish Medical*

Times. I was particularly annoyed that the new ANC government under the tenure of the second post-Apartheid President of South Africa, Thabo Mbeki, questioned the link between HIV and AIDS and believed that the correlation between poverty and the AIDS rate in Africa was a challenge to the viral theory of AIDS. The article would focus on the willingness of the South African government, under the stewardship of Mbeki, to allow the pseudoscience of Peter Duesberg to masquerade as science. I wanted the health minister to explain to me why she had decided to reject the use of AZT in all ANC-run provinces, even though the manufacturer was willing to cut the price of the drug. This was a ridiculous position, as the number of people in South Africa with HIV was now nearing five million, and it was evident to one and all that the drug was the only means of preventing the spread of the disease in new-borns. Thankfully, doctors in the Western Cape were not under ANC control and went ahead with providing the drug despite pressure from these people.

While in Cape Town, I was invited to a bar on the waterfront for a social function that was attended by some senior ANC government officials. At first, everything was excellent, and the conversation centred on the political direction of the new South Africa. We chatted about how they should address the significant social problems of housing and poverty. As the drinks flowed, I expressed my opinion that President Thabo Mbeki's belief that AIDS was caused by poverty, not HIV, was not based on science, and that it was lunacy to assume that the communist health minister's approved diet of beetroots and ginger could save their people from decimation.

The truth didn't go down well intellectually or socially. In their eyes, I had crossed the line. The officials refused to talk any longer and eventually asked the staff to remove me from the bar. What irony! Six years earlier, I had been asked to leave a bar in Cape Town because I had stood up for some poor Blacks who had been refused a drink because of Apartheid and White racial prejudice. Now, I was being ejected from another bar in the same city because I had stood up for them against their own new leaders' scientific ignorance.

As I walked past the homeless children openly sleeping along the dirty pavements of Long Street, I stood for a while and looked over at the hostel where I once lay my head. As I stood there, I thought that the emperor might have changed his clothes in South Africa, but when it came to the future health of the nation, it certainly hadn't done so for the better. Incensed about what was happening, I wrote a strongly worded article for the *Irish Medical Times* on my return to Dublin entitled "A Tragedy That Has Resulted in Countless Needless Deaths in Africa". This article made me personae non grata with Mbeki's regime for a period, and it was cast back to me by some government officials when I visited Cape Town again a few years later. Their ban on antiretroviral drugs in public hospitals has since been estimated to be responsible for the premature deaths of between 330,000 and 365,000 people. This apparent inability of some members of the ANC to respect Western science again featured a few times again in later years in South Africa but none more prominently than in late September 2015. It took me longer than most to discover that its origins were deeply embedded in the culture of a people whose psyche was deeply traumatised by years of colonial oppression.

The incident to which I refer happened when I was lecturing at the Cosmedica Conference 2015 in Johannesburg. A controversy had been brewing all week after some anthropologists assigned some newly discovered fossil skeletons of an of South Africa, in a chamber of the Rising Star Cave system, about 50km northwest of Johannesburg. One of my lectures was demonstrating the new Syneron VelaShape® RF cellulite device at a specialised workshop at Oakfield Farm in Gauteng near the Cradle of Humankind World Heritage Site where the fossil specimens were being exhibited. While there, I decided to visit the exhibition before calls for it to be closed were enacted. The disagreement arose because, initially, features of the newly discovered skeletons were said to resemble fossil specimens from over two million years ago but were redated as closer to 250,000 years ago, and in keeping with the first appearance of larger brained anatomically modern humans. The fact that the fossils were also said to have been buried rather than placed there only added to the intrigue. If proven to be the case, it could have profound implications for the evolution of culture in early humans as the burial of the dead was previously thought have emerged mainly in our species. The South African Council of Churches (SACC) made a statement that, 'It didn't approve the theory that humans come from baboons.' I could accept that creationists claimed that evolution had never occurred but was rather shocked when some members of the ANC tried to make it a racial issue.

One of the sceptics was Dr Mathole Motshekga, ANC MP, a former Premier of Gauteng, and Executive Director of the Kara Heritage Institute. He said, 'The discovery of the new ancestor supports the West's story that we are sub-humans,' and he challenged scientists to a debate over *Homo Naledi*. The former Premier also described the palaeontology discovery to *Die Burger* newspaper as Western "pseudoscience, which seemed bent on trying to confirm that Africans are descendants of baboons".

He made it clear that it was his and the Kara Foundation's point of view, and not that of the ANC but continued, 'That is why today no African is respected anywhere in the world because of this type of theory.' Other prominent South Africans also dismissed the discovery of a new human ancestor as a racist theory designed to cast Africans as "sub human", an opinion that I felt resonated in a country that was profoundly intellectually damaged and bruised by Apartheid.

This was sadly confirmed to me when the former Congress of South Africa Trade Unions (Cosatu) General Secretary Zwelinzima Vavi took to social media, where he tweeted, 'No one will dig old monkey bones into backing up a theory that I was once a baboon.' He recalled that when South Africa was under Apartheid rule, he was a target of racist remarks: 'I been also called a baboon all my life so did my father and his fathers'.

'I am no grandchild of any ape, monkey or baboon,' he said on his Twitter account, which was followed by more than 300,000 people. While at the exhibition, I read that the DNA in the fossils was found to be degraded and attempts to extract it was unsuccessful. There was a lot of anatomical data to view relating to the species; the teeth were small, like modern humans, but the third molar was more significant than the other molars, like australopithecines. The tiny middle-ear bone called the incus resembled those of chimpanzees and gorillas. I stood for a long time looking down upon the ancient fossils lying in the glass and wooden cabinet and wondered for a while about the deepening controversy and whether this mentality had played a part in the earlier stance on not Mbeki's position of accepting not to treat the disease of HIV with medicine.

I found it difficult to understand how the discovery of *Homo Naledi* could not be celebrated as all of humankind's common origins on the continent of Africa. It was even more difficult to perceive how anyone could take the scientific interpretation of the anatomical data therein as a personal offence. But perceptions of what constitutes history amongst the hills and the rocks of South Africa are different. The next day, the government closed the exhibition, and I felt privileged to be amongst the few hundred who saw it. The only saving grace to the *Homo Naledi* experience was when the ANC Deputy President Cyril Ramaphosa said, 'Our common umbilical cord is buried in Africa. *Homo Naledi* shows that "a common ancestor binds us".'

In the fall of 2001, I had my first dermal filler complication. It occurred in a thirty-year-old patient who was getting married the following week. The patient's left upper lip swelled up rather grotesquely but quickly settled with some oral steroids. It taught me not to treat patients within two weeks of a big social event – especially a wedding! That November, I saw a young Spanish male student living in Dublin. The patient looked like he was dying of cancer as his face was grossly emaciated, with substantial fat loss around both his cheeks and temples. He told me that he was suffering from HIV-associated lipodystrophy, a condition characterised by loss of facial subcutaneous fat associated with the infection. The wasting occurred mainly in the face, especially in the cheeks and temples, and I learnt from him that the resultant gaunt features led to many of these patients becoming socially isolated or suicidal. He mentioned that there were many hundreds of patients like him throughout Europe and the United States, and nobody knew what was causing the illness. Over the next few days, I decided to learn more about this fascinating illness – the loss of fat was occurring either because the new drugs were allowing people to live long enough to experience a new phase of HIV/AIDS or else as I suspected the medications were changing the pathophysiology of the fat metabolism in the body itself! Either way, I immediately felt a deep sense of empathy with these tortured patients. After all, there, but for the grace of God, it could have me sitting in that chair!

I decided to treat the Spanish student with New-Fill®, an experimental treatment involving injecting polylactic acid into the patients face to stimulate new collagen to replace the missing fat tissue. The compound was composed of a polylactic acid polymer, identical to the plastic cups found by our water cooler which we also find in plastic cups. It was later renamed Sculptra® but it was difficult to inject as the needle continually blocked, and the patient required as many as sixty injections at each treatment. However, the results were quite remarkable, and after three to five treatment sessions three weeks apart, the patients emerged with almost normal facial profiles. Within a few months, I had treated three similar patients from Italy, Holland, and the United States. It seemed, I had tapped into a special cohort of patients that nobody else in the UK or Ireland was providing treatment for, and over the next few months, St James Hospital in Dublin started referring Irish HIV facial lipodystrophy cases to me.

Visiting the extinct species, Homo Naledi, *in Gauteng*

HIV Lipodystrophy syndrome was a devastating disease to have and many patients with the condition committed suicide as they were unable to interact socially. In truth, some considered the effects of the treatment was worse than the disease itself. Some patients grew large "buffalo humps" on their necks that I also attempted to remove. As the number of these patients attending the clinic continued to grow, because of information on gay internet forums, I knew that this procedure might curtail my aesthetic medicine project. However, I had a responsibility to treat these patients.

Many things worried me about the growing numbers of HIV patients coming through my doors. Firstly, I knew from my earlier experience on the ships that these patients could coming under an assumed name and carrying a friend's blood tests. Secondly, they could pose a health risk to myself and my staff as even with double gloving, there was a lot of blood present during the Sculptra® treatment as we had to inject the dermis where both the collagen was stimulated but also where the blood vessels are. Thirdly, the pharmaceutical we were using continually blocked the needle making the risk of a needle-stick injury quite high. Last, but not least, the possibility existed that when the word got out about HIV patients *en masse* attending the clinic it might keep other aesthetic patients away. It was apparent to me that I needed a safer form of treatment and a better means of getting reliable viral blood results for my international patients.

In January of 2002, I was lecturing on my results at IMCAS Paris and noticed a new filler compound on one of the stands called Bio-Alcamid®. This was a permanent filler made from 96% water and 4% synthetic polymer (polyalkylimide) designed to stimulate collagen growth which formed around the filler. When I used BioAlcamid® on these HIV patients for the first time in 2002, it opened a new, safer method of treatment, in which the person carrying out the procedure was less exposed to needle-stick injuries and the patient had a treatment that lasted for life rather than two and a half years.

As my experience grew, I was invited by my colleagues to New York to demonstrate my procedure, where I treated three HIV lipoatrophy patients. It was the first time that patients had been treated using this method in the United States. One of the patients was 74-years-old and he had been living alone in an apartment contemplating suicidal thoughts. The treatment changed his life and he wrote to me a letter of appreciation from his journey on a world cruise. I later heard he found a new partner and was considering marriage. The ability to change people's lives for the better always made me appreciate the almost immediate benefits this new branch of medicine could achieve. After I had treated about forty patients, I published my findings in the *Journal of Dermatological Surgery* in conjunctions with Dr David Goldberg, a professor of dermatology at New York's Mount Sinai. This BioAlcamid® technique certainly altered the lives of many HIV patients, but sadly since its initial use, numerous reports of adverse reactions were reported, including significant infections. Because of this, BioAlcamid® was taken off the market, and the original Italian manufacturer stopped production. In Canada, class action lawsuits were filed against the company.

I continued to work in St Vincent's Hospital in Dublin was there that September when the news broke that a plane had crashed into the World Trade Centre in New York. As concerned staff gathered around the waiting-room television, the *Sky News* reporter announced that an American Airlines flight had hit the burning North Tower. Almost immediately, I felt that it was a terrorist attack. This was confirmed when a second plane hit the South Tower about the time my shift was ending at two o'clock. As I left the hospital, I knew that the world in which I was living would probably never be the same. I phoned Julie, my receptionist in Ailesbury, to cancel my patients and try to find me a flight to New York.

It proved almost impossible to get a flight into JFK, but I felt a personal attachment to the city where I had once lived and wanted to help in its hour of need. Things eased again after a few days, and I called Pasty Keenan and asked him if he would come to New York and join me at Fitzpatrick Manhattan Hotel for a few days. By the time we reached the city, things were already beginning to settle. The bar in Fitzpatrick's hotel was packed with Irish members of the NYFD and NYPD who had assembled there, sharing their horror with us about what had happened. One of them, Paul McCauley, told me that most of the casualties were in St Vincent's Hospital in Manhattan and he could get us entry near to the site of the destruction, which was now called Ground Zero. Patsy and I left and took a taxi down through the empty streets of Manhattan.

We passed along Broadway, where the shops had replaced their window displays with giant red, white, and blue American flags. The driver left us at Canal Street, and we began slowly walking to the intersection with Fulton Street, where a large plume of greyish smoke rose in spirals, darkening the city sky. An acrid smell of burning plastic hung everywhere in the surrounding air, tinged with a more putrefying smell that I assumed was decaying flesh. White dust, which been hanging around in the air for days, began to settle, blanketing the loft apartments and obscuring the wording on the police barricades. We stood in silence as rows of demolition trucks lined up in formation, moving like soldier ants clearing up after their nest had been attacked. I paused for a while at an impromptu shrine of lighted candles and cards with heart-wrenching messages to the many who were missing, now presumed dead. My eye caught one about Dr Sneha Ann Philip from St Vincent's Hospital on Staten Island. The poster had been erected by her family who believed she perished trying to help victims of the following day's terrorist attacks. I decided to take the poster with me for some reason, probably because she was a colleague. Sometime later an investigation by New York City police delved into her life and found details of a double life, a history of marital problems, possible affairs with other women, job difficulties and alcohol and drug abuse, as well as a pending criminal charge against her. This led them to conclude it was just as likely that she had met a different fate.

Two people handing out prayer leaflets stopped to say a few words. They were eager to chat to us, and Patsy took their pamphlet and read it to me. It said, 'This is a struggle between God and Allah and our God is the greatest.' I looked again at the pamphlet and knew that America would go back to war soon…and maybe, as the booklet said, just to see whose God was the greatest after all.

*

The Ailesbury Clinic was flourishing in 2002, and I decided to introduce a method of fibroblast transplanting called Isolagen. The process involved taking a small biopsy from behind the ear to harvest fibroblasts cells, which were then cultivated in a laboratory and re-injected back into the patient. The US scientists behind the project were keen to get FDA approval, primarily to treat wrinkles but also to treat acne scars and burn victims. I was also trialling Botox® in chronic migraines and had success in over twenty patients. The interest in migraine treatment started when one of our nurses, Tadgh, told me his daily pain had almost completely disappeared after he got Botox®.

In May, I decided to go again to the 2001 Monaco Grand Prix. It was the seventh race of the Formula One season, and I was hoping that it would be won by Michael Schumacher driving for the Ferrari team. The Irish contingent would be hoping to see fellow countryman, Eddie Irvine performs well for the Jaguar team. I asked a young nurse, Julie, who worked with me in the Emergency Room of St Vincent's University Hospital if she would like to accompany me. We both flew to Nice, and after the race, we celebrated the final night on Eddie's yacht. He had made his Formula One debut in 1993 with Jordan Grand Prix and scored his first podium with them two years later. However, his best days were now behind him as his most successful season was in 1999 when he took four victories and challenged McLaren driver, Mika Häkkinen, for the World Championship. We partied well into the night and left the boat just as a full moon rose over the Mediterranean. It was indeed a romantic setting but, yet, romance hadn't blossomed between us. As we looked out over the vast expanse of water, we began to share our dreams, where we saw ourselves going in life, and Julie told me that she would like to work in the cosmetic medicine industry.

Following the trip to Monaco, Julie and I became closer. She resigned her position in St Vincent's and came to work for me at Ailesbury as an aesthetic nurse. The patients liked her, and, within a short time, she was injecting dermal fillers and had become quite proficient in injecting Isolagen fibroblasts. Over the next few months, we started dating more regularly. It was nice to have someone close with whom I could share the experiences of building the clinic, someone who would accompany me on my travels to conferences around the world.

Later that year, fear swept the land as there were over a hundred cases of Bovine spongiform encephalopathy (BSE), commonly known as mad cow disease, in Britain, with the risk of it spreading to contaminate the herds in Ireland further. This neurodegenerative disease of cattle caused abnormal behaviour, trouble walking and weight loss. In North America, doctors became concerned that the collagen they were using to treat faces and lips could become contaminated with the virus, which until then had been sourced in Texas from calves' hooves.

An alternative source, roosters' combs, was proving just as disastrous, as a new avian influenza virus had been detected that could potentially create a new subtype, lethal in humans. The fear of this new disease led to the destruction of 4.5 million cattle.

Such was the fear that US patients now looked towards British and Irish aesthetic clinics to provide safer alternatives, and many patients travelled from New York and Los Angeles to Ailesbury Dublin to get the more reliable hyaluronic-acid dermal filler. The product of choice at that time was Restylane®, which had been invented by the Swedish company Q-Med six years before. It was not available in the United States as FDA trials meant that American doctors would not be able to use these products commercially until at least 2005. Before long, there were many other hyaluronic variants in the marketplace, including Matridex®, Matridur®, Hydrafill® and Teosyl®. In fact, within a short while, there were over a hundred differing hyaluronic products. In 2003, I wrote an article indicating not only were they safer because they would not cause infection but also because they were potentially reversible. My lectures regarding these safer compounds became popular among my American colleagues, and I got invited to New York and Los Angeles to speak about my experiences with them.

*

In the summer of 2003, Ireland hosted the Summer Special Olympic World Games. Events were held in June at many venues including Morton Stadium, the Royal Dublin Society, the National Basketball Arena, all in Dublin. Croke Park served as the central stadium for the opening and closing ceremonies, even though no competitions took place there. I was invited to present medals to the athletes in Morton Stadium on the last Saturday. The philanthropist Denis O'Brien made his private plane available to the Iraqi team so that they could travel from the bombed-out remnants of Baghdad to participate in the games. I took some time to meet them and welcome them to my homeland. During those memorable days, Ireland also became a place, defined, not by exclusion, but by inclusion, embracing togetherness, abhorring human barriers of any kind, striving to change negative stereotypes based on ignorance and prejudice.

Later that year, I published the uncovered story of the rejection of GM foods by Africa nations, during one of their worst famines in my "Cutting Edge" column in the *Irish Medical Times*. For the previous year, I was aware that southern Africa had been in the grip of a devastating famine.

A report from the World Health Organisation (WHO) estimated that nearly 14 million people, including 2.3 million children under the age of five, were at risk of starvation and at least 300,000 would die without outside help. Yet when the US offered over half a million tons of genetically modified grain to countries in the region, many states rejected the offer. They were concerned about the safety of GM foods and how it would eventually affect their exports to European markets. African farmers feared that if they could no longer certify that their meals were GM-free, they would lose their share in the European market. I was awarded the coveted GSK "Irish Medical Professional Journalist of the Year" award for my columns.

With Bono at the UN Awards in New York 2003

In October, I was invited to New York to attend the 2003 United Nations Association of the USA Global Leadership Awards. That year, Bono presented the honours to Dr Alex Godwin Coutinho, Executive Director of the Infectious Disease Institute in Kampala and head of The AIDS Support Organisation (TASO), for his great work in combating HIV in Africa. The singer had long been an advocate of fighting preventable disease, especially in Africa, by raising public awareness and putting pressure on political leaders to make and keep responsible policies. He told me that he has not seen any cases of HIV associated lipodystrophy syndrome in any of his clinics in Uganda. Because none of his patients were taking any of the anti-retroviral medication, it almost proved to me that the anti-HIV medication was most probably to be the cause of the disease. This was later proven when newer medicine emerged, and within a few years the condition largely disappeared and joined the annals of medical history.

*

In January 2004, I went to Miami to learn about thread-lifting and, while there, met the famous French plastic surgeon, Dr Pierre Fournier, considered by many to be the father of cosmetic surgery. Julie and I later met him again by invitation at his house in Paris, where his wife gave a beautiful piano recital, and he presented me with an original framed copy of one of his older 1960 lectures, *The Concept of Beauty,* which I proudly hung back on the walls at Ailesbury. It always amazed me how true innovators of aesthetics never had to promote their wares. There was something humble about their approach to medicine, and they were still willing to help other doctors learn their techniques. I employed that approach at Ailesbury and never charged visiting doctors for mentorship.

During that Miami visit, I also met Dr Abdala Khalil and his wife, Carol, and spent one evening with them having a meal along the shoreline of their beautiful Miami beachside home. Little did I know as we sipped wine on their boat deck that evening, that fifteen years later, I would be inviting Carol over to speak to my medical colleagues in London. There, in my capacity as Chairman of the Aesthetics Conference of the Royal Society of Medicine, she would tell us her story of how she developed a major aesthetic complication resulting in her having to get a forehead transplant after damage done to her by somebody injecting a silicone filler into her face. It was during this period I developed an interest in treating complications, and her husband sent me over some cases for management and treatment.

Carol had contacted me in 2013 after she suffered this horrible complication and had undergone a sixteen-hour procedure on her forehead, in which all the muscles and tissues were removed, down to the bone. After the residual silicone was removed, she had received an autologous forehead transplant by Dr Reza Jarrahy, Associate Professor at the UCLA Craniofacial Clinic and Face Transplant Program. During the procedure, a large section of skin and tissue was removed from her back to replace the damaged skin on her forehead. She told me that only a few doctors were up for the challenge: including one of America's most renowned microvascular surgeons, fellow Northern Irelander, Dr J Brian Boyd, Chief of Plastic Surgery at Harbor – UCLA Medical Center. Over the next few months, she told me that the problem had started in late 2009, resulting in her face expanding, contracting, and becoming distorted. Once the initial damage was done, she was no longer able to go out in public. Corrective procedures worsened the damage until it was so bad, she needed to hide her face – not only from the world but also from her family and friends. After four frightening years of isolation and sustaining emotional and physical pain, her daughter finally had enough of the secrecy and reached out to hospitals all over the country. After the Congress, Carol came back to Ireland with me and told her story to Ryan Tubridy on the *RTÉ Late Late Show*. It was a journey none of us could have ever imagined as we sat outside her Miami home that night.

In 2005, I got increasing requests to lecture at international conferences, and found it a great way to expand my knowledge in new cutting-edge techniques. In late January, I lectured about the application of radiosurgery in cosmetic medicine at IMCAS Paris. As usual, Julie accompanied me on the trip and, later, we flew to Monaco, where I delivered a speech to the Aesthetic and Anti-Ageing World Congress regarding the new Syneron Polaris RF laser. Although she loved to travel, Julie never lost her fear of flying. The take-offs and landings terrified her, but not to the extent that she would opt to stay at home. In April, we travelled together to Moscow, at the invitation of Dr Elena Gubanova, to speak about Isolagen and fibroblast transplantation at the World International Symposium on Aesthetic Medicine. It was fascinating to see the city again after so many years. This was a different Moscow than it had been fourteen years before, a city where the new Russian state saw its glory in its saints and martyrs and the splendour of its churches, arts, science and literature. We travelled on the chandelier-laden Moscow Metro with marble faced stations with their gilded works of art. Somehow, in this new age, the wall frescos and ceiling mosaics told a different story. The peasants, the workers and revolutionary heroes were all still there, but they seemed silenced and unwilling any longer to be the propaganda billboards of a failed communist system. While in Moscow, we decided to visit the GUM store, that large Russian old trapezoidal shopping mall in the Kitai-gorod area. It was here that Stalin had displayed his wife Nadezhda's body in 1932 after she committed suicide as famine swept the Soviet Union during his forced collectivisation of agriculture. The glass-roofed three-storey building, which stretched the length of three football fields along Red Square contained many memories for me, not least the fact that Olga and I had passed many evenings together there fourteen years before, staring into the empty shop windows and watching the last remnants of the Soviet Empire collapse before our eyes.

We were looking at some Russian dolls in a souvenir shop on the second floor when an older lady entered briefly and then left. For a moment, her eyes caught mine and I focused on a black lesion on her left cheek and instantly thought it was a melanoma.

'Did you see that old woman?' I said to Julie, who was still entranced with some Matryoshka dolls laid out in descending order along the counter.

'No, I didn't see her,' she replied. 'Why?'

'I think she has a melanoma on her face!' I replied, making my way out to the corridor, just in time to see her descending the escalator. 'I'm going to have to tell her! Leave those and come with me.'

'Patrick, are you sure? This is not the time to be practicing dermatology.'

We descended the escalator after the older woman as the evening light fell through the glass roof structure and went to the outside of the building. After a short search, I noticed the old lady hail down a taxi and enter it with her shopping.

'What do we do now?' said Julie.

'We'll just have to follow her,' I said, hailing down another nearby taxi before we lost sight of where she was going.

We followed the old green Moskvitch taxi out of the Red Square feeling like we were enacting a scene from the latest *James Bond* movie with the walls of the Kremlin wall rising in front of us, St Basils to our right, and the GUM department store beginning to fade into the distance behind us.

'Are you sure that was a melanoma? How far are we going to follow her? How do we know where she's going?!' Julie asked in rapid succession, not stopping to ask one question at a time.

The evening was already beginning to fall when we reached the old lady's destination. Somehow, I'd the hoped the lady might have lived in one of those classic Italian-architectural buildings with graceful arches, balconies and columns that we passed along the way. She might have even invited us in for tea and Julie could have seen that other side of Moscow, which I had experienced back in 1991. But it was not to be, as her taxi stopped outside an old grey apartment block in a place full of many similar angular, austere buildings. Many of these apartments were constructed during the Khrushchev years, the early 1960s, and the Muscovites called them *Khruschyovka*.

The old lady got out of the taxi but quickly disappeared into the seventeen-floor complex. I had some difficulty telling the driver to wait for us and after running out of options to find suitable words to explain things to him, I decided to pay him and just let him go.

'Why did you let the taxi leave?' said Julie, becoming more exasperated by the minute in the way her day was now developing.

I stood for a while looking up at the building, hoping to catch a sight of the lady. We crossed by some children playing on some swings and made our way to the entrance of the building. She could be anywhere in this concrete labyrinth, and I thought the best thing was to find somebody who could speak English as a translator.

"Do you know an old lady with a black lesion on her face?" seemed to provide a quick answer, until we were brought to a rather surprised elderly African lady living on the third floor.

A small group of onlookers began to gather, and Julie became increasingly uncomfortable with proceedings.

'I think we should go home,' she said.

It was while we were on the third floor that I caught a brief glimpse of someone resembling the old lady entering one of the apartments.

'That's her!' I said, pointing in her direction.

Things happened apace, and there were now at least five of us with a few stragglers following in the rear scurrying in the direction of that brown door.

When I knocked on the door, a younger female answered, but I could see the older lady cowering behind her in the background. One of our group, who had a rather good command of English, spoke for all the assembled gathering.

'Is that your mother?' she asked.

'Yes, what do you want with her?'

'This person is a doctor,' she continued, 'and he would like to get a closer look at the black thing on her face as he thinks it might be dangerous.' The old lady and her daughter spoke briefly together, somewhat huddled away from our prying eyes.

Then the daughter approached us with her mother in full view.

'Yes!' she said. 'The doctors say that it is a melanoma and they are removing it in the hospital next Wednesday!'

That summer I gave a lecture on the use of Botox® in the treatment of migraine to the Migraine Association of Ireland. Although, I had been using botulinum toxin for the treatment of migraine since 2001, the technique was only adopted by both the Irish and UK regulatory authorities in 2010 and approved as a preventative treatment for chronic migraine headaches. During that period, I had some running arguments about its efficacy in treating migraines with some neurology consultants in the *Irish Medical Times*. It is estimated that over three-quarters of a million people in the UK and Ireland are affected by chronic migraines and that this can adversely affect their lives. It annoyed me to think that they would now benefit from the approval by learning the technique and charging their patients for the treatment. The insurance companies would not finance me as I was not a neurologist. At times, payment by insurance companies appears to be unfair, and the rewards seem to be concentrated unjustly amongst a chosen few.

That summer, I started conducting clinical trials on patients on a new form of fat treatment called injection lipolysis. The innovative treatment involved injecting the pharmaceuticals, phosphatidylcholine and deoxycholate (Lipostabil) into a patient's neck, arms or abdomen. This practice evolved from intravenous use of those drug formulations to treat blood disorders. The first report of Lipostabil injection for fat removal demonstrated that infra-orbital fat could be removed by Lipostabil injection by Patrica Rittes in Brazil in 2001. I published a joint study with a professor of dermatology at New York's Mount Sinai, repeating Ritte's work about its efficacy in the reducing infraorbital fat pads, in the *Journal of Cosmetic and Laser Therapy*. This was quite a breakthrough because it meant that patients could get rid of prolapsed fat pads without requiring surgery. Although the treatment worked successfully, it was controversial and difficult to get insurance to cover the procedure as it caused quite a lot of swelling underneath the eye and theoretically could have caused compression of the optic nerve causing blindness. I continued my research by combining the compound with subsequent radiofrequency for the treatment of cellulite. The results of my work earned me an invitation to Salzburg in Austria and, later, to the Grand Hyatt in New York to relate my experiences to the American Society of Mesotherapy.

There followed a few whirlwind months during which I spoke about RF (radiofrequency) at a dermatology conference in Japan, and later at the first International Lipolysis Convention in Salzburg. At the meeting in Austria, I explained it was preferable to inject Lipostabil at a specific angle into cellulitis, in order to physically disrupt the fibrous septal tissue. One of my German colleagues raised his hand and asked me what that precise angle was?

'It's forty-five degrees – the *Garrison* angle,' I jokingly replied.

I was amazed when I heard him mention the "Garrison angle" in a lecture he gave in Paris about a year later. If only my fellow villagers in County Fermanagh could have heard him and knew they were being remembered on the world stage. In September 2005, I was invited to speak about radiosurgery in general practice to the European Society of General Practice on the island of Kos in Greece. The same month, I lectured to dermatologists at the World Congress of the International Society for Dermatological Surgery, which fortunately was held in Co. Wicklow, Ireland that year.

In the fall, as things were going well at the clinic, I decided to buy an Aston Martin V12 Vantage. Its 5.9-litre, 48-valve, V12 engine had a power output of 420 hp. The car had a top speed of 186mph with the manual gearbox and could accelerate from 0–60mph in 4.9 seconds. My father would have loved to drive it. Little did I know then what would happen to the sports car a few years later.

That winter, I went back to New York with Julie to attend the wedding in Club 21 of Sophie, my previous Ailesbury Clinic receptionist. We stayed in Lower Manhattan with Dr Ed Schulhafer, a New Jersey allergist whom I had recently trained in the use of Dysport®, a European form of Botox®, which was gaining popularity in the United States. We also indulged our love of French Impressionists by visiting the Museum of Modern Art on 53rd Street, where we saw pieces by Claude Monet and Paul Cézanne. We decided to spend that Christmas in South Africa and stayed at the Cape Milner Hotel, in Tamboerskloof, under the shadow of Table Mountain. When we arrived on Christmas Eve, fires set by arsonists were burning all over the mountain. The papers said that some British tourists had lost their lives. Julie and I spent our time shark diving, going on safari and visiting wineries. During our visit to Robben Island, I chatted to Joseph Gumbi, who had been incarcerated with Mandela, and to a female ANC member. Both had been very appreciative of my dedication to Mandela's cause. They hugged me and thanked me with tears in their eyes – we had travelled a familiar road together.

The year, 2005, ended on a high when Ailesbury Clinic was voted best medical practice in Ireland at the Irish Healthcare Pharmaceutical Awards in Dublin.

In January 2006, Julie and I returned to Paris, where I spoke at the IMCAS conference about the use of Bio-Alcamid filler in patients who were suffering from HIV lipoatrophy. In April of that year, she told me she wanted to live in London. I had thought that both of us were committed to seeing the Ailesbury brand grow, but in the end, decided not to stand in her way. The relationship didn't survive the move, and we decided to split up a couple of months later. Although I knew it probably was for the best, I also missed the great times we'd had together, especially the romantic dinners in the evenings and dancing in the Dublin nightclubs until the early hours.

With Julie in Club 21 New York

That summer, I decided to set up a hair-transplant unit at Ailesbury Dublin and Cork and flew to Athens to learn a new technique from Kostas Giotas, who had founded a company called Direct Hair Implants. The procedure meant that hair could now be transplanted by follicular unit extraction (FUE) without the need for surgery or scars. By using this method, individual follicular units containing one to three hairs could be removed under local anaesthesia, using tiny punches of between 0.6mm and 1.0mm in diameter. The surgeon then used fine blades to puncture the sites to receive the grafts and could angle the wounds to create a more realistic hair pattern than the older hair plugs. The technique did not originate with DHI, but rather it was created by Dr John Cole (USA), Dr Woods (Australia) and Dr Choi (South Korea). It was another first for Ailesbury to bring the technique to Ireland. Greece was still special to me, and the new development gave me a reason to visit Athens a few times a year, usually to attend hair-transplant conferences and to lecture. The Ailesbury transplant programme was extraordinarily successful, and soon we were DHI's second most successful clinic, transplanting up to 6,000 hairs in one day.

DHI Annual Ball Grande Bretagne Athens

23. Treating the King of Pop

In late June 2006, rumours circulated in the Irish media that Michael Jackson had been sighted near the village of Kinsale, in County Cork. Over the next few days, sightings of the singer gained some credence, especially when *RTÉ* interviewed Bert Hughes of Hughes & Hughes bookshop in Dun Laoghaire, who confirmed a surprise visit from Michael and his children. Speculation became rife that Ireland might have become the land of choice for the singer and his family, as it was known that he didn't want to return to Neverland Valley Ranch in California. In the days that followed, there were other reported sightings of Jackson – in a bowling alley and a chip shop – but I thought little about it.

When the singer failed to show up at a Bob Dylan concert in Kilkenny as rumoured, fans were disappointed, but the speculation about him remained. I wasn't a massive fan of Michael's music back then, much preferring bands such as U2, the Rolling Stones and Pink Floyd, but I certainly recognised his genius when he performed on stage. His creativity crossed not only musical genres but also ethnic lines and made us believe that we could make this world a better place. Like many others, I had followed his recent child molestation court case in California and become acquainted, through the media, with most of the facts.

The problems for Jackson started in 2002 when he allowed a British documentary film crew, led by television personality Martin Bashir, to follow him around for six months. The programme was broadcast in February 2003 as *Living with Michael Jackson*, and it quickly became apparent that the reporter had gone out of his way to paint a very unflattering portrait of the singer.

After the documentary aired, Jackson was arrested when a young cancer sufferer, Gavin Arvizo, accused the superstar of molestation. I think it's fair to say that within media circles, there was a general supposition of Jackson's guilt. As an eccentric, wealthy, African American man, he had always been a target for litigation.

During the 1980s and 1990s, dozens of women falsely claimed he was the father of their children. He had been accused by a boy named Jordan Chandler, in 1993, and had reportedly paid him off. As the Arvizo trial continued, it became apparent that there also was no substantial evidence against the superstar. His accusers were not believable witnesses, and the trial showed that the family had attempted extortion before, trying to elicit money from other stars, including Jay Leno. Arvizo's parents had allegedly used his illness for their gain. I remember the words of *Rolling Stone's* Matt Taibbi when he wrote:

'Ostensibly a story about bringing a child molester to justice, the Michael Jackson trial would instead be a kind of homecoming parade of insipid American types: grifters, suckers and no-talent schemers, mired in either outright unemployment...or the bogus non-careers of the information age, looking to cash in any way they can. The first month or so of the trial featured perhaps the most compromised collection of prosecution witnesses ever assembled in an American criminal case – almost to a man a group of convicted liars, paid gossip hawkers or worse.'

On reflection, at that time, something that struck me as unusual was the fact, that those who had spent time in Jackson's company as children categorically denied any wrongdoing on his part. This included many hundreds of sick and terminally ill children such as AIDS patient Ryan White, whom he supported in his final years battling the disease and Bela Farkas for whom he paid for a lifesaving liver transplant. I felt empathy with his stance with Ryan White who became a national poster child for HIV/AIDS in the United States who had been banned from attending school following a diagnosis of AIDS. As a haemophiliac, White became infected with HIV from a contaminated factor VIII blood treatment and, when diagnosed in December 1984, was given six months to live. Doctors said he posed no risk to other students, as AIDS is not an airborne disease and spreads solely through body fluids, but when he tried to return to school, many parents and teachers in Howard County rallied against his attendance due to concerns of the disease spreading through bodily fluid transfer. My needle-stick injury happened around this period also, and above all others, I knew how poorly the public understood AIDS at the time.

*

One morning in August, I did a radio interview with *RTÉ* presenter Ryan Tubridy about this trend. When I arrived back at Ailesbury, I was a little surprised to find that a smartly dressed woman without an appointment had been waiting for some time to see me. She was black, attractive, spoke with a soft African accent, and had saffron-tinted hair that fell around her face in small ringlets. She introduced herself only as Grace and politely asked if she could make an out-of-office-hours appointment for a very prestigious client. The request was not unusual. Many celebrities send a representative to view the clinic before deciding to attend. Their greatest fear is that they will find the media camped en-masse on the doorstep, awaiting their arrival, cameras in hand.

It *was* a little unusual that, having met me and viewed the clinic, Grace still refused to name the client, although she did say '"he was a very famous singer" when referring to the star. I was curious, intrigued even. Before she left, Grace said that the client wanted no media attention about his medical consultation and that one of the main reasons he had decided to attend Ailesbury was my reputation for maintaining patient confidentiality.

'The singer finds it difficult to trust people,' she said. 'People are always trying to get something from him, so please don't mention our meeting to anybody. The singer already knows your work and he'd like to become your patient.'

She smiled in agreement when I asked if the singer was American but was unwilling to give any more information about him. On the agreed night, my nurse, Carmel, and I returned to the clinic at about nine o'clock. We passed some time cleaning up the clinic and then, right on cue at ten o'clock, the buzzer sounded. An instant later, the door opened, and the visitors entered. Grace kissed me lightly and introduced the male figure behind her. Before she could talk, he extended his hand to shake mine.

'Hi, Doctor Treacy,' he said. 'I'm Michael Jackson.'

It all happened so quickly that I was unprepared. He was the last person I had expected to walk through the door. Startled for a moment, I wondered why he would even feel the need to introduce himself – there would be few people on the planet who wouldn't recognise him. Michael was slightly taller than I had expected, slim, but not too thin. He wore a black fedora; his curly hair was tied at the back, and he had a smile so infectious that it was impossible not to warm to him. His jacket was made of velvety black suede, and it covered a white V-necked jumper that stretched tightly over his light frame. He wore little leather bands on both wrists; the type one gets on the beach during holidays on Greek islands.

We gathered by the glass doors near the clinic's reception area.

He turned back around to me.

'You've already met Grace,' he said, 'and she tells me you're interested in Africa. I know that you do some humanitarian work in Africa.'

'How do you know that?' I asked, wondering if during his research, he had seen some of my YouTube videos, which I'd uploaded about Africa.

I was completely taken aback when he then retrieved an old, curled-up *Health & Living* magazine from his inner jacket pocket and proceeded to read aloud from it.

Slightly bewildered, we all listened intently, as he read from an article that I had written some years earlier. 'There is unchanging magic in the landscape of Africa, but later, we pass many empty villages and vacant huts that are a testament to the destructive power of the plague whose path we follow.' He continued reading, 'I am haunted by these deserted hamlets and, in the restless winds that stir the blue savannah grasses, I listen expectantly to hear the noise of playing children or the sound of barking dogs, but no sound comes.'

He lowered the magazine.

'You know,' he said to me, 'I cried when I read this article. It captures the devastation of HIV in Africa.'

For a moment, I wondered where he had found the article, but then I realised that Grace had probably picked it from a selection on the waiting-room table on the day she was waiting.

'I'm thinking of doing a concert in South Africa for the children who have HIV. Maybe we should do something there together.'

I thanked Michael for his kind compliments about my article and told him that I used to live in South Africa and that I would love to help in any way that I could on an HIV charity concert there. The prospect of doing something about HIV in Africa with Michael Jackson was desirable to me. With his help, a lot of my dreams and aspirations could be turned into reality. I felt I had walked away from the problems of that continent many years before, even though I had been highlighting the issues in the media. The invitation to help one of the most famous people in the world organise a concert, and the thought of meeting Nelson Mandela made me feel that everything I had done up to that point in my life was coming together. I tried to curb my enthusiasm. After all, I had only met him for thirty minutes, and I realised he could just as quickly change his mind – but I hoped he wouldn't.

Jackson removed his dark sunglasses, placed his hat on my desk and took a seat opposite me. It was a surreal moment – I knew it probably wasn't the same hat that I had seen the singer tilt forward on his head or fling jubilantly into the air at the end of a concert, but that was how it felt.

'I've heard much about you, and I'd like to become your patient,' he started shyly.

His voice transmitted in a kind of stuttering falsetto that only served to complete the theatrical effect. It was one of those moments when you are alone with a patient, and you can hear their emotions subsiding into breathing. I got the distinct feeling that he wanted to talk about something but was too shy to mention it. I turned from my desk and took a moment to study the singer's face more closely. His lips appeared to have been tinted bright red, probably coloured in with semi-permanent makeup. It must have been done recently, as that kind of "tattoo" usually fades to a more natural pink within a couple of weeks. His eyebrows and eyelashes were jet black; given his age, I assumed that they had been dyed. His most peculiar characteristic was his skin colour, which was an artificial-looking peach-white, heavily camouflaged with beige foundation and rouge, and populated with lots of unshaven black stubble. There was a large flesh coloured SteriStrip stuck over the tip of his nose, which I presumed was there to hide some damage caused by previous surgery to the area. The whole effect was a strange fusion of David Bowie's *Ziggy Stardust* and Michael Jackson, all wrapped up in Kabuki-style makeup, but somehow, I doubt that Bowie's chief designer, Yamamoto, would have approved of the look. Although I am known for being honest about my opinion on any aesthetic look, I considered it more sensible not to pass any comment on Michael Jackson's look at that time. He interrupted my reverie by leaning forward in his chair and clearing his throat a few times.

The singer's unwavering eyes kept looking deep inside me, waiting for an answer. He then broke the silence and said, 'I'm going to meet the Queen soon, and I want to look my best.'

'Fantastic, when will you be meeting her?' I inquired.

'It's not for a few months yet in London.'

Michael told me the Queen and Prince Phillip were attending the opening of the movie, *Casino Royale*, in Leicester Square and that he'd been invited to the premiere where he would be presented to her. I realised from his conversation that this was uppermost in his mind and that he was quite nervous about it. However, it was still a few months to go, and I suspected he had more to tell me rather than just trying to perfect his look. Meanwhile, I tried to get off the dimple subject until I knew something more about it.

Michael then took a book from the case behind me. It was a copy of Anthony du Vivier's 630-page *Atlas of Clinical Dermatology*. For a while, he sat silently, slowly fingering through the pages. For a while, he sat motionless reading the words therein.

'Nobody knows how devastated that child feels. These pictures only tell some of the stories. They can never show the emotion that the child feels, in here,' he said, pressing a fist tightly to his chest.

I looked over at him. The graphics on the page he had opened were mostly of black African adults and children, some with leprosy but all in various stages of hypopigmentary conditions. One image of a child who had a large white abdominal patch and several more on his legs appeared to catch his attention. He gazed at it for a long time before he began to read from the book aloud.

'Vitiligo is usually symmetrical, but occasionally can be segmental. The patches are completely depigmented and appear white, but not always in the initial stages,' he read, and then stopped and pulled up one of his trouser legs and said, 'You see, I too have vitiligo!'

I was rather shocked to see the extent of his disease. This was not the dermatological condition that we had discussed before. For a long time, neither of us spoke, not daring to give words to our thoughts. Could it be that the world had been wrong all along about him, accusing him of denying his race while he had a medical condition that made his skin appear to be white?

'How bad is it?' I asked.

He seemed to think about the answer for a moment and then sat back in the chair. Shyly, he framed his face with his hands, lifted his shirt to show the porcelain-white patches on his body, and said, 'It's awfully bad!'

Then Michael took off his trousers, and I could see that his legs were so severely affected that they looked like a white man's limbs with large black spots, some as large as six to eight centimetres in diameter. The condition covered most of his body, making me believe that he had had it for many years. He told me that for the previous twenty years he had been attending a Californian dermatologist named Arnold Klein, who had treated his skin for acne and the hypopigmentation caused by vitiligo. My heart went out to him. Someone coping with an illness like vitiligo has enough to contend with psychologically, let alone having to deal with the tabloid newspaper reports that had accused him of wanting to deny his colour.

When he talked about the emotional impact of vitiligo on the African child in the photo, I felt he understood the psychological aspects of the condition. I tried to envisage what it must be like to be accused by the media of denying his people while carrying such a burden alone, painting his skin with creams, trying to control a condition rather than change his race. When he eventually found the courage to tell the world of his illness, it was deemed untrue, an excuse for changing his skin colour.

After he had left, I thought about how he seemed like such a sensitive person. We shared common interests, and it would be nice to get to know him better and help organise his concert for HIV relief in Africa. Michael called me a few days later and said there was something in the paper that he needed to discuss. When he arrived, he took two centre pages from the *Irish Times* and placed them on the blue granite countertop. I was surprised that he would be reading this paper and had a feeling that I was about to learn something else about him.

The article he highlighted was about two children who had been set alight in the back seat of a car, in Moyross, Limerick, in the west of Ireland. Their mother, while visiting a friend, had been approached by two youths, who had asked her for a lift to the county court. She had refused, and, after some abuse, the teens had left. But then they came back with a friend, armed with plastic lemonade bottles filled with petrol. They stuck rags in the bottlenecks and set them alight before lobbing them at the car. The two children sitting in the back were quickly engulfed in a roaring inferno. Gavin, who was five, and Millie, who was seven, writhed in agony as their horrified mother looked on. Sheila Murray managed to pull her daughter, Millie, from the car, while neighbours – including one of the perpetrators, who had been posted as a lookout and hadn't realised the children were in the car – rescued Gavin. Both children had to be sedated before being transferred from the Mid-Western Regional Hospital to Our Lady's Children's Hospital in Crumlin, Dublin.

'I think about those poor children all the time,' Michael said.

'They must be in such pain. They'll give them morphine, right?'

'Do you know the hospital? Will you please take me to visit them there so I can see they're all right?' he asked.

I hesitated, feeling that it would be foolish for him to visit these children so soon after he had been accused of child molestation.

'I don't think that's a particularly good idea, Michael,' I said.

He was noticeably quiet, and I felt that my answer had disappointed him. I shouldn't have said what I had, but I couldn't take it back.

At that time, I was completely unaware at the time that he had visited children in many hospitals, especially paediatric burns victims, all around the world while he was on tour. My answer suggested that I didn't really believe the outcome of the Santa Maria trial. The bright light had now died in his eyes, and his shoulders seemed to collapse in on themselves as he hunched forward in the chair. His whole persona seemed to disintegrate, and the vibrant, powerful personality diminished in front of my eyes. He then took off his black wig and showed me his scalp, his natural hair tightly cropped, wispy in places, with bald patches and a large scar on the crown of his head.

'This is why I want to go there; therefore, I wanted to talk to you today,' he said. 'I was once burnt too, and I know what it's like.'

I was at a loss for words, so I fell back on what I know best – medicine. I got up and asked him if I could look at his scalp. He told me that while filming a Pepsi-Cola advertisement in 1984, a pyrotechnic display had fallen from the set, landed on his head and set his hair alight. When I had finished examining his scalp, we discussed the possibility of treating the area with hair implants. Michael told me that he had had balloon implants inserted in his scalp to stretch the area, cut out the scars and, hopefully, restore his hair. This had gone on for several years, and he confessed that he had given up hope of ever repairing it and instead chose to wear a wig.

The event was more traumatic for Michael, as he had – I later discovered – become addicted to painkillers during that time. Given the amount of underlying scar tissue that had resulted from a failed repair attempt, I almost immediately decided that Michael was not a good candidate for hair implants. My needle-stick injury sustained so many years before sprang into my mind, and I considered how a single incident could change one's life forever. I felt sorry for him. 'But I still don't think it would be wise for you to go there,' I said.

Michael replaced his wig, adjusted it in a small mirror, and composed himself.

'Michael, I'll personally visit the hospital tomorrow and find out how those children are'! I said.

The Murray children were being well looked after, were sedated, and had been made as comfortable as was humanly possible. I also thought that they deserved the opportunity to recover in peace and should not be subjected to a media circus.

Although petrol bomb victims, Millie and Gavin Murray, never got to meet Michael, despite his repeated pleas to see them, they were rewarded in 2013 by been asked to take part in the Michael Jackson tribute portrait, a Los Angeles project, which saw some of the world's most famous stars place a dot in a portrait of the late singer. The portrait was made up of a million dots representing hundreds of thousands of people worldwide. David Ilan, the Los Angeles artist behind the project, travelled especially to Ireland to give the children the award. At the ceremony in the Ailesbury Clinic, he said, 'These children are the perfect people to get the last dots in Michael's portrait because not only are we finally connecting these kids with him but we're also bringing some joy and our collective love and strength to these kids.' I believe Michael would have wanted these children to get the final dots.

One day we were chatting in the clinic when I had to leave to attend a patient who required removal of a dermal filler from her face. Her doctor had placed too much Restylane® under her eye, while filling a tear trough and it now appeared to be bulging. Over the years, I had developed confidence in how to remove these fillers with an enzyme called hyaluronidase. Michael was fascinated when he heard about the procedure and told me he felt that he had too much dermal filler in one side of his face and whether I could remove it. Then he stated that he would like it removed before he met with the Queen at the opening of *Casino Royale* in a few months, and I assured him again that if he felt there was too much dermal filler in his face, then we could quite quickly reverse it with hyaluronidase.

In the end, he suggested we could conference call his dermatologist, Dr Arnold Klein, in California who would probably reassure him about its use.

He asked me whether, I could get him an anaesthetist to put him to sleep for the procedure, again pleading with me regarding his nasal sensitivity and fear of needles. I told him it was slightly inappropriate but assured him that if it was only mild sedation, then I probably could. It surprised me, when he queried what sedation that we would be using and whether it or not it would be Propofol. This anaesthetic is popular with anaesthetists because of its rapid onset of action and very short duration *of* action. It has an excellent recovery profile, and patients usually wake up after a propofol injection in an alert state. However, it is also an extremely potent respiratory depressant, and even small doses may cause the onset of "apnea", or loss of breathing. This effect is even more pronounced when the drug is administered alongside other respiratory depressants, such as opioids. I am already on record on the *Dr Drew Show* on CNN that we administered propofol on more than one occasion to Michael in Dublin, but little did I know, as I listened to him speak about "his milk" that he would die from the same medicine in the hands of a rogue doctor just a few years later.

The next evening, we rang Dr Klein from the clinic. Michael chatted to some people on the phone for a while and then he turned it over to me.

'Patrick, I'd like you to talk to Carrie Fisher,' he said.

'She's an incredibly good friend of mine, and she happens to be with Arnie in the office.' I was surprised at the informality of it all, and I didn't know much about Carrie, other than that she had acted in the George Lucas film *Star Wars*. I needn't have worried, as she was a pleasant woman who spoke with the warmth and ease of those used to dealing with strangers.

'Hi, Patrick. I hear you guys are taking real good care of Michael in Ireland,' she said.

'Yes, indeed, he loves it here.'

'He told me that – he's told me about you too.'

'All good I hope?'

The actor laughed and spoke for a little longer until I excused myself and handed the phone back to Michael.

'She's a special friend of mine. I'm glad the two of you got to talk,' he whispered. Such a small incident seemed to give him genuine pleasure. Throughout our time together, Michael had a habit of passing me his phone and sharing his friends with me.

That was the first and last time I spoke to Carrie Fisher. After finishing the European leg of her book tour in December 2016, she was on a commercial flight, from London to Los Angeles when she suffered a medical emergency around fifteen minutes before the aircraft landed. A passenger performed CPR until paramedics arrived transferred her to the Ronald Reagan UCLA Medical Center, where she was placed on a ventilator. She died four days later at the age of 60.

Meanwhile, Dr Klein got on the phone, and Michael had a few words with him before passing him on to me.

'Hello, Dr Treacy? Arnie Klein here.'

Michael sat to my left, listening to our conversation. Dr Klein and I started chatting academically,

'Did you see my article in the *Journal of Dermatological Surgery* a few months ago?' he asked. 'It was called "Minimally Invasive Esthetics: My Life's Journey".'

As luck would have it, I had read the complete article; the same edition had included a research paper of my own, about Bio-Alcamid facial implants in patients who suffered from HIV lipoatrophy. Soon our conversation became more natural – two colleagues in the same industry sharing what we had achieved in our field. We chatted for a while about HIV, and how we both had developed an interest in the disease. In the infancy of the AIDS epidemic, Arnie had become one of the first doctors to link the illness to Kaposi's sarcoma. He had also helped establish the Elizabeth Taylor AIDS Foundation and Art for AIDS.

I told him about my needle-stick injury and, for a while, forgot about Michael, who was waiting patiently for me to end my conversation. I explained to Arnie that Bio-Alcamid was a one-off, permanent procedure, which reduced the requirement for having to repeatedly put a doctor, or his staff, at risk of accidental injury through exposure to the virus.

'Do you get many HIV patients in Ireland?' he asked.

'I did, but I get fewer now, as the hospitals have begun to treat them aesthetically.'

Michael then stood up and began to pace, obviously tiring of the conversation, which was going on much longer than he had imagined it would. I knew he was nervous about the upcoming events in London, so I focused the conversation to what we were supposed to be talking about.

'Michael feels he has a little too much dermal filler in one side of his face and he'd like me to take some out.'

'And can you do that?' Arnie replied.

'Yes, I've done it a few times before using hyaluronidase!'

'How many units would you use?' he continued.

'About 350, I think.'

I wanted to ask Arnie about the fact that Michael had requested propofol to have the procedure and whether he considered that this was appropriate but felt that was something I could speak to him later. Again, on reflection, it is difficult to imagine that I am the only person still alive who was in that conversation that night. Arnie Klein died on October 22, 2015, at Eisenhower Medical Center in Rancho Mirage, California. No cause of death was announced.

Michael was in the clinic one evening, treating his vitiligo when one of the strangest incidents in my life happened. His mobile rang, and he was answering it while I applied a depigmentation cream to the bottom of his lower legs. He usually only treated his skin condition in areas that could be seen by the general public. With feverish eyes, he handed the phone to me.

'Patrick! chat to him!' he said. 'Go on, it's my friend. He's going to help us with the AIDS concert in South Africa.'

I sighed and took the phone. As the Amelan® cream that I was using was going to solidify, it was hardly the time to start talking to someone who I presumed was another concert promoter. I had heard his distinctive voice speaking in the background, and thought the person was probably an Afrikaner.

'So, are you going to help Michael and me get this concert in Africa organised?' I asked.

'Yes, how are you? We can make everything possible here in South Africa,' the man on the phone said.

'Where are you speaking from?' I continued.

'I'm speaking from Cape Town.'

'Oh, I used to live in Cape Town!' I replied, giving up my annoyance and trying to make the person on the other end of the phone feel more at home.

Michael started to laugh. Feeling that a joke was being played on me, I asked the man on the phone who he was.

'It's Madiba,' he laughed back.

'Who's Madiba?' I replied, absentmindedly, trying to concentrate again on what I had been doing.

'So, how is the weather in South Africa?' I said, trying to be polite and get off the phone as quickly as possible at the same time.

'The sun is shining, every day,' he replied.

'You must come down here. How is Michael keeping?' he asked.

'Michael is fine, enjoying the weather here as well!'

Michael got bothered by my small talk and took the phone back again, just as I realised that the distinctive voice on the other end of the phone – Madiba – was Nelson Mandela! I couldn't believe that the person I had supported, in my small way, in his struggle for freedom had just been talking to me and I had been so abrupt with him.

He continued to speak to him, but no matter how many hand signals I made, he wouldn't hand the phone over again. Maybe it was just Michael's way of saying that he was annoyed that I had not recognised Mandela, but he terminated the call and put the phone in his shirt pocket.

'I wanted to commiserate with him about the recent death of his son from AIDS,' I said.

'Don't worry,' he said, sensing my disappointment. 'Grandfather probably won't remember anything anyway. Not many people know it, but he's in the early stages of Alzheimer's disease. We'll have to deal with his son to help us organise the concert. But I promise we'll go to see him personally when we're in Africa.'

'On the subject of HIV, I saw there was a story going around a few years ago that you refused to kiss the Blarney Stone as you thought you could catch AIDS or something else,' I said.

'Most of that was nonsense,' Michael replied. 'It was a different time when people thought you could catch AIDS from kissing, and there was no cure for it.'

'I know – I once got stuck with an HIV needle,' I said, pulling up my trouser leg to show him the scar where I had been accidentally injected.

He looked at the scar silently, time ticked away, and he just didn't know what to say.

'It's OK,' I said. 'I went to the theatre and got the surgeon to cut a lump out of my leg. I never seroconverted – it was nearly twenty years ago.'

'Then the children with HIV in Africa are the same for you as the photographs in your book were for me,' Michael said.

It was a profound, philosophical statement, and we hugged each other close. For a while, neither of us spoke. There was no need to say anything. I had defeated my opponent at an emotional price, while Michael was still living his nightmare. Our fates were also intrinsically linked by the events themselves: without my needle-stick injury, I would have been less drawn to Africa, and without the HIV article, Michael Jackson may never have become my patient.

Recently, I met Nelson Mandela's granddaughter, Swati Dlamini a private function arranged by Mr. Bruno Doutrelepont in Kilruddery House. Swati is the granddaughter of Nelson and Winnie Mandela and recently participated in the publishing of The Prison Letters of Nelson Mandela in which she wrote the forward. She laughed heartily when she heard the story of me mistaking her grandfather for a concert promoter and had fond memories of Michael Jackson visiting her homeland before giving me a signed hard back copy of the edition.

With Swati Mandela in Dublin

On another occasion that Michael was in the clinic, my nurse Carmel came into the office to get me.

'You'll have to go up to the glass room,' she said. 'He's taking all our creams and putting them into his pockets.'

The glass room was an area in the clinic that is constructed almost entirely of glass, with backlit shelving, where we kept expensive cosmetic products on display. It was big enough to consult and had a table, chairs, and a skin-analysis device. I went up and saw Michael with his back to me, stretching up to the top shelves, removing the more expensive bottles and placing them into his jacket and pants pockets. When these were full, he took a chair to gather a selection of the medical-grade facial creams and put them into a plastic bag that he had found in one of the drawers.

'You realise there's going to have to be a charge for these, don't you?' I asked.

He turned his head and looked at me sheepishly, slowly withdrawing some lotions from his pocket and pretending to polish the glass shelving before carefully placing the products down. I was amazed at the fluidity of his movement, especially since he was in his late forties.

When he had decided which products, he could part with and had returned them to their shelves, he turned to me, showed me what he had left in his hands, and said, 'I'm taking these with me.'

I was surprised at his impulsivity, but presumably, he felt that he could take whatever he wanted when he visited a clinic because he was Michael Jackson.

'There'll be nothing left for the Irish ladies,' I sternly replied.

*

One day, I had to visit Michael, at Grouse Lodge, where he was staying. We arrived by the entrance to the estate. The countryside was slowly swallowing the sun, and the shadows were falling fast over the nearby hills. There were some winding roads surrounded by low stone walls, and now and then the driver would point out security guards watching the property. We passed the studio where Michael was recording his new album and made our way towards Coolatore House. The seclusion of the property had already attracted poets and musicians such as Nobel Prize winner Seamus Heaney and its studios had been used by everyone from REM to Snow Patrol and Shirley Bassey.

Grace was waiting in the dimly lit entrance porch to welcome me. It was a fiercely cold November night, and we made small talk about the weather before she took my green overcoat to hang it up. It was the one that my mother had got for me before she died, and I treasured it. After a while, Michael arrived and took my medical bag inside. We chatted for a short while in one of the lower rooms, which was decorated with dated period furniture and high, newly painted ceilings. A short while later, quite unexpectedly, he got up, saying he had better put the children to bed. He told me to follow him into one of the lower bedrooms, where Prince Michael was already in bed. In the dim light, Michael bent over him and kissed him goodnight.

'I love you, Daddy,' the child said.

'I love you too,' Michael replied.

Michael and I then went into one of the downstairs living rooms, where Paris and Blanket were already asleep with a jacket over them. Michael took one in his arms to carry upstairs and asked me to get the other. I carried the sleeping four-year-old up to bed in my arms. Not knowing the difference, and seeing the long hair, I thought that I was carrying a girl. We were halfway up the stairs when I turned to Michael and said, 'She's a lovely child.'

'Don't let *him* hear you say that,' he laughed. 'He's my youngest son!'

So, this was Blanket, the child that Michael had dangled over the balcony for the fans at the Hotel Adlon in Berlin that night. I still remembered the tabloid images of the nine-month-old child in a blue jumpsuit, with his head covered by a towel, and it started to erode my positive impression of Michael. Which was the truth? The loving father or the erratic individual represented in the British tabloids. Every inch of me screamed that it was the former, and for a moment, I thought about asking him what had happened that night. However, it never seemed to be the right time to ask these delicate questions.

'Why did you call him Blanket?' I asked.

'That's his nickname – his real name is Prince Michael Joseph Jackson II. Blanket is his nickname; it means "blessing".'

We left the children in their beds. Paris shifted, snuggling into him, and he gently kissed the top of her head. I had always thought that Michael Jackson was in his element on stage, but *this* was his element. I was touched by the love and normality of the scene. He was very obviously a doting father, much loved by his children, someone far removed from the media's interpretation of him. More than once, they had intimated that he was damaging his children in some way by keeping their faces hidden behind veils and home-schooling them. When he had made sure that the children were settled, he showed me into another room upstairs. We chatted for a while about how the Murray children were progressing and how he had enjoyed his day with his children. Michael then opened a bottle of wine, and we had a few glasses. 'Do you miss Neverland?' I asked.

'No, Neverland is now over. The media are probably wondering how I'm surviving without a daily ride on the Ferris wheel. They're stupid!'

He went on to explain that Neverland had been his dream home, and he had loved it for a long time, but it had been turned into something sordid. His home had always been more than an amusement park. It had entertained thousands of children: not only those who were sick but those from underprivileged areas, giving them a break from their daily, grinding poverty. 'I built a home where children could feel safe, a sort of sanctuary,' Michael said.

He flopped back into the chair and sighed. I couldn't help thinking that if he hadn't had vitiligo, a lot of the negative press would never have occurred. He looked odd; ergo, he must be odd – that seemed to be the idea, and once that was embedded in the public psyche, the media had to feed the frenzy they had created. Michael Jackson sold a copy.

'Do you think you'll make your home here?' I asked.

'Patrick, I love Ireland, and this would make a great place to raise children. We get to do a lot of things together here. I'm working on it. I just must get myself back out there, sort out my finances, and I'll probably set up home here. I feel it would be a safe place for my children to grow up.'

'Bono does a lot for Africa. Maybe if you came to live here, the two of you could team up?' I said, laughing.

'I don't think Bono likes me,' he replied.

I never went into the finer details of why he felt that this was the case, but I suspected it was related to the charges being laid upon him.

'Treacy, where are you from? he asked.

'I'm from Fermanagh, in Northern Ireland.'

'I grew up in Garrison, a little village by the shores of Lough Melvin. You like Charlie Chaplin, don't you? He used to fish on that lake.

'I love Charlie Chaplin! That's amazing! We must go up and visit that lake.'

'You'd love it; it's stunning.'

I told him that we had a shop, a filling station, and a garage near the lakeshore and that we would go swimming there in the summer.

'Sounds like a wonderful childhood,' he said. 'Did you have a good relationship with your father?'

'Oh, yes,' I said.

I explained that my father had died many years earlier, but that he had been a good man, and everybody had loved him.

'I hope my children say that about me one day, Patrick.'

'I've seen you with them, and I'm sure they will, Michael.'

'Thank you, my friend.'

He had brought my father to mind, and I started reminiscing about the good times we'd shared and how he had always been there for all of us. I told him a story about my father, from when I was still at St Michael's College in Enniskillen. I had entered the Irish Aer Lingus Biochemist of the Year competition with a study on the effects of different sound waves on the growth of mung beans. The project required individual wooden boxes with acoustic wadding, so that the growing plants could be isolated from contamination by other sound waves and be influenced only by those that were generated by an audio frequency oscillator.

The materials were expensive, and I went to bed one night, depressed that we didn't have the money to buy them, I told Michael.

'And what happened?' he asked.

'Well, the following morning, I woke up to find that my father had made the acoustic boxes during the night,' I said. 'Incredibly, he had taken down the large, wooden road display from outside our garage and worked for hours during the night to complete the task.' I explained to him that the advertising display sign had been easily fifteen feet by ten feet and that it had cost my dad a few hundred pounds to erect in the first place. The story absorbed Michael and clapped his hands as he asked me what had become of the project. He was fascinated when I told him that the plants grew to nearly four times their standard size and that the project had won the competition.

'That's just incredible,' he said. 'Why do you think they did that? Did they respond to a special sound that they loved?'

Michael had a long history of producing environmentally conscious videos about the earth and saving Amazonian plants. He listened intently, nodding with naive enthusiasm when I started talking about the acoustic wavelengths that I had used. I half-expected him to use them for some record of saving the planet. I knew he wanted to hear that my plants had loved a sound and that was what had caused them to grow taller.

The truth, however, wasn't at all romantic. The plants possibly didn't grow because of their love for a sound: they might as quickly have responded to a negative growth inhibitor, ethylene gas, which was released from the soil when the sound waves from the audio frequency oscillator blasted them. This was the most plausible scientific explanation put forward by me at my level of research at the time of the experiment. Michael seemed disappointed with my unemotional scientific answer and I got the feeling he thought I was joking with him. I felt I knew him well enough at this stage to throw some humour into the conversation.

'Michael, if I'd known you back then, I would certainly have played them *Earth Song*.'

He studied me for a while and then started laughing.

'No,' he replied, 'it sounds like those plants needed to listen to *Beat It* played way up loud! With Eddie van Halen on a Marshall amp as well – that'd get them growing.'

We laughed together for a long while and poured some more wine.

Michael went quiet for a few moments.

'That was such a great thing your father did,' he said. 'I don't think Joe would have done that for me.' Michael paused, trying to choose his words carefully. 'He wanted to be a musician, but he had kids to feed. Maybe it was failed ambition; maybe he saw the talent, so he worked us and worked us and worked us… I was terrified of him. Sometimes I think we were just his meal ticket. Fatherhood can be difficult, but I hope my children will have better memories of me.'

As we both got a little drunker, he started talking about the Santa Maria trial and strongly hinted, regarding the issue of child molestation, that he had been set up.

'I'd never harm a child – anyone who knows me, knows that. They told me to part with some of my catalogue or the case would be brought against me.'

'Who did? Your record companies?' I asked.

In retrospect, I know that this conversation is of public importance, but he never really answered that question accurately. He said that he had received a telephone call, and I got the eerie feeling that he was terrified of someone.

'They're watching you, watching all of us,' he said.

I felt a cold shiver and slipped naturally into my doctor's "bedside manner", allowing him to unburden himself some more. So many in America still believed he was guilty, despite the verdict, that he felt badly let down by his people – even those he had worked so tirelessly to help.

We got up together, and I went to get my green overcoat, but it wasn't hanging in the hallway any longer. If it had been any other coat, I would have left it and simply asked Michael to bring it with him the next time he visited the clinic. Michael and I searched the lower rooms, and eventually, we found it behind the sofa in the room where Blanket had been sleeping. Michael tried not to laugh but couldn't help himself as he handed it to me.

'Sure, he's a thief and takes after his father!' he said, in a dreadful Irish accent.

It wouldn't be the last time that Blanket took a shine to something belonging to me. A few days later, Michael flew to London and performed at the World Music Awards.

*

In later years, I thought about that statement again about him wanting to build a home "where children could feel safe", a sort of sanctuary. It seems ironic that as I write this instalment, the world has been hit with an unexpected and unpleasant event with HBO's two-part Michael Jackson documentary called *Leaving Neverland*. In the new four-hour documentary, James Safechuck and Wade Robson accuse him of sexually abusing them from early childhood into adolescence. James Safechuck is now 41 and was ten years old when the alleged sexual abuse began. James Safechuck claimed in the documentary that Michael "had secret rooms, alarmed doors and one-way glass to stop anybody spotting superstar abusing kids".

*

The World Music Awards were Michael's first UK performance in nearly a decade, and he was given the Diamond Award for having sold more than 100 million albums in his career. He had already been given the Millennium Award some years earlier, as he had sold nearly three-quarters of a billion records in his career. Although the reception he received was incredible, things started to go wrong for him later in the awards ceremony, possibly around the time the audience discovered he wouldn't be joining Chris Brown to sing *Thriller*. They were not impressed when he finally came out on stage and performed a very feeble version of, *We Are the World* with a children's choir, which sang most of the song. In truth, he only sang the chorus of the charity hit before stopping to repeatedly tell the audience: 'I love you; I love you.' The crowd started booing him as Rihanna came onto the stage.

The British tabloids were relentless in their criticism. The *Daily Mirror* reported: 'When he stopped singing no one could understand why. But when he started rambling, a lot of people lost their patience with him. That's when the booing started, and it got louder and louder until he left the stage.'

I felt deeply sorry for Michael when he returned to Ireland. After a few days, he said he didn't have the confidence to meet the Queen after what had happened at the World Music Awards. I knew how much he feared meeting the Queen and how shy he was beneath his exuberant exterior.

*

Near the end of November, I scheduled another trip with Kostas Giotas, the CEO of Direct Hair Implants, to see about twenty patients in Abu Dhabi who were interested in the Follicular Unit Extraction (FUE) hair transplant. I flew via Manchester, where I had been asked to conduct a training session for some doctors in the use of Bio-Alcamid implants in HIV lipoatrophy patients, as the NHS was considering introducing the treatment to public hospitals in Britain. During the session, Michael phoned me to see how I was and asked the stunned lady who was holding my phone while I was lecturing if he could speak to me. He wished me all the best and asked if I would be kind enough to bring him home a souvenir dinner menu from the Emirates Palace in Abu Dhabi.

When I got back to Ireland from the Emirates, Michael called me again and asked if I would take Blanket to see the dentist. He said that he was in the studio all day and couldn't accompany his son but wanted to send him to Dublin with a driver. Michael's children were lovely, mannerly kids – a credit to him. Blanket was the quietest, in my view, but reminded me very much of Michael. Although he didn't say much, he always struck me as being very observant, taking in all that was going on around him. When the procedure was over, I took him back to my clinic and sat him on the sofa in the waiting room, where he was entirely absorbed by the flashing lights on the Christmas tree. Blanket was now over by the fireplace, standing side by side with a decorative wooden snowman, which was much bigger than him. His eyes seemed to be huge in his head, and his arm was thrown around the snowman's neck. I stood in the doorway and told him that his driver had arrived. He stayed where he was.

I stretched out my hand and wiggled my fingers, signalling him to come to me. He didn't move. His lips sealed in determination, he tightened his grip on the snowman and seemed to be holding his breath.

'Why don't you bring your friend with you?' I said.

He visibly exhaled and, for a moment, I was treated to a beautiful smile, which lit up his whole face and reminded me of his father. He began to walk towards me but was hampered by the weight of the snowman as he dragged it alongside him. I bent down to carry it for him, but he whipped it away – no one was getting their hands on it but him!

Blanket struggled with it out to the door, where the driver also tried to give him a hand – but he was having none of it. It was funny to see the determined little character drag his new best friend to the car. It's an image that I'll never forget.

*

On Christmas Day, the soul icon James Brown died. In a career that lasted 50 years, this gospel singer from Toccoa, Georgia had influenced the development of several music genres, including that of Michael Jackson, whom I texted to send my deepest commiserations. I never received a reply and just assumed that Michael was no longer using his Irish phone. He later contacted me to say that he was now living in Las Vegas and would try and get back to Ireland with his family as soon as he could. The years passed, and other events began to take over his life, though. He never returned to Ireland.

On June 8th, 2009, Paul Martin penned a story for the June 8 British *Daily Mirror* under the title "Jacko Goes Green" that Michael was going to be returning to Ireland for further dermatology treatment. The *Daily Mirror* article stated, "Michael Jackson will make secret trips to Ireland for cosmetic surgery check-ups when he moves to London next month". The moonwalking star visited Dublin's Ailesbury Clinic several times when he lived in Ireland for a spell three years ago. Now the 50-the year-old singing legend is planning to return after striking up a friendship with top cosmetic dermatologist Dr Patrick Treacy. A source revealed: "Michael has been there in the past, but nobody has ever known about it. He has a great deal of admiration for Dr Treacy's work… Michael will fly over whenever he needs his skin treated and for top-up treatments on surgery that he has had done in the past. He is always having his skin looked at because of his vitiligo, a condition that whitens his appearance."'

The piece continued, saying that he felt 'comfortable at the Ailesbury because he doesn't get harassed by paparazzi there. All eyes will be on him so it's great that he can get away to Ireland when he needs to and be off the radar'. The article was interesting, as its source seemed to know as much as me about his impending visit. It also seemed to quash other recent gossip: 'And despite rumours the star is too ill to perform at the 50 "sell-out" gigs the source added:

The Sun Newspaper front cover

"Michael is in good shape and has been leaving the younger dancers in the rehearsals in awe of him.". I later spoke to Paul Martin, who confirmed to me he had heard the rumour from a member of the singer's entourage. Days passed, and I looked forward to Michael returning to Europe. He hadn't called in a while, and I wondered whether everything was OK.

24. The Death of Michael Jackson

I was at home in Ballsbridge when a breaking news report came on television: 'We've just learnt that Michael Jackson was taken, by ambulance, to a hospital in Los Angeles... We're told it was cardiac arrest, and that paramedics administered CPR in the ambulance... It's looking bad.'

I stood in shocked silence, listening to the horrific news. Over the next fifteen minutes, the story developed. I shook my head in disbelief when the news bulletin said, 'We've just learnt Michael Jackson has died. The fifty-year-old suffered a cardiac arrest earlier this afternoon at his Holmby Hills home, and paramedics were unable to revive him.' I thought about his family, about Prince, Paris, and Blanket, and how distraught and afraid they must have been at that moment. What life would they have without their father?

The phone rang. I looked at my watch: it was 11.15 pm on June 25, 2009. TV3's *Ireland AM* wanted to interview with me the following morning. I lay in bed that night, thinking about the enormity of what had just happened. The world had lost not only a wonderfully talented entertainer, a genius in his field, but also one of its greatest humanitarians. I thought about what we could have done together in Africa, building hospitals, and helping children who had been orphaned when their parents had died with HIV. It would be nice to be able to continue this legacy, I thought. Michael had been misunderstood and often taken advantage of during his life, and now there would be nobody to protect his legacy; his children were just too young.

During the breakfast-television interview, I told the Irish listening audience about the side of the singer that I had witnessed, the enormous love between Michael and his children, and I defended his great humanitarian work. The interviewer, Mark Cagney, was very respectful of Michael's legacy and allowed me to tell the nation about the side of Michael that nobody knew. I told some personal stories about how comical and intelligent he was. It was an honest appraisal of the person I had come to know.

Tom Prendeville interviewed me later that day for the *Evening Herald*, and I said that Michael had been the perfect embodiment of the rags-to-riches story, whose celebrity took him from gifted musical child to global superstar. Unfortunately, it also brought him back to America, to a place where he had endured painful lawsuits and unscrupulous people who took advantage of his good nature and kindness. I thought again about his words that night: 'I don't want to die another penniless black man while others benefit from me.' I wondered whether he had managed to fulfil his dream.

I decided to go to Michael's funeral and visit Neverland to pay my respects and say goodbye to him for the last time. The funeral was a very dignified affair, consisting of a private family service at Forest Lawn Memorial Park's Hall of Liberty, followed by a public memorial at the Staples Centre. Half a billion people flooded the internet looking for tickets. Michael's casket was present during the ceremony, which was broadcast live around the world and watched by up to one billion people.

While there, I gave a television interview outside Neverland to *Fox News*, talking about Michael's great warmth and humanity. He had received so much negative press in America that I wanted to redress the balance in whatever way I could. I was still in California when the *Irish Sun* ran a "world exclusive" with my picture on its front page, headlined "Irish Doc Fixed Jacko's Face". The article told how Michael used to come to the clinic late at night and how he felt comfortable in Ireland away from the glare of the media. I wondered where they were getting their information. In early July, William Bratton, chief of the Los Angeles Police Department (LAPD), indicated that the police were looking into whether Michael's death had been a homicide or an accidental overdose but had to wait for the full toxicology reports from the coroner.

In the days that followed, the LAPD grew increasingly concerned about the actions of Michael's physician, Dr Conrad Murray. Some articles stated that Michael had insisted that concert promoter AEG Live hire Murray to accompany him to England. I found this very odd, as he had never mentioned to me that Murray would be coming with him and, besides, Murray was not even registered to work in Britain. Michael knew that I *was* registered in England. Murray became the primary focus of the LAPD investigation when they discovered he had administered propofol to Michael within twenty-four hours of the singer's death. I couldn't understand why someone who would not even use midazolam without an anaesthetist present would use a drug as powerful as propofol in his own home. The LAPD announced that they were referring the case to prosecutors, who might file criminal charges. In the media frenzy that ensued, there were reports about other drugs found at the scene, and that Michael had used aliases to procure prescription medications. Arnold Klein told CNN that Michael had had an anaesthesiologist administer propofol to help him sleep during the history tour in Germany in 1997.

It almost seemed like they were talking about another person. It appeared to me that the media were being influenced by individual lawyers who had an agenda to make it look like Michael Jackson was a drug addict who had killed himself. It was awful for me to know that, in my experience, Michael was not a drug addict, and to see his name muddied once again on the world stage. I called Tom Mesereau, the attorney who had defended him during the child-molestation trial. Michael had spoken highly of Tom, whom *GQ* magazine had named one of its Men of the Year in 2005. He viewed him as a person of integrity, and I felt that Michael would want me to chat with him and help clear his name. When we talked a few days later, I found that he was accommodating. Tom asked me to contact Michael's brother, Randy, and the LAPD with information about some private documentation I had that might help clear Michael's name and preserve his legacy. A few days later, a detective from the LAPD called me and took a lengthy statement. The interview lasted thirty or forty minutes, and at the end of it, the detective mentioned that there was a list of nine or ten doctors who were under investigation, but that I was not one of them. They were subpoenaing medical records from these doctors, who had all treated Michael. The detective said I might be called as a witness when the trial started.

The *Sunday Times* later published an article that said the police wanted to question thirty doctors, nurses, and pharmacists, including Arnold Klein, who had been told that he had occasionally given Michael Demerol. I felt sorry for Dr Klein, as he had always been professional whenever I had talked to him.

*

When Michael died, Wade Robson – the former choreographer whose allegations of abuse later became the centre of that controversial new documentary, Leaving Neverland – wrote in tribute to him: 'Michael Jackson changed the world and, more personally, my life forever. He is the reason I dance, the reason I make music, and one of the main reasons I believe in the pure goodness of humankind. He has been a close friend of mine for 20 years. His music, his movement, his words of inspiration and encouragement and his unconditional love will live inside of me forever. I will miss him immeasurably, but I know that he is now at peace and enchanting the heavens with a melody and a moonwalk.'

*

In Sept 2011, I was invited to New York by the cable-TV host Aphrodite Jones to take part in her documentary series *True Crime with Aphrodite Jones*. Aphrodite and I had chatted on the phone a few times, and she had sent me a copy of her latest work, *Michael Jackson: Conspiracy*. The book examined how the American media had sensationalised the prosecution's case against the late pop star in the Santa Maria trial. Her writing had made the *New York Times* bestsellers list, and I admired her work. During the interview, she asked whether I had ever prescribed anything to Michael for insomnia or had seen needles or syringes in Michael's home. I told her, quite honestly, that I had never prescribed him any drugs for insomnia, and I'd never seen any drugs in his house.

She delved deeper, stating that one of the theories proposed by the defence team was that Michael was remarkably familiar with propofol and had the ability to inject himself. I assured her that any time he had received propofol in Ireland, it had been injected by an anaesthetist and that this had been done at his request. We filmed for two hours, going over the same questions, time and time again. It was almost like I was on trial, but I knew a lot of people in America would be listening to the programme when it aired, and I was keen. I felt that Michael's legacy was being tainted and that saddened me. Investigation *Discovery Channel* posted some snippets from the interview on YouTube, which carried a disclaimer stating that they didn't share my views. The *Irish Sun* took a story on 8th May saying, 'Explosive claims by a top Irish surgeon about the mysterious death of Michael Jackson.' The article claimed that defence lawyers had had the footage pulled as they fought manslaughter charges against Murray.

A few weeks later, Jerry Biederman, executive producer of the Michael Jackson Tribute Portrait invited me to Los Angeles to receive a dot in the pointillist painting by artist David Ilan. The portrait contained hundreds of thousands of dots: it had the blessing and support of members of Michael's family and those who were close to him and was endorsed by Diana Ross.

With cable-TV host Aphrodite Jones in New York

I was to be honoured with a dot in Michael's heart, which was reserved for family and close friends. The snow was falling over the Santa Clarita Valley when I arrived. I made a small speech for the media, saying that I was honoured to be given a place in Michael Jackson's heart, as his legacy as an artist often overshadowed the tremendous good, he did in the world and the way, he unselfishly supported many causes, often at a financial cost to himself. He treated everybody equally, regardless of race, colour, and creed. It was especially annoying to me that the media used against him a condition I was treating him for, I said. While travelling through Los Angeles, Jerry asked me whether I would like to a give a talk to some students at Gardner Street Elementary School, in Hawthorn Avenue, Los Angeles, where Michael had once been a pupil. I agreed, eager to see where he had spent an earlier part of his life.

Before going to the school, I went up to Santa Monica to meet Grace Rwaramba, and we spent a few happy hours strolling along Palisades Park, with its crumbling bluffs and views of the Pacific Ocean. She still seemed deeply troubled by the loss of Michael. When I asked why she had not gone down to Haiti as arranged, she told me that some of the Jackson family were accusing her of being involved in voodoo; she didn't want to visit Haiti because it might make it seem like they were right. We discussed some difficulties that she and Michael had had in Bahrain before arriving in Ireland, where he was happy and, she felt, should have stayed.

Grace felt that it would be too distressing for her to visit Gardner Street and meet Principal Kenneth Urbina and the students. We discussed the talk I would give and agreed it should be entitled "What Would Michael Do?" I told the teachers and students how each of us owed a debt of gratitude to him who had always fought for those in need.

'Michael brought light where there was darkness, hope where there was despair; he never turned away from cruelty when he could give compassion,' I said. The speech borrowed heavily from Elie Wiesel, a Jewish Holocaust survivor, when it mentioned that we cannot be indifferent to the world around us, as that always benefits the aggressor – never the victim, whose pain is magnified when he or she feels forgotten. During my speech, I also said, 'Gratitude is what defines the humanity of the human being and that is what we owe to Michael Jackson, someone I am privileged to call my friend, somebody who often stood alone to fend for the children in the world, for the destitute, for the victims of disease and injustice. Michael was very troubled by the suffering he saw in the world and even more by the indifference to it.

'His first words to me when we met were, "Thank you so much for helping the people of Africa.". There were no airs and graces, no pomp and circumstance, and his only concern was for the lives of other people who lived on a different continent than the one on which either of us was born. I had been to Africa and seen the devastation of the plague of HIV at first hand, and when we discussed it, there were tears in his eyes, and he said we had to do something together for the people of Africa. He planned to hold a great concert in Rwanda, and we would fly there together in his private plane and then go down to see his great friend, Nelson Mandela. Sadly, these events were not to happen, and the world lost one of its great humanitarians.'

While at Gardner Street, the teachers showed me a small desk in the music room, where Michael had once sat. They also showed me some memorabilia and said they would like to have a small area in the back of the classroom set up as a museum to honour their famous student. I took a guitar and sang the Neil Young song *Out on the Weekend*, which included a lyric about going to LA. Somehow, it just seemed appropriate at the time, as we had both once lived in that great city, and it reminded me of my time working with Carnival Cruise Lines some years before.

While I was in Los Angeles, Dr Conrad Murray's preliminary hearing was taking place at the courthouse in Temple Street. There were some fans outside the courthouse with painted placards. I spoke with them, and each had their own story to tell. In the circumstances, I thought it best not to mention to them that I had known Michael. After visiting the courthouse, I went to Forest Lawn Memorial Park to visit Michael's grave. Although it was not officially open to the public, it felt right to be in the presence of his spirit. I got as near as I could to his graveside and prayed for a while.

Murray's trial for the death of Michael Jackson eventually started on September 7, 2011. It was held in the Superior Court of Los Angeles County before Judge Pastor, and I was on the select witness list. During the opening days, I was interviewed by Dr Drew Pinsky, from CNN in Los Angeles. He questioned me whether Michael could have committed suicide by injecting himself with propofol. I was never called to testify. On November 7, he was found guilty of involuntary manslaughter, and later sentenced to four years of incarceration.

After the trial result, I was invited by *TV3's Midweek* programme to give my opinion. I said that while it was sad to see another doctor incarcerated, Dr Murray was guilty of not providing an adequate standard of medical care, and his reckless behaviour and negligent actions had led directly to the death of another human being, who was also a father, brother, and son – and my friend.

In the following days, I wrote a poem to Michael and posted it on my Facebook page. It was seen by many fans around the world, who felt that the words helped to heal their pain.

25. Devastation in Haiti

The year 2010 had barely begun when a devastating 7.0-magnitude earthquake struck the Caribbean city of Port-au-Prince in Haiti, destroying everything from shantytown homes to public landmarks. Early reports said millions were likely to be displaced, with many tens of thousands feared dead. As darkness fell on Haiti's capital, crowds gathered in the streets and began to pray, as rescue teams from all over the world descended on the island. Over the next few days, television showed horrific scenes of the shattered city. Corpses were piled up and lay on bloodstained sheets on the crumpled streets. Residents valiantly tried to prevent their loved ones from being eaten by gangs of prowling dogs. The scenes were almost too horrendous to contemplate. After watching the nightly news updates on the television, I decided that I had to go there and help.

The opportunity to visit Haiti arose after I was invited to an aesthetic meeting in Miami that February, which had been organised by BioForm Medical to get the views of key opinion leaders from around the world, where the field of aesthetic medicine was heading. The meeting entitled "Partners for Aesthetic Advancement" was attended by old friends of mine, Christopher Zachary and Bob Weiss from California, Mariano Busso from Florida, while Ravi Jain from England and I were the European representatives. Plastic surgeon, Randy Waldman from Kentucky was also there, and after a period, he invited me to speak at the prestigious Las Vegas Cosmetic Surgery Congress. Ireland was still in the depths of the recession, and I welcomed concessionary flights to Miami, as it gave me the opportunity to visit the victims of the Haitian earthquake and donate my bursary from the meeting to them.

Before I left Dublin for Miami, I arranged a meeting with two NGO volunteers, my good friends, Peter Hanley, and Peter Gannon who were also keen to go to the island to try to help. By coincidence, Gannon had visited the island in 2009, just before the earthquake, and while he was there, he had met Bishop Pierre Dorcilien, who was from a Christian community involved in education. The bishop and his wife, Gladys, ran a primary-level school called the School of Miracles and Restoration. This school, like many others, had been destroyed during the recent earthquake, and we decided it would be our mission to help rebuild it. God works in mysterious ways and, within a few days, my friends and I were living in a small tent behind the collapsed school in Tabarre, Port au Prince. The bishop and his wife lived in a small hut on the premises, and from the beginning, they made us feel very welcome. On the first evening, as darkness fell, we wandered with the Bishop around nearby camps in Dumornay, where he provided spiritual assistance and talked to his people about their ongoing problems.

In the camps after the Haitian Earthquake 2010

On the second morning, I took a taxi to see the devastated city of Port-au-Prince. It was distressing to hear stories of bodies being burnt in funeral pyres of old car tyres, and shopping trolleys being used to collect the dead when there was no more room in the cemeteries. The earthquake survivors told me how some of the injured had been cut from the rubble with butchers' knives or hacksaws, and how this caused problems later as the stumps, without skin flaps to cover

275

them, became infected. Peter Gannon and I visited Gena Heraty at St Damien's Paediatric Hospital, where she worked as the director of the special needs programme. She told me that the average life expectancy on the island was forty-four years, and the annual income was just over $650. I knew from working in disaster zones previously that the three things survivors immediately need are food, water and shelter. Next, they need sanitation antibiotics and mosquito nets.

The next afternoon, we met with Richard Morse, owner of the famous Hotel Oloffson, which had been immortalised in Graham Greene's novel, *The Comedians*. At night, Richard played in a *rasin* band called RAM, his initials, which mixed elements of traditional Haitian voodoo ceremonial music with rock and roll. He told me not to fear the voodoo religion, explaining that it was just an extension of other, more familiar religions. He laughingly said, 'Protestants have God and the Trinity; Catholics have God, the Trinity, and the saints; and Voodoo has God, the Trinity, the saints and the spirits.'

Later in the week, we met Hugh Brennan, a construction engineer working with Haven, an Irish philanthropic organisation, who promised to provide some sanitation for the shanty town we saw in Dumornay. Within a few days, Hugh had begun training twenty of the camp's inhabitants to make twenty-four toilets. He told me, 'These people require sanitation and our focus is to get them to help themselves. We have learnt from the mistakes of the past and when you get a person to construct something themselves, they are more willing to hold onto it.' It was good advice that I would later follow in Africa. Many scores of NGO volunteers participated in mission trips to the devastated island nation since the earthquake. They came of their own volition and, without their ongoing help, the story of Haiti would have been very different. Their goodwill mixed with the sweat of a courageous populace who laboured all day under the burning sun to try and rebuild their lives.

At the time, I knew the best way we could help these people were to provide financial support and target specialist groups to rebuild their educational infrastructure. This was the only way to bring new hope for all those impoverished people in the huts and small villages of Haiti, struggling daily to break the bonds of poverty, which had primarily been placed on them by others, mostly through slavery and trade embargos. It took me a long time to get over the devastation I had seen in Haiti. In the months after my visit, I maintained Facebook contact with Bishop Dorcilien and his wife, and we formed the Haiti Leadership Foundation, which aimed at building a new Christian village, high in the Haitian mountains, to replace what had been lost. The village would-be built-in memory of the bishop's brother, Ned, who had been assassinated for political reasons some years before. The bishop had survived the attack, and still had the gunshot wounds to prove it.

In May 2011, the bishop and his wife came to Ireland to join the Doolough Famine Walk, which was held annually at Louisburgh, County Mayo, to commemorate local victims of the Irish Famine. On the night of March 30, 1849, near the end of the famine, hundreds of destitute and starving people walked twelve miles to Delphi Lodge in the hope of receiving rations. They set out on foot along the mountain road and pathway in cold, wintry conditions, including snowfall. When they arrived at the lodge, they were refused either food or tickets of admission to the workhouse, and so they began their weary return journey.

It was reported shortly afterward that the bodies of seven people, including women and children, were subsequently discovered on the roadside overlooking the shores of Doolough Lake, and that nine more never reached their homes. Local folklore maintains that the total number who perished was far higher. To commemorate the event, each year, a significant speaker comes to join the pilgrimage who re-enact the walk. The previous year, Gary Whitedeer, a Native American Choctaw Indian, was the walk leader. The Choctaw Indians had earlier showed their generosity in providing Humanitarian relief for the people of Ireland during The Great Irish Famine (1845-1849). It was twenty years (6th April 1991) since the last Bishop spoke and walked the road at Doolough Lake on Famine Walk Day. Within three years of Nobel Peace Prize winner, Bishop Desmond Tutu, walking the Famine Walk, Apartheid was abolished, and South Africa was free. I was finishing my GP Register rotation in Scotland then.

The Irish radio station, *Sunshine 106.8* and some national newspapers interviewed the bishop and his wife about the progress occurring in Haiti after the earthquake. I said, 'There is little doubt that one year after Haiti was ravaged by the fifth deadliest earthquake in history (according to the US Geological Survey), it's hard to find anybody involved in the reconstruction effort which isn't deeply frustrated by the lack of progress.' While on the walk, Gladys developed some breathlessness and we rested by a monument in Doolough Valley, which had an insightful inscription from Mahatma Gandhi: 'How can men feel honoured by the humiliation of their fellow beings?'

In April, I was joined in Dublin by Michael Jackson's nanny, Grace Rwaramba, who was on the way to a wedding in the Middle East. She had found the days since Michael's passing exceedingly difficult and was still devastated by his death. During the meeting, she expressed an interest in going down to Haiti to work as a volunteer. Since then, she hasn't visited the island, but we remain in contact. On the first anniversary of Jackson's death, I did an interview on *Ireland AM* with Aidan Cooney, during which I spoke about the singer's great humanitarian work.

*

That summer, I was also invited to interview with Reverend Catherine Gross on a Chicago Internet radio show and said that his body of artistic work carried a spiritual message relating to all the injustices of humans: racism, inequality, disease, hunger and corruption. During the 1960s, Catherine had joined the Civil Rights movement and marched with Martin Luther King Jnr. The campaigner became a member of PUSH during the 1970s and worked with the Rev Jesse Jackson. She worked as a special educator in Chicago for twenty-five years and helped the homeless of Chicago in that period. We became good friends and she gave me a regular spot on her radio show until sadly, she died in 2017.

*

It wasn't only Haiti, where the forces of nature had turned against humanity wreaking destruction. Earthquakes, heat waves, floods, volcanoes, super typhoons, blizzards, landslides, and droughts killed at least a quarter million people in 2010 – the deadliest year in more than a generation. More people were killed worldwide by natural disasters in this year than had been killed in terrorism attacks in the past forty years combined. 2011, unfortunately, brought no relief. It started an 8.9-magnitude earthquake off Japan's coast, which triggered a 30 feet high tsunami that killed more than 15,000 people. East Africa the worst famine in decades.

And in Dublin, that October 2011, we had the most severe floods ever witnessed in the city in many years. I watched from the window of my home that Monday night as the water level grew higher as the nearby River Dodder burst its banks and flooded our apartment complex, the Sweepstakes. All the parked cars, including my Aston Martin were destroyed. Because of a multitude of errors, including breaking down the protecting walls of the river to clear a blocked bridge at Lansdowne Station, when the river burst its banks, its effect was catastrophic! We lost 242 cars at the apartment complex that fateful evening, totalling more than €19 million. Although we tried to keep the damage private to protect property prices, before they replaced the protective walls; Alan O Keefe in the 27th October edition of the *Evening Herald* wrote the following lines,

'HUNDREDS of thousands of euro worth of luxury cars have been destroyed after the car park of an upmarket Ballsbridge address flooded. As the multi-million-euro floods damage bill continues to rise, the highest concentration of totally submerged cars was at the D4 Sweepstakes residential complex and surrounding developments. It was a virtual "Carmageddon" as scores of cars, including many highly expensive vehicles, were "written off" when the Dodder burst its banks. Cars in parking bays and underground car parks were rendered worthless within a few minutes on Monday night. Two Aston Martin sports worth more than €100,000 and several luxury Mercedes, including a €120,000 S600, and several BMWs vanished under the raging torrents. One 2002 Aston Martin, caked in mud inside and outside, was being towed away when the Herald visited the devastated complex. The 10-year-old sports car's €60,000 value was dramatically reduced by the damage.'

And it wasn't just the forces of nature, which were in turmoil. On the evening of November 21, 2010, Taoiseach Brian Cowen admitted that Ireland had formally requested financial support from the European Union's European Financial Stability Facility and the International Monetary Fund (IMF). His party, Fianna Fáil, fell to the last place in political opinion polls, placing behind Fine Gael, Labour and Sinn Féin, for the first time in the history of the Irish state. At this stage, mass emigration from Ireland had started again, and worse of all, five of my patients committed suicide over the collapse of their financial affairs.

As the recession deepened, I decided to close the Ailesbury Clinic in Douglas, Cork. Where once, I flew parties of medical staff to the clinic to perform liposuction and hair transplant techniques on patients, now we faced mounting bills for leased devices and staff wages. In the end, I decided to cut my losses and like many others see what tomorrow would bring.

26. Humanitarianism

In early 2012, Bishop Dorcilien moved his family and some of his Tabarre community to Mirebalais, a village in the mountains about one hour's drive north of the earthquake's epi centre. It was served by the teaching hospital, Hôpital Universitaire de Mirebalais, which was considered the largest solar-operated hospital in the world. The Bishop's wife, Gladys asked me whether I could help or be influential in asking Irish entrepreneur, Denis O'Brien, Chairman and founder of Digicel Group and Patron of the Digicel Haiti Foundation to help fund a new school for the village. Within a few years. Denis had opened close to two hundred schools in Haiti. Commenting on the opening of the school, he said, 'Education provided in a safe, friendly and conducive learning environment is the bridge to a brighter future for Haiti's children, and we are so happy to be doing what we can to help these children realise their enormous potential.'

In June of that year, Dee Pfeiffer invited me to become an honorary ambassador of the organisation Michael Jackson's Legacy, to help preserve the singer's legacy by providing humanitarian assistance to children in the Third World. She wrote to me,

'Dear Patrick,

As the founder of MJL, we had envisioned yourself, Tom Messerau and Larry Nimmer being honorary ambassadors of our organisation, but we had been waiting for estate approval before endeavouring to ask. Being such a humanitarian yourself, you will likely already know that Liberia is one of the poorest countries in the world. Monrovia itself has several slum districts, and it is in one of these – Caldwell – that Everland will be built.

– Dee'

With Bishop Dorcilien in Port au Prince, Haiti

At St. Damian's Paediatric Hospital Port au Prince

I was honoured to accept the position and felt their first project would have been close to Michael's heart: building the Everland Children's Home to provide a safe place for fifty children from the slums of Monrovia, Liberia.

With some children in Monrovia, Liberia

The new orphanage was under the care of a native called Pastor Dekontee, who had been accepting funds for the project over two years. As the brickwork began, he wrote: *'They killed our dreamer, but they cannot kill his dream.'* Later during the summer, he continued, 'The workmen defied a downpour during Africa's rainy season and sang Michael's songs in the rain, in memory of the humanitarian star who inspired the project.'

In November 2012, Dee had travelled with some friends to Liberia to see Everland for the first time, and to inspect the building. She admitted that progress in Monrovia was slow – they couldn't paint or put up curtains as they'd hoped because the concrete floor wasn't down, nor were the windows in at this point. Although still not complete, she was able to share the very first pictures of her painting the entrance sign to Everland Children's Home Monrovia.

Liberia had always held a fascination for me, being the place where all of Carnival Cruise Lines ships were registered but for Dee, "Liberian Girl" was the ninth single released from American recording artist Michael Jackson's 1987 album *Bad*. The nation was founded in 1822 to serve as a haven for the once enslaved.

With Pastor Dekontee in Liberia

But instead of creating a land of liberty, the freed slaves over the "natives", forcing them to work in the fields and on rubber plantations. Liberia's years of war had their roots in these divisions, and the scars are still visible. More recently, their previous president Charles Taylor had been indicted in The Hague of "aiding and abetting" war crimes and crimes against humanity, making him the first (former) head of state to be convicted by an international tribunal since Karl Donitz at the Nuremberg Trials.

It was decided we should try and open the orphanage in Caldwell on Christmas Day, primarily as it was the only time that I could take the required time off. We were still in the depths of the worsening Irish recession and working every hour of the day to take in whatever money we could to pay redundancy money to our Ailesbury Cork staff. In the end, I decided to use the funds from the Aston Martin to pay entitlements to the seven team members who worked there.

Visiting a church meeting in Monrovia, Liberia

My Christmas Day visit to Liberia was carried by many of the Irish national papers and the aesthetic magazines in London. As I packed my bags, news broke that the outgoing Chief Executive of the Irish Medical Organisation was about to receive a retirement deal worth nearly 10 million euro. It infuriated me, the level of blatant corruption present in Irish society, either in these organisations or within the charity sector. Before I left, I penned a letter to the editor of the *Irish Independent*, which was mentioned on *RTÉ*, the local radio station. It read,

'Dear Editor,

As I pack my bags to go and open an orphanage on Christmas Day in Liberia, where 76% of the population live below the poverty line of $1 (€0.76) a day, I learn that the outgoing Chief Executive of the Irish Medical Organisation is receiving a gold-plated retirement deal worth nearly €10m. He is walking away *with a lump sum of €1.5m and delayed pension payments of €3.75m. I, for one, am cancelling my membership in this organisation. My membership would be better served to keep a family in Liberia alive for two whole years.*

Dr Patrick Treacy Ailesbury Road, Dublin 4'

*

I flew through Brussels and arrived in Monrovia in the late evening, where I was met by Pastor Dekontee at the airport. The sun was already setting as we made our way back to my hotel in Mamba Point, in the embassy belt of the capital. I was astonished to see that there were no streetlights and none of the houses we passed had any lights on in them. There was also little evidence of working traffic lights, nor diesel generators providing electricity, except for a local shop or *shibeen* every few miles along the road. I asked the pastor to stop the car along the route just to see whether there were people in the houses, unaware at that time only two per cent of the Liberian population had electricity and the tariff is among the highest in the world. Some of the houses had paraffin lamps and candles, their light too faint to be seen outside their structure.

'It happened after the civil war!' said Dekontee.

'Have you got a generator?' I replied, wondering what daily life was like for these people on the ground.

'I have a "Tiger", and it can give enough power for a television or a fridge for most of the day.'

I later discovered this was the name many people in Monrovia gave to these imported Chinese devices.

'Most of the tap water stopped as well, and it is not safe to drink,' he continued, passing me a plastic bottle of water to drink. The conversation brought us neatly to the subject of the civil war, and he told me how he had to escape by bus to Ghana for a few years to avoid the conflict.

I was aware that the first civil war began in 1989 when Charles Taylor, fresh from guerrilla training in Muammar Gaddafi's Libya, entered Liberia with around a hundred other rebels known as the National Patriotic Front to overthrow the repressive government of president Samuel Doe. The second war began ten years later when another group, (LURD) emerged in the north. Within a few years, they had turned the nation into the most infamous bloodbath of the 1990s.

The conflict lasted until 2003, and by that time, over a third of a million people had been killed.

'They used drugs, and child soldiers were supplied with khat, cocaine, and other drugs as a means of controlling them.' 'Many innocent children were press-ganged into military service as soldiers or ammunition porters' he said.

We reached the Mamba Point Hotel after about thirty minutes. The hotel was considered Monrovia's most beautiful, and it had once been the residence of the American Chargé d'Affaires. It was now owned by Dublin native Anna O'hUadhaigh-Bsaibes and her Lebanese husband Chawki and had gained a reputation with western war reporters who visited during the country's most tumultuous times. Bono and former Irish presidents Mary McAleese and Mary Robinson had previously stayed there. Anna was there to welcome me when I arrived, probably because she knew that I was coming in from Dublin. We discussed the lack of streetlights in Monrovia and she laughed and said if I thought that was a problem, during the height of the civil war she had to be evacuated by US Navy Seals helicopter to neighbouring Sierra Leone. As she looked down on the city now plunged into darkness, the only lights emanating were from the Mamba Point hotel.

Dekontee wished me a happy Christmas and said he would leave me for a few hours to rest and then we would go to visit Everland Liberia in Caldwell a few days later.

Christmas passed with a little celebration at Mamba Point, although I met some exciting government dignitaries who came to celebrate with us for dinner. One of them brought me to a nearby little bar called *Lila Browns*. It was set in an old colonial home, nestled between the hotel and the Atlantic and popular with expats. It had a great jukebox and I spent a lot of the next few evenings hanging out there, listening to music and being approached by numerous well-dressed females looking for conversation and probably a partner.

During my wanderings over the next few days, I learnt we were staying less than a kilometre away from one of the biggest slums in Africa. The squalid seaside settlement was called West Point, and home to an estimated eighty thousand residents of differing ethnicities, religions, and languages. Along its single paved road, brightly clad prostitutes mingled with women in dark chadors and tooting orange autorickshaws competed with wheelbarrows for a piece of the carriageway. One always felt ill at ease walking through those rows of rusty zinc shacks, lined with food stalls and video shops as the locals continually

286

watched and followed you, ever willing to help you in your wanderings – and probably even keener to steal your purse!

The local beach was packed with local fishermen straddling their long dugout canoes and further along the coast young children selling wares stepped their way through the human faeces that lay everywhere. This part was called '*poo*' beach as its inhabitants openly defaecated there without any sense of shame, and then ran forward to shake your hand. I later heard that there were only four toilets in West Point, and only thirty per cent of the population of Monrovia had access to sanitation. It was hard to believe that less than a kilometre away, we lived in relative luxury at our country lodge type hotel.

Craft shops in Liberia

Some brightly coloured blue and yellow craft shops lay adjacent to the hotel entrance. One, entitled "Liberia Arts and Crafts" sold fearsome looking *gunyege* facemasks, most probably from the Dan northern region. Another displayed some native drums and on the wall outside hung those ever-watching chimpanzee-like *kagle* masks. Both were openly selling ivory although I assumed this was illegal. To the right of dilapidated one storey buildings, local children manned a busy car wash, with vehicles waiting their turn to be pampered on the beach below. It was there that many former child soldiers gathered in small groups to smoke ganja and pass away the hours. The location of their enterprise meant I was continually hassled by these young beggars who collected at the gate of the hotel each morning looking for money from me. Most of the hotel security tried to stop them pestering me with their incessant dawn chorus of '*Please, Mr. Patrick -give me a dollar!*' Little did I know that my growing relationship with the locals may have saved my life.

One night just after Christmas I attended a drinks party on the beach outside Lila B's bar. Some friends and I were listening to some reggae music, and watching some young Chinese tourists paddling in the shallow, turquoise water in front of us. As darkness fell, most of the others went home or back up to the bar. I remained with a female friend whom I'd met a few nights earlier. It was easy to get carried away, listening to the romantic sound of the waves crashing by the shoreline and drinking those never-ending Alabama slammers and brown sugar shots, which we got the barman to put into an empty vodka bottle. As it approached midnight, we made our way down along the white beach to lie together for a while. The moon was shining brightly on her face, and we laughed away the hours as the music gently played in the background.

Suddenly. I noticed that my friend had become silent, and her face looked deadly scared. I heard some voices whispering behind me and realised that we were surrounded by three or four natives who had slowly crept up on us. Being in a rather compromising position, I turned awkwardly around to see a young man brandishing a machete just above my head. To our left, were two others carrying knives. My friend was by now too scared to scream and instead uttered partial prayers as if her death were imminent. Then one of the robbers, who seemed to be their leader came closer to me. He bent down and looked directly at me in the moonlight. He was carrying a machete in his right hand. For a moment he stared into my eyes and then said,

'*It's Patrick!*'

The rest gathered closer, keeping their distance before they all eventually slinked off into the night. There was no sign of friendship from any of the rest of them as they hesitantly departed like hyenas who had been deprived of their prey. It was a close encounter and made me immediately realise the dangers of being alone in this area at night. I was thankful that I had unintentionally paid for my freedom to those persistent beggars who loitered by the gate. Sometimes, like my distant memories in Kurdistan, one doesn't know what way that life will throw its curveballs!

The next morning, Dekontee came to collect me and take me out to Everland Monrovia. We made our way out to the eastern suburb of Caldwell. En route, we had to pass a massive, burnt out Palladian-style construction called the Masonic Grand Lodge. It was founded in 1867 but was the scene of a battle during the civil war, and its ruins became home to thousands of squatters. As we entered the suburb, we had to cross a rusted iron bridge, and the pastor told me that he remembered Taylor's ragtag army shooting people there and throwing the dead bodies into the river below. That was the day he decided to leave Monrovia, shocked by what he saw, especially how the crazed children ran around shooting people with machine guns.

He then pointed to a person walking along the sidewalk. The young man, about mid to late twenties, was dressed in a brightly coloured crimson red suit, and he walked with the authority of a Congolese *sapeur*, oblivious to the filth and debris on the street below him. His hair was braided in dreadlocks, and he wore a pair of giant dark sunglasses, which probably shut out the surrounding populous from his gaze.

'He was a child soldier!' he said.

'You'll see them walking around everywhere. They're crazy people damaged by their memories and years of taking drugs.'

He was correct. The Congolese sapeurs dressed impressively to distance themselves from the reality of their working-class roots, but these latter-day child soldiers performed a similar act of denial; unwilling to accept the way they had destroyed the nation around them. We eventually reached the building, which was only partially constructed and still quite far from opening. I noticed a hand-painted sign lying on the ground. It was the one that Dee had painted while in Monrovia. Dekontee made many excuses about the rains and the workmen, but it was evident to me there was a governance problem, and it was not my role to mention it.

'So, what happens now?' I asked.

'We will do the opening down at the local church on Sunday,' he said.

That Saturday, I interviewed with a Monrovian radio station. The building was very dilapidated with the blue paint missing in patches around the walls as if the underlying wallpaper had long since disappeared. I explained to the interviewer how Michael Jackson suffered from vitiligo, and his underlying skin was both black and white patches outside his face, hands and feet.

On the way back to the hotel, Dekontee expressed a great surprise that the singer had this underlying dermatological condition.

'I never knew that!' he said. 'Everyone in Africa was annoyed that he wanted to be a white man! In fact, the children here sang this song.

'Michael Jackson was a black man
He wants to change to a white man
Chemicals will kill him
Chemicals will kill him.'

There was something both poetic and prophetic about the words. The people around the world misunderstood his pain about vitiligo and would have to be more understanding if he had been more open and honest about his underlying condition. Michael contributed to this interpretation, I as a doctor continued the fallacy being bound by the Hippocratic Oath to maintain confidentiality and in the end, it was chemicals that killed him.

The next day, Sunday, Dekontee brought me to his church and his community gave me such a great welcome, that I settled back into enjoying Christmas in western Africa. The whole building was bedecked in bunting, and the children gathered around me, dressed in beautiful, incongruous clothes usually reserved for Sunday church. Their warm smiles and manners concealed the fact that they were all hungry, and they carried the dignity of their people. They started singing songs of praise and Halleluiah, happy that my arrival had guaranteed them their first hot meal that week. The children mostly spoke little English and had never heard of either England or Ireland. However, they all had heard of Michael Jackson, and it surprised me the power of his influence, even here in deepest Africa where there was neither electricity nor television. It didn't take long to realise that my speech was probably a little complex for them. Although English served as the lingua franca, it had several varieties, including Kru Pidgin English, Kreyol, Merico and even Caribbean English. Thankfully, Dekontee promised to translate the speech for me, and he looked proudly over at me in his new Irish top as I began to talk,

'Michael Jackson felt the pain of the hungry children of Africa, often walking for miles with swollen bellies, dying without dignity in the night as the rest of the world emptied its supermarket food waste into the bins of New York, London and Dublin. He knew and felt deeply about a continent ravaged by civil war and pestilence, where children in this city were forced to hack off the limbs of their parents and eat the beating hearts of other humans. None of these children asked to become involved in an adult war, where man's inhumanity to each other is only outdone by the evil that lies within their hearts.' There was silence as I continued.

'There are times when we all feel that God has abandoned this world: the terrible earthquake in Haiti, the bloody streets of Northern Ireland, and when, at evening-time, shadows fall over the coffin makers in Nairobi, another HIV-infected child is put back into the earth from which they were born. Well, I say to you here today that there is a God who looks down on all this wrong and he brought us an angel in the form of Michael Jackson to help solve it.'

When we had finished, Dekontee told me that he had some members of his congregation who were quite ill and whom he'd like me to see. We got into his jeep and travelled along a long red murram dirt track to one of the houses. An older man was lying on a bed inside. He had recently been in the hospital for surgery for a varicocele, an enlargement of the veins within the scrotum but this had become heavily infected, and he was slowly passing blood in his urine and bedridden. They had no money to bring him back to the hospital, nor did they ask me for any. He had been discharged with amoxycillin, but they were having no effect on his infective problems. Another female lay in another darkened room. She had been the patient's carer but now had a fever, pronounced abdominal pain and "pea soup" diarrhoea.

There was a distinct smell from the patient, which I immediately suspected was from typhoid gastroenteritis. A rash of small, flat, pink spots along her chest confirmed the diagnosis. Typhoid is caught by using water that's contaminated with infected faecal matter and caused by a bacterium known as *salmonella typhi*. The surgical patient then confirmed he was indeed a carrier. Both patients required immediate antibiotics. I was unsure about the treatment for typhoid and went outside to look up on the internet on my phone, and whether the amoxycillin her husband had would be useful for her symptoms. On learning that it would, I gave him the doxycycline, which I was using to protect me against malaria and her his medication. Within a few days, both patients had well recovered.

However, the next patient's symptoms proved to be more psychological. She sat hunched over a sink and said nothing, but instead stared blankly into the distance, unwilling to talk to me or the pastor It appears that a few days earlier, she had developed a form of glossolalia, running around her neighbours' houses and "speaking in tongues". The pastor said that he witnessed the event and that she spoke almost no recognisable words, apart from biblical words and phrases. I had travelled in central Africa enough to know that glossolalia is practiced in Pentecostal churches who widely believe that it is a spiritual gift. However, it soon became apparent that this community did not see it like that, but instead took it as a sign of God's judgement and they had taken her to the local church, where I had been earlier and tied her to the railings outside and whipped her into submission. Her blank stare and resistance to the examination could not deny the fact that Dekontee was probably involved in her molestation.

'Did you see her being whipped?' I asked.

He slowly bowed his head and nodded, he did. I didn't reply, conscious of the fact that as doctors, we must be careful to match our Western education with the same standard of compassion and understanding for those who hold different memories and views. This was a country ravaged by civil wars, where millions faced hunger daily, and children were kidnapped to fight in wars. It was colonised, its peoples enslaved, and Christian missionaries, representing a broad spectrum of competing beliefs came and traversed the continent for centuries. The practice of speaking in tongues had mainly died out of Christian tradition until Pentecostalists revived it at the turn of the twentieth century believing that the second coming of Christ was imminent. Evangelists spread this evangelism throughout the United States and then into Africa.

The patient refused any contact with us, either beaten into submission or fearing what would happen to her next. I placed a hand on her shoulder and promised I would return to see her within a few days. When I saw her again, she sat by the fire, still withdrawn from the world and unable to let me know how she was feeling.

That night, I thought about the role of missionaries in this part of the world. Some, like David Livingstone, saw colonialism as an opportunity to spread the Christian faith, but others used it to subdue the natives and steal their land and property. Reverend Helm fooled King Lobengula of the Ndebele to give away all his estate to Cecil Rhodes. Friar Anthonio Barroso tricked the illiterate Dom Pedro V, King of the Congo, in 1884 to sign an oath of submission to the King of Portugal. This means of people using religion as a means of suppression was nothing new. Authors, like Joseph Atwill, author of *Caesar's Messiah: The*

Roman Conspiracy to Invent Jesus, asserted that it was used by the Flavian Caesars to pacify the citizens of Judea, and it may have been the origins of Christianity itself. He forwards this argument to state the "peaceful" Messiah was invented to urge the revolting Hellenistic Jews to 'turn-the-other-cheek' and "give onto Caesar", hence paying their taxes to Rome.

*

In June 2013, Michael Jackson's Legacy (MJL) started a second project: building an orphanage in Ned Dorcilien's Christian village in Mirebalais, Haiti. The building was to be called *Everland Haiti*, and I was invited there in January 2014, by Bishop Dorcilien and Dee Pfeiffer from MJL to open the new building for thirty orphaned children. Everland Haiti was built on the same ground as a new secondary school, which had been completed with a generous donation of almost $350,000 from my Irish friend Denis O'Brien, owner of Haiti's largest Telecom Company, Digicel. As a result of his benevolence, the number of students that attend schools built by the Digicel Foundation in Haiti now totals over 60,000.

*

It was beautiful to see my old friends again after so many years. I stayed for over a week in Mirebalais with the Dorciliens, being joined there by Rachael Paulson, a humanitarian from New Jersey and founder of "Hands on the World Global". We drove up into the mountains with Cheri Roseau, the teacher from the Tabarre school and for the next week, slept under the cloudless skies of Haiti. There was a sense of history amidst these hills, as it was here that the rebel leader Toussaint Louverture gathered the Haitian slaves in 1791 to fight the English.

'Why were the English armies in Haiti?' Rachael asked.

'I thought it was a French colony.'

'It was, but they were there because they were supporting white colonialists who were opposed to the abolition of slavery,' I replied.

I explained that Louverture took his cue for rebellion from the French revolution, which had occurred two years earlier and proclaimed that all men, including slaves, were born free with equal rights. However, the Parisian revolutionaries soon realised France needed its slaves and overseas possessions to maintain its power and prosperity. In Haiti, the slaves were freed and took their revenge by burning down the memories of the plantations. By 1801, Napoleon decided to restore order and recuperate the formerly wealthy colony. He agreed to appease British demands by signing a peace treaty and deciding not to abolish slavery in any of the French territories.

Although the French managed to capture Louverture, the expedition failed when high rates of disease crippled the French army. In May 1803, the last eight thousand French troops left the island, and the slaves proclaimed an independent republic that they called Haiti in 1804. The Haitian revolution that he inspired affected the whole of the western hemisphere and encouraged uprisings in surrounding countries. It greatly influenced President Lincoln to free the slaves in America. Seeing the failure of his colonial efforts, Napoleon decided in 1803 to sell the Louisiana Territory to the United States, instantly doubling the size of the US.

Although two hundred years had passed since Louverture had freed the slaves, few people on the impoverished island of Haiti were really free and wouldn't be until they were properly educated.

The next morning, we had a small ceremony to open Everland Haiti. During my speech, a great turbulent wind got up and blew the doors and windows of the building wide open. Everything was strewn from the tables across the floor. Many there became startled, thinking it was the spirit of Michael Jackson himself. Bishop Dorcilien and his wife told us not to mention what had happened, as it may have been misinterpreted, fearing that orphan children might not have been brought to the village if there was any suspicion that outside forces or malevolent spirits were present there. After all, voodoo was still widely practiced in this rural hinterland.

While writing this memoir, I am conscious of the global feelings towards Michael Jackson whose reputation has been severely damaged since the screening of *Leaving Neverland.* After watching the documentary, myself, many questions remain. Some critics say that it is more a testimonial than journalistic endeavour, as people defending the singer were not involved or interviewed. I can only attest to the fact that anytime I saw Michael around children, including his own, he acted with total respect and love to them. However, I did have my reservations about him visiting the children in Our Lady's Children's Hospital in Dublin, and we did sit down and discuss the topic of paedophilia together. Paedophiles can be manipulative as witnessed by events surrounding the reign of the Catholic clergy in Ireland. I mentioned this when I was recently interviewed on the *RTÉ* Joe Duffy show, giving my opinion about several radio outlets around the world pulling his songs from rotation.

*

When Nelson Mandela died later in 2013, the world lost another great humanitarian, and I fondly remembered the conversation that Michael and I had had with him about the concert in Africa. My brother was having brain surgery in London, and I decided to stay with him at the hospital rather than attend the funeral. On the day he was buried at his ancestral home in Qunu, I remembered my small part in his struggle for freedom. Those marches on cold winter days outside South Africa House during the eighties, visiting his small lonely prison cell on Robben Island, the 46664 Concert at Green Point Stadium, Cape Town, his 90th birthday party in Hyde Park, his visit to the Special Olympics in Dublin in 2003, and most of all – my failed phone conversation with him in 2006.

*

In 2016, Ireland was at last beginning to recover from the recession. It had been a long painful eight years, trying to maintain a business and keeping my staff paid. In the end, I was unable to maintain the exceptionally high mortgage on my clinic properties on Ailesbury Road and KBC Bank moved to foreclose my clinic properties on Ailesbury Road. This was recognised as the most expensive location in Ireland and many of my neighbours lost millions during the property crash of this period. After the legal proceedings regarding the buildings ended, I decided to take time out. In May of that year, Peter Gannon who had been with me some years before in Haiti joined me on a humanitarian mission to Malawi. Before I left, I gathered some needles, giving sets and lots of pharmaceuticals which I knew were severely needed there. Our mission was to visit some HIV orphanages in Lilongwe, Blantyre, and Zomba, as I was aware that Malawi's HIV prevalence is one of the highest in the world, with ten per cent of the adult population living with the disease. In 2016, one million Malawians were living with HIV, and 24,000 had died from AIDS-related illnesses in the same year. I thought about how HIV had caused such immense human suffering in the continent, where people with HIV-related diseases occupied more than half of all hospital beds and remembered how fortunate I was not to have got the infection.

Visiting a HIV Orphanage in Blantyre, Malawi

On route from Addis Ababa, I was seated on the plane beside a Malawian priest called Fr Emmanuel Chimombo. During conversation, he told me about the oldest Christian mission in Malawi, founded by the White Fathers in 1902. He mentioned that Mua Mission Hospital was located next to the mission in the Dedza District. Patients came from the surrounding villages to be treated there, but like many other places in Africa, they had just one doctor. They had no neurotic medicine for children suffering epilepsy attacks or painkillers for the road traffic accident patients

It was a fortunate encounter as I was carrying enough medicines to keep the hospital supplied for possibly three or four weeks. However, when I later visited the hospital, the problem was much larger than I had expected with maternity, paediatric, general medicine, and surgery wards being treated by that one doctor. It was the fundamental lack of laboratory facilities, such as having the ability to do sputum smears for TB that blocked up the system and patients had to be put in isolation wards until it was verified that they were free of being contagious. Even more annoying was the fact that the doctors had X-ray equipment but no money to buy the films so that no chest films could be done. Most of the staff had worked for the past weeks without any wages and were dedicated to their jobs. I left the doctor my favourite Littman cardiac stethoscope to help him on his daily examinations, and it made me realise my financial problems were nothing compared to what these people had to endure.

Peter decided to stay on for a few weeks, painting the outside buildings. Before we left, I watched him bend down to talk to a mother and her baby on the neonatal ward. The new born was brightly dressed in the colours of the green and golden hues of the Kerry football team, with a matching woollen cap. It was quite obviously a donation from somebody in Ireland.

'May your son score a goal for Kerry in the All Ireland final one day,' he said loudly. There was a silence before the mother became tearful and turned away. I stood for a while to see what had offended her. She then replied, 'Doctor, this is not a boy, it is my new daughter!'

*

In September of that year, I watched as five articulated lorries transferred our Dublin clinic to our new location at David Lloyd Riverview in Clonskeagh. It was only six minutes from Ailesbury Road, and all the staff loved the new location. Marie Loftus, who had published the original article about the rise of HIV in Africa, was now on board as our clinical director. She had also lost property during the recession, understood the aesthetic world, and was the perfect person to help me during the recovery. It was indeed the end of an era but hopefully also the start of a new one.

*

I met up with Peter again in Africa when I visited Uganda on a humanitarian mission in early 2019. On that journey, I travelled with Jim Corr, guitarist from the Corrs, and Norman Page, a childhood friend from Bundoran. Peter was helping at a Christian missionary and orphanage run by Carol Adams in Fort Portal. They operated under the Church of Uganda with a Child Care Outreach programme and operated an NGO called Youth Encouragement Services (YES).

He joined me when we visited Happy Mbabazi, who was organising activities for disadvantaged children through his organisation, Heal the World Miracle Community Organisation (HWMCO). Happy had asked me to write the foreword for a book he had written some years before. We spent a beautiful day rejoicing the children with toys and being entertained by them as they sang their welcome song. The children showed us a small garden they were cultivating with pawpaw, coffee, matoke (banana), guava, and young orange trees. They made us a delicious lunch consisting of cassava, beans, cabbage, avocado, and traditional posho. During a special ceremony, the Irish flag was hoisted, and six young trees were planted in memory of our visit.

A few days later, we all drove southeast to Lake Bunyonyi together. It was a beautiful part of the world, with our truck climbing ever higher into the highlands, surrounded on every side by snow-capped dormant and active volcanoes. Elisha, our driver, was well used to the broken red murram roads, which had been subjected to continuous landslides and were being propped up with landfill every few miles. We stayed in the Bird Nest Resort, and I shared a room with Norman, boasting its balcony with breath taking views over the lake. To the left upriver, I could see the new boat that would take us over to a government primary school, located on Bwama Island. It had been provided by Yvonne Verhagen, Founder and Chair of HWMCO-Nederland.

Yvonne was a Dutch translator and researcher of the MJ Community, who had decided because of a life-changing event to dedicate her life to Africa to provide the children at Bwama Primary School with life jackets and two motorboats with outboard engines to replace their dugout canoes. People lose their life every week on the lake as the canoes continually overturn and most of the natives cannot swim. Another five died yesterday as I write this memoir, of whom two were little children. Her research for the MJ Community had also led her to Happy Mbabazi, and his organisation, the Heal the World Miracle Community Organisation (HWMCO). Yvonne told me her interest in Africa was related to the death of her son Nicky, in a road traffic accident in 2011. He had loved Africa, intrigued by its beautiful nature, especially the mountain gorillas, that lived in the nearby misty Virunga mountains. I had promised her that I would visit them in Nico's memory. Next day we attended the school, and discovered that a British doctor and Christian missionary, Dr Leonard Sharp had made the then uninhabited Bwama island a leper treatment and quarantine centre, back in 1931. At its height, Bwama Island had over six hundred leper patients on it, technically removing them from the communities where they might potentially infect others. The people on the island lived as a community and eventually had children, and they built Bwama Primary School in 1934 for their education. I remembered my journey to Nelson Mandela's cell on Robben Island in South Africa with Julie some years before. Leprosy broke out in the Cape during the mid-1800s, and the patients were placed out on the island with other undesirable citizens of South Africa who struggled to fit into society physically, mentally, and socially. Here, far away from the eyes and conscience of the populace, they remained from 1846 to 1931. We had done similar things very recently to African patients suffering from HIV and Ebola. Each time, these victims of the disease are shunned by ignorant and unforgiving societies, that view them as unclean and hazardous. More than that, each time it is science and medicine, which saves these people and not the religious intolerance and ignorance that perpetuates their cultural beliefs. On one side we have bishops and priests spreading falsehoods about condoms not protecting the populous or whipping patients with mental illness and on the other doctors struggling to contain the infectious pathogens against ignorance and a lack of education.

On Humanitarian Mission to Uganda

Heal the World Miracle Community Organisation (HWMCO)

With Dr Christopher Roland Payne RSM Aesthetic Congress

There are many types of ignorance, one being indifferent to facts or logic. In Africa, it shows itself as a stubborn devotion to uninformed opinions, ignoring contrary ideas, opinions, or data. These people, like Thabo Mbeki in South Africa, often occupy elected offices, and patients die because of their beliefs. But there is another type of ignorance, which is related to a communal gap in knowledge, where the existing data doesn't entirely make sense or add up to a coherent explanation. It is the type of situation where science has not yet provided all the answers and hence has not furnished a cure for the Ebola or HIV or even the reason people speak in tongues. Most scholars agree that Isaac Newton, while formulating the laws of force and gravity and inventing the calculus in the late 1600s, probably knew all the science there was to know at the time, but he just asked the correct questions. Religion tends to wallow in this perceptive ignorance, promising people there will be a better afterlife and keeping a blind adherence to sacred texts and using them to disarm the validity of scientific truth. This became apparent in 1633, when Galileo was forced to stand trial for his opinion regarding the heliocentric theory of the universe.

The school remained after science had controlled the disease. It was taken over by the Ugandan government in 1969 and attracted students from the entire region. We reached the island, stopping over at some of the villages along the shoreline. The children were still on their Christmas holidays, but the teachers came out to welcome us. While there, standing by the blackboard, and looking at the orange and blue lifejackets piled together in a corner, I again remembered Mandela, when he said,

'Education is the most powerful weapon which you can use to change the world.'' It is through education that the daughter of a peasant can become a doctor, that the son of a mineworker can become the head of the mine, that a child of farm workers can become the president of a great nation.'

At that moment, I realised the sacrifice that some of these children must make to become educated. Every day, the Bwama Primary school's pupils had to arrive on the island in dugout canoes. Many come from other islands, but most of the pupils came from the mainland. Another school located in the region would mean that they would have to walk uphill for two hours or longer every day.

On the way back to Bird Nest, we passed by a tiny outcrop of reeds with a horrible history to it. It was called "Punishment Island", where until the 1940s unmarried girls who got pregnant were taken to the island and left to die. In this part of Uganda, amongst others, a young woman could only get pregnant after marriage. Whenever a virgin daughter got married, the family of the bride received a bride price, mostly paid with livestock. A girl became worthless, though, when she got pregnant before she was married. With most of the people, especially girls, not knowing how to swim, a young woman that was dumped on the island, had mainly two options: jump into the water and drown, or wait to die from cold and hunger. The practice was only abandoned in the 1940s, also due to the influence of missionaries; one of them being Dr Leonard Sharp.

Lake Bunyonyi was only about two hours from the Bwindi Impenetrable Forest, and location of the mountain gorillas, one of the rarest large mammal species in the world. Their small, fragile population are now only found on the western rim of the Great Rift Valley, where the drainage basin of the Nile River is separated from that of the Congo River. These are the two largest rivers of the African continent and the second and third largest rivers in the world. We visited the mountain gorilla before leaving Uganda. It was a difficult, arduous trip climbing through the twisted vines and orchids that lined the steep inclines of the tropical forest, and some of our party soon became breathless and fatigued. Still, it is one of the most enjoyable experiences to finally reach the peaceful gorilla families feeding and playing in the misty Hagenia forests. We learnt that the gorillas small and fragile populations were under threat. People have been pushing into the mountain gorilla's forests in central Africa for decades – now there are only about a thousand of these splendid beasts in the wild. The main threat to gorillas is people and the associated increasing pressure on the gorilla's habitat. With so few individuals in the wild, the mountain gorilla is listed as critically endangered. I was extremely impressed with Yvonne's selfless dedication to helping the people of Uganda and invited her to London a few weeks later to talk about her mission work there at the Royal Society of Medicine Aesthetic Congress Gala Dinner that February 2019. She shared the platform with James Kliffen from Médecins Sans Frontières UK. The focus of the "RSM Aesthetic Conference 2019" was aesthetic complications, and I decided the theme for the Gala Dinner afterward would be related to African Humanitarianism.

*

In late January 2019, I was seated next to the Israeli physicist and inventor of IPL® technology, Dr Shimon Eckhouse, during the IMCAS Gala Ball in Paris. He was delayed on a visit to Mombasa that night as security has been stepped up across Kenya since al-Shabab gunmen attacked a Nairobi hotel complex, killing twenty-one people. During our conversation, he told me that he had just come back from visiting the mountain gorillas in Bwindi Impenetrable Forest a few months before. He told me the good news that due to Ugandan conservation measures, the gorilla numbers have recently been steadily rising and it's still not too late for us to protect our mighty mountain cousins. He mentioned that their numbers have increased almost four-fold since conservation efforts began in the 1970s, from around two hundred and fifty to nearly nine hundred today.

*

At the time of writing this memoir, I have also learnt that four rare mountain gorillas, including a pregnant female, have died in Uganda after being hit by lightning. The three adult females and a male infant were found in Uganda's Mgahinga National Park with "gross lesions" on their bodies indicating electrocution. The Greater Virunga Transboundary Collaboration (GVTC) called this a "big loss for the species". Mountain gorillas are also prone to some respiratory illnesses that afflict humans. A common cold can kill a gorilla, according to the World Wide Fund for Nature, one reason why tourists tracking gorillas are not normally permitted to get too close. As the coronavirus infects more people around the world, conservationists are warning of the risk to another vulnerable species: Africa's endangered mountain gorilla.

27. Bringing Hair Transplant to India

Beginning in the early 1990s, before the economic recession, Ireland had experienced unprecedented economic growth. During that period, we witnessed our GDP double in little more than a decade. In this period Ailesbury opened hair transplant clinics in both London and the Middle East, and an opportunity to open further clinics in Saudi Arabia appeared, which required me to engage more staff and formulate a new business plan. There were many reasons for this economic success, especially Ireland's low corporation tax rate. Many countries praised the nation's investment in education and training and its ability to reverse many years of economic emigration. I never believed that this was real economic growth, as it was mostly witnessed in the construction sector, generated by a property-market bubble that left Ireland in a very precarious position by 2007.

Ailesbury was by then the second-most-successful FUE transplant clinic in Europe practicing under the DHI. The method did not require major surgery and was practically painless. We were also beginning to attract many international celebrities from India, the United Kingdom, and the United States to the clinic for the FUE transplant procedure.

In April 2007, I attended the DHI hair transplantation awards in Athens and returned to the Greek capital the following month, as a keynote speaker at the European Society for Laser Aesthetic Surgery (ESLAS) conference. While there, I shared the podium with the late Dr Yves-Gerard Illouz, the French plastic surgeon who was internationally recognised as being the "father" of modern liposuction. Yves had been a true pioneer in the field of aesthetic surgery and made the procedure of removing fat safer for both doctors and patients alike. He had introduced the blunt cannula and paved the way for the tumescent techniques of Dr Klein that we used with the VASER® at Ailesbury Dublin and Cork.

In the Taj Hotel looking over the Gateway to India

He was also best friends with Dr Pierre Fournier, and I considered both doctors to have primarily pioneered the field of medicine we were all engaged in. They gave generously gave of their time to train others. I was deeply sorry to hear of the passing of Yves in 2015 at the age of eighty-six. When I organised the Royal Society of Medicine Aesthetic Congress in London later in 2019, I invited Pierre to open the event, but sadly he was now ninety-five, and living in Morocco and recently unfit to travel. His son remained in contact with my dear friend, Dr Christopher Roland Payne, and wished us his every blessing for the Congress. In June 2007, I received a citation at the Aegean Masters Hair Transplant meeting in Sounion, Greece. As the new FUE method became more popular internationally, I travelled with the DHI CEO Kostas Giotas to Mumbai that December to open a new clinic there. We had been invited by a big Bollywood star who had been a patient and he had gone into a special film role with his head shaven because of the procedure. Hence, it was imperative that we could not be seen together. It had been twenty years since I had last been in India, returning to Ireland from New Zealand.

Standing on the waterfront under the iconic Indo-Saracenic "Gateway of India" stone arch, and watching the fading saffron colours of sunset, I thought again about Trish and marvelled at the unusual combination of Islamic and Hindu styles. The monument stood proudly against the dying summer sun, having been constructed in 1924 to commemorate the visit of King George V and Queen Mary to the city, and from here the last British troops departed, when India gained Independence just twenty-three years later. Surrounded by such history, I considered how Ireland and India shared a ubiquitous history. Both were part of the British Empire who forfeited their youth to fight in wars, which were none of their makings. They were the first two countries to gain their freedom from the British, who partitioned both of their countries. While in India, we were invited to many events, including the premiere of the film *Taare Zameen Par* (Stars on Earth), and received a unique personally signed copy of the product. The film explored the life and imagination of Ishaan, an eight-year-old dyslexic child who excelled in art, but his poor academic performance led his parents to send him to a boarding school. It reminded me somewhat of my own time spent boarding at St Michael's College in Enniskillen.

*

In 2011, I got invited to the DHI hair transplant awards ceremony at the Hotel Grande Bretagne Hotel in Athens. The historic hotel had been used as Nazi headquarters after Athens fell to Germany in 1941, and for three years, Nazis leaders had lived in the hotel. It was close to the nearby Greek Parliament where another political crisis was now enacting. The economic recession had affected Greece severely, and despite heavy rainfall, over 14,000 angry people had gathered to protest cuts in public spending and increased taxes as austerity measures. The protests had been organised by Direct Democracy Now – a Greek citizen grassroots organisation made up of ordinary citizens.

As evening fell, the protestors clashed with the police and hurled petrol bombs and stones, causing a rather dramatic inferno. These measures were in exchange for a €110 billion bail-out, aimed at solving the Greek government-debt crisis. The police sprayed the crowd with tear gas, and I could hear stun grenades. For a moment, I thought about how the recession in Ireland was deepening, as several financial institutions faced collapse due to insolvency. In response to the worsening crisis, the Irish Government had instigated a €64 billion bank bailout, and many people thought that Ireland would require IMF assistance. It was tough times, and I treated many of my loyal patients for whatever they could afford and had to obtain loans on three occasions just to pay my staff.

From my balcony, I could see the angry crowds in the streets below. In the last glimmers of sunset, I looked to Mount Lycabettus in the far-off distance and remembered the open-air amphitheatre at the top, where Van Morrison played twenty-five years before. It was the same night I met Dublin Pat, who joined me as a driver, and we had gone on the last "Turkey run" together. My life had indeed taken a lot of turns since then.

*

In the next period, Kostas Giotas wanted me to move the Dublin hair transplant facility from Ailesbury Road to the Beacon Hospital. This did not suit me as I needed them as an anchor tenant to pay the substantial mortgage on the buildings. In the end, myself and Lorraine Lambert decided to form a new company called Ailesbury Hair Implants. This was successful, and in August 2012, I was invited back to Mumbai, to meet another company, Richfeel Ltd, who were interested in franchising our expertise in FUE hair transplant. Richfeel had dealt in trichology for many years and had fifty offices, mostly in the Mumbai area. The owners of the company were Dr Apoorvah Shah and his wife, Dr Sonal Shah, who had built up the business together. Pritam, their project manager, collected me from the airport and brought me to my hotel. On route, we passed giant hoardings with my image bedecked in blue surgical and headset scrubs emblazoned with the strapline "Richfield presents Dr Patrick Treacy Hollywood Cosmetic Surgeon (Michael Jackson Fame) for hair transplant. Free seminar Call 6776 1406".

As part of the seminar session, I had to talk in a local hotel about the advantages of FUE hair transplant to about two hundred doctors who were interested in learning about the new technique. Androgenic alopecia is a common, chronic hair loss disorder. The condition is characterised by progressive hair loss, and it affects up to 80% of white men and 40% of women. Many products, including FUE hair transplant were being used as hair-loss therapies. During this period, I had experimented with using PRP (plasma rich platelets) to help the new follicles grow. The technique involved taking a patient's blood and spinning it in a centrifuge to separate the heavier red blood cells from the lighter platelet layer, which contained stimulative growth factors and signal messenger to instruct the fibroblasts to work. The solution contains growth factors that influence wound healing, and theoretically could play a role in tissue repairing mechanisms. I had some reservations that injecting the solution into the scalp could cause transection of the new transplanted hair follicle and if the platelets were injected before the FUE their effect many have worn off by the time the new hair was transplanted. I also did not want to introduce the idea to an assembled group of hair transplant surgeons as any one of them could take my idea and copy it. This branch of medicine is tempered by colleagues who steal your ideas, and one learns to be on guard until you have published your findings. I found this particularly to be the case during treatment of chronic migraine with botulinum toxin and later when selecting the number of units of hyaluronidase required to treat vascular occlusion caused by a doctor injecting an artery with hyaluronic acid dermal filler.

Advertising Hoarding in Mumbai

Initially, I welcomed the audience and recorded the historic occasion of a new Irish Indian relationship with Ailesbury Hair Implants Dublin and Richfeel Hair restoration Mumbai collaborating in bringing new advances in the field of hair restoration to India. I was aware that the FUE was already on offer by DHI in India, as I had helped open the first clinic there in 2007. Consequently, I had to show that we were offering something different and exploited the fact that we were now offering mechanised follicle extraction. This extraction was performed using a device with a tiny 0.7mm punch, and the post-procedure holes almost disappeared overnight, whereas the 1mm or 0.9mm punch holes left marks that took a week or more to heal and left small dots in the donor site. It was also impressive that we could transplant six thousand hairs in one day or twelve thousand hairs in two days, which I knew our competitors would struggle to compete with as one of their surgeons told me he couldn't extract six thousand hairs manually in one day.

Ailesbury Hair Transplant Clinics in Mumbai

During the lecture, I slightly mentioned the use of PRP and decided to veer off the main hair transplant topic and told the audience about the commonality and shared experience of the Indian and Irish governments. I told them that we had the same colours in our respective national flags, and that Indian's constitution was strongly influenced by that of Ireland. Both our nation's leaders had come together to write the new Indian constitution. I reminded the audience that the British had partitioned both our countries and that we had suffered disastrous famines whilst under their rule. Most of the audience were unaware that the Bengal Famine of 1943–4, was reminiscent of the Great Irish Famine of a century earlier, especially that the British had taken the corn from the local population and used it to feed their army horses in military campaigns. As the lecture progressed, I mentioned how we both experienced a certain person called Charles Trevelyan. In 1826, as a young man, Trevelyan joined the East India Company as a writer and was posted to the Bengal Civil Service at Delhi, India. I told them that we inherited Trevelyan from the Bengal Civil Service when he took up a senior civil servant with the Lord Lieutenant of Ireland in Dublin Castle. While the famine raged and over a million people died, he callously said, 'The judgement of God sent the calamity to teach the Irish people a lesson.'

*

Trevelyan remains a hate figure in Ireland, forever remembered in the lyrics of our national team's rugby song *The Fields of Athenry*. These words, known to every Irishman mention a fictional farmer who "stole Trevelyan's corn" for his starving family and was sentenced to transportation to the Australian penal colony at Botany Bay. While still in the trust of delivering what was by now a partially political speech, there was a noisy disturbance at the door as two noisy men tried to get by security and enter the fully packed room.

As the disruption became increasingly louder, I became concerned until I distinctly heard one of the people in the melee shout,

'But I know Patrick many years ago!'

I thought for a moment, about who it could be and thought it might have Lokesh, one of the Indian doctors, whom I knew at Bangour Hospital in Edinburgh many years before. To quell the disturbance, I asked security to let them and they walked up to some empty seats at the very front of the room. Despite my best efforts, I couldn't remember the man's face, or where we had met before. One of the men, who was bald and could do with a hair transplant himself, smiled at me continually as if we were long lost friends.

After things had settled, I got back to the infamous Trevelyan and how karma intervened to play a role in his rather dubious legacy. In 1864, some years after the Great Irish Famine, he went back to India and became the governor of Madras. While there he remembered his time in Ireland and gifted an Indian rhinoceros to Dublin Zoo. These herbivores were used to grazing in flood plain areas in Northern India and Nepal. However, the sick animal died just a few weeks later as the zookeepers fed it on an incorrect diet – ironically of Indian corn meal! The audience gave me a standing ovation, and I looked again at the strange man who was seated in front of me and now approached my lectern.

'Hello, Patrick,' he said. 'Do you remember me? I'm Venugopal Naidu, from the Ibn-Al Bitar twenty-one years ago! I've lost a little hair, but otherwise, I'm feeling great. We heard you got kidnapped by Saddam's forces as you never turned up again in the hospital.'

'My God,' I said. 'Venu – after all these years! I remembered him fondly from my days at the Ibn-Al Bitar hospital and he used to change my Iraqi dollars on the black market. Venu had the best rates in the hospital and at one stage was giving 22 times more than the official rate.

'How on earth did you know that I was lecturing here?'

'We were crossing over the New Bandra Bridge, and we heard it on the radio that you were coming to Mumbai, and then we saw your picture advertised,' he replied.

I was astounded – here we were reunited in a small Mumbai hotel on the west coast of India. We both had escaped the Iraqi incursion of Kuwait as well as US-led invasion of Iraq and lived to tell the tale – the power of marketing never ceased to amaze me after that!

On return to Ireland, I was saddened to hear that a fifth patient of mine had committed suicide by jumping off a building. The recession was destroying the Dublin that I once knew, and nobody was going out to clubs or restaurants, and people were embarrassed to drive a nice car. At least that was one problem that had been solved for me.

*

In 2013, I started researching my idea of using PRP to help treat male pattern baldness. I had also been toying with the idea of introducing it with red light to our Ailesbury hair transplant patients and was in the process of writing a paper on the new process. I decided to call it the SMART® Hair Implant Technique. This was an anagram for a multi-procedure hair restoration technique that combined stem cell technology, Motorised micro punch extraction, anabolic nutrition and red-light phototherapy to shorten the time required for complete hair growth and increase follicular graft survival. If the technique worked, it could represent a significant advance on methods of hair implant technology then available by concentrating on a shortened recovery time, increased graft survival and reduced risk of complications. It also could be used as a standalone procedure or as an adjunct to our established FUE hair transplantation.

With Dr Beatriz Molina MyFaceMyBody Awards (London).

In February 2013, I was invited to be the principal speaker at the 4th American Academy of Antiaging Medicine in Mexico City.

The Mexican Faculty had asked me to speak in three lectures. One had to be the Dublin Lift and I decided to include the SMART® Hair Implant Technique.

The last day I decided to speak about the effect of Botox® on the Brain. For a long time, I noticed that patients who had got their frown lines treated had become happier, but it was not true in every case. Most of my lecture was spent on dealing with other features such as treatment of migraine and trigeminal neuralgia.

Randy Waldmann invited me to the Las Vegas Cosmetic Surgery Congress in June of that year to speak about the Dublin Lift procedure. While there, I also presented the results of patients who had benefited from the SMART® Hair Implant technique. It was well received, especially from other colleagues, such as Corey Maas and Neil Saddick from New York. Most of my colleagues felt there was a possible role for the use of platelet rich plasma in the treatment of androgenetic alopecia. I was delighted when a few months later the SMART® Hair Implant technique was awarded Highly Commended "Best Innovative Non-Surgical Procedure" at the inaugural "My Face My Body Awards" held at the London Lancaster that November. The awards were selected by my aesthetic colleagues and peers, and this made it even more rewarding! Maybe the dark, dismal days of the Irish recession were beginning to get behind us!

28. Lasers and Lecturing

While lasers were invented in the mid-60s, it wasn't until the mid-70s that the technology had evolved enough to be used safely for dermatological applications. More complex lasers, like the CO_2 and the Erbium YAG, were limited to a few dermatology and plastic surgery clinics but that all changed in 1998 when Israeli physicist, Dr Shimon Eckhouse, invented a new technology called IPL®, which could be safely used by any medical personnel. He correctly postulated that a Xenon flashlight could be turned into a type of laser using filters and some intelligent software. The principle was simple enough; if one took intense white light (made up of multiple wavelengths) and then applied cut-off filters to restrict the bandwidth to a specific range, it could imitate laser action. Ailesbury got its first IPL laser, operated by Nurse Patrica Molloy in 2000. We set up the large device in one of the rooms at Ailesbury and trained up some of the nurses to use it. The primary principle behind the IPL was selective photothermolysis (SPTL), where light of a specific wavelength was matched on a targeted tissue to obtain maximum effect without damaging the surrounding tissue. This meant it could cause localised damage by selectively heating certain target matter, haemoglobin, or melanin, thereby treating broken vessels on the face or hair follicles, without heating the rest of the skin. An IPL treatment thereby used the power of broadband light to improve the appearance of many conditions and within a short time we were treating a lot of patients for rosacea, solar lentigos, diminishing red faces and using photo rejuvenation for skin texture. The treatment could also be used for hair removal, photo rejuvenation, as well as to help alleviate conditions like acne.

By 2004, Israeli scientists introduced a new type of laser, which promised to enhance photorejuvenation by using the addition of RF (bipolar radiofrequency) to the pulsed light source. Ailesbury trialled the RF devices, as the treatment promised a safer way of tightening and renewing the skin's collagen. In October of that year, I presented my research on the new RF devices to the British

Association of Cosmetic Doctors (BACD) in the Mayfair Hotel in London. The following summer, I presented my findings to the FACE Conference at the Royal College of Physicians, and while there, Syneron asked me to treat a famous New York female singer with the new Aurora RF device at a clinic in Harley Street, London. We had done the trials of this new device in Ailesbury and were considered to have the experience to operate it to its best effect. Some journalists appeared to know she was there and created a flurry outside the building.

Interest in the new RF device was phenomenal as it promised skin tightening with no downtime and probably why I was interviewed by the *BBC World Service* about the new technology. I was attending a conference in New York when they contacted me, and I had to do the interview from the ornate halls of Beaux-Arts Penn Station.

During the nineties, the Lumenis Ultrapulse CO_2 laser resurfacing was considered the cosmetic dermatology "gold standard" for the treatment of acne scarring, deep wrinkles and photodamaged facial skin. In 1995, the device gained popularity within medicine as physicians like Professor Nick Lowe stated ultrapulsed CO_2 laser was the most effective modality for repairing photodamaged skin. Although the laser quickly gained prominence, it had considerable post-procedural problems, including prolonged postoperative recovery, pigmentary changes, and a high incidence of infective adverse side effects such as acne flares, fungus and herpes simplex virus (HSV) infection. Many patients also complained of swelling, burning and persistent redness that sometimes lasted for many months. The delayed healing, the implied risks and long downtime made many patients reluctant to accept this method. I bought an ESC Sharplan CO2 laser, from Mr. Maurice Collins, Blackrock Clinic when he switched his specialism from being an ENT Surgeon treating tonsils and adenoids to becoming a hair transplant surgeon.

In 2006, Lumenis released the ActiveFx® – a new method of facial rejuvenation by fractionalised laser skin resurfacing (FLSR). The new laser technology was a marriage of the American Fraxel® laser, developed by Reliant in 2004, under the supervision of Dr Rox Anderson, Director of the Massachusetts General Hospital and the Lumenis CO_2 lasers, which was partially researched by the Israel Defence Forces. The science of fractional skin treatment meant that the technology created thousands of microscopic treatment zones in each square inch of skin. Each zone was so small that it healed very quickly through interactions with healthy skin surrounding it, resulting in a very safe treatment with a lower risk of side effects and less discomfort than other laser treatments. Facial rejuvenation was revolutionised mainly with the development of the new CO_2 fractional laser. This procedure benefited from faster recovery time, more precise control of ablation depth and reduced risk of post-procedural problems.

In June 2007, Ailesbury introduced the new laser technology to Ireland and in the first few months we were finding our own way with the treatment. I was trained under the careful direction of Mr Max Murison, Consultant Plastic Surgeon who founded the Swansea Laser Clinic and worked with the NHS at Morriston Hospital, in Wales. One of the problems patients with CO_2 facial laser resurfacing is the potential reactivation of herpes simplex virus 1 (HSV-1), which can delay healing and result in severe scarring.

A funny incident happened in the first few weeks that we had the new laser. We had a patient from a rural Irish county who had been living in New York for many years and she wanted to look her best before meeting the rest of her family. It appeared she had fallen on hard times in America and over the years her faced had become cragged as the signs post menopause took its toll. Over this period her parents had relocated to a new more modern house and left the old isolated country cottage get into a state of disrepair. Mary had read about this new laser on our website and flew to Dublin before warning her parents that she was coming home. It became apparent that she was intending to stay in the old cottage where she grew up for a few weeks. The problem was she was a herpetic risk, having had the infection before and being unwilling to commence the recommended two-day anti-viral prophylaxis prior to her treatment.

In the end, feeling sorry for her, I decided to compromise and get her to double her Valacyclovir tablets for the first few days and continue with it twice daily for the next week. I warned her if she was not healing or developed vesicles to inform me immediately and to take another prescription with treble the dose. On day four, she phoned the clinic in quite a panic, saying that she had got severe facial herpes! This can be difficult for any patient as there is a small possibility that it could develop into more serious herpetic encephalitis. Being somewhat of a technophobe, she was unable to send an email or an image of her face to let me analyse the problem. In the end, I decided on a wet winter's evening to travel in the dark to the rural heartlands of Ireland and clinically evaluate her for myself.

These were the days before the widespread use of Sat Nav and with the help of her neighbours, I eventually found the house some fields in from the road. By now, it was about half nine or ten o clock in the evening.

With Dr Nikola Milojević, Dr Richard Sibthorpe, and Dr Ross Perry

The front door was locked so I went around the back and entered the old stone cottage. There I made my way through the kitchen to a room where I heard some people chatting. It was almost like the rosary was been said and it reminded me of similar noises of my youth. I entered one of the dimly lit bedrooms where a small crowd of people were assembled and there was a priest saying prayers beside her. Astonished, I presumed things had taken an awful turn for the worst. Everyone stopped and turned to look around at me. Mary spoke first,

'Oh, this is Dr Treacy, a dermatologist who I called down from Dublin.' Unsure, to what was happening she introduced me to her father and sister. He was an old man with rugged features, more used to the windswept hills of Roscommon than the finer avenues of Dublin. He took off his cap and spoke to me,

"Do you think you can fix her doctor?" "She got this ould cream for herself in New York and it's burned the face of her!"

It soon became apparent that her father was keeping some livestock near the old cottage and when he went to check it, he found Mary isolated there with her face post laser treatment. Determined to keep her laser treatment a secret she refused to see the local GP. Her father in his innocence told the local priest who came to pray by her beside. No doubt, I knew she'd be fully recovered in a few days and kept her secret. Thankfully, she had no evidence of a herpetic infection.

Later that year, Lumenis asked me to become a Key Opinion Leader (KOL) and to lecture about it at both the Aesthetic Cosmetic Medicine Fair in London and later at the Aesthetic Dentist Show in Birmingham. Their October meeting in Marbella again clashed with the UNA-USA Global Leadership Awards dinner at Cipriani-Wall Street, where Queen Rania was recognised for her many philanthropic efforts, including her notable role advocating for the rights, health and safety of children around the world as UNICEF's first Eminent Advocate for Children. Also, at the event were UN Secretary-General Ban Ki-Moon, Her Royal Highness Princess Firyal and Ted Turner, Founder of CNN, who presented the award to Her Majesty.

The new technology quickly became a favourite, and soon many other laser companies followed with newer versions. These included the Deka 30W SmartXide DOT from Italy and Reliant moved into the CO_2 wavelength with their new Fraxel Repair. These fractionalised CO_2 lasers substantially reduced the high level of non-responders seen with quite expensive non-ablative radiofrequency type treatments that often-required multiple painful sessions. The adoption of the newer fractionalised CO_2 lasers was favoured by many physicians as the stratum corneum largely remained intact during treatment and acted as a natural bandage allowing the skin to heal much faster. I started to test different levels of power and laser dwell time on the face and décolletage.

The study between the different lasers was performed in cooperation with Prof Kieran Sheahan from the Pathology Department at St Vincent's University Hospital in Dublin resulting in another publication in *PRIME Magazine*[1]. In September, the great humanitarian, Luciano Pavarotti, died of pancreatic cancer in Italy. He had lasted about the same length of time after diagnosis as my mother had. I had met Luciano on a few occasions and been enthralled by his talent and

---

[1] Treacy Patrick J; Treacy *Comparative split face study on photoaging with two different CO_2 fractionalised resurfacing lasers,* PRIME International Magazine, October 14, 2013

his great spirit of humanitarianism; I attended his funeral in Modena's cathedral. There were many familiar faces at the ceremony including Romano Prodi, Kofi Annan, and Bono.

*

In June 2011, Dr Randolph Waldman invited me to lecture about CO_2-fractionalised skin resurfacing at the Las Vegas Cosmetic Surgery meeting at the Bellagio. The Nevada conference attracted some of the top international aesthetic practitioners, and my lecture concerning laser resurfacing to the face and chest areas was particularly well received. It is true to say most practitioners were quite averse to treating the décolletage or chest area, and my results showed that fractionalised resurfacing could be safely used in this area. While at the Congress, I presented some results on dermal filler complication cases, which I had treated, and gave a lecture on why we should only use hyaluronic acid fillers in facial areas where blood vessels could be occluded.

I was watching television in 2015, when the news broke that Charles H Townes, the Nobel Prize-winning physicist credited with the invention of the laser and its predecessor – the maser had died in Oakland, Calif. He was ninety-nine, a visionary physicist, whose research jointly won him the 1964 Nobel Prize in Physics for his contribution to the field of lasers, sharing it with two Russian scientists. His contribution to everyday life was immeasurable as his work made it possible not only to measure time precisely, survey planets and witness the birth of stars, but also play CDs and scan prices at the supermarket. I won a Young Scientist Award with studies about lasers while still in my teens and had written articles about him for *Aesthetic Medicine* magazine in the past.

29. Speaking in the House of Lords

In January 2008, I presented the results of a trial using Radiesse® dermal filler for hand rejuvenation to IMCAS in Paris, and then left a few weeks later for Seefeld, Austria, to give the same lecture at the World Leaders Congress. I shared the podium with Florida dermatologists Mariano Busso and David Applebaum and while there introduced a novel three-way-tap method of mixing anaesthetic into this compound. This was necessary as the salt calcium hydroxyapatite present in the filler caused patients quite a lot of pain after placement. During my lecture, I advocated that Radiesse® should not be used in areas where great vessels lay, because if they were punctured, it would be impossible to reverse the destruction that they could cause. My suggestion that only reversible hyaluronic acid fillers should be used there was not welcomed by the company.

Some years later, at a meeting in Dublin in the spring of 2010, I again complained about the lack of a standardised injection technique for volumisation and cheek augmentation with this compound. I had used the product for HIV lipoatrophy patients and suggested staying very lateral away from the highly vascular areas and even superior to the alar-tragal line to prevent damaging the transverse facial artery or facial nerve. I protested strongly that injecting it directly into this line anteriorly would leave less experienced injectors at risk of causing damage to the important underlying structures. My prediction of impending vascular complications came to fruition, as more and more complications from other clinics were presenting. I again drew attention to this at a lecture in Las Vegas in 2011. Thankfully, nobody would consider using a non-reversible filler in these areas. Meanwhile, back in Ireland, the recession was deepening, and the economy was worsening, presenting new challenges, Ailesbury was left heavily exposed after failing to secure venture capital to build clinics planned for the Middle East.

With Marie Loftus at the House of Lords

That summer 2008, Ailesbury Clinic was named runner-up for the best aesthetic clinic in the UK and Ireland Aesthetic Medicine magazine awards. I visited the House of Lords again for a surreal event at which Taoiseach Bertie Ahern supped wine with members of the Orange Order to the sound of two giant Lambeg drums crashing away. I shared a table with Princess Rima al-Sabbah from Kuwait and Lord Iveagh, a member of the Guinness family. During the night, the Irish Prime Minister said he was leaving office but would like to have been around to deal with the problems. It was shameful to witness his lack of responsibility in causing Ireland's economic downfall. Within days, the Irish Stock Exchange fell to a fourteen-year low, and we were heading towards a deep recession and the biggest economic collapse since the formation of the Irish State. The following year, I returned to the House of Lords, where I was invited to listen to Rhodes Scholar Dr Edward de Bono lecture on "a thinking evolution", designed to help change global attitudes to humanity. The event again had been organised by Lord John Laird, who had invited leaders in various fields to use their creativity to generate ideas on how to bring about this change for a better world. I had to give a talk about what action the world should take on removing the dictator Robert Mugabe from Zimbabwe. Many people in their speeches accused Mugabe of being a dictator responsible for economic mismanagement, widespread corruption in Zimbabwe, and anti-white racism. After speaking to Dr Edward de Bono who had invented 'lateral thinking', I decided to take a different approach and said to give him the kind of things that he craved for, the Rolls Royce and ceremonial gowns but not let him have any direct charge of the economy. It seemed like ten minutes in this physician's company had changed my total mentality on the subject. He later came to live on a 33-acre island off the coast of West Cork, called West Skeam. The unique had the ruins of a 4th century Gnostic Christian Church, a World War II airstrip, a pier and a possible Viking burial ground.

*

In January 2009, I presented research on a Radiesse® cheek augmentation technique using the calcium salt of bone tissue first to IMCAS Paris and later in the year to the 7th Anti-Ageing Medicine World Congress in Monaco. The technique involved replacing the malar fat pad in patients to restore volume in their cheeks and had been learnt by me treating all the HIV lipodystrophy patients many years before. Because of that Monte Carlo lecture, I was invited as the main lecturer by Dr Paul Garcia and Karim Dominguez Oceguera to the SOCEMMAM Euro-Mexican Congress of Aesthetic Medicine Conference in Mexico City. While there, I took the opportunity to visit one of the UNESCO World Heritage ancient sites, Teotihuacan, also known as the City of the Gods. This archaeological site was 40km northeast of Mexico City, and home to some of the most massive ancient pyramids in the world. I was impressed by this Pre-Columbian city, which reached a population of 150,000 at its height. Karim and I also visited the National Anthropological Museum, in Mexico City to view the artefacts of both the Mayan and Aztec civilisations. I always felt a deep sense of association with the people of Mexico from my days of visiting Puerto Vallarta, Mazatlán and the rest of the Mexican Riviera, while working as a ships doctor with Carnival Cruise Lines back in 1992. This sense of relationship allowed me to travel overland without any fear throughout Mexico in 1994, those days before the nation spiralled into decline with kidnappings and the influence of drugs lords. In that year, I became a regular contributor on TV3's *Ireland AM*. The breakfast programme discussed, amongst other things, the rising tide of obesity, and it allowed me to explain to Irish people the differences among the many fat-removal techniques, including Vaser®, SmartLipo® and the fat-busting injection Lipodissolve.

*

That January, Paul Summerfield invited me to attend a Medical Innovations Briefing in the Royal Society of Medicine, where the Italian Professor, Paolo Macchiarini would speak on the world's first trachea transplant, followed by a reception. It appeared that surgeons in Spain had carried out the world's first tissue-engineered whole organ transplant – using a windpipe made with the patient's stem cells. Five months on the patient, thirty-year-old, mother of two, named Claudia Castillo, who needed the transplant to save a lung after contracting tuberculosis was still in perfect health. The ground-breaking technology meant for the first-time tissue transplants could be carried out without the need for anti-rejection drugs. To make the new airway, the doctors took a donor windpipe, or trachea, from a patient who had recently died. Then they used strong chemicals and enzymes to wash away all the cells from the donor trachea, leaving only a tissue scaffold made of the fibrous protein collagen. This gave them a structure to repopulate with cells from the patient. Scientists from Bristol helped grow the cells for the transplant, and the European team believes such tailor-made organs could become the norm. By using Ms Castillo's immature cells from her bone marrow, the doctors were able to trick her body into thinking the donated trachea was part of it, thus avoiding rejection.

US scientists had already successfully implanted bladder patches grown in the laboratory from patients' cells into people with bladder disease, and it was felt that, in twenty years, virtually any transplanted organ could be made in this way. Between 50,000 and 60,000 people are diagnosed with cancer of the larynx each year in Europe, and scientists thought about half them may be suitable candidates for tissue engineering transplants. It was not the last time that I would come across Professor Paolo Macchiarini on my journey of life.

30. Botox and Its Effect on the Brain

On 29th April 2013, an article by Claire Coleman in the Daily Mail led to widespread public confusion, as it suggested that Botox® probably caused depression rather than treating it. One of my Harley Street colleagues, Dr Michael Prager, was so enraged by the article that he wrote on his Twitter page "What nonsense. The opposite in every aspect, at least scientifically. Sad." The report was based on a study led by Dr Michael Lewis of the School of Psychology, Cardiff, Wales, who followed 25 people who had received Botox® for facial lines and examined the idea of facial feedback – where the expression we make with our faces affect how we feel. The study concluded that botulinum caused the patients to feel worse. This made no sense as all previous studies had found that the treatment of frown lines with botulinum had left patients feeling less depressed.

The scientific evidence in favour of Botox® reducing depression was quite prolific. In 1992, Heckmann from the Ludwig Maximilians University in Munich published opposing data suggesting that treatment of the glabellar (frown) region with botulinum toxin changed facial expressions from sad, and fearful to happy, and this impacted on their emotional experiences. Many therapists, including Sommer in 2003, showed that patients who had been treated in the glabellar (frown) area reported an increase in emotional wellbeing and reduced levels of fear and sadness beyond what would be expected from the cosmetic benefit alone. In 2006, two US clinicians, dermatologist Dr Eric Finzi and psychologist Dr Erika Wasserman published a paper in the *Journal of Dermatologic Surgery,* which concluded that treating clinically depressed patients on their frown lines got rid of their depression. Three years later, in 2009, Andreas Hennenlotter of the Max Planck Institute in Leipzig, Germany, went one stage further and showed that botulinum toxin treatment of the central frown lines stopped the activation of specific brain regions normally seen during voluntary contraction of the corrugator and procerus frown muscles. This indicated that feedback from the facial musculature in this region in some way modulated the processing of emotions.

Then, in 2010, a team of researchers lead by Axel Wollmera and Tillmann Krugerb, based at the Psychiatric Hospital of the University of Basel, Switzerland and the Department of Psychiatry, Medical School Hannover, Germany, conducted a randomised, placebo-controlled, double-blind scientific trial and concluded that botulinum treatment of the glabellar region could reduce the symptoms of major depression. This effect developed within a few weeks and persisted until the end of the sixteen-week follow-up period have indeed turned conventional thinking on its head. Their research, was published in *the Journal of Psychiatric Research*, proved scientifically that injecting "Botox®" into the muscles most linked with low mood, produces alleviation of depression. This is where things were until recently with many authors suggesting that this capacity to counteract negative emotions could be put to some clinical use during the treatment of depression. So, the question was, who was correct – as the answer could have profound implications for the cosmetic industry?

I decided to contact Dr Lewis at the School of Psychology, Cardiff, Wales, to discuss his findings. During the conversation, we discussed Finzi and Wasserman's paper, which had made an impact on social media but was considered by many that the method evaluating depression should have been more rigorous. I was impressed that he was aware that a footnote at the end of the paper by the editor, Alastair Carruthers, stated that 'the findings must be considered anecdotal as there were no appropriate methods of control utilised and there were other methodological weaknesses including limited follow-up, lack of randomisation, the absence of a blind evaluation and especially the small number of individuals included'. I told Michael that I had also written to the journal at the time, that patients' self-reporting of their depressive symptoms by use of the Beck Depression Inventory introduced a significant self-report bias, because of the potential for secondary cosmetic gain. I added that to ensure that patients' psychiatric symptoms are accurately classified, a thorough psychiatric interview must be conducted.

While we were chatting, I discovered his research had been done on another area of the face, the lines around the eyes, known as the crow's feet! The penny dropped – Botox® was acting in two different ways in two different areas of the face! I decided to investigate this further and called my thesis – the Botox® paradox! The more I thought about it – I started to feel that both were correct and the answer to the apparent medical paradox lay with Charles Darwin! Dr Lewis and I promised to collaborate in a medical paper, but I did not let him know my feelings about the matter at that time.

After the telephone conversation, I took out the work of Charles Darwin and read it again. In 1872, thirteen years after publishing his sentinel book on evolution called *On the Origin of Species*, this British genius formulated another theory called the "facial feedback hypothesis", and it was here that I would find the answer to the paradox. Darwin suggested that physiological changes caused by emotion had a direct impact on, rather than being just the consequence of that emotion. He wrote:

'The free expression by outward signs of an emotion intensifies it. On the other hand, the repression, as far as this is possible, of all outward signs softens our emotions... Even the simulation of an emotion tends to arouse it in our mind!'

This theory implied a mutual interaction between emotions and facial muscle activity, and he published his findings in another book *The Expression of the Emotions in Man and Animals*. It was Charles Darwin's third major work of evolutionary theory, following from *The Descent of Man* (1871). It was initially intended as a section of that book but published the next year separately. In this book, Darwin set out ideas about behavioural genetics and explored the animal origins of such human characteristics as the lifting of the eyebrows in moments of surprise and displaying the crow's feet in times of anger. He sought out the opinions of some eminent British psychiatrists, notably James Crichton-Browne, in the preparation of his work, which was his main contribution to both psychiatry and psychology.

Charles Darwin recognised these features as an expression of sadness and attributed them to the activity of so-called "grief muscles" in the glabellar region. He suggested the forehead pattern that they made (omega sign) could be used as a diagnostic criterion for hospital admission for patients suffering from melancholia. In this book, Darwin sought to trace the animal origins of human characteristics, including the movement of specific facial muscles during certain emotions, such as anger or disgust. One theory, which particularly interested me was called the "facial feedback hypothesis", and it implied a mutual interaction between emotions and facial muscle activity. He even provided experimental evidence that voluntary contraction of some facial muscles could channel some feelings, and they were conversely expressed by activation of these muscles. It is evident that the facial musculature not only expresses but also regulates mood states.

I thought again about Dr Lewis's work, which found that people treated for another muscle (around the crows' feet) left patients feeling more depressed and felt that it did not contradict Charles Darwin's original hypotheses, but it supported it. The muscles around the eye are related to happiness and smiling, and to restrict their movement must interfere with the "facial feedback hypotheses" in a converse way to those in the frown area. Accordingly, happiness can make you smile, and smiling can make you happy. Maybe, it was my sixth sense, but I never really felt right about totally removing crow's feet around the patient's eyes.

I ran a trial of thirty-four patients who answered by questionnaire and published my findings and opinion in an article[2] entitled "The paradoxical effect of botulinum on the brain" in the June 2013 edition of *PRIME Journal Magazine*. The study concluded that botulinum toxin injection most probably directly interferes with the "facial feedback hypothesis" originally postulated by Charles Darwin and that it could be used to either cause or relieve depression depending on the area of injection. I said that botulinum toxin to the glabellar region might be an effective, safe and sustainable intervention in the treatment of depression. We must respect the concept as depression affects over 120 million people globally, making it one of the leading causes of disability in the world.

Although there are various effective treatments, the therapeutic response remains unsatisfactory, and depression can develop as a chronic condition in patients. Negative emotions, such as anger, fear and sadness, are prevalent in depression and have long been associated with hyperactivity of the corrugator and procerus muscles in the glabellar region of the face.

Because of the long treatment intervals, it may also be an economical treatment option, and the safety and tolerability record of botulinum toxin injections to the frown area region is excellent. I also said that injecting the area around the eye reduces the smile lines and hence probably gives a different feedback effect, possibly even inducing depression. Accordingly, we should not

---

[2] Treacy Patrick J; *The paradoxical effect of Botox on the brain, Prime International Magazine, June 2013* Page 63-69 May 1, 2013

treat this area liberally with the toxin. The reason that most people are unaware of the impact was that nearly everybody injected both areas at the same time, one negating the effect of the other.

With Dr Dayal Mukherjee, Dr Uliana Gout, Dr Christopher Roland Payne,
Prof Souphiyeh Samizadeh RSM ICG-6 (London)

Christopher Roland Payne, then Chairman of the organising committee invited me in February 2013 to talk at the RSM ICG-6 (Royal Society of Medicine's Interventional Cosmetics Group's 5th Annual Multidisciplinary International Meeting) at the Royal Society of Medicine in London. The meeting would give me the perfect opportunity to present my results about the effect of Botox on the brain. While there, I took advantage of going to the library and seeking out *The Expression of the Emotions in Man and Animals,* a book Charles Darwin published in 1872, thirteen years after the *Origin of Species* and one year after *The Descent of Man.* Darwin had been collecting material for this book for over thirty years; he intended to show how the expressions of the emotions in man were analogous to those in animals. If proven, this would support his theory that man and animals were derived from a common ancestor.

Darwin, of course, was a past fellow of the Royal Society and in this book, he sought to trace the animal origins of human characteristics, such as the pursing of the lips in concentration and the tightening of the muscles around the eyes in anger. This was taking emotion to a new level and concerned genetically determined aspects of behaviour.

It was published thirteen years after *On the Origin of Species* and alongside his 1871 book *The Descent of Man*, showed his consideration of human origins. In the late 1860s and early 1870s, he had corresponded with the French physician, Duchenne, regarding his experimental manipulation of human facial expression of emotion, by applying Galvanic electrical stimulation directly to facial muscles. He received permission from Duchenne in 1871 to reproduce a set of over sixty photographic plates to illustrate his view that the different muscles in the human face are separately responsible for each emotion. The facial feedback hypothesis stated that facial movement could influence emotional experience. He gave the example of an individual who is forced to smile during a social event will come to find the event more of an enjoyable experience. Darwin studied this material very carefully and wondered whether there might instead be a set of core emotions that are expressed with great stability worldwide and across cultures.

I looked more closely at Darwin's *The Expression of the Emotions in Man and Animals*. The first edition was published in 1872, thirteen years after the Origin of Species and one year after *The Descent of Man*. Darwin had, however, been collecting material since 1838. He intended to show how the expressions of the emotions in man were analogous to those in animals, supporting his theory that man and animals were derived from a common ancestor, but he knew that he was going to have opposition from many people, including the Church. His emphasis on a shared human and animal ancestry was also in sharp contrast to the arguments deployed in Sir Charles Bell's *Anatomy and Philosophy of Expression* (1824), who claimed that the facial muscles were divinely designed to express uniquely human feelings. Darwin had listened to a discussion about the emotional expression at the Plinian Society in December 1826 when he was a medical student at Edinburgh University. The meeting had ridiculed Bell's theological explanations, pointing instead to the striking similarities of human and animal biology, and ended in uproar. Forty-five years later, Darwin made his feelings known but expressed his special indebtedness to Sir Charles Bell for his book.

In addition to the mass of information from these sources, Darwin made his observations on animals, particularly his pets and the orangutans and monkeys in the London Zoo, a short walk from where he lived. He also studied the expressions of psychiatric patients because he thought their emotions were more fixed and exaggerated. He quoted Sir James Crichton-Browne's description of patients with "melancholia" (depression) and "hypochondria" as showing the contraction of what he calls the grief-muscles, causing a transverse furrow across the forehead. He postulated that most expressions of emotion are inherited and seemed to favour their origin as acquired habits rather than natural selection.

*

In February 2013, I was asked to be the keynote speaker in the 4th World Congress of Anti-Ageing Medicine in Mexico City, which was sponsored by the American Academy of Anti-Ageing Medicine, in the Fiesta Americana Hotel on Reforma Avenue. The other keynote speakers were Dr Luis Miguel Parra from Columbia and my good friend, Dr Paul Garcia from Venezuela. It was great to meet up with Paul and Karim Dominguez Oceguera once again and we discussed Chávez after winning his fourth term as Venezuelan President in the October 2012 Presidential Election. Paul was originally from Venezuela, and he had invited me to speak at a conference in 2009 at the Hilton hotel on Margarita Island, Venezuela's tourist playground. The government, unfortunately, seized the hotel before the congress happened. What used to be the Hilton Margarita now stood as a bold symbol of Hugo Chávez's leftist revolution, but sadly with a gift shop offering a range of ceramic Chávez mugs and sculptures. A presidential decree transferred its assets, including 280 rooms, 210 suites, shops, restaurants and a casino to the tourism ministry.

While in Mexico City, I left the conference on the second day as the lectures were all in Spanish and I wandered downtown to Tianguis Cultural del Chopo, a gathering place for the city's various youth subcultures, with outdoor vendor stalls selling punk clothes or offering body piercing. When Paul eventually found me, he was angry that I had left the conference without security or letting them know where I was going to. 'It's dangerous in Mexico,' he said, 'You could be kidnapped and held for ransom.'

I felt he was a bit overboard as I was used to travelling across the country and had previously journeyed alone overland from Puerto Vallarta to Mexico

City in the nineties. However, he was correct as this was a different era, and the kidnapping surge in Mexico was fuelled in large part by the insatiable US demand for drugs.

Beginning around 2006, criminal groups began to use kidnappings to help fund personnel and vast caches of assault rifles to defend their "plazas". In 2013, a record 1,700 kidnappings took place, according to data from the Mexican National System of Public Security (SNSP). A few weeks later, I was shocked when Karim phoned me and told me that Paul himself had joined these statistics. He had been kidnapped and held for ransom, and the criminals threatened to cut off his finger if his family didn't pay for his release. Eventually, the kidnappers settled for taking his credit cards and stole over $50,000 from him, which ultimately, he recovered from the bank. When we met up together at the AMWC in Monaco a few months later, we had a few beers to celebrate his release and pondered on what could have been.

In August 2014, I got the opportunity to present my work on "Botox and the Brain" at the ICAD Conference in the Frei Caneca Conventions Centre, São Paulo, Brazil and later at the 1st AMWC Aesthetic & Anti-Aging Medicine World Congress – Latin America, which took place in November of that year in Medellin, Colombia. I also gave it as a joint presentation with a lecture warning of the rising problems with vascular complications at the Las Vegas Multispecialty Congress 2014.

On the way back from Medellin, Colombia, I decided to spend a few days in New York and visit U2's World AIDS Day (RED) performance in Times Square. It was rumoured that Kanye West and Carrie Underwood would be performing at the event, but that Bono was rather ill back home in Dublin, as the singer remained under doctors' orders to refrain from performing until fully recuperated from his injuries, sustained in Central Park a few weeks previously. Appearing at the personal invitation of U2, Bruce Springsteen and Chris Martin graciously donated their time and talents to save the World AIDS Day event from cancellation. It was "U2 Minus 1," but Bono appeared on screen, speaking from Dublin.

'This year is a World AIDS Day like no other,' he said. 'The world reached a tipping point in the fight against AIDS – more people were newly added to life-saving treatment than were newly infected with the virus. A lot of people are calling it the beginning of the end of AIDS. Maybe, indeed I was entering a new phase of my life.'

While there, another exciting thing happened. It started after I decided for some reason to take the Metro to Roosevelt Avenue and hopefully replenish my memories and maybe even visit Mooney's bar in Queens where I'd worked during the late seventies. My friend, Thomas Maguire, said how the area had changed entirely with Asian-Americans and Hispanics now replacing the Irish families who used to live there. On route to Woodside and being solely guided by the dying battery of a Samsung phone, I got off at 74th and Jackson Heights. The area had indeed changed, reflected in the number of Thai, Filipino, and South American eateries that were now flourishing everywhere. In the 1930s, Woodside was the largest Irish American community in Queens, but in the early 1990s, many Asian American and Latino families moved into the area, and the neighbourhood was now filled with many cultural restaurants and pubs.

While standing and establishing my bearings, I was approached by a young girl in her mid-twenties, dressed in long colourful tie-dyed cotton attire. My first instinct after my recent iPhone loss was "here we go again", but something was exciting about the strange encounter as she took my hand and led me to a small shop across the street. I had just time to see the flashing neon "fortunes told" sign outside the door before she guided me through rails of sarees and I realised she was most probably from India, Sri Lanka or even Bangladesh. Eventually, she reached the end of the shop where another person was seated under some flashing colourful bulbs emblazoned with the title of "World Famous Sri Lankan Astrologer and Palm Reader" Pandith Sri Guruji. The cost was only $10; so, when I'd come this far. I decided to give it a try.

'You are a politician,' he said, taking my hand. 'And you work in the Third World!' I denied that I was a politician but decided to string him along for ten dollars' worth of entertainment, being without a phone or mission on a cold New York December afternoon. Then he surprised me and said my hand reading was difficult and that he was going to fetch his more experienced brother.

In truth, I expected a scam and had allowed about fifty dollars before I would quit. His older brother arrived, dressed in a long magenta open-necked tunic with a long necklace hanging over his sternum.

'He doesn't speak much English,' the first reader said.

He took my hand and studied it carefully.

'You are a doctor,' he said through his brother's translation.

'You have been to the Third World –Africa,' he continued. 'You have been writing a book, and it will be published. You will get a great award for your work!'

With that, he left, as if he had done his spiritual duty and not wishing to get involved in any financial matters. Then he returned with a little talisman shaped like a bullet.

'Keep this to tell your fortune – it will shine brightly when you need it!'

1st AIDA Award for PLUS technique (Abu Dhabi)

His predictions became amazingly accurate. Sean O'Keefe arrived in my office the next Monday morning and said that Liberties Press wanted to publish "Behind the Mask" as soon as possible. His mention of awards was also exact. My hypothesis on the potential neurological effects of botulinum on the brain became accepted, especially in the Latin world. In 2015, I was awarded the CCME Mexican Congress Medal for "Excellence in Medical Aesthetics" in Cuernavaca, Mexico for my work in helping to identify the effect of botulinum on the brain.

31. When Did We Learn to Hate the Sun?

On Aug 2016, Carol Dooley from *Sunshine Radio 106.8* interviewed me on a recent study from Pelle Lindqvist, MD, of Karolinska University Hospital in Huddinge, Sweden, which showed that non-smokers who stayed out of the sun had a life expectancy like smokers who soaked up the most rays. The study, from a very reputable source, was published in the *Journal of Internal Medicine* on March 21st but had gone mainly unnoticed by both the public and my colleagues. It was well known that people who seek out the sun were generally at lower risk for cardiovascular disease (CVD) and non-cancer/non-CVD diseases such as diabetes, multiple sclerosis. They also had fewer incidences of pulmonary diseases, and the results are dose-specific – sunshine benefits are related to exposure. The study concluded that women with active sun exposure habits were mainly at a lower risk of cardiovascular disease (CVD) and non-cancer/non-CVD death as compared to those who avoided sun exposure. As a result of their increased survival, the relative contribution of cancer death increased in these women. Non-smokers who avoided sun exposure had a life expectancy like smokers in the highest sun exposure group, indicating that avoidance of sun exposure is a risk factor for death of the same magnitude as smoking. Compared to the this (sun exposure) group, life expectancy of avoiders of sun exposure was reduced by 0.6-2.1 years. This was important as we spent so much of our time encouraging patients to stop smoking but also to avoid the sun.

The researchers had studied 30,000 Swedish women over twenty years and concluded that avoiding the sun "is a risk factor for death of a similar magnitude as smoking". More importantly, compared with those with the highest sun exposure, life expectancy for those who avoided the sun dropped by 0.6 to 2.1 years. They acknowledged that longer life expectancy for sunbathers seems paradoxical to the common thinking that sun exposure increases the risk for skin cancer. There was an increased risk of skin cancer. However, the skin cancers that occurred in those exposing themselves to the sun had a better prognosis. For a long time, I had thought that the Western world's restrictive guidance against sun exposure over the past four decades might be particularly ill-advised. It makes little sense to impose global rules regarding sun exposure to everyone on the planet, whereas patients exist in different geographical locations with various risk profiles.

There is also the great elephant in the room – the more medicine says to wear sunscreen, the higher the levels of skin cancer went up. Something doesn't add up – and I suspected that sunscreen could be a contributory factor! This may happen by allowing people to stay out in the sun too long or possibly blocking a vital ingredient required to protect us against the sun's radiation. Sunlight exposure and fair skin are significant determinants of human vitamin D production, but they are also risk factors for cutaneous malignant melanoma (MM). There is epidemiological evidence that all-cause mortality is related to low vitamin D levels. In 2011, the *Journal of Clinical Oncology* published a randomised, clinical study of over 1,600 people showing that regular sunscreen use reduced the incidence of melanoma by 50-73%. When used as directed with other sun protection measures, broad-spectrum sunscreen with an SPF of 15 or higher helps prevent sunburn and reduces the risk of early skin aging and skin cancer (melanoma and squamous cell carcinomas) associated with UV radiation.

The longer life expectancy amongst women with active sun exposure habits was related to a decrease in CVD and non-cancer/non-CVD mortality, causing the relative contribution of death due to cancer to increase. The results of this study provide observational evidence that avoiding sun exposure is a risk factor for all-cause mortality. In the United States alone, more than 42 000 cases are diagnosed annually, resulting in more than 7,000 deaths. In 2014, 1,041 people were diagnosed with melanoma in Ireland, which has the highest rate of deaths in Europe from aggressive skin cancer. Another worldwide study by the German dermatology group, Derma Plus, in 2016 showed that Ireland has 859 new cases of melanoma a year, of which 16% of people, or 137, diagnosed with the disease died

If solar radiation is a primary risk factor for malignant melanoma, it is reasonable to conclude that reducing sun exposure via topical sunscreen use would be associated with reduced disease risk. However, the available epidemiological data are contradictory. Some studies suggest that sunscreen use is associated with an increased melanoma risk.

Establishing Ailesbury Hair transplant clinics in Dubai in 2010

I have had a long history in dealing with skin cancer, particularly cutaneous malignant melanoma. In 1989, I published a sentinel paper on the increasing level of malignant melanoma in the Rochester, Minnesota, population between the period 1950-1985 at the Mayo Clinic. I presented an article of my experiences with this condition at the 56th meeting of the (RCSI) Biological Society, earning me an award. In 1997, I worked in Toowoomba, Queensland, which had the highest melanoma incidence in the world of seventy-five cases per 100,000 people, and some of the patients were also part of the melanoma vaccine study Brisbane's Princess Alexandra Hospital. The sustained increase in malignant melanoma incidence over the past few decades highlights the fact that this disease represents a significant public health management issue worldwide.

It is possible that sun exposure advice that is very restrictive in countries with low solar intensity might be harmful to women's health. In other words, cardiac disease is much more prevalent than skin cancer, and we should take this into account, especially as high-level SPF was being put into every cosmeceutical sold in Ireland – a nation that ranks amongst the lowest sunshine levels in the world! Ireland gets typically about one thousand two hundred and fifty hours of sunshine each year, while many other cities around the world are nearly three times this level.

- Treacy Patrick J; Popescu NA; Kurland LT; *Cutaneous malignant melanoma in Rochester, Minnesota: trends in incidence and survivorship, 1950 through 1985,* Mayo Clin Proc. 1990 Oct, 65(10):1293-302.
- J Intern Med. 2016 Oct;280(4):375-87. *Avoidance of sun exposure as a risk factor for major causes of death: a competing risk analysis of the Melanoma in Southern Sweden cohort.* Lindqvist PG1, Epstein E2, Nielsen K3, Landin-Olsson M4, Ingvar C5, Olsson H6.

32. Research Awards

In October 2012, I published a paper called *Combining Therapies for the Ageing Face – The Dublin Lift[3]*. The background to the technique was to establish the clinical effectiveness of combining multiple established rejuvenation treatments synchronously to the ageing face to see if it was possible to increase the aesthetic effect, patient safety and, hopefully, reduce patient downtime. Until then, there were a variety of different dermatologic treatments available for facial rejuvenation. These included red light, chemical peels, dermal fillers, microneedling, microdermabrasion, Botox® injections and IPL (intense pulsed light). In later years, new technologies such as RF (radiofrequency devices), CO_2 laser resurfacing, and platelet-rich plasmas (PRP) had emerged, but each treatment has its relative benefit, as well as risks.

I always felt that the best way to rejuvenate skin was to make use of the body's own healing mechanisms. If one falls on the ground and cuts oneself, the body immediately sets up a repair mechanism to restore lost function. This process is different depending on whether the skin is broken or not. If the skin breaks and blood is spilt, then repair mechanisms involving platelets and signal messengers come into play. If we could recreate this process in ageing skin with a controlled series of steps taken to achieve new skin, we could mimic what nature had already provided us. I decided to merge three or four of the available technologies synchronously to bring some order and efficiency to the facial rejuvenation process.

The first part was to set up a controlled wounding phase. To achieve this, I started by wounding the skin by using low-powered Lumenis Ultrapulse fractionalised CO_2 to provide a rich source of fibroblasts. This method was limited as it took five days to heal, increased the expense incurred to the patient,

---

[3] *Combining Therapies for the Aging Face – The Dublin Lift, Prime International Magazine*, Vol 2 No 7 Page 20–31 October 1, 2012

and not every clinic was lucky enough to own such a device. Looking for a cheaper alternative, I considered collagen induction therapy (CIT), an aesthetic medical procedure that involves repeatedly puncturing the skin with tiny, sterile needles. Typically, this is done with a specialised implement called a microneedling device. Similar evidence of collagen production and reduction of acne scars had been well documented from these devices, and they were cheap and readily available.

The second part was to simulate wound healing in the body by providing platelets and growth factors to convert the fibroblasts into collagen and elastin. I had already lectured on platelet-rich plasmas (PRP) at IMCAS Paris some years before and demonstrated how this technique could be used to promote healing and facial rejuvenation. These platelet injections were first used by Ferrari and Valbonesi in 1987 in open heart surgery and later in orthopaedic and cosmetic use. The technique involved taking a patient's blood and spinning it in a centrifuge to separate the heavier red blood cells from the lighter platelet layer, which contained stimulative growth factors and signal messenger to instruct the fibroblasts to work. The benefits of red-light phototherapy on skin and hair had been known since 1967, after the Hungarian doctor, Endre Mester, noticed that shaved mice experienced better quality skin and faster hair re-growth after exposure to 633nm light. He became a pioneer of low-level laser therapy (LLLT) showing that red light could boost blood circulation, stimulate collagen and fibroblasts production, and develop new capillaries in skin rejuvenation. During World War II, Mester worked as a surgeon at Saint John's Hospital and in the "Rock Hospital", located in the tunnels underneath Budapest and welcomed the 1956 Hungarian uprising against Communism.

The red light provided the final stage in guiding the fibroblasts to make new blood vessels and collagen. I called the procedure the DUBLiN Lift, a multi-procedural facial rejuvenation technique that combined, growth factors, dermal needling or low-level CO_2 fractionalised resurfacing and red-light phototherapy together to inexpensively increase the efficacy of fibroblast conversion into new collagen for facial rejuvenation. The DUBLIN facelift was an acronym of the procedures involved: D – Dermaroller, U – Ultralase laser, B – Blood growth factors, Li – Light (near red 633nm) and N – Neurotoxin. My research was well accepted, and I was invited to speak about it at conferences around the world.

*

I spoke about the Dublin Lift at the EADV (European Academy of Dermatology and Venereology Congress) in Istanbul in October 2013 and remembered those long summer evenings I spent hanging out with my drivers in Sultan Ahmed, during the period of the Turkey Run some thirty years before.

As well as treating aesthetic patients, I was interested in seeing the effect on my medical ones. One of my patients had become very wasted after a protracted treatment for cancer of the oesophagus. The condition was known medically as cancer-related cachexia, and it caused devastating structural changes in the face, manifesting mostly as muscle and fat pad wasting. This loss of weight, skeletal muscle and adipose tissue was not caused simply by anorexia but rather by the release of small peptides and catabolic cytokines that appear to produce some of the systemic effects of cancer. Most of the research to date in treating the condition had focused on the use of pharmaceutical agents and parenteral nutrition in the restoration of total body mass rather than being concerned with facial aesthetics.

I was somewhat surprised how little had been published about the use of using external mediators (growth factors, microneedling, and red light) to help stimulate collagen in those patients with the condition who are recovering from cancer.

The patient was fifty-three years old, and I had previously used some Radiesse® – calcium hydroxyapatite to address her loss of malar fat pads but noted that it failed to treat the associated cachexic problems of poor skin texture and facial sagging, which caused the patient deep psychological concern and social isolation. In the end, I decided to use a multi-procedural facial rejuvenation technique (DUBLiN Lift) by combining cross-linked hyaluronic acid dermal fillers, PRP growth factors, dermal needling or (low-level CO_2 fractionalised resurfacing) and red-light phototherapy to try and address these other problems. During the procedure, I substituted hyaluronic acid dermal fillers instead of calcium hydroxyapatite because of the theoretical suspicion that bone material could be formed by the consequential use of injected growth factors. The procedure worked well and addressed both the facial volumisation and the skin-texture problems quite well.

The research on the Dublin Lift won me my first prestigious AMEC Aesthetic Award in Paris in 2014, in the category for "novel techniques in facial rejuvenation". This is a peer-reviewed award for the "Best medical case in non-surgical facial rejuvenation". When I lifted the prize, I said, 'It is hoped that the use of this technique and these external factors may prove to be safe and aesthetic physicians in the future may support oncologists using oral medications and parenteral nutrition in restoring these patients to full health.' I wrote up my results and published the paper in *Prime Magazine*[4] a few months later. The research also won the MyFaceMyBody Award "Best medical research for wound healing" (London), November 2016.

At this stage, I had a lot of experience in treating these complications and advocated the use of hyaluronidase to reverse any problem when it occurred. In 2006, when Michael Jackson required these products to be removed from his face, he had to cross the Atlantic to Ireland for reversal treatment. European doctors had a lot of experience with these hyaluronic fillers, having been using them since 1996. It took another nine years for the FDA to sanction its use in the United States. I found it challenging to get anyone to agree to my concerns, so I asked my friend, Catherine Decuyper, the Euromedicom congress organiser, if we could introduce a *"mea culpa"* session at the next AMWC Monaco. This was originally used by Randy Waldman in Las Vegas as a special session where doctors could present serious complications that had happened to themselves and see if the audience agreed with how they dealt with it.

Respectfully, it took a lot of courage for an eminent doctor to stand up on stage in front of his colleagues and admit they had caused a problem in a patient. It was an immediate success, and it was evident that the doctors were more interested in real experiences rather than watching their largely diva colleagues showing photograph after photograph of how wonderful they were while treating their patients. I believe this was a turning point where delegates were exposed to the fact of aesthetic complications and eager to learn how to prevent them. Many colleagues, including Bob Khanna agreed that it was also a breath of fresh air to be shown real life issues and not be subjected to a gallery of images of doctors showing how impressive they were. As I was on the Euromedicom Scientific Committee, I wanted to make sure that from now on, doctors should take control and we should increase our focus on human anatomy, proper injection techniques and how to deal with complications.

---

[4] Treacy Patrick J; *Treating facial cancer-related cachexia by aesthetic medicine*, *PRIME International Magazine, January 2, 2015*

AMEC Award for HELPIR technique (Paris) 2014

In September 2014, I published a paper[5] with *PRIME International* entitled "Reversal of a dermal filler induced facial artery occlusion" that set out a protocol about how to treat a blocked artery caused by a dermal filler. This was one of the first publications on this topic and in the paper, I proposed using the reversal enzyme at ten times the dose being advocated in some forums, quite aware that it would do no damage to the patient's healthy tissue. The paper also showed the chronological changes that occurred whenever a facial artery was blocked, and it suggested that we should all carry the reversal agent, hyaluronidase, as potentially this problem could happen at any time to any person and possibly even cause blindness in some of our patients in the future.

My protocol included using lignocaine both as a vasodilator and numbing agent, and I changed it in 2014, to include bacteriostatic saline rather than normal saline as it didn't sting as much. I also used Hyperbaric Oxygen Therapy (HBOT) – 100% oxygen at pressures higher than atmospheric pressure. HBOT has been successfully used as adjunctive therapy for wound healing, especially non-healing wounds such as vascular insufficiency ulcers and infected wounds like clostridial myonecrosis, compromised skin grafts and flaps, and thermal burns.

Although rarely reported in the literature, complications related to the interrupted blood supply to the nose can occur with nasolabial or glabellar fold dermal injections. It seems I tapped into an unreported underground pool of problems as many doctors came to me after the lectures with images of patients who had developed severe vascular adverse events in the glabellar and nasolabial regions after treatment with both biodegradable and non-biodegradable injectable fillers. Soon I was getting referrals from all over the world and the National Hyperbaric Treatment Centre was being filled with vascular occluded patients in various levels of progress.

With the increase in the availability of these hyperbaric chambers across the country, and with an increasing number of studies proving the benefits of adjunctive use for various kinds of wounds and other indications, HBOT was immediately considered as part of the overall management plan. When I gave the complications lecture at AMWC in Monaco, I also suggested using oral nitrates such as Viagra rather than nitroglycerine paste as they worked during the night and didn't cause the syncopal episodes that the topical compound did. After that,

---

[5] *Treacy Patrick J; Reversal of a dermal filler induced facial artery occlusion, PRIME International Magazine, September 1, 2014*

I was invited to give the lecture on complications to doctors in many cities around the world, including Las Vegas, Sao Paulo, Abu Dhabi, Paris and Cartagena.

Most of the audiences seemed interested in learning how to treat complications that occurred immediately, such as bruising, erythema, pain and tenderness, swelling and itching. This was natural as it caused embarrassment to the patient, but these events usually resolved within a few days without sequelae.

However, many other events such as delayed onset nodules, granulomas and biofilm other occurred three months after the filler had been injected. It was great to have an extensive database of patients who I had treated for other physicians over the past decade. In Monaco, I suggested that dermal fillers complications should be divided into early and delayed in terms of the time of occurrence and minor and significant in terms of severity Although rarely reported in the literature, complications related to the interrupted blood supply to the nose can occur with nasolabial or glabellar fold dermal injections. It seems I tapped into an unreported underground pool of problems as many doctors came to me after the lectures with images of patients who had developed severe vascular adverse events in the glabellar and nasolabial regions after treatment with both biodegradable and non-biodegradable injectable fillers.

*

In December 2014, Balraj Juttla of *PRIME Magazine* asked me to be Guest Editor of the magazine for the Nov/Dec issue. I was honoured and decided to write about the recent Ebola outbreak in Liberia and the response from the media, 'As I write this editorial, one of the first medical deaths from Ebola has happened in the township of Caldwell right beside Everland Liberia. There is a deluge of the Western press focusing on barricading the patients in Monrovia and closing the Liberian border, believing that isolating affected nations will be enough. As a scientist, I feel this is absurd. If airlines discontinue air travel in and out of this Ebola-stricken nation, they will no longer be able to receive the resources they need to control the virus, and it will then spread to all neighbouring countries. Conversely, we need to send as many doctors and nurses as humanely possible, well-trained volunteers (including military) to hang the drips and isolate the sick patients. As a doctor, our primary duty is to help the sick.'

During 2014, I was treating about two patients with blocked blood vessels every week and giving information to many worried doctors around the world by email or social media. Some of the cases had happened many months or even years before and had left scarring, which I treated in Dublin by a CO_2 laser. There were two cases, one from Columbia and one from the Philippines, which eventually required plastic surgery. Neither case had used a reversible filler.

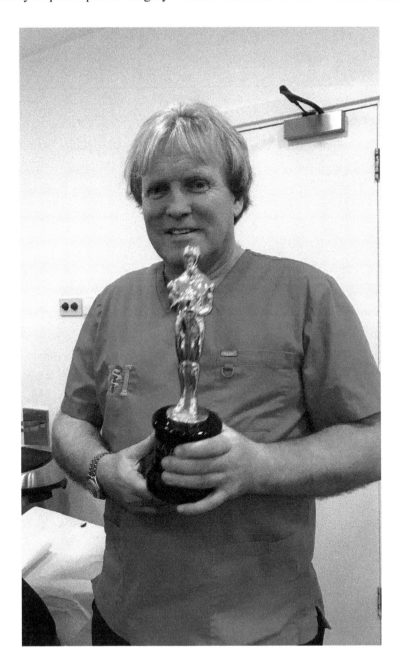

Wining the Ist AIDA Trophy in Abu Dhabi (2017)

While much of the physiology of wound healing was understood, I felt that many gaps still existed in our understanding of the everyday phenomenon. My mission was to not leave things in the hands of God, but rather to try and prevent dermal scarring when vascular occlusion and necrosis occurred after a doctor had accidently injected a facial artery. To do this, I had to start at the very beginning, and needed first to understand skin and then how it heals itself. There would be minimal room for experimentation or error and my best patients to work with would be those facing the worst outcomes.

I knew that skin was the soft outer tissue covering of all animals with backbones, although it has a different type of structure in those animals that fly or remain under water. It is there to protect us against pathogens and to keep water in our body. It also regulated our temperature by allowing water to evaporate through sweat glands. We humans are mammals, having separated ourselves from reptiles and birds, in the late Triassic period, possibly 220 million years ago. All mammalian skin is composed of two layers: the epidermis and the dermis. This is important as I now believed scarring occurred because the epidermis did not replenish itself properly in these vascular occlusion cases after it was damaged. The same effect happened during burns, probably in both instances because the blood supply to the area was cut off, along with all the healing cells and chemicals. Timing of treatment was also essential to wound healing as eventual reepithelialisation can decide the outcome of the event. If the epithelisation of tissue over a denuded area is slow, a scar will form over many weeks or months; if the epithelisation of a wounded area is fast, the healing will result in regeneration.

The first thing on my agenda was to try and make the outer layer (epidermis) grow back again. The three phases of healing required blood. Within the first few minutes of injury, platelets in the blood begin to stick to the injured site. This activates the platelets, causing a few things to happen. They change their shape, and they release chemical signals to promote clotting. This results in the activation of fibrin, which forms a mesh and acts as "glue" to bind platelets to each other. So, in any wound, the initial gap is filled by blood, that is missing in these patients. The blood vessels are sealed during a burn and blocked off during an occlusion. Because there is no formation of fibrin polymers to provide initial stability to the wound, the dermal matrix machine below goes into action to form collagen and scarring. It was then I realised that I had to add platelets and growth factors to initiate the epidermal repair mechanism.

During the spring of 2015, I gave the complications lecture at FACE London, IMCAS Paris, and AMWC Monaco. During this time, I was toying with the idea of using platelet-rich plasma to help the wound healing process. Plasma is the liquid portion blood, which provides a medium for red blood cells, white blood cells and platelets to circulate through the body. Platelets are blood cells that cause blood clots and other necessary growth healing functions. Platelets play a key role in the body's natural healing process. Platelet-rich plasma (PRP) can harness those abilities and amplify the natural growth factors your body uses to heal tissue. The treatment was already being used to accelerate the healing of injured tendons, ligaments, muscles and joints. Maybe we could use it to provide the chemical that were absent when a blood vessel was blocked.

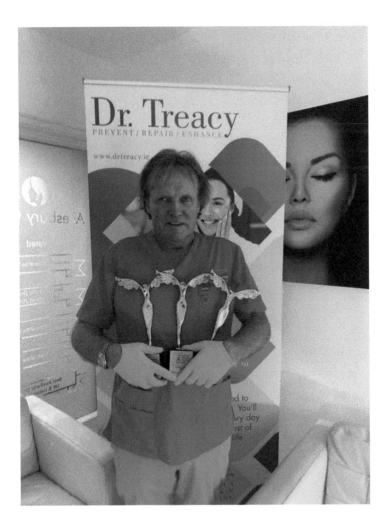

Holder of three AMEC Awards in 2019 (Monaco)

While researching for my upcoming summer complication lectures for IMCAS in Shanghai and AAAM Singapore, I decided to update my data and review suitable publications from Chinese scientists. One of my interests was to see whether epithelial cells could be developed from mesenchymal stem cells. I came across a recently published paper[6] by Yi-Shuan Sheen and Sabrina Mai-YiFan, that got me thinking. The paper demonstrated how the application of using red light to help the production of keratinocytes and hence epithelial tissue. Low-level laser (light) therapy (LLLT) was a fast-growing technology used to treat a multitude of conditions that require stimulation of healing, relief of pain and inflammation and restoration of function. The photons are absorbed by mitochondrial chromophores in skin cells. Consequently, electron transport, adenosine triphosphate (ATP) nitric oxide release, blood flow, reactive oxygen species increase, and diverse signalling pathways get activated.

So, what would happen if I used PRP and red light together to try and restore the outer layer of skin, the epithelium. This was certainly bringing the mountain to Mohammed and shining a light on the event. Wound healing is a complex process in which the skin, and the tissues under it, repair themselves after injury. The process occurs in three phases called haemostatis, inflammation and tissue growth. I decided to look at these in more detail. I had begun to believe that the reason these patients scarred was there was no blood present in either these patients or burn victims. It crossed my mind that stem cells could also be potentially activated, allowing increased tissue repair and healing.

Platelet-rich plasma (PRP) was the other mechanism that I was using. It derives from the centrifugation of the patient's blood, and it contains growth factors that influence wound healing, thereby playing an essential role in tissue repairing mechanisms.

I arrived in Shanghai that April, at the same time as the Chinese Grand Prix. The race was the third round of the 2015 season, and Lewis Hamilton was the defending race winner and went into the weekend with a three-point lead in the world championship over Sebastian Vettel. It was great to be able to attend Formula 1 again, as my attendance had stopped completely since the beginning of the Irish recession. While there I met Dr. Charles Mukunta, an orthopaedic

[6] Yi-Shaun Sheen MD Sabrina Mai-Yi Fan Chih-Chieh Chan MD *Visible red light enhances physiological anagen entry in vivo and has direct and indirect stimulative effects in vitro* Lasers in Surgery and Medicine Volume47, Issue1 January 2015

trauma specialist from Zambia and we discussed some complex road traffic accident patients, which he had treated in Africa. I was quite aware of the causalities from these accidents, while travelling through the continent, having personally attended them on many occasions. Together, we watched Vettel win the race from his teammate, Nico Rosberg.

In June, I gave an updated version of the lecture at Aesthetic Medicine Live in London and went into more detail about wound healing. I showed the doctors at the conference some diagrams during the lecture demonstrating ordinary would healing occurs. My diagrams showed that when skin is split, the epidermal cells at the edges of the wound lose contact with other epithelial cells and with their basement membranes. This loss of contact acts as a signal to trigger the migration of the cells. The result of this coordinated migration and cell division is the gradual covering of the epidermal defect. This signal was missing during wounds caused by vascular occlusion, but we could imitate it by providing the growth factors, signal messengers and other chemicals artificially from the outside. During the lecture, I mentioned that 633nm light could enhance keratinocyte proliferation, suggesting my suspicions about possible enhanced epithelial-mesenchymal interaction. The origins of the mesenchymal cells participating in tissue repair are poorly understood. The epithelial-mesenchymal transition (EMT) is an essential mechanism in tissue repair. Several signalling pathways (TGF-beta, FGF, EGF, HGF) and hypoxia may induce EMT, which occurs when epithelial cells lose their epithelial cell characteristics and become mesenchymal. My suspicion was that if we added mesenchymal stem cells from fat or another source, shone some red light and then added the growth factors and signal messengers from PRP we would have a chance of restoring the epithelial tissue.

The next thing was to obtain some patients who were, in my opinion, going to scar. This was a period when hospital ER departments were not required to stock hyaluronidase, or if they did were unwilling to use it on these patients who had blocked branches of their facial arteries. The patients were just referred on to plastic surgery outpatients who did little to aid their recovery. At this stage, I had seen about five of these patients in my clinic in Dublin and had treated one who had developed the problem almost a week before. The opportunity arose when I treated a patient who had an occlusion for eight days. They had attended a nurse on day two who naturally mistook the violaceous hyperaemia for bruising, then her GP who erred in thinking the sloughing of the fourth day was an infection and by the time she reached the hospital she was turned away as there was nothing they could do. I began treatment and she had her skin totally repaired without blemish within 100 days. My suspicions were confirmed, the treatment worked!

*

In July 2015, I attended U2's Innocence + Experience tour in New York. Before the concert, I met up with my Facebook friend, Julianne Mosher, whom I'd delivered at sea off the coast of Mexico twenty-three years before. It was an enjoyable experience to meet in such circumstances. The concert was exciting, with the stage becoming a giant walkway leading to another small circular step in front of me. A giant screen hung above, with digital scripts running along with it. The show began with the four members of U2 together on the mainstage, backlit in red with a single giant lightbulb hanging near Bono. He got up and walked along the walkway when singing songs about his youth, including *Cedarwood Road* and *Raised by Wolves*.

*

On October 22, 2015, Dr Arnie Klein died at Rancho Mirage, California. Cosmetic dermatology brought him great wealth, and his Beverly Hills clinic was decorated with million-dollar Warhols, and he owned multiple mansions. Well known for his philanthropy, he became an early advocate and fundraiser for AIDS research. He said to have raised over $250 million for the cause and was one of the first physicians to diagnose a case of Kaposi's sarcoma (cancer associated with HIV/AIDS that causes skin lesions) in Southern California. He had asked me a few months before to help him retain his licence in California by writing him a reference to give to the Medical Board. This is part of what I wrote,

'As a clinician, Dr Klein devoted time to discuss relevant journal articles that we had both written and published. He was competent in providing help to me in a broad spectrum of cosmetic dermatology treatments, and I benefited from the ability to discuss these issues with a world-renowned cosmetic medical expert. I felt his commitment to education and teaching was highlighted by his willingness to openly share his previous aesthetic experience with others. His compassion and ethics as a colleague to me always appeared to be exemplary.'

I was sad to learn later that Arnie died pennilessly and his body remained on the ice at a coroner's office in California because no family members came forward to claim it.

*

During this period, I gave the complications lecture in Las Vegas (June), Johannesburg (July), Moscow (September), Abu Dhabi (September), London (September), Paris (October), Mumbai (November) and Miami (November). While in Miami, I was given an award at the 20th World Congress in Aesthetic Medicine Lecture Award for my lecture on complications. It was nice to be back in Miami again after eleven years, and I met up with some good friends in the aesthetic industry, including Dr Alan Bauman and Dr Michel Delune who had been there at the AAAM Congress back in 2004. Vicky Eldridge, editor of *Aesthetic Magazine*, kindly wrote in the December edition,

'Renowned cosmetic doctor, Dr Patrick Treacy, picked up the 20th World Congress in Aesthetic Medicine Lecture Award for his lecture "Diagnosis and Management of Dermal Filler Complications" in Miami. He has been a long-term advocate of making corporate take some responsibility for the problems associated with their dermal filler products and highlighting these issues openly in his lectures as well as forwarding new theories and protocols for the aetiology of both vascular filler complications and biofilm. Dr Treacy also gave the award-winning address at Aesthetic Medicine Live 2015.'

I had just got back from Miami when I was informed of a seven-day dermal filler induced vascular occlusion. As this patient was at high risk of scarring, I realised that was imperative to restore epithelium to the compromised area as quickly as possible to reduce the potential of dermal scarring. I had to increase the mitotic activity of the epidermal cells to repair the epidermal thickness and decided it was the correct patient to employ platelet-rich plasma and red light to reduce this happening. Platelet-rich plasma (PRP) was known to regenerate tissue regeneration and promote healing. It contains growth factors that influence wound healing, thereby playing an essential role in tissue repairing mechanisms. Platelets form a rich source of essential growth factors, such as platelet-derived growth factor (PDGF), transforming growth factor-b (TGF-b) 1 and 2, and vascular endothelial growth factor (VEGF) – all of these are involved in the angiogenic cascade which assists in hard and soft tissue wound healing. I was aware that we couldn't yet differentiate between the growth factors in the platelet rich plasma, and the repaired tissue was going to be controlled by them all. Hence, it probably would become quite vascular due to the presence of growth factor (VEGF), a signal protein produced by cells that stimulate the formation of blood vessels and restores oxygen supply to tissues when blood circulation is inadequate. Its normal function was to create new blood vessels after injury, and new vessels (collateral circulation) to bypass blocked vessels. Therefore, I would possibly have to treat this with one of our IPL vascular lasers – the same one that Shimon Eckhouse had invented in 1998. It had also been known for some time that low oxygen (hypoxia) was a stimulant for forming new blood vessels and it was better to try and control this by using hyperbaric oxygen (HBOT), early in the process. As no blood is present when the arteries become blocked with dermal filler, it was a case of bringing the mountain to Mohammed if Mohammed couldn't come to the mountain.

That November, a series of coordinated terrorist attacks occurred in Paris, killing 130 people, including 90 at the Bataclan theatre, where an American band was playing. In December, I went to the city to see U2. They were joined on stage by the Eagles of Death Metal, who returned after their Bataclan concert was invaded and halted by three of the gunmen. Bono welcomed them on stage saying, 'They were robbed of their stage three weeks ago, and we would like to offer them ours tonight.'

Meanwhile, I gave an updated version of my complications lecture that January at IMCAS Paris 2019, and later at the Royal Society of Medicine (London) a month later. By the time I lectured at AMWC Monaco in March, the patient had made a one hundred per cent recovery without evidence of a scar, although I did have to fine tune the final epithelium with a gentle run of a CO_2 laser. The technique indeed appeared to work, and I improved on it with the next few cases. I gave my updated protocol for complications in London, first to the doctors at the FACE Conference in June, and later for Dr Bob Khanna, President of the International Academy of Advanced Facial Aesthetics that September.

I decided to call it the HELPIR technique, an acronym for H – Hyperbaric oxygen, E – Epithelial stimulation, L – Low-level light laser (633nm), P – PRP, I – IPL and R – Resurfacing laser.

*

352

In January 2016, there was increasing concern about the growing incidence of blindness being caused by dermal fillers at the IMCAS Congress in Paris. A recent paper by Katie Beleznay and James Alastair Carruthers, published in *Dermatologic Surgery* (2015), showed ninety-eight cases of vision changes from filler were identified. The sites that were high risk for complications were the glabella (38.8%), nasal region (25.5%), nasolabial fold (13.3%) and forehead (12.2%). Autologous fat (47.9%) was the most common filler type to cause this complication, followed by hyaluronic acid (23.5%). The most common symptoms were immediate vision loss and pain. Most cases of vision loss did not recover. No treatments were found to be consistently successful in treating blindness.

Most of the cases were apparently in Korea, but there were many also in Europe and the US, including one by a colleague of mine and a member of the British College of Aesthetic Doctors (BCAD). The problem involved filler entering an artery in the region of the temples, nose or even the nasolabial area, between the lips and the nose. There was much conversation about how to treat this problem if this happened. Some favoured direct intravitreal administration of hyaluronidase but most felt that the globe would get worse by action of the enzyme. This is because the vitreous humour in the eye is also composed of hyaluronic acid, just like the dermal filler. A recent paper by Tanvaa Tansatit, Prawit Apinuntrum and Thavorn Phetudom, published in *Aesthetic Plastic Surgery* (2014) favoured the retrobulbar approach and concluded, *'In ophthalmic artery occlusion by hyaluronic acid injection, retrograde cannulation of the ophthalmic artery may have the potential for restoration of retinal perfusion and minimising the risk of blindness.'* Most doctors, including many of my colleagues, favoured it also as it was already used by ophthalmic surgeons as a type of regional anaesthetic nerve block used in intraocular surgery. In this technique, a local anaesthetic is injected into the retrobulbar space, the area located behind the globe of the eye and the injection blocks cranial nerves II, III and VI, stopping the extraocular muscles from moving.

I didn't agree with this, saying that doctors had to be trained in this method, it was dangerous, and we were at the end of the day treating blood vessels and not muscles or nerves. I told them that I favoured using the supraorbital notch just under the inner part of the eyebrow, which was immediately palpable by running one's finger under the eyebrow until one felt a little depression. It was easy for me, as I used it every day during laser resurfacing. The supraorbital notch was also closer to the retinal artery and the ophthalmic artery than the other method. I postulated that this notch and the surrounding area of the supraorbital and supratrochlear arteries on the forehead easily could give us a potential site of reversal for the introduction of hyalase rather than by direct retrobulbar or intra-orbital injection. In the end, there was no conclusion, but everyone agreed it must be timely because the eye has minimal ability to withstand a lack of blood supply. With so many new injectors who may not have complete knowledge of the underlying facial anatomy, I said this easily identifiable landmark might help their management of these complications.

In the July/August issue of *Aesthetic Surgery* Journal, Wei Chen, Lin Wu, and Xing-Ling published an article on a patient who experienced visual acuity impairment and ischemic oculomotor nerve palsy after injection of hyaluronic acid filler into the dorsum if the nose.

That summer, Ailesbury Clinic won the Irish Health & Beauty Award "Best Cosmetic Surgery Clinic in Ireland 2016" (Dublin), and I got runner-up as "Aesthetic Doctor of 2016" at The Safety in Beauty Diamond Awards in London. This run of good fortune was followed up by two peer-recognition awards for the now recognised HELPIR technique, both at the Kolkhida Congress Tbilisi, Georgia, and the International Cosmetology Congress (ICC) held in Cairo.

*

While in Tbilisi, Georgia, I was interviewed by the Russian media about the HELPIR technique. It seems that my method and dosage of hyaluronidase for reversal of these vascular occlusions was called the 'Treacy Protocol' in some of the East European nations. The city of Tbilisi is located on the crossroads between Europe and Asia, reflected in its architecture, which was a mix of medieval, classical, and Soviet buildings. This location meant it lay close to the old Silk Road and through the centuries was part of both the Iranian and Russian Empires. The conference organiser Dr George Sulamanidze and his wife,

Dr Albina Kajaia, took me to see the old city Mtskheta, which lay at the confluence of the Mtkvari and Aragvi rivers. This was really where West met East and was the interface between the Roman and Orthodox religion.

George told me Mtkvari became a UNESCO World Heritage site in 1994 and served as a burial place for the kings of Georgia until the end of the kingdom in the 19th century. We visited Svetitskhoveli Cathedral, where the Pope had recently visited. It is now considered an endangered cultural landmark, having survived a variety of adversities, notably by the invasions of Arabs, Persians and Timur, and latterly during Russian subjugation and the Soviet period. Many of its priceless frescoes were lost due to them being whitewashed by the Russian Imperial authorities, as part of an effort to give the cathedral a "tidier look", when Emperor Nicholas was scheduled to visit. In the end, the Czar never even came. 'The next time you come, Patrick, we must go another hour up that road to the small town of Gori, which is the birthplace of Stalin.

*

I travelled to the International Cosmetology Congress (ICC) in Cairo, Egypt that August, where I received a lecture award regarding treatment of complications. I was saddened to see how Cairo had changed since I'd been last there in 1983 and was aware that the reign of long-standing President Hosni Mubarak and the more recent President Mohamed Morsi had ended. We passed near the Rabia Al-Adawiya Mosque where the protests had occurred. Although, the Dusit Thani Hotel where we were staying that had a facade of affluence, Egypt was facing high levels of unemployment and immense poverty. The conference was superb with excellent entertainment and dancing provided, but I was told most of the population was struggling with unemployment and some Luxor taxi drivers faced destitution. Egypt had also just floated its currency and embarked on an economic reform programme supported by a \$12 billion IMF loan.

In August, I read with special interest a recent article in the *Journal of Dermatologic Surgery* from Australia by Dr Greg Goodman and nurse Mike Clague, entitled "A Rethink on Hyaluronidase Injection, Intraarterial Injection, and Blindness: Is There Another Option for Treatment of Retinal Artery Embolism Caused by Intraarterial Injection of Hyaluronic Acid?" They demonstrated a novel possible remediation of potential occlusive eye injury that they noted in one of their patients. In the article, they mentioned a female patient who was being injected deeply in her temples and brow with hyaluronic acid when she noted a flashing sensation in her right eye and partial loss of vision.

International Cosmetology Congress (ICC) in Cairo

The physician injected hyaluronidase (hyalase, 375IU/mL) widely in the brow and forehead area where there seemed to be swelling contemporaneously with the visual changes. Widespread hyaluronidase in this area did not make any change to the visible symptoms. However, the practitioner then injected approximately 0.8mL (300 units) of hyaluronidase twice in short succession into the area of the supratrochlear and supraorbital notches with the second injection bringing instant relief of visual symptoms and return of eyesight. Subsequent ophthalmic review and magnetic resonance imaging illustrated no retinal artery or product intracerebral event.

This was precisely what I was saying about injecting the supraorbital notch and may have been the breakthrough I was looking for. I published an article in the September edition of *PRIME Magazine* saying:

'About the recent discussion at the FACE 2016 conference in London on the injection of facial fillers, I read with particular interest the recent article in the Journal of Derm. Surgery by Greg J Goodman, MD, FACD, and Mike D Clague,

BSc Medicine, Dermatology Institute of Victoria, South Yarra, Australia1on a novel possible remediation of potential occlusive eye injury that they noted in one of their patients. It is suggested by the authors that physicians be trained in the anatomy of the essential vessels of the face. Where possible we should continue to inject peripheral end-vessel embolisation with hyaluronidase into this broad field but also inject hyaluronidase in and around the main feeding vessel. The supraorbital and supratrochlear vessels are accessible, and the notches where they exit the superomedial aspect of the orbit and both communicate with the ophthalmic circulation. I commend the authors on an excellent article, highlighting the often-overlooked side to injecting with facial fillers.'

That September, I gave the lecture to the AWMC Eastern Europe in the World Trade Centre in Moscow. It was obvious to me that Russia was suffering from the sanctions that had been imposed on it by other Western countries over their annexation of Crimea and the situation in Ukraine. The Russians were proud people, whom I'd seen up close during the fall of the Soviet Union in 1991. The number of doctors attending AWMC Eastern Europe had fallen quite dramatically, and there was talk that the conference might not be held the following year. I visited some of the downtown nightclubs to get the feelings of the people, who were as pleasant as ever. The number of high-grade cars, including top of the range Mercedes and Bentleys on the streets of Moscow was in total contrast to the Lada Sputniks and Moskvitch-based kombi hatchbacks of the Soviet era, although one had to be careful of curb-crawling unlicensed taxis were still everywhere in existence.

I returned from Moscow and went to Paris to receive the AMEC Anti-aging & Beauty Trophy for the HELPIR technique from Catherine Decuyper for the "Best Clinical Research Case in Aesthetic Medicine". The presenter of the award kindly read these words, 'Physicians to date have not focused on the outer layer of skin to modify the wound. Dr Treacy used novel means at his disposal to stimulate fibroblasts and provide new epithelial tissue. These techniques included the use of low-level laser light and platelet-rich plasma to encourage fibroblast stimulation.'

With Dr George Sulamanidze and wife, Dr Albina Kajaia (Georgia)

It was undoubtedly true that we had achieved a possible milestone in medicine by using whatever was at hand. In November, I lectured in Abu Dhabi on complications and returned to London, where the HELPIR technique received the MyFaceMyBody Award for the "Best medical research for wound healing" (London). While in the Emirates, a friend from home sent me a WhatsApp photo-shopped black and white image of a newborn child with an elephantine male phallic symbol. Being a doctor, I was dissuaded from forwarding it further in case someone might think it was real and thinking little more about it and it joined the hundreds of other images on my phone. Little did I know it could become useful in the future.

In November, I also went to Cuernavaca, Mexico and received the CCME Mexican Congress Medal in Mexico for "Excellence in Medical Aesthetics" from Dr Federico W von Son de Fernex. The city was nicknamed the "City of Eternal Spring" by Alexander von Humboldt in the 19th century, and Aztec emperors had summer residences there. On route, I had to make a detour through London as my flight to Frankfurt got cancelled after Lufthansa pilots went on strike. Meanwhile, all hell was breaking out at home as one of my nurses thought a good friend had had a heart attack, and as he refused to go to the hospital, she sent me his ECG while I was travelling over the Atlantic. There was no taxi waiting for me as my flight was changed and we had to pull over every few miles to read the ECG strips as they downloaded. The Mexican military was also involved in a drug cartel raid in one of the villages on route. It was now five o'clock in the morning before the eight cardiac strips downloaded, and I could confidentially report our patient was fine.

The problem was it used up my international allowance and then I couldn't find out my hotel name being unable to access my email. Eventually, I showed the old taxi driver in the little Spanish, which I remembered from the ships, how to use a personal hotspot and I arrived at the hotel at seven thirty to be welcomed by Federico's sister, Karla. I never went to bed but went to the conference to speak at about nine thirty that morning. My old friend, Dr Roberto Blum from Ecuador was already on stage, and he welcomed me into the auditorium.

After a short while, I could see that he was lecturing about penile enlargement. His method involved grafting fat cells from elsewhere in the body onto the penis, and he was explaining that the organ could lose fifty per cent of the new volume within a year of surgery, so the patient often required multiple procedures to achieve the desired result. He then asked me publicly whether I did this surgery in Ireland. 'Of course, we do!' I replied. 'In fact, we even have a paediatric department,' I continued, smirking to myself and showing him the

WhatsApp image that my friend had sent to me in Abu Dhabi. He continued his lecture unfazed, and to this day, I don't know whether he believed me or not.

33. Cuban Editorials

In that month, businessman Donald Trump won the 2016 United States presidential election and became the 45th president. His populist, nationalist campaign, which promised to "Make America Great Again" and opposed political correctness, illegal immigration, and many free-trade agreements gained attention around the world. That Christmas holiday 2016, I went to Cuba, where I was joined by my brother, Raymond, and his family. I visited Ernest Hemmingway's property, Finca Vigía, where he enjoyed the island lifestyle, hanging out in Havana and entertaining guests. It still contained many of the original furnishings, hunting trophies and his artefacts. When not fishing or travelling, Hemingway wrote a great deal from his Cuban home. He once said, 'Writing, at its best, is a lonely life. A writer grows in public stature as he sheds his loneliness but the most often his work deteriorates.'

I visited some of the clinics there, interested to see that according to the World Health Organization, Cuba provided a doctor for every 170 residents and the HIV rate was almost the lowest incidence in the world having eliminated mother to child transmission and disease from blood transfusion and intravenous drug use. I reflected on the summer weeks spent at an HIV orphanage in Blantyre, Malawi, where the HIV prevalence rate was nearly 200 times that of Cuba. Balraj Juttla had again asked me to write the Guest Editorial for *PRIME Magazine* for the upcoming 2017 edition. I said, 'I write this guest editorial at the bar of the Floridita Restaurant in Havana, where Hemingway once sipped daiquiris with socialites like Jean-Paul Sartre, Ava Gardner, and Errol Flynn. The Afro-Cuban band who are playing behind me effortlessly exude a rhythm of sexuality and rebelliousness, although their passion is probably tempered in respect of the recent death of their revolutionary leader, Fidel Castro.'

Across the bar, in the very back corner, was a life-sized bronze statue of Hemingway on his favourite barstool, created by Cuban artist Jose Villa Soberon. I had shared many of his experiences, visiting his home in Key West where he wrote *A Farewell to Arms*, spending time in Mombasa and the Serengeti, which inspired the *Green Hills of Africa* and even drinking a few pints in El Callejon and Cerveceria, Madrid that grew the seeds for *Whom the Bell Tolls*. I looked again around me, thankful to be alive to enjoy these days under a Caribbean sun. I thought about a line from Santiago in *The Old Man and the Sea*, 'Every day above earth is a good day.'

Bronze Statue of Ernest Hemmingway

Donald Trump was sworn in as the 45th president of the United States on January 20 after his stunning upset over Democratic rival Hillary Clinton. Meanwhile, I was attending IMCAS Paris, where I was made Academy Board Member and IMCAS Scientific Committee Member. During the Congress, I was approached by Dr Elena Gubanova, professor of dermatology in Moscow, to make a small video for the Russian media. It was twelve years since she had invited me to Russia to speak about Isolagen at the World International Symposium on Aesthetic Medicine. The next month, I attended the Royal Society of Medicine Aesthetics 9 meeting in London where I gave a talk on "Management of vascular complications, including hyperbaric oxygen and multimodality stimulation of wound healing (HELPIR)".

Lecturing about HELPIR to the British College of Aesthetic Medicine

Dr Christopher Roland Payne gave Mr Jonathan Britto the title of incoming Chairman of the Aesthetic Conference Committee, and I was made Chairman-Elect. It was agreed we would rotate the title between Dermatologist, Plastic Surgeon and Aesthetic Physician.

Because the HELPIR method had a potential to treat all wounds and not just one related to vascular occlusion, I decided to test my theory against the assembled plastic surgeons who had to deal with these injuries daily. My lectures mentioned that a wound is a disruption of the healthy structure and function of the skin and underlying soft tissue, which may be caused by a variety of mechanisms, including acute traumatic injury to the skin (abrasion, puncture, crush, burns, etc.). Anything that decreases blood flow in the skin for a prolonged period has the potential to cause the ischemic breakdown of the skin. Platelet-derived growth factors are released into the wound that causes the migration and division of cells during the proliferative phase. I then mentioned that wounds required blood products for proper repair and that burns, or vascular occlusion, lack these blood products for appropriate reconstruction. These wounds will then form dermal scars. The HELPIR technique demonstrated that PRP and red light stimulated epidermal repair.

Nobody disagreed with my postulation, but it was more challenging to prove that mesenchymal cells can return to an epithelial phenotype, a process called mesenchymal-epithelial transition (MET). The Chinese doctors had recently shown in a co-culture condition, dermal papilla cells irradiated by red light could stimulate keratinocytes, the building blocks of the epidermis. Factors mediating this effect included fibroblast growth factor 7 upregulated in mRNA and protein levels. My good friend, Dr Christopher Roland Payne then asked me if I could put that science into simple language and I smiled and replied,

'Let's consider we are building the pyramids. The fibroblasts are the primary slave workers who produce the internal structure, the PRP growth factors are the bosses who control them, and the keratinocytes are specialist slaves who make the outside covering, and they require a bonus before they will work. First, we need to get more workers, or fibroblasts and we can do this by wounding the skin as in microneedling (Dublin Lift). Then we need the bosses to direct them, and we do this by supplying platelet-rich plasma (PRP). Then the specialist workers are enticed to produce keratinocytes by shining a red light on them (LLLT).'

The problem was I could not prove that this keratinocyte proliferation was related to enhanced epithelial-mesenchymal interaction. As there were not too many mesenchymal stem cells in the blood, I needed another source to see whether I could improve the effect. What we needed was somebody who was an expert on mesenchymal stem cells to speak at the next Royal Society of Medicine Aesthetic Congress and I was determined to find him.

Award for HELPIR technique Monaco (2016)

During 2017, I continued lecturing about my work in Kyiv, Miami, Abu Dhabi, and even to a few hundred Dutch dermatologists on board the *SS Rotterdam*. This old "Grande Dame" of the seas had been a former ocean liner and cruise ship, but was now a hotel ship in Rotterdam, the Netherlands, since 2010. In 1959, she made her maiden crossing of the Atlantic with the then Crown Princess of the Netherlands to New York. When Carnival Cruise Lines took over Holland America Line in 1989, she remained in service settling into a routine of winters in the Caribbean, with the occasional world cruise. We had crossed paths during my time as a ship's doctors with the MS *Fantasy*, and it was great to stay on board her cabins so many years later. I published my findings about how to perform the HELPIR technique in the The PMFA Journal sometime later.

'How I Do It - Management of dermal filler induced facial artery occlusion using the *HELPIR technique*'. By *Patrick Treacy*. PMFA Journal 5 February 2020

34. Given a Laureate

In March, the HELPIR technique won the Irish Healthcare Award for the "Best Medical Research Award" in Dublin. Tony O'Brien, the Director General of the Irish Health Service Executive, awarded me the trophy. While still on stage, I publicly made the point that there was a certain irony in the fact my research work was receiving awards all around the world, and that compromised patients were flying into Dublin for treatment, but none of our public hospitals were properly diagnosing these problems or keeping the reversal agent "hyaluronidase" in their emergency rooms. To be fair, he did promise to investigate the problem before he resigned over the Cervical Check controversy a little time later. It emerged he had read a memo from the National Screening Service in March 2016 informing women about false negative smear tests discovered during a clinical audit were being suspended pending legal advice.

In September, I received correspondence from a north European doctor who had treated a healthy young woman with hyaluronic acid filler to her nose to hide a hump, resulting in complete loss of vision on her right eye, and within one hour, she developed eyelid ptosis and paralysis of the muscles within or surrounding the eye. The doctor had immediately injected a total of 750 units of hyaluronidase, but it was unclear if it ever got intravascularly. The ophthalmologist was seen within 20 minutes, and CTI and MRI reports initially suspected of a small thrombosis in the cavernous sinus but was later rejected. Cases of blindness occurring after dermal fillers were becoming more common, and it was estimated there were at least one hundred documented cases at this time. Most of these were recorded in Korea. We discussed the benefits of the retrobulbar or supraorbital injection approach. The ophthalmologists favoured the retrobulbar approach and had intended to teach other doctors in the hospital. They were aware of my paper "Dermal Filler and Blindness: Is There Another Treatment Option…?" but understandably used the one they knew. The patient was thankfully slowly recovering but could still only see intense light with the affected eye. In October, I was awarded the 1st AIDA Trophy in Abu Dhabi for the "Best Clinical Case in Aesthetic Medicine in Dermatology & Aesthetics". It was the first time the award was given, and it was reported on television and the national papers. Most interestingly, I got invited to Baku, where the Azerbaijan Aesthetic and Anti-Age Medicine Congress awarded me the Art of Beauty Trophy for my "Contribution to the Development of Aesthetic Medicine". There was no doubt my technique had been accepted worldwide and had now won awards in four continents.

That August, I won the MyFaceMyBody Award "Ultimate 100 Global Aesthetic Leaders" (London) and the following month, the British College of Aesthetic Medicine (BCAM) awarded me their "Quality & Research" award in London. The BCAM award was presented by my peers, and it was very appreciated as BACD had almost become like a family to me. Their inaugural meeting was held at the Law Society in London in 2001, with a committee which included Dr Patrick Bowler, Dr John Curran, Dr Tracy Mountford and Dr Mike Comins. Their next meeting in 2002 had 65 attendees, including myself.

While in Baku, the Azerbaijan College of Medicine also kindly gave me a Laureate through the Aesthetic Conference National Organising Committee. It was my first time in the city, the largest city on the Caspian Sea and of the Caucasus region. It had recently become a famous venue for international events, hosting the Eurovision Song Contest and the F1 Azerbaijan Grand Prix as well as UEFA Euro 2020. During my visit, I was brought into a live studio and interviewed live on Azerbaijan television in front of millions of people about my relationship with Michael Jackson. The programme was hosted by Ranar Musayev and three other colleagues, and they even brought on a Russian female impersonator who had surgically altered her appearance to look like him.

On my return to Dublin, I was invited by Dr Federico W von Son de Fernex CCME Congress to attend a stem cell conference in Playa del Carmen in Riviera Maya, Mexico. Federico wished me to talk about the HELPIR technique, and how it could be used to restore necrotic skin after dermal filler vascular occlusion. Most of the Congress was in Spanish, and there were no translators as two million pesetas worth of audio-visual equipment had been stolen when an articulated lorry was hijacked on route to Cancun. It was great to meet Dr Roberto Blum again, and we laughed about the photoshopped image of the child with the enlarged penis, During the conference, I met Dr Diego Correa, Assistant

Professor at the University of Miami, Miller School of Medicine, who is one of top mesenchymal stem cell researchers in the world.

Irish Healthcare Award for Vascular Occlusion Research

He had spent over eighteen years of basic and translational research experience in the areas of adult Stem Cell Biology and Regenerative Medicine, with emphasis on Adult Mesenchymal Stem Cell (MSC) Biology. He was also founder and owner of Lumos Biomed Consulting, a company consulting in the areas of Regenerative Medicine, Stem Cell Biology/Therapy and Biotechnology.

Nurse Ciara Murphy with myself

Diego and his wife and family came with me to visit Tulum, the site of a pre-Columbian Mayan walled city about one hour down the coast from Playa Del Carmen. On route, we chatted about the melanoma vaccine and the progress he was having with research on it in Miami. It was now twenty years since I had been involved in the trials in Queensland. We eventually reached the ruins, situated on thirty-nine-foot-tall cliffs along the east coast of the Yucatán

Peninsula. This city, one of the last built and inhabited by the Maya, was at its height between the 13th and 15th centuries and managed to survive about seventy after the Spanish occupation of Mexico. The Spanish settlers brought disease to them, resulting in extremely high fatalities, disrupting the society, and eventually causing the city to be abandoned. It was so sad to see how the Spanish colonialists treated the natives, almost a reflection on what the British had done to the Australian Aborigines.

Dining with Dr Alvaro Skupin and his wife, Dr Nancy Álvarez

That evening, I attended the Gala dinner and was seated beside Dr Alvaro Skupin and his wife, Dr Nancy Álvarez. He was President of the Latin American Society of Stem Cells (SOLCEMA) and considered an innovator in the development of protocols for stem cell treatments derived from adipose tissue. His wife, Nancy, was a sex therapist and best known for hosting the talk show *Quién Tiene La Razón?* (Who's Right?), where she helped counsel families and couples with their interpersonal problems. We talked for a while about this his work, which appeared to be related to patients who had been diagnosed with chronic degenerative diseases, including Parkinson's, and he was convinced that the mesenchymal stem cells provided a viable and effective therapy by improving the body's natural capacity for regeneration. He then said, more than 70 diseases and medical conditions had been successfully treated with stem cell transplants, including hair loss, erectile problems and it held promise for the treatment of refractory systemic lupus erythematosus (SLE). I asked him whether stem cells could be used to treat patients who had sustained blindness after vascular occlusion, but he had never heard of it. It all seemed instead a little snake oil to me, few things in medicine could reverse the constant factor of decay and ageing, but I was happy that at least some doctors were working on it.

Dr Skupin gave me his card with details of his offices in Miami and Santa Domingo. When I got home, updates showed the patient's eye muscles had recovered, but her retina was intact. However, her blindness unfortunately remained. The year 2017 ended on a high note with Ailesbury Clinic being awarded "Best Clinic in Ireland" at the Aesthetic Awards (London). January 2018 arrived, and Sinead O'Connor invited me along as her plus one to celebrate Shane MacGowan's 60th in the National Concert Hall. It was now thirty years, almost to the date since I watched him play down in Dunedin, and Damien Dempsey summed it up when he said, 'This is for all those people who said Shane wouldn't see 30.' Sinead sang a haunting version of Shane's *You're the One* accompanied by just piano and flugelhorn. Cerys Matthews sang *The Broad Majestic Shannon* which was dedicated to the late Dolores O'Riordan. It felt strange to be honouring one musical legend in the shadow of another's death. While there, I had a long chat with Johnny Depp who spoke reverently about his love of Irish culture, which of course he obtained through his mother, Betty Sue Palmer.

Later that month, I attended the 20th-anniversary IMCAS Congress in Paris. While chairing one of the sessions at the Congress, I was approached by Nurse Mike D Clague, from South Yarra, Australia, who thanked me for my letter to *PRIME Magazine* supporting the potential use of the supraorbital notch in the treatment of dermal filler induced blindness. In February, I took over as the Chairman of the Royal Society of Medicine Aesthetic Conference in London. During the Congress, I listened to Associate Professor Ivor Lim, Plastic Surgeon from Singapore, whom we had invited from Singapore to talk about extracting mesenchymal stem cells from New Zealand red deer. The morning session had an optional symposium for his cosmeceutical product Calecim by Dr Mitchel

Goldman, Dermatologist, San Diego, entitled, "The safety and efficacy of red deer umbilical cord extract cream for facial rejuvenation".

It seems the parent company, CellResearchCorp harvested stem cells from the umbilical cord lining of red deer. These red deer were organically and ethically raised in New Zealand. Professor Lim said they chose red deer as its source of umbilical cord lining as there are no known diseases that are transmitted from deer to humans. The red deer were free ranging on the farm, where they were reared for the antler velvet, they naturally shed. During the lecture, Dr Goldman discussed how embryonic stem cell storage and treatments involved the destruction of an embryo. However, umbilical cord stem cells came from the blood left over in the umbilical cord after birth, and the baby was not harmed in any way. The umbilical cord, which connects the calf to its mother, is typically discarded or disposed of after birth. While harvesting this "medical waste" did not involve any harm to mother or calf, many countries have laws that prohibit products with human-derived ingredients. Hence red deer umbilical stem cells are used.

I liked the idea as all mammals share similar signalling proteins, including those released by stem cells which are used to communicate with other cells. Red deer cord lining stem cell proteins thus also have regenerative and restorative effects on human skin. Later that year, I started used these type of stem cells to try and grow new hair follicles, especially in androgenic alopecia. Hair loss is determined by a large assortment of factors: some inherited (androgenetic alopecia), while others are associated with hormonal conditions such as thyroid organ disease. We also must screen for autoimmune conditions, nutrition, and even psychological stress, especially in women. The results were quite impressive and hopefully it will provide another means of therapy to use in the treatment of in cases of androgenic alopecia (AGA)

*

I met Jay-Z when he was presented with a United Nations special humanitarian award at a special ceremony in the Waldorf Astoria in New York. Jay Z is one of the most successful artists in the hip-hop industry and received the global leadership award in recognition of his documentary Water for Life with MTV, and for his collaboration with the United Nations to attract support for safe, accessible drinking water in Africa. Jay-Z took on the fourth Millennium

373

Development Goal by creating play pumps, merry-go-round structures that use children's pedal power to pump water from wells into underground tanks, reducing child mortality. He said, "I'm not a politician; I'm just a regular person with a heart". He had just played at Glastonbury and we discussed both humanitarianism in Africa as well as the concert. He reminded me of Michael Jackson's 'Man in the Mirror', when he told me later "If you see a problem like that and do nothing about it, there's something wrong with you."

With Jay-Z at UN Humanitarian Awards in New York

The ceremony's host, actor Michael Douglas, presented Jay-Z with the award, which honoured him for his raising funds and awareness for the world's water crisis. I spoke with Katherine Zeta Jones for a long time discussing our common heritage and living in Los Angeles. I joked with Michael about his television series, 'The Streets of San Francisco', which starred Karl Malden and himself as two homicide Inspectors in *San Francisco*. The 60-minute episodes of the show ran on RTE at about 11pm on a Saturday night. My father was fixated on it and it meant my friends and I could not get a lift into the dances in Bundoran until it ended. He laughed and saw the funny part of the story .

With Sinead O' and Alan Amsby in Dublin

With Michael Douglas and Katherine Zeta Jones at the UN Humanitarian Awards in New York

With Johnny Depp at Shane Mc Gowans Birthday Party in Dublin

With Dr. Raj Kanodia and Ailesbury Management in Dubrovnik

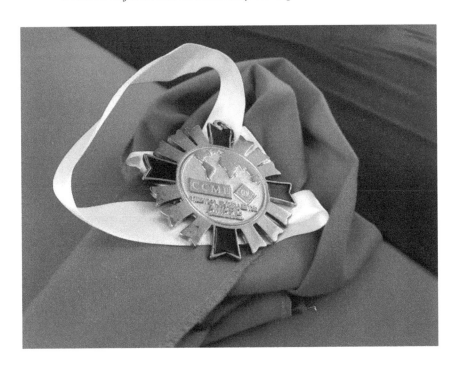

The CCME Medal for Excellence (Mexico)

35. Trying to Make the Blind See

In February, I learnt that the visually impaired patient was open to considering mesenchymal stem cell therapy as she had read about a similar case in the Baltimore Sun. The case involved a person called Vanna Belton from Baltimore who had been blind for more than five years, but after undergoing surgery where stem cells extracted from her bone marrow were injected into her right eye, she claimed she could see again. At twenty-nine, she developed optic neuritis, a demyelinating inflammation of the optic nerve, most often associated with multiple sclerosis, which could lead to a complete or partial loss of vision in one or both eyes. In just a few weeks, Belton lost her sight almost completely, with no explanation as to the sudden onset of the condition. She tested negative for multiple sclerosis, and she was initially told that her sight would eventually improve, but this did not happen.

I contacted Dr Diego Correa about the case as it happened in Miami, where he was also working. He said that the doctor in charge of the study didn't follow proper procedure for clinical study, and he strongly advised against it, as it was an unconventional stem cell study, costing around $20,000. Despite her own doctor's misgivings, Belton decided to go through the four-hour procedure, where the bone marrow was extracted from her hip so that stem cells could be taken from it, and it was then injected into her right eye's retina and directly into her left eye's optic nerve. That said, the doctor involved, Dr Jeffrey N Weiss, a former Harvard University professor and board-certified ophthalmologist from Margate Florida, was actively enrolling blind patients to take part in this non-FDA approved stem cell studies. However, Diego did say there was a good chance this could indeed work on the patient, but the placement of the cells would be awkward and required an ophthalmic surgeon involved. There was one surgeon with the experience to perform orbital decompression (for example, in patients with Graves' disease and advanced exophthalmos). Of interest, he also said that Dr Katherina Le Blanc was world respected in stem cells and works in the Karolinska Institute.

Meanwhile, I contacted Dr Alvaro Skupin, who said he was willing to treat the patient but would do it in the Dominican Republic, where he had individual facilities rather than in Miami. He wanted a referral letter from the ophthalmic surgeon who had first treated the patient. In that period, Dr Skupin ran into some adverse health, and when we contacted the ophthalmologist a few weeks later, he said he was not willing to do any experimental surgery on the patient.

I learnt that the hospital involved was also unwilling to get involved in any potentially unethical or pioneering procedures after the recent stem cell scandal surrounding thoracic surgeon, Paolo Macchiarini. The controversy occurred after a television station aired a documentary following his work at the Karolinska University Hospital and a University hospital in Russia. A young Russian woman who had the operation died, although her life had not been in immediate danger. He was the same surgeon that I had been invited to hear at his talk in the Royal Society of Medicine in London in 2009. He stated then that he wanted to pioneer similar transplants as he had done in Barcelona using synthetic windpipes. In 2010, the Karolinska Institute recruited him to perform stem cell transplants, but soon allegations of clinical and scientific misconduct were brought against him. An investigation concluded that of the nine patients that received the treatment, in Sweden and elsewhere, seven had died. The two still alive had to have their synthetic tracheas removed and replaced with a windpipe from a donor. It was a PR disaster for the Karolinska Institute, whose professors decided each year who would receive the Nobel Prize in medicine.

In March, news broke that two almost blind patients had their sight restored in a pioneering trial by Professor Pete Coffey of UCL at Moorefield Hospital in which stem cells were used. The findings, published in the journal *Nature Biotechnology*, were the result of a partnership between Moorfield's Eye Hospital NHS Foundation Trust, the UCL Institute of Ophthalmology and the National Institute for Health Research (NIHR). Both patients, a man in his eighties and a woman in her sixties, suffered from a severe visual impairment caused by age-related macular degeneration (AMD) but reported their sight was much improved a year later. The patients had previously been unable to read, even with glasses, were now able to read again after the procedure, which is the first of its kind.

At least, I knew the technique worked, but we were not going to be the first to perform it. I was glad of the pioneering accomplishment as AMD is the most common cause of blindness in developed countries, and in the UK, it affects around 600,000 people. The macular degeneration causes the central vision to deteriorate, making it impossible to focus on text or objects, causing colours to lose vibrancy and making it difficult to recognise faces. While the peripheral vision is not affected, meaning patients don't have total sight loss, it can make it very difficult to live independently and can lead to legal classification of blindness. In that month, I received the MyFaceMyBody Specialist Award for "Scientific Contributions to the Aesthetic Industry" in London.

In April, I attended AMWC Monaco, intending to talk about the use of mesenchymal stem cells in patients, whom I'd treated successfully with chemical burns. At first, I had used adipose tissue-derived stem cells (ADSCs) but later switched over to the stem cells from red deer. ADSCs are mesenchymal cells with the capacity for self-renewal and the ability to differentiate into fat cells, cartilage cells, muscles cells, bone cells and nerve cells among other cell lineages. I felt that I had not enough research cases and decided instead to speak about a new procedure that I had invented called the PLEASE technique in Abu Dhabi later that year.

In June, I went to London to receive the "Aesthetic Doctor of the Year 2018" UK & Ireland at the Safety in Beauty Diamond Awards and the following month to IMCAS Asia in Bangkok. I briefly spoke about the new technique and demonstrated how on the day of the procedure we took a blood sample and processed it to obtain Platelets Rich Plasma (PRP) that were added to the red deer mesenchymal cells and activated by a red light to enhance epidermal tissue. It again was an acronym for Platelets, Light Emission, Adipose Stem Cells. In Thailand, even the taxi drivers were forever thankful to the people of Britain for helping rescue the twelve boys who got trapped inside a cave underneath a mountain while exploring in the northern Chiang Rai province with their football coach. Their dramatic rescue bid had gripped the attention of the world.

In September, I gave a lecture on the PLEASE Technique at the AIDA Congress in Abu Dhabi. At this stage, I had treated about ten patients successfully, with various pathologies, including some chemical burns, and a few vascular occlusions. I also gave a lecture on how the face ages with time and "why do we want to change our faces?".

The face had always intrigued me as it was the area for which most patients sought cosmetic treatments. Everyone is aware that the convex lines of a youthful appearance tend to flatten and droop as one grows older. The younger face is characterised by a balance captured in the classic shape of the inverted triangle. The reversal of this "triangle of beauty" as ageing proceeds is considered generally less aesthetically appealing. But there was more to this simple explanation as older patients tended to want to look well and did not necessarily want to look younger than their age. I reasoned that it was probably more to do with the fact that the most important stimulus of social interaction was the face, and it carried a primary means of social communication. This was important as the way the public responded to the symmetry and health of a patient's face was just as important a factor in determining why someone would want to treat their face as them wishing to look younger. In other words, people respond socially to someone who doesn't look tired or depressed, and this facet of life is inbuilt into our psyche.

It is known that a newborn child will respond preferably to a beautiful person with symmetrical features before its mother to the age of three months. From a face, we could immediately identify a patient's gender, sex, age and race but also ethnicity, physical health, sexual orientation, emotional state and pain. Some of my lectures were based on the work of Professor Karl Grammer, Emeritus Professor at the Institute of Evolutionary Anthropology, University of Vienna and I decided to invite him to speak at the Royal Society of Medicine Aesthetic Congress the following February in London.

In October, I was invited as the keynote speaker to the 4th World Aesthetic Congress, which took place on board a cruise ship, the *Symphony of the Seas* sailing between Rome-Naples-Barcelona. The *Symphony of the Seas* was an Oasis-class cruise ship owned and operated by Royal Caribbean International. As of January 22, 2019, she was the largest passenger ship in the world by gross tonnage, at 228,021 GT, surpassing her sister, *Harmony of the Seas*. I lectured to 350 female aesthetic doctors from Russia and the CIS nations and was awarded a Diploma in Aesthetic Medicine from the Russian College. It was great to be back at sea again on the cruise liner.

That December, Ailesbury Clinic won the "Best Aesthetic Clinic in Ireland 2018" at the Hi-Style Awards (Cork). It was a great morale boost and turnaround for our Cork clinic, which was now back up and functioning under Sabrina Campbell for the previous five years but had just undergone a significant refurbishment. I spent that Christmas and early January 2019 in Uganda and was keen to visit Dr Alex Cauthino again while in Kampala, but the university was still closed for holidays. It was now sixteen years since we had met in New York, and there were 1.3 million of the population infected with HIV, of which 73% were on anti-retroviral medication. As I stood outside Makerere University, I wondered how different my journey in life would have been if I had never been stabbed by that needle-stick injury in Dublin so long ago.

*

In January 2019, I gave a lecture on "Twenty Years of Treating Aesthetic Complications" at IMCAS Paris and was invited to provide the same talk at the 1st Qatar International Cosmetology Conference and the Pakistan Academy of Aesthetic Dermatology and Surgery the following July.

In February, Marie Loftus and I organised the 11th Aesthetic Conference at the Royal Society of Medicine in London. It was an excellent congress with an international faculty composed of many of my friends and colleagues and people who populated my medical journey through life. The theme of the congress was identifying and dealing with aesthetic complications. Professor Karl Grammer spoke about "Evolutionary aesthetics and human beauty", while Dr Mitchel Goldman, Dermatologist, San Diego spoke on "The safety and efficacy of red deer umbilical cord extract cream for facial rejuvenation"'. My friend, Carol Bryan, was by now founder of Saving Face Initiative, and she kindly flew in from Los Angeles to give a talk entitled "My many faces – how dermal fillers caused me to require an autologous partial face transplant". It brought me back to that night when we shared some wine in Miami. Ms Donna Corden followed her persuasive speech, and Lindsey McEnroe, Clinical Director of True You Skin Clinics, who both gave a similar lecture on "How a flesh-eating bug caused me to require an autologous partial face transplant". My Georgian friends, Mr George Sulamanidze and his wife Dr Albina Kajaia, from Tbilisi, gave a live demonstration of a non-surgical facelift – threads vs fillers – and Associate Professor Ivor Lim, Plastic Surgeon and Group Chief Medical Officer, Cell Research Corporation, Singapore, gave a talk on the latest trends in stem cells research. To complete the day, my research on the PLEASE Technique won the Royal Society of Medicine Aesthetic 11 Conference Poster Award 2019.

Meeting Carol Bryan again at the RSM Aesthetic Conference (London)

The theme of the Gala Dinner hosted by the RSM afterwards was related to humanitarianism in Africa. To this end, I invited James Killen from MSF (Médecins Sans Frontières), an independent, neutral, and impartial emergency aid organisation, to speak about their work on the continent. MSF was founded in 1971, in the aftermath of the Biafra secession, by a small group of French doctors and journalists who sought to expand access to medical care across national boundaries and irrespective of race, religion, creed or political affiliation. It received the 1999 Nobel Peace Prize in recognition of its members' continued efforts to provide medical care in acute crises, as well as raising international awareness of potential humanitarian disasters. My friend, Yvonne Verhagen, Founder & Chair of HWMCO-Nederland, spoke about her work in Uganda providing transport and education for the children attending Bwama Primary School on Lake Bunyonyi. We ended the event by getting my good Irish friends, actor Patrick Bergin and musician Jim Corr to sing a few songs. Patrick spoke about his famous movie *Mountains of the Moon* detailing the story of the English scholar-explorer and orientalist, Sir Richard Burton.

Burton was the first European to discover Lake Tanganyika and to penetrate hitherto-forbidden African Muslim cities. He published forty-three volumes on

383

his explorations and almost thirty volumes of translations, including an unexpurgated translation of *The Arabian Nights*. The movie details his fascination with discovering the source of the White Nile. Ironically, both Jim Corr and I had pictures of the Ugandan River Katonga, which flows into Lake Victoria, before emerging as the Victoria Nile and travelling northwards, passing through two other Equatorial Lakes – Kyoga and Albert. Jim later accompanied me on guitar singing, and we sang *The Needle and the Damage Done* by Neil Young. The song first appeared on the *Harvest* album in 1972.

Although the song describes the destruction caused by the heroin addiction of musicians, he knew including his friend and Crazy Horse bandmate, Danny Whitten, it seemed to end the aesthetic conference, which had focused on dermal filler complications perfectly. After all, my last few years had been spent dealing with facial damage done by needles.

'I've seen the needle and the damage done

A little part of it in everyone

But every junkie's like a settin' sun.'

After we had finished, Marie Loftus suggested the song title would make a good name for a book that I was writing about my research into skin necrosis caused by aestheticians inadvertently injecting dermal fillers into facial arteries causing subsequent vascular occlusion.

*

In May, I was invited to attend the Western Canada Aesthetic Congress in Calgary, Alberta by Jason Olandesca. Canada is where many of my father's sisters had emigrated to and settled, and I was looking forward to some of their grandchildren coming to meet me there. It was a long way from the village of Garrison, Co. Fermanagh across the Atlantic in that war period. Calgary is situated in Alberta, at the confluence of the Bow and the Elbow rivers, in an area of foothills and prairie, about fifty miles east of the Rockies. Every year, it hosts the Calgary Stampede, an annual ten-day rodeo, exhibition, which attracts over one million visitors per year. It was snowing lightly when we reached Mount Royal University and there were about five hundred delegates present for my complications lecture. Near the end someone who was noon medical entered the room and approached the stage. "Are you Patrick Treacy" he asked? I was unsure if some of my Canadian relatives were playing a joke on me. "I am" I replied.

Getting "whitehatted" in Canada

"Then please be upstanding!". I was quite astonished when he got up beside the microphone and commenced a 'white hatting' ceremony on stage. Receiving a Smithbilt "White Hat" in Calgary is an internationally known honour. It started when oilman Bill Herron introduced Smithbilt hats in the Stampede Parade of 1947 the tradition of being presented one began in 1950 and remains a Calgary symbol of hospitality. Although most Calgarians are many generations removed from the farm or ranch, the community still adhere to some aspects of the cowboy identity: a sense of resistance to government and independence. The mayor's white hatting ceremony is considered the equivalent of bestowing the keys to the city, among its recipients have been Queen Elizabeth II, Prince William, Vladimir Putin, Tony Blair, Bill Clinton, George W Bush; the Dalai Lama, Pope

John Paul II, as well as Bob Dylan, Ozzy and Sharon Osbourne, Luciano Pavarotti, and Oprah Winfrey.

36. Top Aesthetic Doctor in the World

In September, Ailesbury Clinic was awarded "Best Aesthetic Clinic 2019" Ireland at the Irish Healthcare Centre Awards in Dublin. It was the fourth year in a row we had achieved this award, albeit from different conferring organisations. That November, I was invited to Las Vegas by Dr Michel de Lune as the key speaker to the 16th Annual American Academy of Aesthetic Medicine Congress 2019 to be held at the Westin Las Vegas Hotel and Spa. Michel wished me to speak on both my new HELPIR and PLUS techniques and the use of platelets and stem cells in treating damaged tissue. He reminded me of attending one of the first AAAM's in Miami as a fresh-faced young fledgling delegate in aesthetic medicine fifteen years before, listening to the great Dr. Pierre Fournier. Now he had aged and was living in Morocco and was too ill to attend the Aesthetic Conference we held in the Royal Society of Medicine earlier in the year. Unfortunately, I was also due in Monaco on the same day as a nominee for the AMEC Award for my research into stem cells and platelet rich plasma in treating burns. I was in Las Vegas, and Marie Loftus went in my place to Monte Carlo to collect the award.

Again destiny played a role, as I should have stayed in Las Vegas a little longer, because two nights after I had left, the My Face My Body Awards were held in the Bellagio and I learnt that I had won "Best Aesthetic Doctor UK 2019" and more importantly "Best Aesthetic Doctor in the World 2019". It was an incredible honour that had been bestowed upon me by my peers.

As I reach the end of this manuscript, I foresee there are many exciting things for me in the months ahead. During the Covid pandemic, I have written two books on the 'Living History of Medicine' and the 'Living History of Aesthetic Medicine' and look forward to their publication. The first book relates to the history of medicine as a living entity, reflecting on the battles that have been won or lost in the ever-changing struggle against disease. I speculate that this living history lies within man himself and too often the human side of this story is neglected. As doctors, we have been trained to focus on the signs of disease and consequently, we pay little attention to the people who discovered them.

With Professor Bob Khanna in London

When we read in our pathology texts about the interesting triad of defects in an illness such as Hand-Schuller-Christian disease, we tend to forget about the doctors who faced great personal hardships to bring us the information we now use to treat the disorder. Hence, I take the reader on a journey with Osler's famed 'Goddess of Medicine' and explain how she is continually on the move, fleeing from battles, tyranny, and oppression, seeking to find a home where man can study pathology in peace. She has moved from Edinburgh to Dublin, from London to Vienna, from Berlin to Maryland, then onwards to California to guide doctors in the wonders of new technologies, translating the genetic blueprint, manipulating defects in the data code of our existence and help us all fight the more complex diseases like the coronaviruses of the new millennium. My good friend, Christopher Roland Payne has kindly agreed to write the foreword. The second book the 'Living History of Aesthetic Medicine' includes French plastic surgeons, such as the late Yves-Gerard Illouz and Pierre Fournier, Georgian George Sulamanidze, and his Russian father Marlen Sulamanidze. It includes Canadian Jean Carruthers as well as hair transplant specialist, American Dr William Rassman. It is in recent memory that I have enjoyed their respective hospitality in their native countries and often in their homes.

With dermatologists Dr Doris Day and Heidi Waldorf in Las Vegas

Recently in Bhutan developing cosmeceuticals

Exciting plans for the future development of the Ailesbury brand will include a new "Dr Treacy" cosmeceutical skincare range, one which I have been working on now for many years. As part of this process, I recently travelled across the Himalayas to the kingdom of Bhutan and visited the apple orchards and the willow-lined roads of the Paro Valley to find a special ingredient to add to some of the creams. Presently, we are working to introduce plant stem cells into the range and are getting international certification for the pharmaceuticals. Next year hopefully when a sense of normality once again prevails, I look forward to bringing these exciting new developments to congress and doctors around the world.

Published Works

Patrick Treacy has published many scientific papers, including sentinel papers about the rising incidence of cutaneous malignant melanoma in the Rochester, Minnesota population from 1950-1985 and protocols for the reversal of dermal filler complications.

Treacy Patrick J; Popescu NA; Kurland LT; *Cutaneous malignant melanoma in Rochester, Minnesota: trends in incidence and survivorship, 1950 through 1985, Mayo Clin Proc. 1990 Oct, 65(10):1293-302.*

Treacy Patrick J; Goldberg D; *Use of a BioPolymer Filler for Facial Lipodystrophy in HIV-Positive patients undergoing treatment with Anti Retro Viral Drugs, Journal of Dermatologic Surgery, Volume 32, Number 6, June 2006, pp. 804–808(5)*

Treacy Patrick J; Goldberg D; *Use of Phosphatidylcholine for the correction of lower lid bulging due to prominent fat pads, Journal of Cosm Laser Therapy, September 2, 2006*

Treacy Patrick J; *Combining Therapies for the Aging Face – The Dublin Lift, Prime International Magazine, Vol 2 No 7 Page 20–31 October 1, 2012*

Treacy Patrick J; *The paradoxical effect of Botox on the brain, Prime International Magazine, June 2013 Page 63-69 May 1, 2013*

Treacy Patrick J; *The efficacy of dermal fillers in the treatment of atrophic acne scars, Prime International Magazine, Vol 3 No 2 Page 40-49, March 1, 2013*

Treacy Patrick J; *Treacy Comparative split face study on photoaging with two different CO_2 fractionalised resurfacing lasers, PRIME International Magazine, October 14, 2013*

Treacy Patrick J; *Reversal of a dermal filler induced facial artery occlusion, PRIME International Magazine, September 1, 2014*

Treacy Patrick J; *Surgical correction of semi-permanent lip filler nodules, PRIME International Magazine, October 1, 2014*

Treacy Patrick J; *Treating facial cancer related cachexia by aesthetic medicine, PRIME International Magazine, January 2, 2015*

Treacy Patrick J; *Non-Surgical Rejuvenation of the Periorbital Area, PRIME Magazine International, May 3, 2016*

Treacy Patrick J; *Reversal of a nine-day old vascular occlusion by using the HELPIR technique, PRIME International Magazine, November 2016*

Treacy Patrick J; *Management of dermal filler induced facial artery occlusion using the HELPIR technique PMFA Journal Feb/Mar 2020 Vol 7 No 3*

References

Émile Van Ermengem – Wikipedia

Retrieved from: https://en.wikipedia.org/wiki/%C3%89mile_van_Ermengem.

Iopidine Use for Eyelid Drooping After Botox? Doctor …

Retrieved from: https://www.realself.com/question/botox-iopidine-eyelid-drooping.

Patrick Treacy – Wikipedia

Retrieved from: https://en.wikipedia.org/wiki/Patrick_Treacy.

Thabo Mbeki – Wikipedia. (n.d.).

Retrieved from: https://en.wikipedia.org/wiki/Thabo_Mbeki

Patrick Treacy – Wikipedia. (n.d.)

Retrieved from: https://en.wikipedia.org/wiki/Patrick_Treacy.

Homo Naledi – Wikipedia,

https://en.wikipedia.org/wiki/Homo_noletti (accessed June 03, 2019).

South Africa's New Human Ancestor Sparks Racial Row ,

https://www.businessinsider.com/afp-south-africas-new-human-ancestor-sparks-raci (accessed June 03, 2019).

I Am No Grandchild Of Any Ape, Monkey Or Baboon – Vavi On ,

https://www.bikehub.co.za/topic/153959-i-am-no-grandchild-of-any-ape-monkey-or-b (accessed June 03, 2019).

Polyalkylimide – Wikipedia,

https://en.wikipedia.org/wiki/Polyalkylimide (accessed June 03, 2019).

Eddie Irvine – Wikipedia, https://en.wikipedia.org/wiki/Eddie_Irvine (accessed June 03, 2019).

Saving Face, Advocating For The Safe And Ethical Practice ,

https://www.prweb.com/releases/2017/01/prweb13992439.htm (accessed June 03, 2019).

What You Should Know About The New Michael Jackson Documentary, https://www.forbes.com/sites/joevogel/2019/01/29/what-you-should-know-about-the- (accessed June 03, 2019).

Ryan White - Wikipedia,
https://en.wikipedia.org/wiki/Ryan_White (accessed June 03, 2019).

Fermanagh Surgeon Reveals How He Became Michael Jackson's ..,
https://www.belfasttelegraph.co.uk/life/features/fermanagh-surgeon-reveals-how-h (accessed June 03, 2019).

It's All About M.i.c.h.a.e.l – Picture(+story) – Wattpad,
https://www.wattpad.com/343821676-it%27s-all-about-m-i-c-h-a-e-l-%E2%9C%AF-pictu (accessed June 03, 2019).

Carrie Fisher – Alchetron, The Free Social Encyclopaedia,
https://alchetron.com/Carrie-Fisher (accessed June 04, 2019).

Gary Dretzka « Movie City News,
http://moviecitynews.com/author/gary-dretzka/page/5/?iframe=true&width=100%2 (accessed June 03, 2019).

Michael Jackson – Cardiac Arrest Tmz.com,
https://www.tmz.com/2009/06/25/michael-jackson-rushed-to-the-hospital/ (accessed June 03, 2019).

What You Should Know About The New Michael Jackson Documentary,
https://www.forbes.com/sites/joevogel/2019/01/29/what-you-should-know-about-the- (accessed June 03, 2019).

Eti Breaks Down Why The New Michael Jackson Documentary Is...,
http://www.etinside.com/?p=25266 (accessed June 03, 2019).

Dr Patrick Treacy, Propofol And the Book Behind The Mask,
https://mjexodus.forumfree.it/?t=71754870 (accessed June 03, 2019).

America's Role During Ending The Holocaust – 1028 Words ..,
https://www.cram.com/essay/America-s-Role-During-Ending-The-Holocaust/P3DBW5F2BX (accessed June 03, 2019).

The Perils Of Indifference Theme Of Humanity – Shmoop.com,
https://www.shmoop.com/historical-texts/perils-of-indifference/humanity-theme.ht (accessed June 03, 2019).

Haiti…six Months On! – Dr Patrick Treacy – Prlog,
https://www.prlog.org/10804747-haitisix-months-on.html (accessed June 03, 2019).

Afri Hosts 31st Annual Famine Memorial Walk This Weekend .., https://www.irishcentral.com/news/annual-famine-memorial-walk-mayo (accessed June 03, 2019).

Haiti…six Months On! – Dr Patrick Treacy Prlog, https://www.prlog.org/10804747-haitisix-months-on.html (accessed June 03, 2019).

2010 A Deadly Year For Natural Disasters – Us News – 2010 .., http://www.nbcnews.com/id/40739667/ns/us_news-2010_year_in_review/t/s-world-gone (accessed June 03, 2019).

Carmageddon: Floods Destroy Hundreds Of Thousands Worth Of .., https://www.herald.ie/news/carmageddon-floods-destroy-hundreds-of-thousands-wort (accessed June 03, 2019).

Post-2008 Irish Banking Crisis – Wikipedia, https://en.wikipedia.org/wiki/Post-2008_Irish_banking_crisis (accessed June 03, 2019).

Denis O'Brien's Digicel Foundation Opens 174th School In .., https://www.irishcentral.com/culture/education/denis-o-brien-s-digicel-foundatio (accessed June 03, 2019).

The Poverty Line – Independent.ie, https://www.independent.ie/opinion/letters/the-poverty-line-28951452.html (accessed June 03, 2019).

Patrick Treacy Speech On Opening Everland Children's Home .., https://www.prlog.org/12052874-patrick-treacy-speech-on-opening-everland-childre (accessed June 03, 2019).

Story Of Jesus Christ Was A Hoax Designed To Control The .., https://www.express.co.uk/news/science/693817/Jesus-Christ-HOAX-Biblical-christi (accessed June 03, 2019).

Napoleon – Wikipedia, https://en.wikipedia.org/wiki/Napoleon (accessed June 03, 2019).

Eti Breaks Down Why the New Michael Jackson Documentary Is ., http://www.etinside.com/?p=25266 (accessed June 03, 2019).

Blood-borne Infections In Healthcare Workers In South Africa, http://www.scielo.org.za/pdf/samj/v104n11/14.pdf (accessed June 03, 2019).

Punishment Island In Lake Bunyonyi: A Place Where .., https://www.healtheworldmiraclecommunityorganization.com/index.php/2017/11/16/punishment-island-in-lake-bunyonyi-a-place-where-unmarried-pregnant-girls-were-lef (accessed June 04, 2019).

Sir Charles Trevelyan, 1st Baronet – Wikipedia,

https://en.wikipedia.org/wiki/Sir_Charles_Trevelyan,_1st_Baronet   (accessed June 03, 2019).

Dr Patrick Treacy Looks At The History Of Lasers In ..,
https://www.slideshare.net/ptreacy/dr-patrick-treracy-looks-at-the   (accessed June 04, 2019).

Following The Death Of The Inventor Of The Laser, Charles ..,
https://www.slideshare.net/ptreacy/following-the-death-of-the-inventor-of-the-laser-charles-townes-dr-patrick-treacy-looks-back-at-the-history-of-this-groundbreaking-technology-and-examines-how-its-use-in-aesthetics-have-evolved-62-67-am-ma (accessed June 03, 2019).

Queen Rania Accepts Una-USA Global Humanitarian Action ..,
https://www.queenrania.jo/en/media/articles/queen-rania-accepts-una-usa-global-h (accessed June 04, 2019).

Dr Patrick Treacy Looks At The History Of Lasers In ..,
https://www.slideshare.net/ptreacy/dr-patrick-treracy-looks-at-the   (accessed June 04, 2019).

The 'Botox Paradox': – SlideShare,
https://www.slideshare.net/ptreacy/pme-3-46671opinion (accessed June 04, 2019).

Does Botox Help or Cause Depression? – Ailesbury Media ..,
https://www.prlog.org/12131892-does-botox-help-or-cause-depression.html (accessed June 04, 2019).

Facial Feedback Hypothesis – Wikipedia,
https://en.wikipedia.org/wiki/Facial_feedback_hypothesis (accessed June 04, 2019).

Patrick Treacy – Wikipedia,
https://en.wikipedia.org/wiki/Patrick_Treacy (accessed June 03, 2019).

Darwin In The World Of Emotions – Europe PMC Article ..,
http://europepmc.org/articles/PMC1279921/ (accessed June 04, 2019

Bruce Springsteen Rocks Out With U2 For World Aids Day ..,
https://www.cbsnews.com/news/bruce-springsteen-rocks-out-with-u2-for-world-aids- (accessed June 04, 2019).

Avoiding Sun as Dangerous as Smoking – Medscape,
https://www.medscape.com/viewarticle/860805 (accessed June 04, 2019).

Endre Mester – Wikipedia,
https://en.wikipedia.org/wiki/Endre_Mester (accessed June 03, 2019).

Prime Supplement – Dr Patrick Treacy – Slideshare.net,
https://www.slideshare.net/ptreacy/prime-supplement-dr-patrick-treacy
(accessed June 04, 2019).

Wound Healing – Wikipedia,
https://en.wikipedia.org/wiki/Wound_healing (accessed June 04, 2019).

Dermal Filler Complications And How To Deal With Them,
https://www.linkedin.com/pulse/dr-patrick-treacy-discusses-dermal-filler-how-dea (accessed June 03, 2019).

A Rethink on Hyaluronidase Injection, Intraarterial.,
https://www.aafps.com.au/wpcontent/uploads/2016/11/A_Rethink_on_Hyaluro nidase_I (accessed June 04, 2019).

Cuernavaca – Wikipedia,
https://en.wikipedia.org/wiki/Cuernavaca (accessed June 03, 2019).

Macchiarini Scandal Is A Valuable Lesson for The .,
https://www.nature.com/articles/537137a (accessed June 03, 2019).

Cure for Blindness? Stem Cell Trial Restores Sight In Two ..,
https://www.rt.com/uk/421857-cure-blindness-stem-cell/ (accessed June 04, 2019).

Prime Supplement – Dr Patrick Treacy,
https://es.slideshare.net/ptreacy/prime-supplement-dr-patrick-treacy (accessed June 04, 2019).

– Dr Patrick Treacy, Dublin, 29 August 2020